UNDERSTANDING EDUCATIONAL MEASUREMENT

UNDERSTANDING EDUCATIONAL MEASUREMENT

ERNEST McDANIEL
Purdue University

WCB Brown & Benchmark
PUBLISHERS

Madison, Wisconsin • Dubuque, Iowa

Book Team

Managing Editor *Sue Pulvermacher-Alt*
Production Editor *Karen A. Pluemer*
Visuals/Design Developmental Consultant *Marilyn A. Phelps*
Visuals/Design Freelance Specialist *Mary L. Christianson*
Marketing Manager *Elizabeth Haefele*
Advertising Manager *Nancy Milling*

A Division of Wm. C. Brown Communications, Inc.

Executive Vice President/General Manager *Thomas E. Doran*
Vice President/Editor in Chief *Edgar J. Laube*
Vice President/Sales and Marketing *Eric Ziegler*
Director of Production *Vickie Putman Caughron*
Director of Custom and Electronic Publishing *Chris Rogers*

Wm. C. Brown Communications, Inc.

President and Chief Executive Officer *G. Franklin Lewis*
Corporate Senior Vice President and Chief Financial Officer *Robert Chesterman*
Corporate Senior Vice President and President of Manufacturing *Roger Meyer*

Cover Illustration by Wordsworth Illustration.

Cover and interior designs by Terri W. Ellerbach.

Illustrations by Wordsworth Illustration unless noted otherwise.

Copyedited by Karen Dorman

f

For Tippen

Since the beginning of educational measurement no fact has been more frequently revealed, and its implications more commonly ignored, than the great variability in the achievement of pupils in the same grade.

Walter W. Cook, 1951

Brief Contents

Contents

part one
Principles of Measurement

part two
Measuring Educational Achievement

part three
Measuring Human Behavior

Preface

This book stems from the belief that there is an increasing need within teacher education for a text that introduces students to the essentials of measurement and evaluation using a style that injects human interest, imagination, and humor into the subject matter. This book will focus exclusively on topics essential to effective classroom teaching and will treat these topics in a manner that emphasizes the human context that surrounds and guides their use. In addition, this book is intended to help students overcome their perception of measurement as an abstract activity interesting only to those who are mathematically inclined.

A number of admirable texts are available that treat measurement topics thoroughly and competently. I have cited many of these texts throughout the chapters of this book, and the reader will profit from exploring these sources more fully. This book, rather than attempting to be comprehensive and detailed, drives home a few essential concepts and skills through a focused presentation and a style that I hope will be seen as friendly and engaging.

There are, to be sure, some statistical formulas, but the emphasis is always on the conceptual material, not the arithmetic operations. Students who enjoy number crunching can apply the formulas to specific examples, and those who want to skip these passages may do so without feelings of guilt or concern that they are missing building blocks in their conceptual development. Dozens of students who have used this text in draft form have confessed to "math fright" at the beginning of the course and returned later to express gratitude for the good foundation they acquired for later courses in statistics.

Educational measurement is an intensely human activity. No test ever arrives in the classroom independent of numerous decisions made by people on the basis of what they know, believe, and value. I like the human context in which measurement decisions are made. I see teachers as valuing broad goals in education and welcoming ways of designing tests to incorporate a philosophy of education with which they feel comfortable. Thus, readers will find an undercurrent of applause running throughout this book for teachers moving away from pure textbook learning and toward the development of thinking processes and positive attitudes toward self and subject matter. From a measurement perspective, this concern is expressed in an emphasis on higher cognitive processes in achievement tests and in a direct treatment of the measurement of thinking growing out of my own research in this area. Newer trends in performance assessment and portfolio assessment also represent, at base, an interest in humanizing education in the sense of becoming more responsive to individual ways of growing. These approaches to evaluation encourage students to become more reflective and self-actualized.

There is a second aspect of testing as a human endeavor that is totally neglected in most measurement texts. As authors of texts, we are too busy teaching how the IQ score is computed to provide even a glimpse of the men and women who struggled to solve measurement problems. For example, there is Alfred Binet, the French psychologist with a passionate interest in understanding everything about the human mind, a fascinating personality who spent long hours giving tests to his two daughters, invented a mechanical device for recording the artistry of piano players, wrote really macabre plays for the Paris theater, and attacked many of the myths that were currently held about indices of character and personality. His colleagues were chagrined when he demonstrated that they could not, on the basis of handwriting, tell the difference between prominent Frenchmen and criminals.

I have included an entire chapter on Binet in this book, and where appropriate, have provided brief biographical comments on some of the other figures in testing. It seems amazing that in other academic fields we recognize a Pasteur, a Mendel, a Mach, a Faraday; but in testing, we somehow see tests of intelligence, aptitudes, or interests appearing on the scene as disembodied entities, separated from their authors' personal motivations and theories of human abilities.

The story of testing is a human story reaching back to Sir Francis Galton, and we will see in a moment that you are linked to Galton through a handshake that spans a hundred years. Galton established a laboratory in Kenniston, England, in 1884, where he measured people for a variety of human traits in the interest of answering questions about human abilities. An American, James McKeen Cattell, visited Galton in his laboratory and we can imagine at the parting, Cattell extended his hand and said, "It has been a pleasure." Cattell returned home to conduct a series of researches in testing, and was the first American to use the term "mental test" in a journal article. In due time, Cattell recruited a young man who had been his son's roommate in college to come to New York and assist him in compiling data about prominent American men of science. Fredrick Kuder performed this work and went on to make his own significant contributions to testing. As Kuder left Cattell, we can imagine that he extended his hand and said, "It's been a pleasure." At the annual meeting of the American Psychological Association in Los Angeles in 1984, Kuder reminisced about his professional experiences and after the talk, Ernest McDaniel, a professor of measurement at Purdue University, extended his hand and said, "It has been a pleasure." And now, to all readers, I extend my hand to welcome you to the field of educational measurement. I hope you will like it.

Acknowledgments

I am deeply indebted to the following individuals who reviewed the material for this text and offered suggestions that resulted in a number of significant changes in the final book:

Ralph F. Darr, Jr. University of Akron

Patricia A. Cook University of Indianapolis

Robert E. Bonner Bartlesville Wesleyan College

Landa Trentham Auburn University

Glen Nicholson University of Arizona

T. Patrick Mullen California State–San Bernardino

Ernest Davenport University of Minnesota

I wish to thank Mark McDaniel, who teaches cognitive psychology at Purdue, for his suggestions on the chapter on measuring intelligence.

Paul Tavenner of Brown & Benchmark Publishers saw the manuscript through its developmental phases, and I appreciate his efforts and those of the many specialists who contributed their skills to the final publication.

Jill Brady competently handled a variety of secretarial tasks and word processing activities associated with the development of the manuscript.

I am also grateful to the many students who identified errors and made suggestions. Their responsive interaction with the material reinforced my belief that the subject of testing can be interesting and enjoyable.

Well, I have done it. . . . I've signed up for a course in educational measurements. I know it's going to be loaded with statistics and dry and boring, but I need it for my program. I wonder if I will get what I really want from this class. I would like to do a better job of interpreting scores of standardized tests. I would like to make better tests for my students and I would like to know what to think about such things as "intelligence" and "aptitude."

chapter one

An Introduction to Educational Measurements

Measurements and evaluations are interlinked with almost every activity of teaching. Teachers with a measurement background are able to construct, select, and use tests more skillfully than teachers without training in measurement. A text in measurement written for teachers should present the principles of measurement, which form the basis for selecting tests and interpreting results. It should explain how to write good classroom items and how to analyze the items after the test has been administered. It should include enough statistics so that test manuals and research reports can be read with understanding. It should also acquaint the reader with the major test instruments in the fields of academic abilities, interests, and personal adjustment.

With these objectives in view, this book is organized into three main sections: (1) understanding general measurement principles, (2) constructing and analyzing classroom tests, and (3) examining specific tests in the areas of intelligence, interests, aptitudes, and adjustment. This chapter introduces each of these three areas and provides an overview of the major ideas in each one.

Principles of Measurement

Measurements provide a precise rather than a vague basis for making educational decisions. A teacher, judging a student's mathematical ability as "pretty good," may assign extra work to do after regular homework is completed. A teacher, knowing that the student exceeds 97 percent of a national sample, may recommend a special program for mathematically gifted.

While measurement lends precision to the study of human behavior, tests may suffer a number of shortcomings. Tests seem scientific. Tests seem to emanate from highly authoritative sources. For these reasons, tests may be dangerous; they may lull us into the belief that we are using highly objective, scientific tools when we are not.

Teachers need to know what qualities to look for in evaluating tests and need to feel comfortable with the specialized terminology that professionals use when talking about tests.

Statistical Concepts

A brief introduction to statistical concepts provides the foundation for consideration of measurement principles. Notice we are not calling this section statistical calculations. Our concern is with the concepts. When specific calculations are needed, it has become easy to ask a computer to perform these calculations. These exercises can be done with ease because the computer has already been loaded with statistical packages that automatically perform the needed calculations.

Descriptive statistics are used to describe a group of measurements such as a distribution of test scores. Some teachers visualize a distribution of scores as a landscape with each test score placed in its appropriate place, low scores to the left, high scores to the right. If you like, you can think of a bell-shaped, normal distribution curve as a mountain of answer sheets with a peak and two sloping sides.

Within this territory the middle point, usually the average or mean, is the key landmark. You can build a surveyor's tower there. From this surveyor's tower, you can see the extent of your domain, the range from end to end. You can also calibrate your surveyor's scope so when you spot a test score, you can tell how many "standard deviations" it is from your position at the mean. The standard deviation is the second landmark, and a solid understanding of it makes for easy transition into applied measurement terms.

Correlation coefficients are the indispensable tool of the measurement person. Correlations tell us the degree to which two variables are associated with one another. If we give a test twice to a group of students and correlate the scores, we have a reliability coefficient. If we correlate scores for math aptitude with math achievement, we have a validity coefficient. I realize these are terms that have not yet been defined, but I am illustrating how an understanding of correlations is a prerequisite to the following discussions about the qualities of a test. Let us now turn to these essential qualities of a good measurement device.

Validity, Reliability, and Norms

It is impossible to talk about tests or test scores without using a specialized vocabulary. Understanding this vocabulary involves more than definitions; it involves learning about a set of procedures that are employed to "test the test."

When evaluating a test, you will be seeking information relevant to three characteristics: reliability, validity, and norms. You may want to think of test evaluation as asking three major questions:

1. Reliability: Does the test give consistent scores on subsequent occasions?
2. Validity: Does the test measure what it claims to measure?
3. Standardization: Are the norms based on a representative sample?

These three criteria for judging tests will be appropriate whether the test was published in Iowa City or in Princeton. These criteria for judging tests will also be essential no matter what the test is designed to measure: reading readiness, for example, or self-concept, or teacher competency. Learning to use these three principles of measurement will enable you to be a better consumer of tests and a far better interpreter of test information.

The essential information for evaluating tests is in the test manual. Without some background in measurement, however, there may be a tendency to leaf through the manual vaguely hoping for some important information to leap off the pages. If you understand that the quality of a test depends on its reliability, validity, and the way it was standardized, then these headings in the manual become the signposts indicating that relevant information will follow. Although test terminology may appear technical, we will see that the terms describe common sense concerns raised by anyone asking the question: "How good is this test?"

Designing and Constructing Classroom Tests

Constructing classroom tests is one of the many applications of measurement principles. Many teachers believe writing tests should be left to the professionals, a belief easily maintained since textbook publishers are quick to supply a list of questions accompanying every chapter. Professionals do construct the items: professional item writers, not professional educators. Many item writers try to emphasize main ideas and higher cognitive processes; some are more successful than others. Examine the test provided by the publisher covering a unit you have taught. How many items deal with the big ideas or ask the students to apply or analyze material?

Teachers as well as publishers sometimes succumb to writing quick, memory-level items. A study of 342 teacher-made tests revealed that most teachers use short answer tests measuring knowledge of terms, facts, and principles (Fleming & Chambers, 1983). The tests require students to remember but not apply knowledge. Such tests are easy to construct, but they send wrong signals to students about the things we value in education.

Fortunately, there is nothing mysterious about constructing better classroom tests. Three steps will lift your test out of the ordinary and provide a sounder basis for evaluating student achievement: test planning, item writing, and item analysis and revision. You will soon be reading a chapter on each of these steps, but an advance word may be in order.

Test planning begins with drafting a test blueprint or table of specifications designating the subtopics of the unit and the cognitive processes that will be required in answering the items. The cognitive processes are typically defined by the Bloom Taxonomy which emphasizes comprehension, application, synthesis, and analysis. The table of specifications is your best guide to writing tests that capture your teaching emphasis and reflect cognitive processes above the memory level.

Armed with the test blueprint, there is one and only one point at which tests become good or bad: writing the individual test items. Some items are so wordy and bulky that getting through the test is a matter of reading comprehension and endurance. Other items contain obviously wrong alternatives so that correct answers can readily be chosen by students who have only a hazy grasp of the material. Far too many items use direct phrasing from the textbook, thus giving a break to students who may recognize the correct answer without understanding it. The curatives for these ills in item writing lie in a few simple rules of item construction. Procedures for item analysis and item revision will round out your skills in constructing objective test items.

Although multiple-choice items can be constructed to measure comprehension and application, the essay test stands out as holding the greatest potentiality for measuring analysis and synthesis of conceptual material. The down side of essay tests is their susceptibility to many hazards in scoring. Scoring of essay tests, however, can be vastly improved by using some well-known precautions. While the research evidence is uneven, essay tests appear to encourage students to think about the issues and motifs in subject matter.

A new family of measurement procedures is arriving on the scene under the general term performance assessments. A popular book by Mitchell (1992) provides a good introduction to this new movement. Performance assessments include such tasks as essay writing and problem solving in mathematics and science. A distinguishing feature of performance assessments is scoring procedures directed at the processes employed by the learner. Ideally, the scoring yields insight into how the student approaches the problem and reveals snags and difficulties which can be remedied by subsequent instruction. While there are some continuing questions about the psychometric qualities of these approaches, i.e., the extent to which they meet the criteria for reliability, validity, and standardization procedures, performance assessments may have offsetting advantages in signaling clearly to students some of the more broadly conceived aims of instruction. This congruence between performance testing and many of the educational reform goals has prompted the inclusion of performance tests in statewide testing in this country and in national testing programs abroad.

A related aspect of the general movement to restructure classroom practices is a renewed interest in the measurement of thinking. In our discussion of the measurement of thinking, we make a distinction between formal thinking, which focuses on such reasoning processes as induction and deduction, and "everyday thinking," which centers around the way situations are perceived, organized, and interpreted. The existing tests of critical thinking grow out of the formal reasoning tradition, and most use a multiple-choice format. This text offers an approach to the measurement of thinking that rests on the assumptions of "everyday reasoning." Scores depend on the way students interpret complex situations. The scoring rationale gives weight to developing the student's own point of view, explaining rather than simply describing the situation, and considering many factors rather than making simple right-wrong judgements. Teachers can apply the scoring procedure to situations that are open to a variety of interpretations, such as taking sides on controversial issues.

The discussion of measuring thinking processes will complete the section on constructing classroom tests. One of the most important goals of any course in measurement is to help teachers write, analyze, and evaluate classroom tests. Tests are always written with an eye on larger educational goals, and an underlying message of the chapters on test construction is the importance of thinking about subject matter content. This orientation is maintained as attention ranges from the construction of multiple-choice items to the more complex task of assessing thinking processes directly.

Measuring Human Behavior

Teachers interested in the cognitive abilities, aptitudes, interests, and adjustment of their students will find a number of standardized tests in each of these areas. In many cases, well-established instruments dominate the market. For example, in the area of individual intelligence testing, the Stanford-Binet and the Wechsler tests are at the pinnacle of all tests available. These are the tests of choice when it comes to making difficult diagnostic decisions. Although the tests are administered by psychologists, teachers need to know about them since they receive the reports and recommendations.

Our introduction to this section starts with Alfred Binet, whose extensive work with his own daughters and with school children led to the development of the first intelligence test almost 100 years ago. The story

of Binet helps us see the intensely empirical nature of this most significant work in intelligence. The test did not reflect a full-blown theory specifying what intelligence was or was not. Rather, the test reflected years of trying out a wide variety of tasks, coupled with great, inventive insight. The insight provides the simple logic of intelligence tests: find out how normal children at a single age level perform. Now, test a child of unknown ability. At what age level is it functioning? If a child of eight functions more like a six year old, this is a matter for concern and further study. Binet's insight was that carefully documented performance of normal children could be used as markers for establishing the "mental level" of children of unknown ability.

Today there are many questions about intelligence tests. Is there one "general ability" or many abilities? Do the tasks included on intelligence tests reflect skills useful in the larger society? More pointedly, can we measure basic cognitive processes that are essential to the information processing demands required in learning and retrieving information?

If abilities are the engine that run the human ship, interests are the rudder. The measurement of vocational interests has a history reaching almost as far back as the measurement of intelligence. Interests tests can be used to stimulate career explorations during the middle and high school years, and informal measures of interest can be used by teachers at all levels in individualizing reading programs and instructional units.

Sociometric techniques help identify children who have no friends.
Copyright © Michael Siluk

It may also be useful on some occasions to look at learning strategies, attitude toward school, self-concept, or how well a student is fitting into the social group. Our discussion of affective measures provides a brief overview of instruments that might be used by teachers to gain an understanding of the personal and social adjustment of students. Asher and Coie (1990) report that when elementary children are asked to name the three best friends in their class, about 10 percent of the children are not named by any of their classmates. Sociometric techniques can help teachers identify children who may have no friends in the setting where they spend most of their day. This section concludes with some illustrations of the way close observation of behavior reveals underlying needs.

New Trends in Testing

This book ends with a chapter on new trends in testing. Three trends have been chosen to illustrate that educational measurement, like all fields, is constantly undergoing growth and change. Additionally, the three trends identified in the last chapter appear to be movements that will show rapid growth and development in the decades to come. We refer to portfolio assessment, dynamic assessment, and computer-based adaptive testing.

Portfolio Assessment

Let's look for a moment at Brad, who is not a real boy but a composite of thousands of children who are making progress in school, progress that will not show up on a standardized test.

> Brad came to the desk with a big smile. He couldn't wait any longer to show his teacher the two grasshoppers and a spider he had captured the day before. Brad is two years behind grade level in reading and clueless about fractions. Yet Brad was considered by the other teachers to be one of their most successful accomplishments. Brad had transferred into their school as a third grader, withdrawn and sullen with a self-concept that must have been minus five on a scale from one to ten. Now, at least, he seems to feel good about himself and to have a good attitude toward school. Maybe the fractions will come later.

This interchange reminds us that achievement tests measure a relatively narrow band of the total development for which teachers, particularly elementary teachers, feel responsible. It also offers in a nutshell the rationale for portfolio assessments, attempts to document growth and development as a highly personal journey of each individual student. Portfolios are rapidly spreading as teachers reach for "authentic assessments" of a broad range of student achievements.

Dynamic Assessment

Critics of intelligence tests claim that they provide an unfair assessment of ethnically diverse or mentally handicapped individuals, who may have had little opportunity to learn the mental skills and knowledge required. Further, by painting a static picture of what has been learned, the tests may reveal little about what one might learn with help. Drawing their theory from Vigotsky, an almost forgotten Russian psychologist, advocates of dynamic assessment believe that learning potential is revealed by close observation of behaviors during repeated teaching-testing cycles. Under the leadership of Reuven Feuerstein in Israel, a growing number of reports are describing the use of dynamic assessment with subjects ranging from emotionally disturbed adolescents to prison inmates.

Computerized Adaptive Testing

It is but a short step from dynamic assessment to computerized adaptive testing. In both cases, there is a high level of interaction between the student and the examiner, the examiner observing carefully what the student can and can not do, and making adjustments accordingly. When the test is administered by a computer, judgements are made about the student's level of ability after each response and a new item is selected at an appropriate difficulty level. Little time is wasted administering a long string of items that are too easy or too difficult, and the student is working at a level that is challenging but not discouraging.

Computer adaptive testing can be designed not only to measure the proficiency of the student, but also to detect poor strategies in solving problems. When erroneous patterns begin to appear, the computer can offer remedial hints to get the student back on track, then test to see if the newly learned strategy transfers to similar problems. Additionally, computer adaptive testing can use moving displays and realistic situations as test items. For these and other reasons, computer adaptive testing will become an increasingly common feature of the measurement scene.

Ending Comments

Testing invariably reveals a wide range of individual difference within a single class. Teachers are concerned about meeting the individual differences within their classes, but the general public and many legislators seem to work on an unspoken and unexamined assumption that all children can and should be at "grade level." There are mounting pressures for tighter promotion policies driven by external testing programs. A news magazine recently announced in bold headlines: *Children in Georgia Must Pass Competency Test to Graduate from Kindergarten*. Is this going too far?

Concerns about statewide competency tests were voiced when the trend was first emerging (Jaeger & Kehr, 1980), and these concerns continue today. Definitions of competency appear unclear and arbitrary, teachers feel pressured to concentrate on the "basics" at the expense of higher order learning, and decisions which may best be made by the teacher are increasingly influenced by district and state policy. Now there is pressure to publish test results so that school-by-school and state-by-state comparisons can be made.

There are many issues in this situation. Linn (1988) raises a number of questions about making comparisons among states, districts, or schools. Is there a minimum set of knowledge and skills essential for all students? How similar are the curricula of the schools participating in the testing? To what extent does school achievement reflect the socioeconomic levels of the students? Additionally, does the norm of a test represent a standard which all students should achieve?

Sometimes teachers contribute to the tendency to see grade levels as fixed standards and work hard so that the pupils will be "ready" for the next teacher or school; all this in spite of Cook's (1951) classic summary of the wide range of individual differences in all classes and the futility of

expecting strict grading, grouping, or promotion policies to solve the problem. Cook points out that there is a range of 8 years in reading ability by the time children reach the end of elementary school and adds, ". . . if the low achievers in the eighth grade were demoted to the fourth, they would still be low achievers in the fourth grade" (p. 12).

There should be little trouble deciding the teacher's responsibility in the midst of conflicting demands. The teacher's responsibility is to the child at hand, not to the next teacher or the next school. Of course, by helping the pupil take his or her next developmental step, the current teacher is doing the best thing possible for both the child and the next teacher. In today's climate where education and testing have become highly politicized, teachers and school administrators must continue to ask to what extent external testing programs facilitate or hinder the work of the teacher and how much such tests contribute to school improvement.

It is well to keep in mind that instructional practices are shifting to new forms and the whole construct of achievement is undergoing change. Classrooms are moving away from memory of content as a dominant educational goal. The Holmes Group (1990), an important force in educational reform, visualizes "learning communities" where students examine, interrogate, and interpret information, constructing and reconstructing knowledge as they go along. Special video-based materials developed by the Cognition and Technology Group at Vanderbilt University (in press), *The Adventures of Jasper Woodbury,* give middle school students opportunities to work together in posing mathematical problems, finding relevant information and seeking solutions. The whole language movement is beginning to blur boundaries between subject matter and skill development. An elementary magnet school in St. Paul, Minnesota, is built around a museum concept. There students acquire knowledge of the rain forest, for example, not to remember it but to transform it into museum exhibits and assembly programs which communicate important information to other students, teachers, and parents.

In these new inquiry communities, conventional tests may play some role. It seems likely, however, that the most significant learning cannot be captured by existing instruments. Evaluation in the coming years may well focus on such abilities as problem sensing, problem finding and problem formulation. We may need to develop simulations that tell us what students have learned about organizing their work or finding relevant information through computer searches. We may find ways of measuring growth in student autonomy and in the development of reflective cognitive styles. These new movements in education will bring new challenges to testing and create many opportunities to contribute to educational measurements.

Summary

In summary, we study tests because they represent an approach to understanding human behavior. Tests provide more precise information about the abilities and performance of individuals than do our subjective impressions. Such information is important in making instructional decisions about students and in studying the effects of different teaching methods.

Teachers are frequently called on to construct their own tests as a basis for assigning grades and evaluating their instruction. Designing tests, writing test items, and studying the effectiveness of test items are important skills for teachers at every level of schooling from the first grade through university teaching.

At other times, teachers must select published tests or interpret scores from standardized tests. To evaluate and interpret tests, teachers need enough technical vocabulary to read the test manual and to know what to look for in deciding whether a test is good, bad or, as in most cases, somewhere in between.

Test evaluation leads naturally to consideration of the underlying characteristics that tests are designed to measure. After all, what is achievement? Is it the material a student remembers or does it include the ability to apply knowledge to new situations? Examining tests of achievement, intelligence, aptitude, and interests leads to a more thoughtful consideration of these traits and abilities.

The three sections of this book will provide major organizing ideas and numerous examples leading to increased competency in selecting measurement instruments, constructing tests, and interpreting test scores.

References

Asher, S. R., & Coie, J. D. (1990). *Peer rejection in childhood*. Cambridge, England; New York: Cambridge University Press.

The Cognition and Technology Group at Vanderbilt. (in press). The Jasper Series: A generative approach to improving mathematical thinking. In *This year in school science*. Washington, DC: American Association for the Advancement of Science.

Cook, W. W. (1951). The function of measurement in the facilitation of learning. In E. F. Lindquist (ed.), *Educational Measurement*. Washington, DC: American Council on Education.

Fleming G. M., & Chambers, B. A. (1983). Teacher-made tests: Windows on the classroom. *New directions for testing and measurement,* No. 19, 29–38.

The Holmes Group. (1990). *Tomorrow's schools*. East Lansing, MI: The Holmes Group.

Jaeger, R. M., & Kehr, C. (1980). *Minimum competency achievement testing: Motives, models, measures, and consequences*. Berkeley, CA: McCutchan.

Linn, R. (1988). State-by comparisons of achievement: Suggestions for enhancing validity. *Educational Researcher, 17*(3) 6–9.

Mitchell, R. (1992). *Testing for learning*. New York: The Free Press.

Measurement in education is the art of attaching numbers to aspects of human behavior. It is an art because intuitive and creative processes are at work in thinking about and defining such fuzzy ideas as intelligence, aptitudes, and achievement. But measurement is also a science. We insist on proof that test scores give us accurate information. We don't want crystal balls and stargazing. Statistical concepts? Yes, they bring precision to our discussions. And after that, understanding reliability, validity, and norms will take the mystery out of test jargon.

part one
Principles of Measurement

I looked up angrily from the journal I was reading. The author was referring to the means and standard deviations of reading tests for two groups of students. It was so frustrating. Why couldn't these researchers just say whether whole language was better than phonics? Do they think we have time to take a year off to learn statistics?

chapter two

Elementary Statistical Concepts

. . . until the phenomena of any branch of knowledge have been submitted to measurement and number, it cannot assume the status and dignity of a science. (Galton, 1879. Cited in Pearson, 1924)

One of the earliest investigators to use measurement as a means of studying human behavior was Sir Francis Galton, an aristocratic Englishman of broad-ranging interests. He had a motto: "Whenever you can, count!" And count he did. He counted the number of fidgets per minute of persons attending lectures and used his counts as an index of boredom. When he traveled through the cities of Great Britain, he tallied the beauty of the women he passed on the street and constructed a beauty map of the various cities of England. London, according to his count, had the highest proportion of beautiful women (Newman, 1956).

Galton's fascination with human behavior led him into many areas: the inheritance of abilities, visual imagery, memory for odors, fingerprinting and many other fields. In 1884, he established a laboratory where fellow Britons could pay fourpence to be measured for height, weight, strength of grip, breathing power, color blindness, keenness of hearing, and other characteristics. Among other purposes, Galton hoped that the measurements would be useful in determining whether promising youth actually grew up to be successful individuals.

Galton's story has a message. It is easy to view measurement and statistics as cold, technical, and of interest only to persons with mathematical minds. Galton's primary interest was not charts and statistics, although he constructed them at the drop of a hat. Galton's interests were first, last, and foremost in human beings, and in learning all he could about human diversity and potential. In observing people, however, Galton's contention was that precise measurements are more helpful than global impressions. When interpreting and comparing measurements, statistics provide the essential tools.

Snow and Statistics

The Eskimo have several words for the different kinds of snow surfaces on which they depend. In a similar fashion, statisticians see more complexity in a set of numbers than we do. Most of these perceptions, however, can be shared without assuming a special background in mathematics. Almost every day, for example, we talk about some kind of average. We may comment that, on the average, it takes about half an hour to drive to work. But, we also know that there is some variability around this average. Depending on weather and traffic conditions, we may deviate from the average as much as ten minutes on any given day. Without being conscious of it, we habitually use the concepts of averages and deviations.

Here is where snow and statistics are related. The statistician knows that there are several different kinds of averages and has separate names for each. There are also several ways of expressing deviations from these averages. In getting acquainted with this vocabulary, we are delving into the area of **descriptive statistics**, which are the concepts and vocabulary that are useful in describing a group of test scores. These specialized terms are the "bread and butter" words used by authors of test manuals and research reports. Learning the vocabulary and becoming familiar with the concepts are the keys to a sense of security in reading test manuals and research reports on measurement.

In this chapter, we will see how a list of test scores can be organized into an orderly frequency distribution. Our discussion will center around ways of describing such distributions of test scores by talking about measures of central tendency and measures of variability. We will see that the shape of the distribution and the kind of data collected will play a role in deciding which measure of central tendency to use in describing distributions of scores. As we progress, we will discover that one measure of variability, the standard deviation, is the building block for an important class of scores, standard scores. Standard scores, in turn, also contribute to our understanding of how correlation coefficients are obtained. We end the chapter with an introductory note on **inferential statistics**, the procedures for testing hypotheses.

It is necessary to first say a word about numbers and the scales used in measurement.

Types of Scales

Numbers appear to be quite straightforward and easy to understand. For example, we know that eight marbles are twice as many as four and that zero means no marbles at all. We shall see, however, that these assumptions do not fit all kinds of scales. Rowntree (1981) uses the purchasing of a secondhand bicycle to illustrate four different kinds of scales: nominal, ordinal, interval, and ratio. Consider the following features, which might be important in deciding which bike to buy:

Make of bicycle	Price
Color	Size of frame
Age	Number of gears
Condition (poor, acceptable, excellent)	

These qualities can be used to illustrate the kinds of scales that numbers might represent.

Nominal Scale

Make and color are obviously categories. If we were coding these categories into a computer in order to keep a record of several bicycles, we might use the following codes: Raleigh = 1, Falcon = 2, Fuji = 3, and so on. Color could also be coded: red = 1, blue = 2, and white = 3. By this process, we would have created a **nominal scale**. Numbers in a nominal scale serve only one function: they name the category. The obvious fact about a nominal scale is that the numbers have no quantitative meaning at all. We cannot do arithmetic with such numbers.

Ordinal Scale

The condition of a bicycle is also a category, but in this case, the categories can be ranked, or ordered, from better to worse. Ranking the bicycles from highest to lowest will produce an **ordinal scale**. Some bicycles of adjacent ranks, however, will have very little differences between them while others, differing by only one rank, may show marked differences in condition. For this reason, the ordinal scales do not have equal intervals and it is not possible to say that a bicycle with a rank of four is twice as bad as one with a rank of two. This characteristic of ordinal scales makes them poor units for further arithmetic analysis.

Interval Scale

Interval scales refer to characteristics that can be measured in amounts. The interval scale has equal intervals, but no zero point. Temperature, for example, is an interval scale in that an object of zero degrees is not completely lacking in heat. With these scales one cannot say, for example, that Monday's temperature of forty degrees is twice as warm as last Friday's temperature of twenty degrees; one can only say that Monday is twenty degrees warmer. Most measurements in education and psychology are interval scales. Since interval scales do represent quantities or amounts, further mathematical work can be done with them.

Ratio Scales

Ratio scales have equal intervals, and also have a true zero point. Measures of time, dollar value, length, and area are all ratio scales since all have an actual zero point. The age of a bicycle in years, the price, the size of frame, and the number of gears can all be expressed in terms of the amount of each characteristic and, in addition, have true zero points.

In educational measurement, we are almost always dealing with interval scales, i.e., scales which have equal intervals but no true zero point. Knowledge of the various kinds of scales is useful in preventing us from performing calculations on nominal or ordinal scales without realizing that these are not good units for further computations. In addition, the measure of central tendency that we select will depend, in part, on the kind of scale used in recording the data.

Discrete and Continuous Variables

To round out our discussion of scales, we need to note that data can reflect either discrete or continuous variables. Discrete variables are those that are encoded in specific steps with no intervening spaces. In our example of the bicycles, the number of gears is a discrete variable which changes in a step-by-step fashion with no values between each step. Discrete variables imply counting. Continuous variables, on the other hand, are variables that can change in value by infinitely smaller units. The frame size of the bicycle, for example, can become large or small in steps of one inch, or in increasingly smaller fractions of an inch. Continuous variables imply measurement.

Frequency Distributions

Phillips (1982) observes: "If the basic element in measurement is a score, the corresponding concept in statistics is a **distribution** that includes many scores—in short, a **frequency distribution**" (p. 2). We will see how frequency distributions provide the basic framework for interpreting test scores and communicating the performance of a group of students.

Let us build an understanding of descriptive statistics by taking one student in one class and seeing what can be done to interpret the student's score and to describe the class performance. If Bob Anderson, a student in our class, earns a science test score of twelve, we really know very little about his performance. If we say the test had 20 questions on it, we may feel that the score is low since he missed 40 percent of the items. If we discover that the highest score on the test was sixteen, we begin to revise our original evaluation. While it is possible to keep adding information bit by bit, the most efficient way of interpreting Bob's score is to see where it falls in a frequency distribution.

Kachigan (1982) illustrates the construction of a frequency distribution from the list of scores in table 2.1.

From this list of scores, the data are organized as shown in table 2.2 so that the teacher can quickly see the number of students earning each score, or the **frequencies**. In addition to the frequencies, three additional statistics are shown in table 2.2: relative frequencies, cumulative frequencies, and cumulative relative frequencies.

Table 2.1 *Test Scores of 36 Individuals*

Individuals	Test Scores	Individuals	Test Scores
Anderson, B.	12	Kornfield, L.	11
Andrews, T.	9	Lee, R.	10
Barclay, S.	8	Logan, B.	14
Bishop, C.	10	Marsh, N.	8
Brody, R.	15	Melrose, G.	10
Carlton, M.	11	Moran, C.	9
Clark, D.	7	Noble, V.	10
Cox, S.	14	Parker, L.	12
Dewey, D.	10	Potter, D.	13
Edelman, P.	13	Rhodes, F.	8
Farrell, J.	11	Rubin, B.	10
Frank, R.	7	Schultz, R.	11
Gibbs, J.	9	Silver, W.	9
Gray, W.	11	Stack, E.	13
Harmon, G.	12	Thomas, J.	12
Hodge, N.	14	Vargas, R.	11
Irving, T.	6	Weiss, C.	10
Kent, N.	16	Wheeler, E.	9

Table 2.2 *Frequency Distribution of 36 Test Scores*

(1) Test Scores	(2) Tally of Individuals	(3) *How many?* Frequencies	(4) Relative Frequencies	(5) Cumulative Frequencies	(6) Cumulative Relative Frequencies
6			1	2.8%	1	2.8%
7	||	2	5.6	3	8.3
8	|||	3	8.3	6	16.7
9	|||||	5	13.9	11	30.6
10	||||| ||	7	19.4	18	50.0
11	|||||		6	16.7	24	66.7
12	||||	4	11.1	28	77.8
13	|||	3	8.3	31	86.1
14	|||	3	8.3	34	94.4
15			1	2.8	35	97.2
16			1	2.8	36	100.0
		36	100.0%		

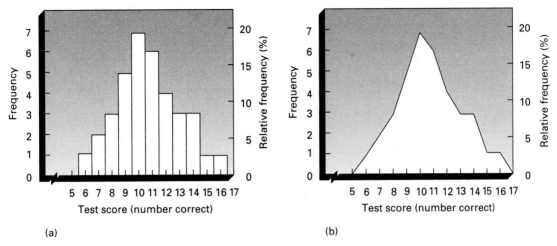

(a)

(b)

Figure 2.1 *Alternative methods for portraying the frequency distribution of the test scores of 36 individuals as given in table 2.2.*
Reprinted with the permission of Radius Press from *Multivariate Statistical Analysis* by S. K. Kachigan. Copyright © 1982 by Sam Kash Kachigan.

The **relative frequencies** (column 4) simply express the number of students earning each score as a percentage of the total class. Thus, 2.8 percent of the students who took the test earned a score of six. These percentages are obtained by dividing any given frequency by the number of students in the class.

The **cumulative frequencies** (column 5) show the number of students who are at or below a particular score. The cumulative frequencies are obtained by accumulating (adding) all the students (frequencies) up to and including a particular score level. Remembering that Bob Anderson earned a score of twelve, we note that he equaled or exceeded 28 of the students in the class.

The **cumulative relative frequencies** (column 6) show the percent of students falling at or below a given score level. These percents are obtained by dividing the cumulative frequency (column 5) for a given score by the number of students in the class. We find from studying this last column that Bob Anderson, with his score of twelve, has equaled or exceeded about 78 percent of the students who took the test, a rather good performance.

The frequency distribution is not only an important tool in helping teachers organize and interpret test results, but it also provides a useful stepping stone to an understanding of the normal curve. In figure 2.1, Kachigan presents a **histogram** (part a) showing the frequency distribution for the thirty-six students as a bar graph, with the height of the bar indicating the number of students earning each score. Connecting the tops of these bars with a continuous line creates the **frequency polygon** shown in part b. Again, the height of the line indicates the number of students obtaining each score on the test.

Figure 2.2 *Progression of a histogram to a theoretical continuous distribution.*
Reprinted with the permission of Radius Press from *Multivariate Statistical Analysis* by S.K. Kachigan. Copyright © 1982 by Sam Kash Kachigan.

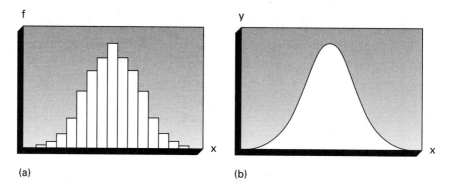

Notice that the frequency polygon for the class is a little jagged and that the right side is a little different from the left side. If many hundreds of students took the science test, however, the frequency polygon would begin to look more symmetrical, and if we could measure even more finely the differences in knowledge among the students, the line connecting the tops of the bars would begin to smooth out. Figure 2.2, adapted from Kachigan (1982) shows the more regular and symmetrical displays that might be expected from testing an infinitely large number of students.

It will be apparent to students with some introduction to statistics that part b of figure 2.2 resembles a **normal distribution**. We will have more to say about normal distributions later in this chapter.

Not all distributions of test scores fit the pattern of a normal curve. Figure 2.3 from Hinkle, Wiersma, and Jurs (1988) illustrates some of the various shapes that distributions may take, along with the technical terms statisticians use to name these shapes.

It is not necessary to memorize all these specialized names. It is, however, important to keep in mind the concept of skewed distributions illustrated in curves b and c of figure 2.3. Each of these curves is skewed, or pulled, to one side or the other. Curve b is skewed to the right, with the long tail extending to the right, and might illustrate a test that was too hard for the group. Curve c has a long tail to the left, hence it is skewed to the left. Curve c indicates that many students are stacked up at the high end of the score distribution. This pattern of scores might indicate a test that was too easy for the group.

Measures of Central Tendency

To this point, we have introduced the concepts of different numerical scales, frequency distributions as a means of organizing data, and curves as a means of displaying frequency distributions graphically. We now turn to

(a) Rectangular or uniform distribution

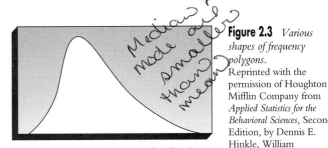

[handwritten: Median & mode are smaller than mean]

(b) Positively skewed distribution

Figure 2.3 *Various shapes of frequency polygons.* Reprinted with the permission of Houghton Mifflin Company from *Applied Statistics for the Behavioral Sciences,* Second Edition, by Dennis E. Hinkle, William Wiersma, and Stephen G. Jurs. Copyright © 1988 by Houghton Mifflin Company.

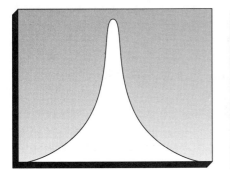

[handwritten: Median and mode are lots larger than mean]

(c) Negatively skewed distribution

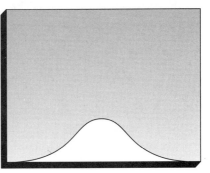

[handwritten: Median mode mean close to same]

(d) Normal distribution

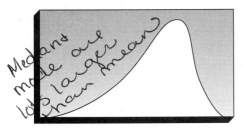

(e) Leptokurtic distribution

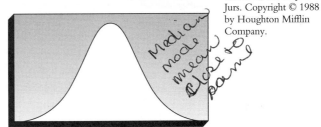

(f) Platykurtic distribution

a discussion of ways of summarizing frequency distributions statistically. We will find that we need only two statistics to describe almost any distribution of scores: a measure of central tendency and a measure of variability. The measure of **central tendency** tells us where the scores tend to stack up, that is, where the center of the distribution is located. Measures of **variability** tell us how the remainder of the scores scatter around the center, that is, whether the scores are spread out over a considerable distance from the center or whether they are bunched in close to the center. In this discussion, you will see that our choice among the various statistics to describe a distribution will depend both on the kind of scale that the data represent and on the shape of the frequency distribution we are describing.

The three most common measures of central tendency are the arithmetic mean, the median, and the mode. Let us examine each of these.

Arithmetic Mean

The **mean** is the most useful of the various measures of central tendency. It is calculated by adding all the scores and dividing by the number of scores. Adding the scores of the students from the science class introduced earlier and dividing by the thirty-six students who took the test yields a mean of 10.69. The mean is the familiar "average" encountered in reports of the average educational level of a particular group or the average number of soft drinks consumed each year.

The mean provides the optimal measure of central tendency when the scores are on an interval scale and the shape of the distribution is symmetrical. The mean, however, is susceptible to distortion by a few high scores. It doesn't take many millionaires to make the mean income of a neighborhood misrepresent the actual income of the rest of the residents.

Median

The **median** is the "middle one" in a distribution of scores arranged in order from lowest to highest. More accurately, it is the midpoint because, in distributions where there are an even number of scores, there will be no score at the midpoint. The analogy of a seesaw is often used in describing the median. For an even number of people, the median is the point at which the board would be balanced with half the people on one side and the other half on the other side. This is the case for the sample of thirty-six science students in our frequency distribution. The median will be midway between the eighteenth and the nineteenth student. Examining the frequency distribution, we note that the eighteenth student has a score of 10 while the nineteenth student has a score of 11. Since the midpoint between these two students would be 10.5, the median for this distribution is 10.5.

Note that in obtaining the median, we do no calculations on the test scores, but rather count from either end of the distribution to the middle. For this reason, the median is most appropriate for ordinal data, i.e., cases where we have ranks of individuals rather than actual scores. Additionally, since no calculations are done with the scores, the actual size of extreme scores does not influence the median. If we are examining the average income of 100 persons in a neighborhood where the highest income is $60,000 a year, the median income will not change at all if the top person moves away and is replaced by a person who earns a million dollars a year.

Mode

The **mode** is the most frequently occurring score. Inspection of the frequency distribution of the science class which has served as our example reveals that most students earned a score of 11; thus, the modal score for the class is 11. The mode is always at the highest point in a curve of a frequency distribution and it provides a quick index of central tendency. The mode is not useful in statistical work, but there are occasions when it might be the best representation of a group. If a supply sergeant for a company of soldiers could order only ten pairs of shoes this month, and all must be of the same size, it would be a good idea to order the modal size for the company.

The mode is an indispensable term for describing central tendency in highly irregular curves. For example, some curves look like a camel with two humps. This configuration is communicated instantly in the literature by describing the curve as **bimodal.** In addition, the mode is the only measure of central tendency that is appropriate when dealing with nominal scales. It would not make sense, for example, to obtain a mean or median for bike color after coding each color as a number. It would, however, make sense to note that the modal color was two, indicating that most bikes were blue.

Relationship between Measures of Central Tendency and Skewness

For a normal, bell-shaped curve, the three measures of central tendency that we have been discussing will all fall in the same place.

For skewed curves, however, the median or the mode may communicate a more accurate picture of the distribution of scores. As mentioned earlier, skewed curves have long tails, which represent a few people getting scores that are far from the middle. These extreme scores tend to pull the mean toward them. As can be observed from figure 2.4, the mean is likely to be the poorest indicator of central tendency for such distributions.

Measures of Variability

In addition to a measure of central tendency in describing distributions, it is also necessary to have a measure of the variability of the scores. Are the scores in a distribution spread out over a large area or are they clustered

Figure 2.4 *Relationship between skewness and measures of central tendency.*
Reprinted with the permission of W. H. Freeman and Company from *Statistical Thinking,* Second Edition, by John Phillips. Copyright © 1982 by W.H. Freeman and Company.

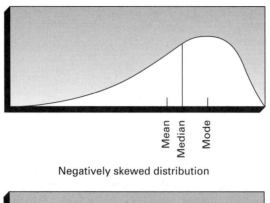

Negatively skewed distribution

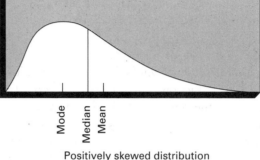

Positively skewed distribution

closely around the mean? To describe this aspect of a frequency distribution, we speak of measures of spread, scatter, dispersion, or simply variability. Two simple measures of scatter are used in describing frequency distributions: the range and the semi-interquartile range. Three additional indices of scatter prove to be more useful in doing statistical work with test scores: average deviation, variance, and standard deviation. Each of these measures of variability will be described in turn, and the standard deviation will be singled out for additional discussion.

Range

The range is a fairly crude measure of the variability of scores within a group. It is simply an identification of the lowest and highest scores earned. It may also be stated as the difference between these scores. Note how much is added to the description of the set of science test scores when the teacher is able to say, "The average score on my test was 10.69, but the scores ranged from 6 to 16. I really expected a bigger range than 10 points."

As useful as it is in providing a quick picture of the variability of the scores, the range suffers a distinct weakness. It is highly susceptible to extreme scores. In the test we have been considering, suppose that the top score were 20 rather than 16. By changing only one score, the range would jump from 10 to 14 points, an increase of 40 percent.

Semi-Interquartile Range

We have noted that the range is based on only two scores, and extreme performance on either end can distort the picture conveyed by the range.

The semi-interquartile range solves this problem by reporting one half of the range within which the middle 50 percent of the class lie. The middle 50 percent lie in the **interquartile range**. The interquartile range is obtained by dividing the class into quarters from low to high and then noting the scores that mark the bottom quarter and the top quarter. For the thirty-six science students in the frequency distribution we have been considering, nine students will fall in each quarter. To obtain the interquartile range, start at the lowest score level and count toward the middle until you come to the ninth student and note the corresponding test score for that student. In our example, the score is 9. Repeat the procedure starting at the highest score and counting toward the middle. The ninth student will have a score of 12. Subtracting the bottom quartile (as these points are called) from the top quartile gives you the interquartile range. For the science class, 9 from 12 gives an interquartile range of 3. Dividing this in half provides a semi-interquartile range of 1.5.

The semi-interquartile range is typically used to describe scatter around the median and in the case of our continuing example, the statement describing the distribution would be: "The median of the science test was 10.5 with a semi-interquartile range of 1.5." From this we deduce that about a quarter of the students fall between the median and a score 1.5 below the median, and another quarter of the class falls at the median plus a score 1.5 above the median.

The measures of variability we have been discussing are most appropriate when dealing with ordinal data or when the scores form a skewed distribution.

The second family of indices of variability to which we now turn is based on the deviations of scores from the mean. Let us see precisely what we mean by the term **deviation**. Table 2.3 shows the scores of our thirty-six science students.

To keep our numbers simple, we have rounded the mean obtained by the thirty-six students from 10.69 up to 10.7. Examining the first student, we find that he earned a score of 12. This score is 1.3 score points

Table 2.3 *Test Scores, Deviations from the Mean, and Squared Deviations for 36 Students*

Score	x	x²	Score	x	x²
12	1.3	1.69	11	.3	.09
9	1.7	2.89	10	.7	.49
8	2.7	7.29	14	3.3	10.89
10	.7	.49	8	2.7	7.29
15	4.3	18.49	10	.7	.49
11	.3	.09	9	1.7	2.89
7	3.7	13.69	10	.7	.49
14	3.3	10.89	12	1.3	1.69
10	.7	.49	13	2.3	5.29
13	2.3	5.29	8	2.7	7.29
11	.3	.09	10	.7	.49
7	3.7	13.69	11	.3	.09
9	1.7	2.89	9	1.7	2.89
11	.3	.09	13	2.3	5.29
12	1.3	1.69	12	1.3	1.69
14	3.3	10.89	11	.3	.09
6	4.7	22.09	10	.7	.49
16	5.3	28.09	9	1.7	2.89

how far away from the mean or middle

above the mean and this deviation (x) is recorded under the column for deviations. The second student earned a score of 9. This score is 1.7 points below the mean and this deviation is recorded. Note that the deviations are recorded without the plus or minus sign. We will soon be adding up all the deviations and if we include the signs, the sum will be zero. In fact, one definition of the mean is the point at which the sum of the deviations from that point is zero. With the meaning of deviation established, we are now ready to proceed.

Average Deviation

The **average deviation** is the sum of the deviations from the mean divided by the number of scores. It is easy to see that some people are farther away from the mean than others. We have determined how much each person deviates from the mean by subtracting the mean from the individual's score and ignoring the sign. The average deviation is obtained by adding up all these deviations and dividing by the number of cases, in this example, 67 is divided by 36 to obtain 1.9 (rounded). The average deviation allows one to make statements like: "My students earned a mean of 10.7 on the science test, and on the average, they deviated from the mean almost 2 points." Generally, the mean plus or minus the average deviation will include 50 percent of the students tested.

Variance

Variance is another measure of the variability of scores around the mean. It is obtained by squaring each deviation, adding up the squared deviations and dividing by the number of cases. In table 2.3, you will notice that we have squared the deviations for each student and entered these in the x^2 column.

The variance is not a very good intuitive measure of variability, but we introduce variance as a stepping stone to the most commonly used and most useful measure of variability, the standard deviation.

Standard Deviation

The **standard deviation** is nothing more than the square root of the variance. Yet, because it is so basic in testing, it is worthwhile to trace the steps in deriving the standard deviation from a set of data. Remember that the standard deviation is a measure of variability, so we start by converting each score to a deviation (x), the distance a score is from the mean. We then square these deviations (x^2), add them up, and divide by the number of cases. As we mentioned, this is the variance. Since we squared all the deviations, we now need to "unsquare" them, so we take the square root of the result to this point. This gives us the standard deviation.

Let us return to our original class of thirty-six science students. In table 2.3, we have shown the original scores for each student coupled with deviation of this score from the mean (x) and the squared deviation (x^2). Using the figures in this table, we have determined that the sum of the squared deviations is 191.64. This sum divided by the thirty-six observations equals 5.32, the variance. The square root of the variance is 2.31, the standard deviation.

For those who would like to see these operations summarized as a formula, we let "x" stand for the deviation of a score from the mean, the Greek letter sigma, "Σ", stand for "sum up," "n" for the number of observations, "SD" for the standard deviation, and write the following formula for the standard deviation.

$$SD = \sqrt{\frac{\Sigma x^2}{n}}$$

Between the mean and plus and minus one standard deviation, there will generally be 68 percent of the cases. We will talk more about this in a moment, but for now we should know that a small standard deviation means that most of the cases are packed in close to the mean. A large standard deviation means that the cases are spread out.

Figure 2.5 *Test A: Standard deviation = 2 Test B: Standard deviation = 8*

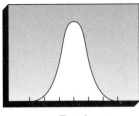

Test A
Small standard deviation

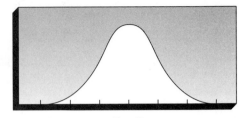

Test B
Large standard deviation

Once we have learned what the standard deviation is, we can visualize the shape of the distribution. If the standard deviation is small, we know at once that the distribution curve is narrow, pinched in, and confined within a narrow range (Test A in figure 2.5). If the standard deviation is large, we know that the curve is spread out, with scores stretching far away from the mean (Test B).

This is a good point at which to stop and look back. We have learned that frequency distributions are a good way to organize a set of data or test scores. We have seen that these distributions can be displayed graphically through the use of histograms and frequency polygons. As the number of observations become increasingly large, the frequency polygons become more symmetrical and bell-shaped. These distributions can be described by providing a measure of the central tendency and of the variability of the scores. For curves that represent interval or ratio data and are relatively "normal" in shape, the mean and the standard deviation are the most useful measures of central tendency and variability. Finally, we learned that given the standard deviation, we have a reasonably good idea about whether the curve is squeezed in with a limited amount of scatter among the scores or spread out with scores distributed relatively far from the mean. In the next section we will put these concepts to work.

The Normal Curve

In this section, we will introduce and discuss the **normal curve**, a graphic representation of a theoretical set of test scores. Our basic assumption in measurement is that almost any large set of test scores will fit this curve. We will find that familiarity with the normal curve furthers our understanding of the important building block, the standard deviation.

The normal curve is the familiar bell-shaped curve found in every book on measurement and statistics. Where did this normal curve come from and what is it? The normal curve was first published by the English mathematician, De Moivre, in 1733 after working on the theory of games and chance. Laplace and Gauss derived the curve independently, and occasionally the curve is referred to as the Gaussian curve.

History

We have already seen how a curve can represent the distribution of a set of test scores. Adolph Quetelet, an early Belgian statistician, found that when he inspected very large sets of measurements collected on people, the heights of French army conscripts, for example, or the chests of Scottish soldiers, the results fell into the bell-shaped curve. He felt it was almost as if nature aimed at some ideal form, and missed on either side, but with fewer and fewer misses at greater distance from the middle.

In educational measurements, the baseline of the curve represents test scores ranging from low to high. The height of the curve at any point represents the number of people stacked up at a particular score. One might visualize these people crowded together, each above his or her test score.

To statisticians, the normal curve is much more than just a picture of a test distribution. The normal curve is a mathematical model that, given the mean and standard deviation, provides the ability to predict how many people will fall at any particular place in a series of measurements.

We have already learned that a distribution of test scores can be described by a measure of central tendency and a measure of variability. We further learned that one measure of variability, the standard deviation, is computed by obtaining the square root of the variance. We shall now see that the standard deviation has a fixed relationship with the areas under a normal curve. This fact allows us to perform some useful feats with it. For example, knowing the mean and the standard deviation of a set of scores, you can tell immediately what score will fall at the 84th percentile.

You can perform these feats if you think of the standard deviation as a kind of yardstick laid along the base of the normal curve, as shown in figure 2.6. The normal curve has known mathematical characteristics specifying that when the standard deviation yardstick is laid on the baseline with one end at the mean, 34 percent of the people under the roof of the normal distribution curve will be clustered above the yardstick. Since the curve is symmetrical, it does not matter whether the yardstick is placed to the right or to the left as long as one end is touching the mean.

If you lay the yardstick down again, starting where you left off, i.e., one standard deviation beyond the mean, note that not as many people will be standing on this yardstick. After all, the roof of the curve is coming down, and there isn't much room for them. In fact, about 14 percent of the people under the normal curve will be standing on the yardstick

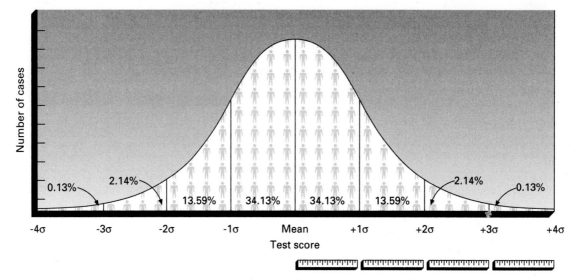

Figure 2.6 *Normal curve with four standard deviations shown to the right of the mean.*

the second time it is put down. Laying the yardstick down a third time reveals that only about 2 percent of the people will be this far away from the mean. You could go beyond this point, but it is hardly worth the effort since there would be so few cases found. For all practical purposes, the normal distribution curve extends three standard deviations beyond the mean in each direction.

The standard deviation marks off a precisely defined percentage of people when the distribution is normal. This is true even though the size of a standard deviation will change when it is computed from one set of scores to another. Assume that two tests have been administered to a group of students and that both tests have a mean of 20. Let us also assume that Test A has a standard deviation of 2 and Test B has a standard deviation of 8. Determine what percent of the students fall within each of the score ranges shown here.

	Score Range	Percent of Students
Test A	20 to 22	_____
Test B	20 to 28	_____

No matter what the computed size of a standard deviation may be, it bears a constant relationship to the distribution of scores from which it was calculated. By definition, we know that in a normal distribution of scores, 34 percent of the students will fall between the mean and plus one standard deviation. If you indicated this percentage in your answers, you have grasped the relationship that we will use as we progress to the next step.

Going from Standard Deviations to Standard Scores

Standard deviations serve as the major element in computing a class of scores known as standard scores. These standard scores are quite useful in comparing an individual on two different tests, almost like comparing apples and oranges. Suppose that a parent asks your help in determining whether her daughter is doing better work in math or in English. Her daughter, Maria, has a score of 46 on her math test and a score of 65 on her English test.

At first glance, Maria appears to be doing much better in English, especially when you learn that each test contains 100 items. But you need the more complete information about each of the two tests that is shown here.

	Math Test	English Test
Number of Test Items	100	100
Maria's Score	46	65
Class Mean	40	50
Standard Deviation	6	15

By considering this information in the light of your knowledge about standard deviations, you can reason your way to an answer for Maria's mother. Try it. Did you arrive at an answer?

You may have thought through the problem in the following way. Maria is six points above the class average on the math test. From the tabulation, we see that the standard deviation in math is six points; thus, she is one standard deviation above the mean in math.

Similarly, Maria is 15 points above the average on the English test. The standard deviation for the English test is 15; thus, she is one standard deviation above the mean in English. It appears that Maria is doing equally well in both classes.

You also have enough information to express Maria's performance on each test as a percentile score. The reasoning goes like this. If Maria reaches the class mean, she has exceeded 50 percent of the students. Noting that she is one standard deviation above the mean, we remember that 34 percent of the students are between the mean and one standard deviation. Adding this 34 percent to the 50 percent, we see that Maria has equaled or exceeded 84 percent of the students. She is at the 84th percentile in both classes.

z-Scores

Without realizing it, you have converted Maria's score to a z-score. A **z-score** is a standard score that expresses a test score in standard deviation units, i.e., tells you how many standard deviations from the mean a particular score may lie. We will learn later that there are several kinds of standard scores, such as the SAT scores, that are useful in comparing performance on two different tests. All standard scores, however, are derived from the basic z-score.

A z-score is a standard score in which the mean is set equal to zero and the standard deviation is set equal to 1. Thus a z-score of 3 means that a student is three standard deviations above the mean. A z-score is computed by the following formula:

$$z = \frac{(X - \overline{X})}{SD}$$

Where   X = score obtained by student
$\overline{X}$ = the mean of the group
SD = the standard deviation of the group

For Maria's math score of 46 in a distribution with a mean of 40 and a standard deviation of 6, we can substitute and get

$$z = \frac{46 - 40}{6}$$

Similarly, for Maria's English score of 65 in a distribution of scores with a mean of 50 and a standard deviation of 15, we get

$$z = \frac{65 - 50}{15}$$

A glance at the two z-scores reveals that Maria's performance is identical on the two tests in different subject areas.

z-scores are easy to compute and very useful, but look what happens when we take another example: Jacob is also in Maria's math class. He earned a score of 31 on the same test. What is Jacob's z-score? Go ahead and work it out, then we will take a look at the results. Remember, the mean in the math class was 40 and the standard deviation was 6.

Have you done the arithmetic? If so, you arrived at a z-score for Jacob of -1.5. This score is easy enough to interpret. It means that Jacob is one and a half standard deviations below the mean on the math test.

For some people, scores containing negative numbers and decimals create feelings of insecurity. In a later chapter, we will see that z-scores serve as the basis for computing other standard scores that eliminate these troublesome features.

We have come a long way in our study of descriptive statistics and its applications. We have learned about the normal distribution curve, measures of central tendency, and measures of variability. We have seen how the standard deviation is used in arriving at a particular standard score, the z-score. We have also observed that the z-score makes it possible to compare accomplishments on two different tests by placing performance on a single scale.

We will now see that viewing a test score in terms of deviations from the mean contributes to an intuitive understanding of how correlation coefficients work.

The Correlation Coefficient

Most people understand that a **correlation coefficient** is an index of the degree of association of one variable with another. Correlation coefficients summarize relationships that can be observed by constructing a **scatterplot**. In the following example (Rowntree, 1981), ten students have completed a test, each providing a score for the theoretical aspects of the subject and a score for practical applications. Is there any relationship between these two sets of scores?

Within the formula of a correlation coefficient, the student's performance on each test is transformed into z-scores. Thus, student A, who appears to be below the mean on both tests, would have a relatively large negative z-score for both theory and practice. If these two negative z-scores were multiplied, the cross product would be positive. If, on the other hand, a student were above average in one test and below average in the other, the cross product of the z-scores would be negative. The Pearson Product Moment Correlation Coefficient is simply the mean of the cross products obtained for every student in the group. The calculation is generally done with the aid of statistical packages preloaded onto a computer disk. For our purposes, it is important to note that the raw data entering into a correlation coefficient need not be of equal units. Different units and different scales, such as height and weight, can be entered into a correlation formula since the formula converts incoming information into comparable z-scores.

Correlation coefficients can vary from +1 through 0 to −1. Interestingly, correlation coefficients of +1 and of −1 both indicate perfect correlations between two variables. For a positive correlation, an increase in

Student	Theory	Practice
A	59	70
B	63	69
C	64	76
D	70	79
E	74	76
F	78	80
G	79	86
H	82	77
I	86	84
J	92	90

one variable is associated with an increase in the other; for example, intelligence and achievement are positively correlated. On the other hand, negative correlation means that as one variable goes up, the other variable goes down; an example would be amount of rainfall and attendance at a baseball game.

Scatterplots of data in which two variables are positively and highly associated with each other will show multiple dots in a cigar-shaped cluster bunched around an imaginary line running diagonally across the plot from lower left to upper right. For negatively associated variables, the imaginary line will run from upper left to lower right. If the correlation is near zero, the dots will be randomly scattered throughout the plot. Figure 2.7 shows a plot of the ten students taking the theory and the practicality tests.

For the scatterplot of the ten students taking the theory test and the practice test, we can see that there appears to be a strong, positive relationship between the two sets of scores. Students who do well on the theory test tend to do well on the practice test.

It is important to dispel two mistaken conceptions about correlation coefficients. One mistaken idea is that correlations communicate the percent of agreement between two sets of data. This is not true. The correlation coefficient is simply an index of the relationship. In order to see how much of the variation in one variable can be accounted for by the other, it is necessary to square the correlation coefficient. For example, if we obtain a correlation of .60 between SAT scores and first semester grade point averages in a particular college, we could say that 36 percent (the square of .60) of the achievement in college can be predicted by the SAT scores. We might go on and assert that 36 percent of college achievement might be attributed to the ability measured by the SAT and the remainder of achievement might be attributed to other factors.

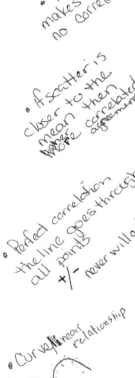

handwritten margin notes:
- If scattered makes circle no correlation
- If scatter is closer to the mean then more correlated/agreement
- Perfect correlation the line goes through all points +/- never will get
- Curvelinear relationship

Part 1: Principles of Measurement

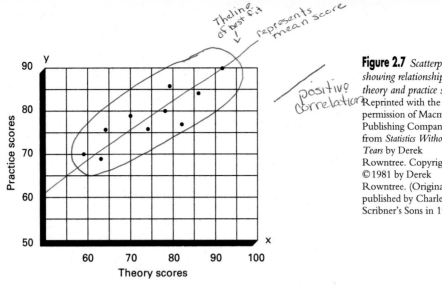

The line of best fit ↓ *represents mean score*

positive? correlation

Figure 2.7 *Scatterplot showing relationship of theory and practice scores.* Reprinted with the permission of Macmillan Publishing Company from *Statistics Without Tears* by Derek Rowntree. Copyright ©1981 by Derek Rowntree. (Originally published by Charles Scribner's Sons in 1981.)

tells you nothing about why

The second misconception about correlation is the mistaken idea that correlation indicates causation. Note that in the preceding paragraph, we used the term "might" in saying that 36 percent of the variation in achievement might be attributed to the ability measured by the SAT scores. In fact, the correlation only indicates the degree of association between two variables. It has been reported that there was a significant correlation between the incidence of sunspots observed by astronomers and the number of residential mortgage loans negotiated during a given year. It seems farfetched to believe that sunspots cause people to buy homes, and this may be a good example to remember if we become too enthusiastic about drawing causal conclusions from correlation coefficients.

The correlation coefficient is an essential tool in further considerations of testing. Correlation coefficients are used in examining test reliability and test validity, and in studying the full range of human characteristics.

How High Should a Correlation Coefficient Be?

It is logical to ask how high a correlation coefficient should be, but this is like asking how tall a person should be. The answer to the latter question will depend on whether we want someone to play basketball or be a jockey. If we correlate scores from two administrations of the same test, as we do when examining test reliability, we expect correlation coefficients of .8 or higher. If we correlate test scores with an index of complex performance, school achievement for example, a correlation coefficient of .6 would be considered very good.

Rowntree (1981) visibly winces when asked for guidance in interpreting correlation coefficients, but then reluctantly offers the following pointers:

.0 to .2	very weak, negligible
.2 to .4	weak, low
.4 to .7	moderate
.7 to .9	strong, high, marked
.9 to 1.0	very strong, very high

While there is no simple answer to the query, "How high should a correlation coefficient be?," Rowntree's guide provides a useful orientation until we gain more experience with the various applications of this highly useful statistic.

A Word about Inferential Statistics

In a moment we will be summarizing our discussion of descriptive statistics, the concepts and vocabulary used in describing a set of measurements. While it may seem that we have covered a lot of ground, almost everything hinges on only two important ideas: The mean and the standard deviation. One is a measure of central tendency; the other is a measure of variation of scores around the mean.

Think how powerful these ideas are. Imagine that you have been captured by a wicked king who announces, "Off with your head," but sets a condition. Your life will be spared if you can foretell the age of one man who will be brought from the collection of 100 prisoners in the dungeon below. You are clueless, but a sympathetic court jester slips you a note showing the mean age of all prisoners held in the dungeon: 40 years of age. Your very best guess is to give the king this age.

The king may realize that your chances of survival are small, so to even up the odds, he may announce that your estimate of the age of the prisoner who will be arriving must be within four years of the actual age. Let us say that the helpful jester has included in his note the information that the standard deviation of the ages of the prisoners is 2. Your best bet about the age of the man who will be walking through the door is still 40, but you can now exhibit a self-confident smile. You know that approximately 95 percent of the unseen prisoners will have ages which are within plus or minus four years. Of course, there is the improbable chance (about 5 in 100) that the prisoner who will come walking through the door is younger than 36 or older than 44.

Your feeling of confidence rests on a third fundamental tool in statistics, the marvelous probabilities associated with the areas under a normal curve marked off by the mean plus or minus a distance expressed in terms of the standard deviation. Thus, you know, assuming a normal distribution, that 95 percent of the cases are contained within plus or minus two standard deviations.

It is but a short step from the analogy of the prisoners in the dungeon to a vision of a collection of means in the dungeon. A researcher computing a mean is obtaining one specimen from an unseen population of possible means. If the researcher repeated the study, it is very unlikely that the same mean would be obtained. The amount of variation of the means in the dungeon is given by the standard deviation of the group of means, but this standard deviation has a special name: the **standard error of the mean**. If the researcher repeats the study, the chances are about 95 in 100 that the second mean will be within plus or minus two standard errors of the original mean.[1]

Now, let's take the last major leap of the imagination. Consider a researcher who has calculated the means from an experimental and a control group. The researcher examines the difference between these two means and wonders whether the difference might have occurred by chance. In this case, imagine that the researcher's dungeon is filled, not with prisoners, not with means, but with a population of *differences* between two means. The standard deviation of this distribution of differences is known as the **standard error of the difference.** About 95 percent of the differences between two means will fall between plus and minus two standard errors. Differences bigger than two standard errors would appear only about five times in a hundred if one reaches into the dungeon of differences and pulls one out by chance.

This leads to an understanding of statements seen in research journals comparing the achievement of two randomly selected sets of students, one group taught by a new method and the other by a more traditional method. The difference between the two means is reported and, with luck, the author can state: "This difference was significant beyond the .05 level." There may be little magic in setting the .05 level as indicating "significance," but it is a widely accepted convention in much educational and psychological research.

Almost all inferential statistics are about ways of estimating such parameters[2] as the standard error of the difference and using these parameters to make inferences about the probabilities that an observed difference would or would not have occurred by chance alone.

---

[1] We assume that the sample mean is the best estimate of the mean of the underlying population.

[2] A parameter describes a hypothetical, unseen, underlying population while a statistic describes a particular sample drawn from the hypothesized underlying population.

While many important details must be omitted, this orientation to inferential statistics illustrates that an understanding of the mean, standard deviation, and the normal curve generalizes to distributions of means and distributions of differences between means. Kachigan (1982) provides clearly written elaborations of these ideas.

Summary

The essential statistical concepts are the mean, the standard deviation, and the shape of the normal curve.

The mean is the Rock of Gibraltar of statistics. The mean characterizes a group of scores and we see this fact revealed every day as we learn about average reading achievement, average income, or average kilowatt hours of electricity used in the nation each day. In addition, the mean provides the high ground from which we view any given score, letting us know at a glance whether a given score is above, at, or below average.

The standard deviation describes the sea surrounding this rock. The horizons of this sea may be close to the rock or stretch out a considerable distance. Similarly, the standard deviation tells us whether the scores are bunched in close to the mean or spread out over a considerable distance. The standard deviation also allows us to state how far above or below the mean any given score lies. When a score is described in terms of its distance from the mean in standard deviation units, we speak of it as a z-score.

As the number of test scores becomes increasingly large, the shape of the distribution of scores more closely approaches the bell-shaped, symmetrical curve of the normal distribution. This is convenient because, when dealing with a normal distribution, there are known probabilities associated with scores occurring at any standard deviation unit from the mean. Thus, a z-score of 1 tells us at once that this score exceeds 84 percent of the other scores in the group.

In much of inferential statistics, the logic of z-scores and the related probabilities are applied to the task of evaluating the probable variation within a group of means or the probable variation in the difference between means. Thus, an observed difference between two means may be changed into a z-score, and using the known probabilities, the investigator can determine whether the observed difference is sufficiently large that it would not occur by chance alone. This is the essential judgement in hypothesis testing. If the difference between means of experimental and control groups is "statistically significant," then the experimenter has a basis for believing that the experimental treatment actually made a difference.

References

Hinkle, D. E., Wiersma, W., & Jurs, S. G. (1988). *Applied Statistics for the behavioral sciences* (2nd ed.). Boston: Houghton Mifflin.

Kachigan, S. K. (1982). *Multivariate statistical analysis: A conceptual introduction*. New York: Radius Press.

Newman, J. R. (1956). Commentary on Sir Francis Galton. In J. Newman (ed.), *The world of mathematics* (Vol. 2). New York: Simon & Schuster.

Pearson, K. (1924). *The life, letters, and labours of Francis Galton* (Vol. 2). Cambridge, England: Cambridge University Press.

Phillips, J. L., Jr. (1982). *Statistical thinking*. San Francisco: W. H. Freeman.

Rowntree, D. (1981). *Statistics without tears*. New York: Charles Scribner's Sons.

I leaf through the test manual looking for hints on how to interpret Shaun's score, but all I find is information about reliability, validity, and the way the test was standardized. I see a reliability coefficient, but it has little meaning for me. That kind of thing is mostly for the test specialists, isn't it?

chapter three
Reliability

A good test can be visualized as resting on a three-legged tripod: reliability, validity, and adequate standardization. If any leg is weak, the test is in danger of falling.

Let us take a closer look at the first leg, reliability. **Reliability** refers to the stability of a test score; that is, the ability of a test to provide a consistent measurement on repeated occasions.

No measurement, in fact, has perfect reliability. If you were to pass a book and a ruler through a class of students, asking each to measure the length of the book, the measurements would vary by an eighth to a fourth of an inch. If we can't measure a solid book with a wooden ruler and get the same measurement twice, think how much more difficult it is to get consistent measurements when we are measuring human traits such as intelligence, interest, or personality.

The scores of every test will, to some extent, be unreliable. The test manual provides information about the unreliability associated with the test. The problem is a tendency to skip over this information because of the specialized language. A typical sentence may read: "A split-half reliability, corrected by the Spearman-Brown Prophesy formula, of .87 was obtained for a sample of 200 fifth grade pupils." The sentence seems too technical to be comprehensible, and besides, do we really need it? In this chapter, you will acquire the skills necessary to decode such sentences and you will also come to believe that you do, indeed, need the information.

It seems natural to believe that if a measurement is not reliable, it is not likely to be useful. Let's imagine that you have walked into the shop of Sam, the tailor, to be measured for a new garment.

> Let's start with the waist. Um . . . 32 inches. Didn't you have boys who wrestled when they were in high school? My boy ran track. He was a little light for most sports. Let's see . . . better get that again . . . 39 inches. Went up to Harvard business school when he graduated. He's an MBA now. Lives in California. Here, let me show you a picture of my first grandson. Better check that one more time . . . 29 inches.

If you listened carefully to Sam's monologue, you have just one option: run! Your waist may be 32 inches, 39 inches, 29 inches, or none of the above. Sam did not get a consistent measurement each time he applied the tape, and it seems unlikely that any garment he makes will fit you. It is easy to see why reliability is an essential criterion to apply to any measurement instrument. Without reliability, we do not have a test; we have a random-number-generating machine.

The term reliability as used by measurement specialists has a very restricted meaning. It is not an overall assessment of the "goodness" of a test, nor does it address the problem of whether the test measures what it claims to measure. Reliability answers a single question: If I administer this test again to the same student, is the score likely to move up or down by a large amount or to remain relatively stable?

The True Score Plus Error

An essential background for our discussion of reliability is the concept of the **true score.** Observed test scores are composed of two components: the true score and the error. The true score is the score we might obtain if human beings never changed from day to day and if all tests were perfect. Since people do change and since all tests fall short of perfection, any single test score contains error. Knowing the reliability of the test helps us know whether the errors are likely to be large or small.

There are several ways of determining the reliability of a test. Some of these procedures capture more of the possible errors associated with testing than do others. For this reason, it is useful to analyze in more detail the sources of test errors. Remember that we are using the term **measurement error** in this discussion to designate variations in test scores that are unrelated to the underlying ability or trait we want to measure.

Sources of Measurement Error

We observed earlier that measuring a book with a ruler would include errors of a fourth of an inch or even more. Some of the errors might be caused by the way the ruler was placed on the book and the angle from which the markings on the ruler were read. These errors in measuring a book arise within the process of the measurement procedure itself.

As we move from measuring physical objects to measuring people, entirely new sources of error come into the picture. While the book stays constant in length, the performance of people changes from one day to the next. On any given day, students may feel mentally alert or sluggish, tired, and hungry. These factors affect students' ability to concentrate and their motivation to put forth their best efforts. These factors will be particularly relevant when measuring attitudes or personality. Such changes in the person from day to day are important sources of measurement error.

Additionally, the sample of tasks used to measure a particular trait or ability will change from test to test. In measuring achievement in American history, for example, there are thousands of items that might be used. Two 50-item tests from this underlying pool of items will measure different aspects of the students' knowledge even if the tests are designed to be identical. A student taking both tests will get slightly different scores even if his or her knowledge of history, the true score, remains unchanged. Observed scores change because the sample of items change. Variations in test items from one test to another are an inevitable source of measurement error. This is true for intelligence tests, aptitude tests, personality tests, and interest tests as well as achievement tests.

A related source of error is the size of the sample of test items. On the whole, the shorter the test, the less reliable it is. Consider an attitude test of ten items. If, on retaking the test, you changed your mind on three items, the score would shift by almost a third. It seems unlikely, on the other hand, that you would change your mind on one third of a ninety-item attitude test.

For a few tests, scores are highly dependent on the speed with which a person works. Scores on most clerical speed and accuracy tests are very responsive to the rate at which the individual works. The score a student obtains while working slowly with attention to accuracy will be quite different from the score earned by the same individual working rapidly. For such tests, changes in the individual's speed of work is a source of measurement error.

With a better understanding of the sources of measurement error, we can now turn to the various procedures for determining test reliability. We shall see that some of these procedures do not reflect all the sources of measurement error in their index of reliability.

Procedures for Determining Test Reliability

There are two approaches to studying the reliability of a test:

1. Test-retest—administering the test a second time and observing the relationship between the two sets of scores.
2. Single-administration methods—administering the test once and calculating an index of internal consistency.

These procedures constitute the core material in understanding reliability. Test manuals, research reports, and teachers' journals may simply state that reliability was obtained using the test-retest procedure without

Table 3.1

Name	First Testing	One Week Later
Maria	18	20
Bill	9	11
Myles	16	13
Dave	12	9
Eduardo	9	8
Fred	15	18
Chong	15	15
Chris	8	12
Iris	13	12
Lamarr	8	10

further explanation. Your comfort level in reading such reports is dependent on knowing what is involved in each approach and why it makes sense. We will examine each of these approaches separately.

Retest Reliability

The **test–retest** procedure is the most commonsense approach to finding out whether a test will yield about the same score if administered to the same individuals at a later date. The procedure involves testing a group of students and retesting the group a second time. The retesting may occur the next day or several weeks later. The time between testing should not be so long that life events or new learning would have time to affect the trait or knowledge being measured.

In the following example, a test was administered, and the students were retested a week later. The results are arranged in table 3.1 so that the two test scores are shown by each student's name.

In examining these scores, we can see that most students did not earn identical scores during the retest. Still, for most students, the second score seems fairly close to the original. It would be helpful if we could summarize in a precise form the degree of agreement between these sets of scores. This is precisely what the correlation coefficient does. In the special case where we are correlating a test with itself, we call this a **reliability coefficient.**

In the last chapter, we suggested that the correlation coefficient could be calculated by converting the performance on each test to a z-score, multiplying the z-scores of each student, summing these products, and obtaining the mean. We have transformed the original scores to z-scores and done the arithmetic; the results are presented in table 3.2.

Table 3.2 *Computation of Correlation Coefficient Using Standard Scores*

Test 1	Test 2	Test 1 z-score	Test 2 z-score	Product of z-scores
18	20	1.64	1.97	3.23
9	11	−.95	−.49	.47
16	13	1.07	.05	.05
12	9	−.09	−1.04	.09
9	8	−.95	−1.31	1.24
15	18	.78	1.42	1.11
15	15	.78	.60	.47
8	12	−1.24	−.22	.27
13	12	.20	−.22	−.04
8	10	−1.24	−.77	.95
				7.84

$$r = \frac{7.84}{10} = .784$$

In table 3.2, small *r* is the conventional symbol for a correlation coefficient. We can see that the correlation between the two administrations of the test is .78. This would be the reliability of the test.

In actual practice, the original scores are entered directly into a computer. The computer employs a preloaded statistical package, which runs the numbers through a calculational formula to get the correlation coefficient. A widely used formula is shown below.

$$r = \frac{N\Sigma XY - \Sigma X \Sigma Y}{\sqrt{[N\Sigma X^2 - (\Sigma X)^2][N\Sigma Y^2 - (\Sigma Y)^2]}}$$

where:

r = Pearson product-moment coefficient
Σ = means to add
X = score on the first variable
Y = score on the second variable

We entered the students' scores from table 3.1 into a computer programmed to calculate a correlation coefficient using the above formula and obtained an r of .79.

A report of this reliability exercise, as it might appear in a test manual or in a research article, would read: "A reliability coefficient of .79 was obtained by the test-retest procedure with 10 fourth grade students with one week intervening between the two test administrations."

The test-retest procedure is the most obvious method of determining test reliability, but going back to the classroom with the same test creates some problems. Informing kids they have to take the test again seems to confirm their suspicions that all adults have long-term memory deficits. In addition, it is a certainty that immediately after last week's test, students assembled in the hall to exchange information about the desired answers. These factors work to lower the test-retest reliability. A variation of the test-retest procedure provides a solution to these problems.

Parallel Forms Reliability

Parallel forms reliability is obtained by retesting the same group of students with an equivalent form of a test. The second test is called an alternate form or a parallel form of the first test. Using a parallel form gets around the problem of credibility when returning to retest the students. More importantly, using a parallel form of the test helps solve the problem of practice effects and learning from the initial test.

Parallel form reliability is a more strict procedure for establishing reliability than is the simple test-retest procedure. This is because use of alternate forms of the test introduces a source of measurement error not present in the test-retest procedure, i.e., variations in scores due to the sample of items comprising a test. If you ask your students to take two forms of a test designed to measure arithmetic calculations, you will obtain two pictures of each student's calculating ability. If these pictures are about the same, then you have confidence that the sample of items comprising the initial test is providing a stable (reliable) measure of the underlying calculating ability. If the scores from the two forms are very different, the reliability of the test is low. You have no guarantee that the score from either form provides a picture of the child's ability that will be consistent from one set of calculating exercises to another.

The test-retest model with parallel forms illustrates the basic logic of test reliability. As we examine the split-half procedure, we shall see that it bears a striking resemblance to this model, but arrives at the reliability coefficient in a much more efficient way.

Single-Administration Methods

It is actually a lot of trouble to construct a parallel form of a test, print it up, schedule new testing dates, and arrange with the schools to repeat the testing. It would be more convenient and less costly if one could get a reliability coefficient without actually administering a test twice. The next approach to determining test reliability relies on test data obtained from a single administration of the test.

Split-Half Reliability

The **split-half reliability** procedure divides the existing test into two halves at the time it is scored. The reliability coefficient is obtained, as before, by calculating the correlation between the two sets of scores. The split-half technique bypasses the trouble and expense of the test-retest procedure.

One way of viewing the split-half procedure is to consider it a way of generating two short parallel forms from the original test. One set of items is assigned to "Form A" and another set to "Form B." Actually, rather than creating two tests, two scoring keys are made. In considering which items should go on each key, it is common to assign the odd items to one key and the even items to the other, which is the "odd-even" procedure for splitting the test into two halves. With two scores available for each student, the data can be organized as in an ordinary test-retest form and a correlation between the two sets of scores computed.

At this point, an important rule about reliability comes into play. Other things being equal, reliability is a function of the length of a test; the longer a test, the more reliable it is. The more we shorten a test, the more reliability we lose. Since we have taken a long test and split it into two short halves, the obtained reliability coefficient underestimates the reliability of the undivided, full-length test.

The correction formula that steps up the obtained reliability coefficient to its appropriate value bears the names of its developers, Charles Spearman and William Brown. The **Spearman–Brown Prophecy Formula** uses the reliability coefficient from the split-half procedure to estimate the full-length reliability of the test. Here is how it looks:

$$\text{Full-length reliability} = \frac{2r}{1 + r}$$

where r is the correlation
between the half-length tests

Assuming that the uncorrected correlation between the two halves of the test is .70, we have the following numerical example of how the Spearman-Brown formula works to increase the obtained correlation to the appropriate value for the full-length test.

$$\text{Full-length reliability} = \frac{2\,(.70)}{1 + .70}$$

$$= \frac{1.40}{1.70} = .82$$

We can see from this example that the reliability coefficient of .70, which underestimated the reliability of the full-length test, was corrected to a co-efficient of .82.

Actually, the split-half procedure is always accompanied by this second step of correcting the underestimated reliability by using the Spearman-Brown formula. For example, a publisher might administer a new test to 200 fifth grade students and compute a split-half reliability co-efficient. The publisher does not want the reliability for half a test, but for the whole test, which is being marketed. The Spearman-Brown correction formula elevates the reliability estimate to its appropriate value. Following this procedure, the manual will include a statement similar to this: "The reliability of the test was determined for 200 fifth grade pupils using a split-half procedure corrected by the Spearman-Brown Prophecy Formula."

A word of caution is necessary before leaving split-half reliability. The split-half procedure can not be applied to tests that have very strict time limits, such as a test that asks students to cross out all misspelled words within three minutes of working time. The result will be artificially high reliability coefficients. Only a test-retest procedure (preferably with alternate forms) would be appropriate for such highly speeded tests.

The split-half technique has become a popular way of establishing reliability. The test publisher has to administer the test only once. The papers are scored to obtain a score for each half of the test, the correlation is obtained and corrected by the Spearman-Brown formula, and the reliability is reported. It seems that nothing could be easier. But the next procedure is, indeed, easier.

Coefficient Alpha

We have discussed the logic of obtaining reliability estimates by splitting the test into two halves and observing the extent of agreement between each half. To get a high reliability with the split-half procedure, it is essential that the two halves of the test be equivalent; that is, the items comprising each half must be sufficiently similar to be measuring the same underlying characteristic. The key idea is that high **internal consistency** of the test will be reflected in a high split-half reliability. Yet, it is not necessary to split a test in two in order to estimate internal consistency. There are several statistical procedures that treat the data as if each item is considered a test and the level of agreement among items is ascertained. The most general of these procedures is coefficient alpha.

Coefficient alpha can be applied to both conventional tests where answers are marked "right" or "wrong," and to responses receiving different weights where, for example, the responses might be "strongly agree," "agree," "disagree," and "strongly disagree." Coefficient alpha is defined by the following equation:

$$\text{alpha} = \left(\frac{n}{n-1}\right)\left(\frac{SD_t^2 - \Sigma SD_i^2}{SD_t^2}\right)$$

where n = the number of items in the test
SD_t = the standard deviation of the test
SD_i = the standard deviation of each item
Σ = "take the sum of" and tells us to add up the standard deviations of the items

The statistical packages installed on the mainframes of most universities include routines for calculating coefficient alpha. Not only do these programs provide an overall reliability coefficient for the test, but they generally show the reliability of the test with any item deleted. Thus, if you have constructed your own test, using a statistical package to generate a coefficient alpha is a convenient means of obtaining a reliability coefficient, and an easy way of checking whether any given item is adding to or subtracting from the reliability of the score.

Kuder-Richardson Reliability

Kuder-Richardson reliability is based on the Kuder and Richardson Formula 20, frequently known simply as KR-20. It is a form of coefficient alpha that is applicable when items are scored as "right" or "wrong." In this case, the standard deviation of each score can be replaced by the proportion of students answering a question right (p) times the proportion answering the item wrong (q).

The Kuder-Richardson Formula 20 looks like this:

$$\text{KR-20 reliability} = \left(\frac{n}{n-1}\right)\left(\frac{SD^2 - \Sigma pq}{SD^2}\right)$$

where n = the number of items
SD = the standard deviation of the test

p = proportion passing the item

q = the proportion failing the item

Σ = "take the sum of" and tells us to add up the pq products obtained for each item in the test

Later, Kuder and Richardson created an easier version of Formula 20 and, naturally enough, issued it as Formula 21. The KR-21 formula assumes that all items are of equal difficulty and substitutes a term involving the mean M $(1 - M/n)$ for pq in the formula immediately above. The complete formula is shown below.

$$\text{KR-21 reliability} = \left(\frac{n}{n-1}\right)\left(\frac{M(1 - M/n)}{SD^2}\right) = \text{Coefficient alpha}$$

where M = the mean of the test

n = the number of items

SD = the standard deviation of the test

The Kuder-Richardson Formula 21 will consistently underestimate the test reliability provided by the KR-20. It is quite useful, however, because it can be quickly calculated by the classroom teacher with a pocket calculator, using just the mean and the standard deviation of the frequency distribution.

The Kuder-Richardson formulas are in widespread use as they are convenient ways of obtaining the reliability of a test from a single test administration. The test manual will report, "The Kuder-Richardson Formula 20 reliability coefficient for this test is .89." Individuals publishing in research journals will not even bother to spell it out, but will simply report, "The KR-20 reliability of this test is .89."

Quick Review

We have established the common methods used in obtaining an index of test reliability. Each time a reliability is reported in a test manual, the procedure used to obtain the reliability coefficient will be identified. A summary of these procedures is shown below.

Repeated-administration methods

   Test-retest—Same test repeated on a subsequent occasion.

   Parallel forms—Retest with an equivalent form.

Single-administration methods

   Split-half—Two scores generated from a single test, correlated, and corrected with the Spearman-Brown Prophecy Formula.

   Coefficient alpha—A measure of internal consistency derived from analysis of responses from a single administration.

Table 3.3 *Sources of Variation Represented in Different Procedures for Estimating Reliability*

	Experimental Procedure for Estimating Reliability				
Sources of Variation	Immediate Retest, Same Test	Retest, After Interval, Same Test	Parallel Test Form Without Interval	Parallel Test Form With Interval	Single-Administration Methods[a]
Variation arising within the measurement procedure itself	X	X	X	X	X
Changes in the person from day to day		X		X	
Changes in the specific sample of tasks			X	X	X
Changes in the individual's speed of work	X	X	X	X	

Note: X indicates that this source of variation can affect reliability from this method of testing.
[a] The single-administration methods are Kuder-Richardson Formulas 20 and 21, coefficient alpha, and split-half.
Reprinted with the permission of Macmillan Publishing Company from Measurement and Evaluation in Psychology and Education, Fifth Edition, by Robert M. Thorndike, George K. Cunningham, Robert L. Thorndike, and Elizabeth P. Hagen. Copyright © 1991 by Macmillan Publishing Company.

Kuder-Richardson—Special forms of coefficient alpha measuring internal consistency for tests with items scored "right" or "wrong."

Although all of these procedures are roughly comparable, they do not all capture the same measurement errors. For example, the test-retest method reflects changes in the individual from day to day, but does not include errors reflecting the particular sample of items on the test. The parallel form procedure captures not only day-to-day variations in the students, but variations in the sample of items making up the tests. The split-half procedure and the internal consistency approaches, on the other hand, do not take into consideration changes in the person that might occur from day to day, but they do reflect the changes that might occur because of the sample of items comprising the test.

Table 3.3, from Thorndike, Cunningham, Thorndike, and Hagen (1991), summarizes the various sources of measurement error that are captured by the different procedures for estimating test reliability.

As you can see from this table, the parallel test, administered with a period of time between the original and the retest, reflects all the sources of measurement error that we have discussed. When several reliability coefficients are provided by the test publisher, this is the preferred reliability coefficient.

Reliability Coefficients Influenced by Group Characteristics

When evaluating reliability coefficients, it is necessary to examine the description of the manner in which they were obtained. We will obviously have more confidence in a reliability coefficient obtained from 200 students than we will from one computed on 30 students. Also, the range of abilities in the group used for the study will affect the size of the correlation coefficient. Other things being equal, the larger the range of abilities in the group, the higher the correlation coefficient. Note that we want the reliability coefficient to reflect the stability of the test, not the wide range of abilities in the sample of students. For example, if an achievement test is designed for use in grade three through grade five, the publisher might report a test-retest reliability based on a sample of 600 pupils enrolled in grades three through five. This reliability would be artificially high. On the retest, it would be unlikely that many fifth grade pupils would score like third or fourth grade pupils and vice versa. The high reliability coefficient would not be a good index of the amount of stability you might expect if you retested your third grade group. The publisher should report, and you should expect, reliability coefficients computed separately for each grade level.

size
ability

How High Should a Reliability Coefficient Be?

All the procedures we have discussed provide an index of reliability. All are reported in terms of a coefficient that ranges from zero to one. It now remains for us to establish some guidelines that may be used in evaluating reliability coefficients of various magnitudes. For example, is .79 high, medium, or low?

While providing a guide is somewhat risky, we do have some basic reference points. In educational and psychological measurements, the highest reliability coefficient we will find is around .95 and that will be for an individually administered intelligence test. Generally, we can feel comfortable interpreting test scores with reliability coefficients in the .90s and upper .80s but should exercise caution as test reliabilities drop into the lower .80s and .70s. Reliability coefficients below .70 warn us that the test scores will be very unstable. Yet, if there is nothing else available, even a test with reliability this low may be better than trying to estimate an ability with no instrument at all.

Until you have gained more experience, the following may serve as a rough guide to the interpretation of reliability coefficients of various sizes.

Reliability	Interpretation
.95 & above	Excellent
.90 to .94	Very good
.85 to .89	Good
.80 to .84	Useful
.75 to .79	Exercise caution
.70 to .74	Borderline stability
.65 to .69	Large amount of measurement error
.60 to .64	May be useful in obtaining group means
.59 & below	Consider other alternatives

Using Reliability Coefficients

The ability to use knowledge about test reliability when selecting tests or interpreting scores is one of the major benefits of studying educational measurement. Certainly, when selecting among several tests, the preferable test will exhibit higher reliability than the competing tests. Rather than making a simple comparison of the reliability coefficients, you will favor a slightly lower coefficient obtained with parallel forms over a somewhat higher coefficient based on a measure of internal consistency. In addition, you will have more confidence in a slightly lower reliability coefficient obtained on a large sample of students within a single grade level than you will for a higher coefficient obtained on fewer students spread out over a wide range of grade levels.

When interpreting scores to individuals, the reliability coefficients help you decide how much confidence to place in the test scores. Imagine, for example, that you are counseling two high school students who have come to see you about taking an art aptitude test. They are Juana and Susan, inseparable friends among the graduating seniors. It seems that Juana has plans to go to the Chicago Art Institute after graduation and Susan is thinking about going with her, ". . . if I have any art aptitude." Both students want to take the test.

You find an art aptitude test in your test files and quickly scan the manual:

> . . . students view plates with two similar pictures . . . subject is asked to select the better of the two . . . good format . . . clear directions . . . test-retest reliability of .70 . . . validated against ratings of student products in art school . . . easy to administer and score . . . norms for both high school and art students . . .

You administer and score the test, noting that one of the young women is at the 75th percentile, the other at the 50th.

When Susan and Juana return the next day for an interpretation of the scores, however, the answer sheets are nowhere to be found. It seems that there is nothing to do but have them take the test again. This time you score the tests immediately and write down the results.

As you begin to interpret the results, the phone rings. Your office mate discovered that she had inadvertently taken home the two answer sheets and reads the score for each student. As she reads the scores, you add them to your notes . . . and then stare at the paper:

Percentile Scores

	Yesterday's Test	Today's Test
Juana	75	61
Susan	50	64

What do you say to the waiting students?

Obviously, there is very little to say. The higher student on yesterday's test is the lower student on today's.

Now cover up the results of today's test. Would you have had any hesitancy counseling the young ladies on this set of test results? In everyday situations, tests are not given twice. The counselor looks at one set of figures and starts talking. Yet the test manual contained the critical information that would have introduced a note of caution: ". . . reliability of .70."

How far-fetched is this example? Table 3.4 tells us how often two individuals, one at the 75th percentile and one at the 50th percentile, will change their positions if measured with tests of various reliabilities.

How often will two students, one scoring at the 50th percentile and one scoring at the 75th percentile, change places after the second testing? Looking at the table, we can see that if the test has a reliability of .00, the chances are 50–50 that on a retest, two students will change places. The test in our example had a reliability of .70. From the table, it appears that there is about a 27 percent chance that the young ladies would actually change places, the high student dropping down to become the low one of the pair, and the low student moving up. With reliability this low, there is about one chance out of four that the counselor would have to completely reverse the advice about who should go to art school and who should stay at home. Note from the table that with a reliability of .80 the chances for a serious reversal in scores is one in five, and for a test reliability of .90 the counselor is still not completely safe. Even with a test this stable, about one in nine pairs of scores will show order reversals if we retested the pair of students.

Table 3.4 *Percentage of Times Direction of Difference Will Be Reversed in Subsequent Testing for Scores Falling at 75th and 50th Percentiles*

| | Percentage of Reversals with Repeated Testings | | |
Reliability Coefficient	Scores of Single Individuals	Means of Groups of 25	Means of Groups of 100
.00	50.0	50.0	50.0
.40	40.3	10.9	.7
.50	36.8	4.6	.04
.60	32.5	1.2	
.70	27.1	.1	
.80	19.7		
.90	8.7		
.95	2.2		
.98	.05		

Reprinted with the permission of Macmillan Publishing Company from Measurement and Evaluation in Psychology and Education, Fifth Edition, by Robert M. Thorndike, George K. Cunningham, Robert L. Thorndike, and Elizabeth P. Hagen. Copyright © 1991 by Macmillan Publishing Company.

Shertzer and Linden (1979) lament the fact that reliability data may not be obtained on the same kinds of people a teacher or counselor may be working with, or worse, reliability data may be simply ignored as counselors and teachers rely on the reputation of the author or publisher to signal high test quality:

> Regrettably, reliability data are often inadequate. More regrettable, is the fact that many counselors never question the reliability of the data they use. Either they do not realize the necessity of doing so or they accept on faith that the tests or other appraisal measures they use are reliable. Neither publication nor development by people who are highly regarded guarantees the reliability of any appraisal measure. Only appropriate data obtained from representative samples of people with whom an appraisal device is to be used demonstrate reliability (p. 86).

The Standard Error of Measurement

In diagnosing learning, the teacher will be examining relatively short segments of achievement batteries: vocabulary, comprehension, arithmetic computation, and arithmetic problem solving. Each of these short subtests has its own degree of unreliability. You will want to know how stable each of these subtests may be so that you will know how much confidence you can put in the scores. We will introduce the standard error as an indicator of how much variation you can expect when examining a particular test score. The standard error applies to all test scores. It is especially useful when deciding whether differences in a test profile are large enough to warrant interpretation.

The standard deviation was treated at some length in the preceding chapter. Knowledge of the standard deviation is useful as a bridge into the concept of standard error, a different way of expressing the reliability of a test. Thus far, we have described the reliability coefficients as an aid in selecting from among available tests and we suggested that a low reliability coefficient should serve as a warning that there will be substantial variability in scores if an individual were retested. But a reliability coefficient does not tell the user *how much* variation might be expected around an individual's test score. A standard error will provide this information.

It seems useful to consider the nature of the standard error conceptually before talking about how it is computed. Suppose you gave one small boy the same intelligence test repeatedly until you obtained 100 scores. Assuming no fatigue or learning during the many testing sessions, the repeated testing would yield a normal distribution of scores. Most of the scores would be bunched up around the middle and the rest would be distributed farther out. You could compute the mean and the standard deviation of this group of scores. The mean of this distribution would be the best estimate of the true score of the boy's intelligence. The standard deviation would be an index of the errors around this mean. The standard deviation of this distribution would be known as the **standard error of measurement.**

No one will ever find a child docile enough to sit still for continuously repeated testing, so the curve in figure 3.1 is a strictly hypothetical picture of the distribution of used answer sheets after the testing has been completed.

The key aspect of this distribution is that, unlike the distribution curves we discussed earlier, these are not people under the roof of the curve, but test answer sheets, each sheet stacked up over the score that the small boy earned on a particular administration of the test. We have marked off the proportion of these answer sheets that will be included between plus and minus one standard deviation, plus and minus two standard deviations, and plus and minus three standard deviations, just as we did earlier. From now on, since we will be talking about this particular distribution of scores, we will call these standard deviations by the proper name (for this kind of distribution), standard errors (SE).

How are these standard errors useful? The next time you look at a test score, you can see in your mind's eye this orderly stack of answer sheets from which one test score has been pulled. You can assume that the

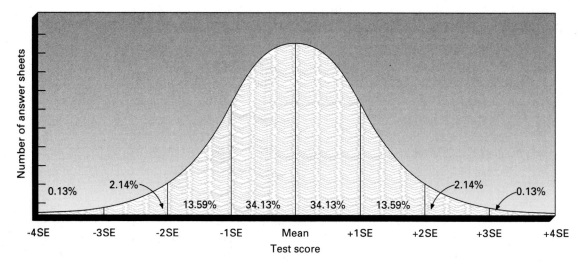

Figure 3.1

Theoretical distribution of answer sheets completed by one child tested 100 times.

individual whose test you are about to interpret was pulled from the mean of this distribution of scores. You can next find the standard error of the test by consulting the test manual. From this, you can mentally compute the range of scores within which this youngster's true score probably lies.

In our example of the small boy, we will assume that the calculated standard error is 3 IQ points, about what one would find for an individually administered intelligence test. Armed with this knowledge, we are now in a position to establish confidence limits around the single score shown on the test we have in hand. If the test record shows an IQ of 100, we know that the chances are about 68 in 100 that if we retested him, his score would fall between 97 and 103 (plus & minus one SE). Maybe we want to be more certain that we have bracketed his IQ accurately. Thus, we can go out plus or minus two standard errors and say to ourselves: "His true IQ is probably somewhere between 94 and 106; at least, if I retested him my chances are about 95 in 100 that I would get a score in this range." You can see that the standard error of a test score is an exceedingly useful way of thinking about the reliability of a given score.

What if our one and only testing of the small boy yielded an IQ of 112? Does this reasoning about the standard error still work? Yes, the reason being that whatever score you get for the single test administration is most likely to be at the mean of the stack of answer sheets that will accumulate if this boy is repeatedly tested. Thus, while you are looking at an IQ of 112 in this example, you mentally calculate that the true score may fall between 109 and 115 (plus or minus one standard error) and highly likely to fall between 106 and 118 (plus or minus two standard errors). Of course, there is still a 5 percent chance that his true score may be even far-ther out from the obtained score; that is, it may fall somewhere between plus and minus three standard errors.

As we mentioned earlier, the standard error is not actually computed from the impossible situation of repeatedly testing one individual. Rather, it is computed from the following formula:

$$SE = SD \sqrt{1 - r}$$

where SD = the standard deviation of the test scores
      r = the reliability of the test

An example will help you see how easily the standard error of a test can be computed. Suppose that the reliability of a spelling test, deter-mined by a test-retest procedure, is .85. The standard deviation calculated for the same class for whom the reliability was computed turns out to be 12. Substituting these numbers into the formula for the standard error of the test, we have

$$SE = 12 \sqrt{1 - .85}$$
$$SE = 12(.387)$$
$$SE = 4.6$$

From this, we would expect the scores on the spelling test to vary by almost 4.6 points if we retested an individual student. That is, we translate the words "would expect" to mean that the chances are about 2 in 3 (68 percent) that if retested, the student would fall within these limits. To be 95 percent confident in establishing the limits of variation on a retest, we would use plus or minus two standard errors, or plus or minus 9.2 in this example.

Let us see what would happen to the standard error if the spelling test had a reliability of only .60.

$$SE = 12 \sqrt{1 - .60}$$
$$SE = 12(.633)$$
$$SE = 7.58$$

In this case, the standard error is 7.6 (rounded). We notice that as the reliability of a test goes down, there is an increase in the standard error of the test. With a large amount of random error in a test, a student who is earning a B in spelling could drop to a C, or climb to an A, if we simply gave the test again.

Figure 3.2

*Profile for two arithmetic
skills showing zone of
variation by chance
(± 1 SE_M) for each
score.*

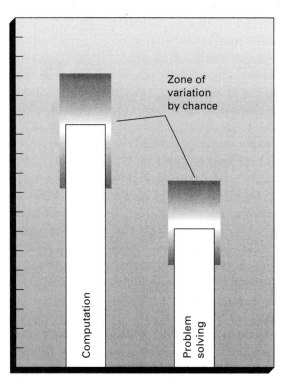

It is particularly important to be aware of standard errors of measurement when interpreting test profiles. In deciding, for example, whether there is a true difference between "arithmetic computation" and "arithmetic problem solving," we need to remember that each score has a standard error, and that the standard error of the difference between the two scores will be larger than the error associated with a single score. To illustrate the role of standard errors of the difference in interpreting profiles, we have reproduced a segment of a hypothetical test profile for a pupil with a score of 44 for arithmetic computations and a score of 36 for problem solving (figure 3.2). The scores have been plotted on a scale of standard scores so that the scores on one test are directly comparable to those on another.

At first glance, it appears that the student might profit from some special work in understanding arithmetic problems; after all, the score in this area is 8 points below the score in computation. From the manual we note that the standard error for "arithmetic computations" is 6 score points, and the standard error for "arithmetic problem solving" is 4. We have drawn shaded bars to show the zone within which each score is likely (68 times out of 100) to vary if the pupil were retested. One can see visually that if the pupil fell a few points in computation and gained a few in problem solving, both quite likely by chance alone, there would be no difference in scores between the two skills.

Aiken (1991) suggests that when we are interpreting test scores from a profile, we draw a band having a width of one or two standard errors around the score points to make it less likely we will interpret differences in performance that are not really significant. Following Aiken's suggestion will reduce the danger of overinterpreting small differences; of telling parents that their child is doing better in one skill area than another when in fact the difference may be due to chance.

We have come a long way in our study of test reliability. We have also seen that the standard deviation helps us understand the standard error, an estimate of limits within which the true score probably falls. We have seen that the concept of standard error is particularly important when interpreting test profiles.

Correction for Attenuation

Before leaving reliability, it is useful to point out that research workers understand that the reliability of tests sets the upper limit on the size of the correlation that can be obtained between two variables measured with these tests. Since researchers are frequently interested in an estimate of the correlation between two scores without the errors of measurement indicated by the low reliability of their instruments, they frequently **correct for attenuation** due to unreliability.

Thorndike, Cunningham, Thorndike, and Hagen (1991) provide the following example of a possible correction for an observed correlation of .56 between a reading comprehension test and a mathematical reasoning test . The reliabilities of the two tests were .71 and .90 respectively.

The correction for attenuation is provided by the following formula:

$$r_{1\infty2\infty} = \frac{r_{12}}{r_{11}r_{22}}$$

where $r_{1\infty2\infty}$ is the correlation of the underlying true scores

r_{12} is the correlation of the observed scores

r_{11} and r_{22} are the reliabilities of the two measures

Substituting in the formula, we get

$$r_{1\infty2\infty} = \frac{.56}{(.71)\,(.90)} = .88$$

From this calculation, we see that the researcher can report that a correlation of .88 between reading comprehension and mathematical reasoning would be obtained if these two abilities could be measured with error-free tests.

Summary

The importance of the first leg of the tripod, reliability, should be apparent. Reliability looms large in our decisions about what tests to select and how boldly or cautiously to interpret the scores. A knowledge of test reliability also helps us read the research literature and understand better some of the specialized procedures used by researchers in interpreting their data.

The reliability of tests is examined by several widely used procedures:

Test-retest—a test is administered on two occasions to a group of students and a correlation coefficient is calculated for the two scores earned by each student in the group.

Parallel forms—a comparable form of the test is administered during the second testing session and the two scores obtained for each student are correlated.

Split-half—following a single administration, half the items are scored on one key, half on another and the two sets of scores are correlated. The result is always "corrected" for the length of the test by using the Spearman-Brown Prophecy Formula.

Coefficient alpha—a procedure for calculating the internal consistency of the test, i.e., the extent to which all items appear to be measuring a single underlying trait or ability. The procedure is very general and can be used either when items are marked right or wrong or when responses get a specific value as in an attitude scale where responses range from strongly agree to strongly disagree.

Kuder-Richardson—widely used forms of coefficient alpha, applicable when responses are marked right or wrong.

Estimates of reliability computed by these various procedures are remarkably close to each other. However, the test-retest with parallel forms tend to show lower reliability coefficients, because this procedure reflects the most realistic sources of variation that can lead to changes in an individual's score from one testing to another.

Reliability is related to the length of a test, which means that subtests on achievement batteries must be viewed with caution since they usually contain a limited number of items.

Low reliability coefficients alert you to the fact that scores are relatively unstable, but they do not tell you specifically how much variation you might expect on retesting. The standard error of measurement does give you this specific information. Remember that the obtained score plus or minus one standard error indicates the limits within which the retest score would probably fall (68 chances out of 100). Standard errors are usually reported in terms of raw scores, and it is frequently surprising to see that a small amount of change in the raw score makes for a big shift in percentile or grade equivalent scores.

The reliability figures are in the test manual for all to read. The American Psychological Association has published standards for test manuals specifying that full reliability data be published. If not, the test will get unfavorable reviews from the academic community and use of the test will be discouraged. But test publishers are only obligated to publish the figures, not to interpret them for you. Test manuals contain persuasive writing as well as technical information. Your best protection against being persuaded to use a poor test is your ability to read and to evaluate the information presented in the manuals.

References

Aiken, L. R. (1991). *Psychological testing and assessment.* Boston: Allyn & Bacon.

Shertzer, B., & Linden, J. D. (1979). *Fundamentals of individual appraisal.* Boston: Houghton Mifflin.

Thorndike, R. M., Cunningham, G. K., Thorndike, R. L., & Hagen, E. P. (1991). *Measurement and evaluation in psychology and education.* New York: Macmillan.

I studied the two tests on my desk. Both claimed to measure readiness of kindergarten children to move on into the first grade. They looked pretty much the same. How can I find out which one of these tests is doing the better job, or if either test will do the job at all?

TEST

2
3
4

RELIABILITY

VALIDITY

STANDARDIZATION

In the last chapter, we discussed reliability as the first leg of a tripod supporting a good test. We now turn to the second leg: validity. **Validity** refers to whether a test measures what it claims to measure. With this chapter, you will be developing an understanding of validity that will help you read test manuals and articles. You will be developing a cautious attitude toward tests. You will become sensitive to the kinds of evidence to look for in deciding how valid a test may be. These are essential skills and attitudes in becoming a wise user of tests.

Where is the claim about what a test measures? It is in the title of the test. We tend to reason from test titles. If the test is called an intelligence test, we believe that the score actually measures intelligence. We talk about achievement and aptitude with full confidence that the tests measure what they claim to measure. But just a moment. Following is a list of three test items from tests of intelligence, aptitude, and achievement. Can you identify the kind of test from which each item was reproduced?

1. Which of these words would come first in a dictionary?
   more
   pile
   mist
   pick
   mine

2. _____ is to masculine as woman is to _____

3. What percent of 300 is 12?
   0.4
   25
   36
   40
   none of the above

The items are, in order, from tests of intelligence, aptitude, and achievement. You can't always tell a book by its cover—or a test either. What are these tests actually measuring? This is a logical question, and this is exactly the question that test experts ask when evaluating any test. Does the test measure what the authors claim it measures? Is this a *valid* test?

Messick (1989) reminds us that it may be inappropriate to think of "test validity." We are actually interested in the meanings, interpretations, and applications of the test scores. Further, Messick suggests, the validation of the inferences we make about the test is no different than the kind of hypothesis testing that goes on in any scientific enterprise: "Hence, test validation embraces all of the experimental, statistical, and philosophical means by which hypotheses and scientific theories are evaluated" (p. 14). Finally, Messick notes that validity is a matter of degree, not all or none.

Approaches to Test Validity

There are several different approaches to determining the validity of a test: face validity, content validity, construct validity, and criterion related validity. We will take each one in turn.

Face Validity

Face validity means that the test looks as if it is measuring the trait the test author desires to measure. For example, a test of mechanical aptitude may consist mostly of pictures of shop tools and tool names to be matched with the pictures. Everything *looks* reasonable. An applicant for a factory job will have no quarrel when asked to take this test. In fact, this is the main value of face validity: customer satisfaction. Aside from this benefit, there is no value at all in face validity. Appearances are no substitute for evidence that the test is measuring what it claims to measure. Since face validity is no indication of validity at all, let us consider it an unfortunate misnomer and move on.

Content Validity

Content validity refers to the match between the sample of items on the test and the underlying domain that the test is attempting to measure. This approach to examining test validity is reserved almost exclusively for achievement tests. In achievement testing, the author is claiming to measure what was taught. To live up to this claim, the test must be a reasonable sample of the material covered. In testing a pupil's knowledge, of course, one cannot test everything that has been taught. The teacher must select a small sample of items to stand for the large amount of material that has been covered. One professor likens this process to rolling a shopping cart through a supermarket, taking one item from each shelf. The question is, does the shopping cart contain a reasonable sample of everything that is in the supermarket? Put another way, would the contents of the cart provide a valid picture of the contents of the store? Content validity asks whether the small sample of material on the test fairly reflects the larger body of material that the teacher covered.

Content validity may not be much of a problem when a teacher is constructing a test for her own class. While some topics may be overrepresented on the test because it is easy to write questions on these topics, most teachers try to test for the concrete facts, important understandings, and thought processes they have emphasized in their teaching. When a publisher constructs a test for classes over the nation, however, content validity becomes a larger problem. The test publisher typically examines widely used textbooks, course objectives, and curriculum guides, and then constructs the achievement test so that it contains a representative sample of all the material covered. The problem is that the local teacher does not teach from an amalgam of all texts, she teaches from a particular text. There will not be an exact match between the content of a national standardized test and the material taught in any given school system.

You will learn more about this important point later. Content validity is one of the most easily understood concepts in measurement, yet some major errors in test interpretation are made because of a tendency to ignore the question of content validity.

Construct Validity

Construct validity is the extent to which the test is measuring a theoretical concept or trait. Throughout history, humans have found ways to summarize their observations, to *construct* ideas that help them explain or understand their experiences. Maybe the first cave dwellers noticed that some of their companions were better at chipping stone tools than others. Maybe they admired the one who first attached a stone tool to a wooden handle. It is doubtful that they rubbed their chins and observed: "That one must be the most intelligent one among us!" But someone, sometime, had to come up with the idea of "intelligence." That is, someone constructed an idea that seemed to summarize a number of observations. These "constructs" come to guide our perceptions and soon we are acting as if our constructs are real. "Intelligence," "aptitude," "achievement," and "anxiety" are all constructs. Establishing the construct validity of a test is a matter of accumulating a convincing set of evidence that the trait or characteristic of interest is actually being measured.

If one decides to build a test to measure one of these constructs—"anxiety" for example—how will he or she go about proving that the test actually measures this internal state? In this case, the author may try to think of a situation that is usually anxiety-producing—say, a trip to the dentist. Working with a dental clinic, the author may arrange to obtain a psychogalvanic reading (indicating how much sweat is present) from the palms of people in the waiting room. The test author reasons that if this test is really measuring the underlying construct, anxiety, then scores on the test should be correlated with the psychogalvanic readings. People with high anxiety, as indicated by their psychogalvanic reading, should score high on the anxiety questionnaire. If the test author does, indeed, find that there is a high correlation between the test scores and the readings from the psychogalvanic meter, then the study has helped establish the construct validity of the anxiety questionnaire.

The construct validity of a new test is demonstrated by accumulating a pattern of expected correlations. Reason dictates that some variables should be positively related to the new test, and other variables should show little or no relationship to the new test. Thus, we might expect a measure of anxiety to correlate positively with a questionnaire of "perceived threats" and to a second questionnaire called "safety consciousness," but have no relationship with measures of intelligence or educational level. This powerful approach to construct validity is called **convergent** and **discriminant validity**. That is, the set of data collected should show a cluster of high correlations among tests where we would theoretically expect the scores to go together (convergent validity), and little or no correlation among scores of tests that we judge should be unrelated to the trait being measured (discriminant validity).

Campbell and Fisk (1959) suggest that convergent and discriminant validity can best be studied by generating a correlation matrix showing the relationships among scores for at least two traits measured by at least two methods. They offer data collected from an earlier study by Kelley and Prey (1934). Kelley and Prey were interested in four personality traits of children: courtesy, honesty, poise, and school drive. They used two methods to get at these traits: the judgement of classmates (peer ratings) and a word association test completed by each child. The correlations among the scores for four traits are shown in table 4.1. This arrangement allows examination of the correlations among the traits *within* each measurement method and *across* each method.

This multitrait-multimethod matrix is quite revealing. The correlation coefficients in parentheses are the reliability coefficients for each test. The upper left block of correlations are all high, but should they be? Why should a student who is courteous, for example, also have a high drive to do schoolwork? Since all these correlations are among the traits as measured by peer ratings, perhaps there is a large amount of "method variance" in these scores. There would appear to be little ability for this method to *discriminate* among the four traits.

The lower right block of correlations shows lower reliability for the traits measured by the word association test and lower correlations among the traits as measured by this method, due largely to the lower reliabilities.

The block of correlations of most interest is in the lower left corner. Here we see how much agreement there is between the two methods when measuring the same trait. These correlations are shockingly low. For

Table 4.1 *Personality Traits of School Children from Kelley's Study*
(N=311)

	Peer Ratings				Association Test			
	Courtesy	**Honesty**	**Poise**	**Drive**	**Courtesy**	**Honesty**	**Poise**	**Drive**
Peer Ratings								
Courtesy	(.82)							
Honesty	.74	(.80)						
Poise	.63	.65	(.74)					
School Drive	.76	.78	.65	(.89)				
Association Test								
Courtesy	.13	.14	.10	.14	(.28)			
Honesty	.06	.12	.16	.08	.27	(.38)		
Poise	.01	.08	.10	.02	.19	.37	(.42)	
School Drive	.12	.15	.14	.16	.27	.32	.18	(.36)

example, the two measures of the identical trait, courtesy, correlate only .13. Similar low correlations between the two methods are shown for the remaining traits. These low correlations indicate essentially no *convergent* validity; that is, the two methods are not providing a similar picture of the traits under study.

Criterion Related Validity

Criterion related validity refers to the relationship between test scores and a criterion. A **criterion** is an established index of the trait or behavior that the test claims to measure. A test claiming to measure religious values should exhibit higher scores for a group of ministers than for people in other professions. A scholastic aptitude test should be highly correlated with the grade point averages of college students. Scores on a new test of intelligence should be highly correlated with an established, individually administered intelligence test. All these are examples of criterion related validity.

Criterion related validity has two subdivisions depending on when the criterion data are collected, **concurrent** validity and **predictive** validity.

Concurrent Validity

Concurrent validity is established when the test scores and the criterion data are collected at about the same time, i.e., concurrently. Suppose you are the personnel person for a factory and need to find a test that will help select good workers for the job of assembling pump parts. A particular mechanical aptitude test looks good and you decide to give it a try. You give it to all of the assemblers now working in the factory. As a criterion, you obtain current production records and compute the number of units each worker assembled per hour during three 8-hour shifts. You calculate the correlation coefficient and find a high correlation between production rates and test scores. You decide to use this test in selecting from the new group of applicants. In this case, you have just conducted a study of concurrent validity. The data from the test and the data on the criterion were collected concurrently or at about the same time.

Concurrent validity is a perfectly acceptable and widely used type of criterion related validity, but in this example, the study is flawed. It may well be that the people who produced many pump parts each hour are the older, more experienced workers. During the years in which they gained this experience, perhaps they were also acquiring the skills and knowledge tested on the mechanical aptitude test. Thus, the high correlation between the test scores and the records of production might reflect experience on the job. A study that would sidestep this problem is a study of predictive validity.

Predictive Validity

In **predictive validity** studies, the test is given at one date, and used to predict performance at a later date. In the example we have been following, the personnel person would administer the mechanical aptitude test, not to workers, but to applicants. These results would be saved until after the new employees had been trained and had worked for a period of time. Production records would then be taken and correlated with the aptitude test. If the correlations are high, the personnel person would feel that the test is valid for the purpose of selecting new assemblers. If the correlation is low, the personnel person might feel that the test would add little to existing methods of selecting new workers.

One of the problems with criterion related validity is that the criterion itself may be only partially reliable and valid. Production records may reflect a number of variables besides the skill of the assembler—the light and temperature at the workstation, for example, or the delivery of parts to be assembled.

If you have produced a new mechanical aptitude test designed for use with adolescents, what could you use as a criterion of mechanical aptitude? One possibility is grades in high school shop courses. Consider, however, the various factors that enter into grading: absences, tardiness, attitudes, neatness, spelling and grammar, and willingness to work hard. In a shop course, the grade may also reflect observance of safety rules, cleanliness of work area, and care of tools. It may be good to include these behaviors in shop grades, but the more that such variables are factored in, the less likely it is that the grade will represent pure "mechanical aptitude." The presence of these behaviors in the grades assigned to students will *lower* the correlation between the mechanical aptitude test and grades in a shop course. A better validity study would be based on shop instructors' ratings of the items produced in the shop courses. The rating of products would provide a more objective criterion of mechanical aptitude than would grades. When reading and evaluating criterion related validity studies, it is important to think about the adequacy and stability of the criterion used as an index of the behavior or trait in question.

A quick summary of the various approaches to validity is presented below.

Face validity   Face validity is based on the appearance of the test. The test may look good, but this procedure produces no real evidence that the test does or does not measure the qualities it claims to measure.

Content validity   This way of expressing the validity of a test is generally limited to achievement tests. Content validity refers to whether the content of the test is a representative sample of the content of the course.

Construct validity   Construct validity is concerned with psychological qualities that the test measures. Construct validity is supported when a set of hypotheses about the theoretical relationships with other variables is borne out by data.

Criterion related validity   This approach to test validity involves measuring the relationship between test results and other behaviors thought to be trustworthy indicators of the same trait or ability. Both concurrent validity and predictive validity are examples of criterion related validity.

Concurrent validity   Concurrent validity is established when the test scores are shown to be related to criterion data that are collected at about the same time.

Predictive validity   Predictive validity is established when test scores are shown to predict future behavior, i.e, to predict criterion data collected at a later period of time.

How High Should a Validity Coefficient Be?

The most common way of reporting both construct validity and criterion related validity is the correlation coefficient. Do not expect to find validity coefficients as high as the reliability coefficients we discussed earlier.

Remember, in reliability studies, we are correlating a test with itself. In validity studies, we are correlating a test with a criterion measure or some aspect of behavior in which we have an interest. Usually the criterion behavior is rather complex, such as performance in college. Thus, we might expect considerably lower coefficients in validity studies than in reliability studies. The well-known Scholastic Aptitude Test of the College Boards generally correlates between .45 and .65 with first semester college grade averages.

The predictive power of a correlation coefficient is given precisely by the square of the correlation coefficient. Let's see how this works when the SAT scores correlate .65 with college grades. The square of .65 is .42, which means that we can account for about 42 percent of the variance in college grades by the scores on the SAT tests. Variance, as you may remember, is the mean of the squared deviations, but we can roughly translate this term as variation. The amount of variation in college grades that can be predicted from the SAT scores may not sound too impressive. Typically, however, we are not trying to predict precisely what grade average a student is likely to earn in college. More frequently, we want to know whether the student is likely to pass or fail a particular program of study in a particular college. There is a great difference in the level of precision between trying to predict the exact grade point average that a student will earn and trying to predict into which of two categories a student is likely to fall.

When the level of prediction is a simple twofold pass-fail criterion, how useful is a test that seems to have a low validity coefficient, say around .50? The graph in figure 4.1 helps provide an answer.

As you can see from this graph, a cadet falling in the lowest level of the Pilot Selection Battery has only an 18 percent chance of completing the program. At the top level of the test battery, about 95 percent succeed. Now that is pretty useful information, and remember, the correlation among the test and the criterion was "only" .49.

You will develop a feel for validity coefficients as you go along. In general, validity coefficients for educational and psychological tests will seem to you to be quite low, but tests with validities of .40 and higher can contribute useful information when you need to make decisions about students. Certainly higher validity coefficients are desirable, but we don't find them very often.

Figure 4.1

Percent of cadets completing pilot training at each aptitude level. The correlation coefficient is 0.49. Reprinted with the permission of Macmillan Publishing Company from *Measurement and Evaluation in Psychology and Education, Fifth Edition,* by Robert M. Thorndike, George K. Cunningham, Robert L. Thorndike, and Elizabeth P. Hagen. Copyright © 1991 by Macmillan Publishing Company.

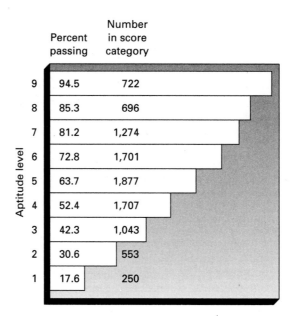

Aptitude level	Percent passing	Number in score category
9	94.5	722
8	85.3	696
7	81.2	1,274
6	72.8	1,701
5	63.7	1,877
4	52.4	1,707
3	42.3	1,043
2	30.6	553
1	17.6	250

Reading the Manual

With the exception of content validity, to which we shall return in a moment, the validity section of a test manual may provide correlations between the test and some criterion, but not always. The publisher may provide mean (average) scores for well-established groups to demonstrate expected relationships. For example, in the manual of a widely used scale for the study of values, it is reported that ministers scored higher than other groups on the Religious Values Scale, and students in the Harvard Business School scored higher than other groups on the Economic Values scale. These data offer evidence that the test is measuring what it claims to measure.

In evaluating validity information, a good rule is to look for the numbers and ignore the verbal claims. If you are choosing a readiness test to help decide whether children should leave kindergarten and enter first grade, you should ignore statements by the test publisher asserting that "this test will help teachers decide which children are ready for first grade work." Rather, you should look for predictive validity studies showing correlations between the readiness test administered at the end of kindergarten and a standardized reading test given at the end of the first grade, or correlations between the readiness test and ratings of first grade teachers on adjustment to the curriculum. Without such data, you are responding to the gleam in the publisher's eye rather than to the hard facts about what the test can do.

An Example

Let us consider a hypothetical case of a school superintendent of a large urban system examining the mean achievement for the school district. Imagine yourself in the place of this superintendent when she discovers that her school system is distinctly below average on the social studies section of the standardized achievement tests.

Suddenly, you are more than a little angry with those social studies teachers who have spoiled the press release you were mentally preparing. They will see that you mean business. You resolve to see the social studies supervisors in your office at 8:30 Monday morning! With this decision made, you continue to examine the score reports when your intuition suggests a new plan of action: "On Monday morning, I think I will visit some of the social studies classes in the schools."

Monday morning you find yourself entering a geography class in a modern middle school. For a moment, it seems that you may have arrived at class change. The seats are empty. You soon spot the kids down on the floor and you look more closely. Thick chalk lines mark some sort of boundaries. Some kids bear badges announcing, "border guard." Indeed, letters on the floor are now forming into words: Uganda, Kenya, Tanzania. Posters announce the various tourist attractions. As you watch, the border guard to Kenya turns away a visitor because he is unable to list Kenya's natural resources. As you observe all this, you tune in on the last sentence fragments of the teacher's voice: "... and so, in view of the fact that these areas will play an important role in the world these children are growing into, we are stressing the emerging nations of Africa and Asia. . . ."

"Emerging nations," you muse to yourself, back in your office checking the manual of the achievement test. "Let's see, Copyright, 1984. Previous copyrights: 1971, 1959, 1945, 1937." Visions of Franklin D. Roosevelt swim in your mind. That was the great depression. The good-neighbor policy. Yes, that's it. Before the jets shrank the world, that was about all the geography anybody took seriously—our good neighbors to the North, Canada, and our good neighbors to the South, Mexico and beyond.

You open the test to the social studies section. There it is, and all remarkably stable: the St. Lawrence River still separates Ontario from New York, the Andes still stretch from Colombia to Chile, and Montevideo is still the capital of Uruguay. But this is not the content your children are studying.

The plain fact is that the national standardized test lacked content validity for measuring social studies achievement in your system.

Figure 4.2

Percent of textbook topics covered by each test. Data from D. J. Freeman, T. M. Kuhs, A. C. Porter, R. E. Floden, W. H. Schmidt, and J. R. Schwille, "Do Textbooks and Tests Define a National Curriculum in Elementary School Mathematics?" in *The Elementary School Journal,* 83 (5): 501–513, 1983.

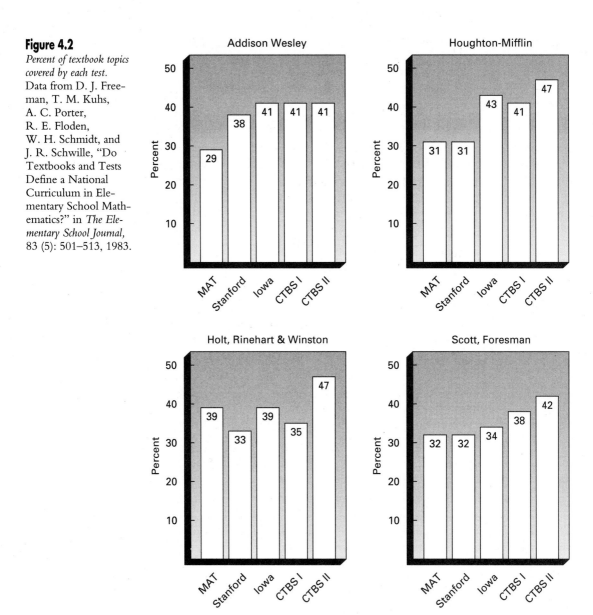

Has our imaginary example been too far-fetched? Figure 4.2, based on the work of Freeman et al. (1983), shows the overlap between text coverage and test content for fourth-grade mathematics. These investigators analyzed the student exercise items in widely used mathematics texts published by Addison-Wesley, Holt, Rinehart & Winston, Houghton Mifflin, and Scott, Foresman. The tests analyzed were the

Metropolitan Achievement Tests, Stanford Achievement Tests, Iowa Test of Basic Skills, and the Comprehensive Tests of Basic Skills (Level I and Level II).

From figure 4.2, it may be observed that teachers who are using the Addison-Wesley textbook and measuring achievement with the Metropolitan Achievement Tests are at quite a disadvantage; only 29 percent of the topics on which they are focusing their efforts will appear on the standardized test. A school teaching under these circumstances will appear more deficient in mathematics achievement than another school teaching from the Holt or the Houghton Mifflin text and measuring achievement with the Comprehensive Tests of Basic Skills, Level II. Examination of this figure reveals that in no case is there a perfect match between what is taught and what is tested. None of the standardized tests has perfect content validity, no matter what text series is adopted.

Concluding Remarks

We might expect some breakdown of the strict boundaries between the various kinds of validity in this chapter. Of course, to pass the National Teachers' Examinations, we need to keep in mind the various approaches to test validity and not mix them up. But in examining the validity of most tests, we will find ourselves using all these approaches almost simultaneously. We will look to see if the test appears to measure the stated objective (face validity). We will view the items as a sample of some larger group of items that might measure the objective (content validity). We will ask ourselves for a tighter definition of the underlying trait or ability being measured and we will look for evidence that the trait or ability is present in the criterion measures used (construct validity). We will examine correlation coefficients between the tests in question and better-established tests or behavioral indices (criterion related validity). We will seem to be doing all of this at once as we seek to evaluate the test in light of the claims made for it by the test author.

Validity Is Related to Purpose

In our discussion, we have been talking as if a test "has" validity. This is a convenient way of talking about a test, but in the final analysis we have to ask if the test scores will do the job we want them to do. A test may be a good indicator of intelligence, but is it a valid instrument for the purpose of selecting automobile salespeople?

This view reflects an established maxim in testing: validity is always related to the purposes of the tester. In the final analysis, questions of validity must always be answered in terms of your local situation.

An example of a local validity study is seen in the work of Beden, Rohr, and Ellsworth (1987) who wanted to know if the *Woodcock-Johnson Psycho-Educational Battery* (Woodcock & Johnson, 1978) would be useful in helping identify children with learning disabilities in their school district. They substituted the achievement section of the new battery for scores obtained from four relatively time-consuming achievement tests being used to make placement decisions. A trained screening committee examined the folders of thirty children who had been referred for learning disability testing, and made decisions. These decisions were compared with the actual decisions of a screening committee using the same folders that instead contained the four achievement scores of the original time-consuming procedure. The results showed that identical placement decisions were made for twenty-three out of the thirty students. In the seven cases where the two committees disagreed on the need for special placement, the differences between the new testing and the standard testing played a role in only three cases. The investigators concluded that the decisions would be the same for most students under either testing program. They suggested that considerable time and effort would be saved if the Johnson-Woodcock battery replaced the four tests currently in use for children being evaluated for learning disabilities. The new test seems to be valid for their purposes.

Summary

The most essential question in psychometrics is "Is this test valid?" Simply put, we want to know whether a test measures what it was designed to measure. There are no yes-no answers to questions of test validity. Rather, validity is a matter of degree. In determining the extent of test validity, we search the test manual or independent research reports for evidence that the test measures what it claims to measure. We have found that there are several approaches to validating a test:

Face validity—the appearance of the test suggests validity. This is not a scientific or systematic procedure and a test with high face validity can be totally lacking in any of the more fundamental components of validity mentioned below.

Content validity—a systematic study of the test items to determine whether the items are a representative sample of the underlying domain. While content validity can be applied to any test, it is an indispensable part of establishing the validity of achievement tests. We provided an illustration of how a superintendent of schools might draw wrong inferences about the quality of social studies instruction in her school system by failing to attend to the content validity of the standardized achievement test used in her system.

Construct validity—evidence that the test has captured the human trait or ability it claims to measure. This approach usually involves a network of theory, which specifies that the test will have high correlations with some variables, low with others. The pattern of expected correlations is typically examined in a convergent-discriminant validity study.

Criterion related validity—evidence that the test is related to other variables of interest, i.e., mechanical aptitude and shop grades. Criterion related validity may be obtained in a study of concurrent validity or in a study of predictive validity.

Concurrent validity—both the test data and criterion data are collected at about the same point in time. Example: the mechanical aptitude test is given to all students in a high school shop course and the scores are correlated with instructor ratings of shop performance collected the same week.

Predictive validity—the test data are collected and used to predict future performance. Example: mechanical aptitude tests administered during the fall testing program are used to predict grades in a high school shop course completed during the spring semester.

In the preceding chapter, we learned to look for very high reliability coefficients, say .85 and above; in validity studies, we might be content with correlation coefficients that are much lower. Remember that in judging reliability, we were correlating a test with itself, such as in a test-retest study. In looking at validity, however, we are correlating a test with a different test or with a work sample. Many additional variables such as effort, motivation, and opportunity will influence performance on the work sample; these variables may not have operated on the test score. Thus, high validity coefficients are difficult to obtain. Further, in many pass-fail situations, tests with modest validity coefficients can be useful in predicting outcomes. Finally, validity questions are related to the test users' purposes and can be answered most satisfactorily by local validity studies.

References

Beden, I., Rohr, L., & Ellsworth, R. (1987). A public school validation study of the achievement sections of the Woodcock-Johnson Psycho-Educational Battery with learning disabled students. *Educational and Psychological Measurement, 47,* 711–717.

Campbell, D. T., & Fisk, D. W. (1959). Convergent and discriminant validation by the multitrait-multimethod matrix. *Psychological Bulletin, 56,* 81–105.

Freeman, D.J., Kuhs, T.M., Porter, A.C., Floden, R.E., Schmidt, W.H., & Schwille, J.R. (1983). Do textbooks and tests define a national curriculum in elementary school mathematics? *The Elementary School Journal, 83* (5), 501–513.

Kelley, T. L., & Prey, A. C. (1934). *Tests and measurements in the social sciences.* Ann Arbor: University of Michigan Press.

Messick, S. (1989). Validity. In R. L. Linn (ed.), *Educational measurement.* New York: American Council on Education/Macmillan.

Thorndike, R. M., Cunningham, G. K., Thorndike, R. L., & Hagen, E. P. (1991). *Measurement and evaluation in psychology and education.* New York: Macmillan.

Woodcock, R. W., & Johnson, M. B. (1978). *Woodcock-Johnson Psycho-Educational Battery.* Boston: Teaching Resources.

Parent conferences tonight, which means I have to interpret the standardized test results. The principal has asked that we use stanines because the other scores suggest more precision than they actually have. But I am not comfortable with stanines because I really don't understand them. Also, parents keep asking me to point out the lowest scores so they can help their child at home. Sometimes I think the lowest score isn't all that different from the next to lowest. Does that matter?

Norms, Standardization Procedures, and Expectancy Tables

VALIDITY

STANDARDIZATION

RELIABILITY

We have noted that a good test can be thought of as supported by a tripod. Adequate reliability is one leg of the tripod, adequate validity is a second. We now turn to the third leg of the tripod: adequate standardization. The standardization procedure provides **norms** that allow the test user to convert the raw score on a test into a more interpretable number. One such readily interpretable number is the percentile score, which shows the percent of students falling below a particular student. Tables for converting raw scores into more meaningful scores are based on a standardization group, and it is essential for the test user to examine the nature of this group for hidden biases. A test may have excellent reliability and be reasonably valid, but faulty norms could still lead to serious errors in interpreting the test scores. Adequate standardization is indeed the third leg of the tripod supporting a good test.

We open this chapter with a brief discussion of raw scores and two approaches to making raw scores more meaningful: criterion referencing and norm referencing. We then ask you to assume the role of a counselor using a norm-referenced test to help a student make a decision about attending college. This exercise is followed by a discussion of the key idea in test standardization: the representativeness of the sample on whom the test is normed. The norming procedure makes possible a variety of derived scores such as percentiles, grade equivalents, age scores, stanines, and IQ scores. This chapter defines these scores and the advantages and disadvantages of each. Expectancy tables, better than norms for estimating future performance in a known situation, are then introduced. This chapter ends with a reminder that test norms, useful as they are, perpetuate a statistical conception of normalcy.

Raw Scores

Counting up the number of right answers that a student earns on a test provides a **raw score.** It is difficult to tell what a raw score means. Is a score of 30 on a math test high or low? It helps to know that there are 50 items on the test, but did these items include calculus or stop at business arithmetic? Even if the test is 50 items of business arithmetic, we are not sure just how good it is to attain a score of 30.

There are two ways to approach the problem of interpreting test scores: criterion referencing and norm referencing. The terms help distinguish between two commonsense approaches. Let us address criterion referencing first.

Criterion-Referenced Tests

Criterion-referenced tests provide measures that can be interpreted in terms of the ability to perform clearly defined tasks. For example, a teacher using a criterion-referenced test for reading skills would be able to examine a score and then state that "Chang has mastered initial word attack skills." Note the difference between this statement and the statement that "Chang has done better than 90 percent of other first grade students on this reading test." Above all, a criterion-referenced test should lead to a clear description of what a student can do. Popham (1978), an early proponent of criterion-referenced tests, points out that the term is unfortunate. A better name would be content-referenced or domain-referenced.

Criterion-referenced tests can be distinguished from norm-referenced tests (described below) by their construction and by the context in which they are used. A criterion-referenced test depends on a detailed specification of the behavioral domain of interest, and it will contain many items dealing with highly specified skills and attainments. For example, in a test for reading skills, the various components of word attack skills would be defined and items constructed to measure each component. The defining characteristic of a criterion-referenced test is that it is constructed to reflect a detailed and finite analysis of a behavioral domain judged to be important.

This feature makes criterion-referenced tests most useful in formative evaluation. **Formative evaluation** is used to monitor learning during the instructional process. Formative evaluation helps the teacher diagnose particular difficulties and adjust instructional strategies. For this reason, criterion-referenced testing is helpful to the classroom teacher and almost indispensable for programmed learning and computer-assisted instruction in which past performance is used to branch the learner into either new units or a review of earlier material.

Criterion-referenced testing is frequently linked to mastery learning, even though this linkage is not implied in the definition. An instructor using a criterion-referenced test may decide that answering 90 percent of the items is required to go on to the next unit, or to finish the course of study. This approach assumes that the content or skills being taught are essential for some later behavior. If, for example, a fifty-item arithmetic test is based on a study determining the most frequent kinds of arithmetic problems encountered in actual business situations, then it might make sense to say that 90 percent of the items must be correct in order to "pass" the test.

There is, however, a problem with criterion-referenced tests when the outcomes of instruction are less clearly defined. For example, it may be difficult to establish behavioral objectives or to determine the level of "mastery" desired in an art history course where one of the goals is to develop an appreciation of the work of van Gogh, Gauguin, Toulouse-Lautrec, and others who broke with the traditional school of painting. There is a tendency in the construction of criterion-related tests to ignore more general goals of instruction that do not lend themselves to measurement.

Criterion-referenced tests must be closely tied to local instructional programs. Some observers have suggested that teachers might be paid during the summer months to develop tests for their school districts. Popham (1978) expresses doubt about the ability of such groups to analyze a behavioral domain carefully and to construct technically competent items. He is not encouraged by the prospect of committees of teachers constructing criterion-referenced tests for school districts. "Such a practice is like commissioning a band of grasshoppers to kick an elephant to death" (Popham, 1978, p. 241). Still, a case can be made that teachers, working with a test expert, might be the most logical group to design and construct tests that would be responsive to their instructional programs and that would meet their needs for diagnosis and remediation of learning problems.

Criterion-referenced tests allow the teacher to speak of the competencies of the student being tested rather than simply observing how well the student has performed with respect to the rest of the group. The ability to wisely interpret criterion-referenced tests depends on the teacher's knowledge of the test content and the kinds of instructional adjustments that may be indicated for students with high, medium, or low scores.

A moment's reflection will persuade us that this last statement about criterion-referenced tests applies also to norm-referenced tests. Knowing how a student ranks in a group will be of little value unless we also know the nature of the tasks that the student had to perform to earn a particular rank. Yet, the distinguishing characteristic of the criterion-referenced test is its very large sample of items covering the behavior of interest, and the absence of normative data that might be used to provide additional meaning to the scores.

Norm-Referenced Tests

The second, and by far the most common, approach to the problem of interpreting test scores is **norm referencing,** i.e., interpreting test performance by comparing a single student's score with the scores earned by a group. Going back to the task of evaluating a score of 30 on a fifty-item test, we are likely to ask what the average student scored on the test. If the median score for the group tested was 25, then we know that a score of 30 places the student in the upper half of the class. Comparing a student to a large sample of others who have taken the same test provides a readily understandable way of evaluating performance. Using the performance of a group as a reference, one can convert raw scores into more easily interpretable scores such as percentile scores. Percentile scores indicate the percent of the group tested that the student in question equaled or exceeded. If a student has a percentile score of 76, this means she equaled or exceeded 76 percent of the people taking the test. Counselors interpreting these scores generally say to a student, "You did better than 76 percent of the others taking this test."

Norm-referenced achievement tests are typically used in **summative evaluation,** i.e., evaluation designed to summarize achievement at the end of a course or unit. Since a broad range of material is covered, any given skill or concept is measured by only a few items. While criterion-referenced tests lead to statements about the kinds of tasks an individual can perform, norm-referenced tests lead to statements about the status of an individual in a group.

Interpreting a test by reference to norms seems very straightforward, but we shall see that there may be hidden dangers for the untrained test user.

An Exercise in Using Norms

Suppose you are a high school counselor working for a school system in Kentucky. In this exercise, a senior has come to you for help in deciding what to do after graduation. Brad opens the conversation.

"I came to see you to find out if I ought to go to college."
"What do you mean, Brad, "ought" to go to college?"
"We took the College Qualification Test last month, and I figure that if my scores are high enough I ought to go to college."

Looking up Brad's score on the College Qualification Test you find that he has earned a raw score of 100. That sounds pretty good, but there are 200 items on the test. Using the chart in figure 5.1, go ahead and convert Brad's score to a percentile and then write your response to his query about going to college.

It is important that you write your response to Brad's query at this time because you will be referring back to it later. This example will lose its value unless you take a moment to write your answer to Brad's question, "Should I go to college?"

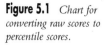

Figure 5.1 *Chart for converting raw scores to percentile scores.*

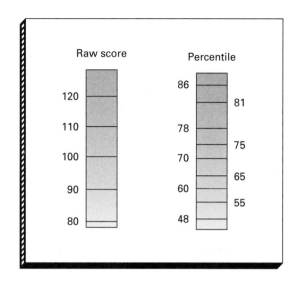

Have you written your response? You may have been very direct in making suggestions to Brad or you may have been cautious and asked Brad for information about his school grades and intended major.

"Well, to be honest, my grades won't set any world records. Mostly Cs, some Bs, and a couple of As, too. But by the time you get through all that basketball practice and the games, you don't have a lot of time left.

I'm not sure what I will major in yet, but my friends say it doesn't matter your freshman year anyway."

If you didn't take a definite position about whether Brad should go to college based on his test scores and his report, go ahead and do so now. What do you advise?

If you were uncomfortable making the decision, what additional information did you want?

The critical information you need is a description of the standardization procedure that provided the norms. Whom are these norms based on? Figure 5.2 shows a more complete display of the conversion table.

This new information may come as a surprise. The norms are based on students within a single state rather than students from a more representative group of states. In addition, using these norms leads to a comparison of Brad with other high school seniors. Yet not all high school seniors go on to college. It would be more relevant to determine Brad's standing among entering college freshmen. You ask Brad where he is thinking of attending college.

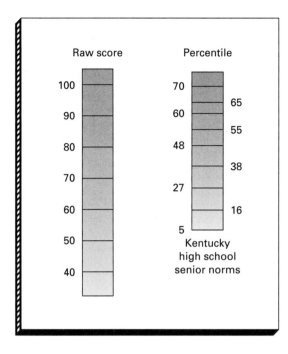

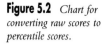

Figure 5.2 *Chart for converting raw scores to percentile scores.*

"Well, I want to go to college in the south. I know a fellow who went up north. When he came back, he had forgotten his southern upbringing. I guess part of going to college is it makes you into a gentleman."

Based on this information, you decide to use the norms provided in the manual for freshmen entering colleges in the southern region of the United States (figure 5.3). Obtain Brad's percentile score based on this group, and then give him your appraisal of his chance for success in a college in this region.

Brad listens to your comments about attending one of the colleges or universities in the south. He then responds:

"Well, I wouldn't say that I just have to go to a college in the south. A lot of the expense is room and board. If I went to Ohio I could save a lot of money. I have an aunt living in Columbus. Ohio State is there. How would I do if I went up there, to Ohio State?"

You consult the test manual again and find the percentile score for Brad based on national college norms (figure 5.4). After converting his raw score to a percentile score for this norm group, what do you say to Brad?

Take a minute to write a sentence summarizing your advice to Brad at this point.

Chapter 5: Norms, Standardization Procedures, and Expectancy Tables

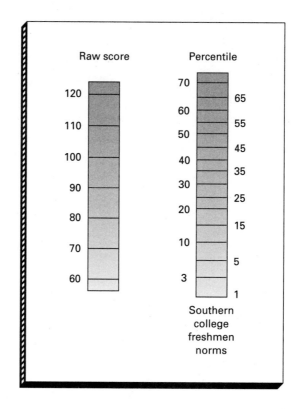

Figure 5.3 *Chart for converting raw scores to percentile scores.*

Are you ready to compare your last comments with your first advice to Brad about college attendance? If so, you will observe a marked shift in the tone and tenor of your comments. Is this the same person? Indeed it is, and notice that his test score has not changed. Brad still has the 100 correct responses he has always had on the test. What has changed is the **norm group** that you are using in evaluating Brad's performance.

The moral of this story is never interpret a test score to anybody unless you know how the test was standardized; that is, unless you know what group was used to obtain the test norms. This admonition holds whether you are interpreting IQ scores, grade equivalents, stanines, percentiles, or whatever. All these scores originate as raw scores, the number of right answers on the test. In order to make these raw scores more interpretable, they are converted to scores that rank the student among other students in a group. The key question to ask is "what group?" Failure to ask this question leads to the danger of using inappropriate norms and painting a distorted picture of the individual in question.

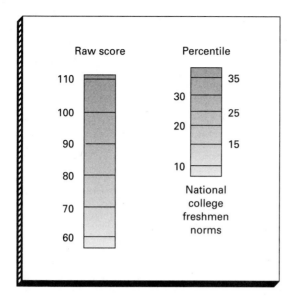

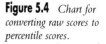

Figure 5.4 *Chart for converting raw scores to percentile scores.*

Information about the procedures used in developing the norms for a test is presented in the test manual. The publisher will tell you how the test was **standardized;** that is, how the group on which the norms are based was selected.

Selecting the Group for Norming the Test

The key decision in evaluating the standardization procedure is determining if the sample of people used in norming the test was selected so as to be **representative** of the more general population of interest. For example, if a publisher offers norms for students entering professional art schools, we would expect such norms to be based on a representative sample of such schools, not just well-known art education programs on the east coast. Far more important than having a large number in the sample is that the sample be representative of the underlying population.

The norms developed for standardized achievement tests provide a good example of efforts by publishers to obtain samples of children representative of the United States with respect to the following characteristics:

Geographic—The United States represents very large political and geographic variations. Pupils going to school in one part of the country may have school experiences that are quite different from those living in another part. All sections of the country must be represented in the group on which the test is normed. The U.S. census data provide the proportions of the population living in the various regions, as shown in table 5.1.

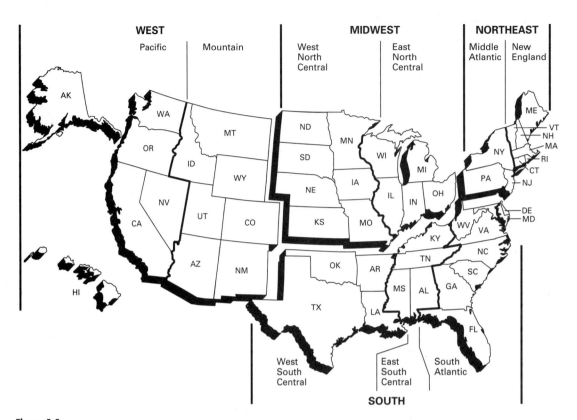

Figure 5.5 *Map showing U.S. census divisions.*
Source: U.S. Bureau of the Census.

Test publishers may use even finer breakdowns in order to obtain geographic representation in their norm groups. The map in figure 5.5 shows the census divisions and regions that guide publishers as they select a sample representative of the geographic regions of the United States.

Rural-Urban—The publisher will want to include children from big cities, small towns, and rural areas. The publisher will select children not only from Dallas, but also from Tyler; from Indianapolis and also from Pine Village; from Seattle and from Sequim Bay; from Minneapolis and from Red Wing. Figures from the U.S. census provide the basis for the proportion of the norm group that will be drawn from each kind of community.

Socioeconomic—Frequently, the educational level or the occupation of the parents is used to indicate socioeconomic level. The census figures in table 5.2 show the breakdown of occupational groups.

Table 5.1 *Geographic Distribution of Population*

	Percent
Northeast	20
Midwest	24
South	34
West	21

Source: Statistical Abstract of the United States, 1991.

Table 5.2 *Distribution of the Work Force by Occupations*

	Percent
Managerial and professional specialty	26
Technical, sales, and administrative support	31
Service occupations	13
Precision production, craft, and repair	12
Operators, fabricators, and laborers	15
Farming, forestry, and fishing	3

Source: Statistical Abstract of the United States, 1991.

Table 5.3 *Distribution of the Population by Ethnic Groups (rounded)*

	Percent
White	84
Black	12
All Others	4

Source: Statistical Abstract of the United States, 1991.

It is evident from these percentages that the test publisher will need in the norm group fairly specific proportions of children from managerial and professional families, business and service families, skilled and blue collar families, and farm families.

Ethnic—Adequate representation of the various racial and ethnic groups that make up the population of the United States is an essential feature of the norm group. The 1980 census provides the breakdown of the U.S. population shown in table 5.3.

A norm group that is representative of the children in the schools must include a proportional percent of each of these ethnic groups.

The Norms

It should be evident by now why representativeness is the most important aspect of the norm group, much more important than size. A norm group of five thousand people selected so as to represent all of the diversity in the country will be far superior to a norm group of fifty thousand white, middle-class people selected from the cities of New York, Chicago, St. Louis, and San Francisco.

The publisher will describe in the test manual the procedure used to select the norm group. You have to examine this section of the manual in order to answer the critical question: With what group of kids am I comparing this student when I am interpreting her test score? For example, until recently, a person using the Peabody Picture Vocabulary Test to estimate the intelligence of a school youngster would have found that the percentile scores were obtained on a norm group composed entirely of children from Tennessee. Now, however, a much more representative sample comprises the norm group for this test.

What does the test maker do with the norm group, once identified? For achievement tests, the publisher arranges for the selected schools to administer the test. The results are entered into a computer, which calculates the mean and other statistical data for the thousands of pupils taking the test at each grade level. These data are then used to construct tables that allow the test user to convert the raw score to one that can be more easily interpreted.

Derived Scores

As we move on to discuss achievement, intelligence, aptitude, interest, and personality tests, we shall see that the raw scores are converted into more readily interpreted forms. There are a number of different names for these **derived scores,** but they all have one thing in common: they communicate the individual student's rank in the norm group. From the derived scores, you can tell at a glance whether a student is above, at, or below the average; that is, the average of the standardization sample. The result of norming the test is always a table that allows the user to convert any raw score to a derived score that instantly compares the individual with the "national" sample. Following are some of the widely used derived scores.

Grade Equivalents

This is one of the most common ways of interpreting performance on achievement tests. The procedure for obtaining the **grade equivalent scores** is strictly empirical. If the test is standardized on sixth grade

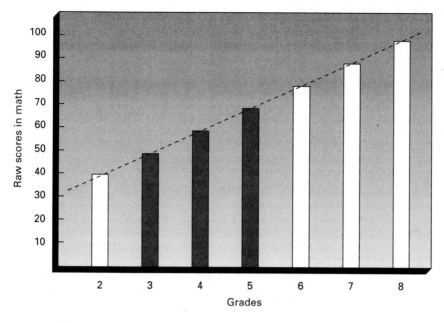

Figure 5.6 *Actual and extrapolated performance on a math test administered to fifth graders.* Reprinted with the permission of Macmillan Publishing Company from *Educational and Psychological Measurement* by George K. Cunningham. Copyright © 1986 by Macmillan Publishing Company.

children tested during the second month of school, the average achievement of that group becomes the raw score that is converted to a grade equivalent of 6.2. Such scores are easily interpreted and generally understood to indicate the grade level at which a child is working. Grade equivalent scores provide reasonably good guides for evaluating school achievement, but there is a connotation that a child who is "off the norm" by a few months may not be making normal progress. Also, grade equivalent scores are not nearly as precise as is implied. For example, a test might have actually been given only in grades 3, 4, and 5, and the grade equivalents within each grade and beyond these grades arrived at by **interpolation** and **extrapolation,** as illustrated in figure 5.6.

The way in which grade equivalent scores are generated has important consequences for interpretation. A grade equivalent of 8.3 earned by a fifth grade child does not necessarily mean that he knows the eighth grade material; it may simply mean that he is very good in comparison to others who have studied the fifth grade material. On the other hand, the student may have hit the ceiling of the test and, in fact, may well be above the grade level shown, but the scale does not go any higher. "Off level" testing (using the next higher series of tests) may provide a more realistic picture of the levels at which highly talented children might perform. On the whole, departures of six months or so from the norm are not occasions for much concern or much celebration. Departures of two years from the grade level norm may flag special attention, but even this rule of thumb is not altogether true. For the Iowa Test of Basic Skills, for example, only about 10 percent of the fourth grade children will be two years behind in language usage, but by the time a class has reached sixth grade, almost 20 percent of the children will be two years below the grade median (Peterson, Kolen & Hoover, 1989). Thus, two years below grade level has quite different meanings at the two different grade levels.

Additionally, because different publishers use different methods for scaling the test, the grade equivalents from one test to another are not necessarily comparable. Thus, some of the puzzlement that might occur when a teacher compares present and past grade equivalents for a transfer student may be resolved by understanding that grade equivalents are not always comparable units.

There are two essential points to keep in mind when interpreting grade equivalents. One is that the grade equivalent representing normal progress for your class is no more than the mean or median of a distribution curve of a national sample of students at that grade level. About half of the students will be below this point, the other half above it. There is no way that all students will or can be at grade level.

The second point to remember is that the grade equivalent score is not a firm recommendation for a change in grade placement. It is sometimes instructive to look at the conversion tables and note how few raw score points are needed to make a relatively large change in grade equivalent scores. Excellent work with the material at hand can appear as competence with advanced material that has not been covered. High grade equivalent scores may mean that the student will not profit from more of the same instruction, but it does not necessarily imply a change in grade placement.

One of the most important uses of grade equivalent scores is the signal that such scores send to teachers about the need to adjust schoolwork for many students. We visited a seventh grade class with copies of a few pages of an upcoming text. We asked the students to record the time from the wall clock when they finished reading the material, and to complete a brief multiple-choice test over the material read. We compared the results of this exercise to the students' grade equivalent scores for reading. The results for three students are shown graphically in figure 5.7.

We can see from this figure that the student with a reading grade equivalent score of 4.5 required more than twice the time to finish reading the passage than did the student with a grade equivalent score of 10.8. Even with this extra time, the student with the lower reading score comprehended only about 12 percent of the material. Using test scores to

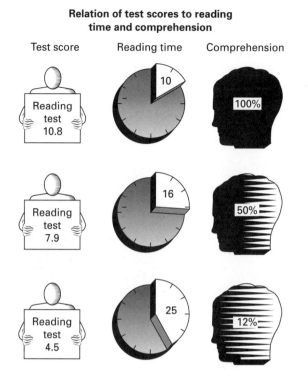

Relation of test scores to reading time and comprehension

Test score   Reading time   Comprehension

Reading test 10.8   10   100%

Reading test 7.9   16   50%

Reading test 4.5   25   12%

Figure 5.7 *Using Test Scores.*

adjust school work to match the students' capabilities is more important than the form (grade equivalents, percentiles, stanines) in which the scores are reported.

Age Scores

If, when the test is standardized, the ages of the children have been collected, it is a simple step to obtain the average age score earned by each age group. Any child who takes the test later can then be compared to these age norms. The result is easily interpreted: "He is reading like an average eight year old." This form of interpreting scores is particularly appropriate for developmental scales. The problem is that age norms convey the idea that all normal eight year olds read at a particular level. Too often, the statistical mean of the norm group becomes the target that a child must hit to be considered as making normal progress for his age. Expressing academic progress as an age score may carry with it unwarranted connotations of mental disabilities or advanced development.

Table 5.4 *Example of a Conversion Table for ACT Composite Scores*

Score	Percentile Rank	Standard Score
32	99	70
31	96	66
30	89	62
29	78	59
28	67	55
27	54	52
26	42	48
25	31	44
24	21	41
23	13	37
22	6	34
21	1	30
20	1	26

n = 177 freshman female liberal arts majors at a midwestern university.
From Principles of Educational and Psychological Testing, Second Edition, by Frederick C. Brown.
Copyright © 1976 by Holt, Rinehart and Winston, Inc. Reprinted by permission of the publisher.

Percentile Scores

Percentile scores are among the most widely used derived scores because of their ease of interpretation. Each raw score is converted to show the percent of students falling at or below that score. Thus, a student at the 70th percentile has equaled or exceeded the scores of 70 percent of the students in the norm group. The major disadvantage of these scores is that they do not represent equal steps in raw scores. For example, around the 50th percentile, an increase of a few raw score points could mean a sizable change in the percent of people passed. Out at the end of the scale, an improvement of several raw score points could mean only a small change in percentile points. This phenomenon can be observed in table 5.4.

From this table, we may note that an improvement of a single point in the student's raw score, a change from 27 to 28, results in a change of 13 percentile points. At the upper end of the scale, however, a change in score from 31 to 32 results in a gain of only 3 percentile points. It is useful to remember this characteristic of percentile scores when comparing the status of an individual in two different content areas. Large differences in percentile scores near the middle of the distribution may not signify correspondingly large differences in actual achievement. The problem of unequal units also makes percentile scores a poor choice for statistical analyses. Raw scores are much better for research studies because they represent more equal intervals on the scale.

Standard Scores

There is a class of derived scores called **standard scores** because they are based on the standard deviation of the norm group. These scores include z-scores, stanines, T scores, college board scores, normal curve equivalents, and deviation IQ scores. We will examine these scores and discover that each is simply a variation of the z-score, which we introduced in chapter 2.

Stanines

This word is a combination of the words "standard nine." It refers to a nine-point scale developed by the United States Army Air Forces during World War II. **Stanines** are derived scores in which the raw scores are converted to a scale of nine equal units, each unit being one half of a standard deviation. Stanines also **normalize** the score distributions that may be skewed to the right or left. This is done by assigning stanines to scores depending on the percent of the group tested that falls within the prescribed limits for half a standard deviation at given positions on the normal curve. Recall that the normal distribution curve reflects the fact that many people earn scores falling in the middle (around the average) of any series of scores, and few people are in the tails (very high or very low scores). The Army Air Forces considered this characteristic of the normal curve when grouping scores into the nine stanine units as shown in table 5.5.

Stanines were a practical invention. In the days of slow calculating machines, it took much less time to enter and compute with a single-digit number than with a two-digit score. Time was important. Thousands of men were being tested daily on a number of tests, and studies had to be done quickly to see which tests would predict success or failure in such jobs as piloting and navigating aircraft.

Stanines seem to contradict a basic goal of measurement, the quest for precision. Stanines are relatively crude indices of performance. They compress all the scores earned on a test into nine categories. But, in some ways, viewing performance as falling within a broad band rather than at a specific point may be more consistent with reality. Tests are not as precise as we tend to think they are, and besides, for most decisions, varying a few points one way or another may not make much difference.

Stanines have some advantages in interpreting performance to parents. They are less common than other kinds of converted scores and not as easy to understand, but they have the advantage of communicating a general level of achievement that is not likely to be overinterpreted. In addition, stanine scores do not carry the connotations of underachievement or overachievement that are often associated with age and grade equivalent scores.

Table 5.5 *Percent of Group Included in Each Stanine*

Percent of People Tested		Stanine
Top	4 percent	= 9th
Next	7 percent	= 8th
Next	12 percent	= 7th
Next	17 percent	= 6th
Middle	20 percent	= 5th
Next	17 percent	= 4th
Next	12 percent	= 3rd
Next	7 percent	=2nd
Bottom	4 percent	= 1st

T scores

T scores were introduced because the use of z-scores involved negatives and decimals, which seemed to open the way for errors in copying and interpreting. A T score is a standard score with a mean of 50 and a standard deviation of 10. Since scores are not likely to fall more than 5 standard deviations below the mean, negative scores are eliminated. Additionally, by multiplying a standard deviation by 10, decimals are eliminated. Thus, a z-score of -1 would convert to a T score of 40 and a z-score of 1.5 would convert to a T score of 65. T scores may also contain procedures of normalizing the distribution of scores as noted by Thorndike, Cunningham, Thorndike, and Hagen (1991, p. 68).

CEEB Scores

The Scholastic Aptitude Test of the College Entrance Examination Board makes use of a standard score (**CEEB score**) with a mean of 500 and a standard deviation of 100. Note that 600 on this scale is simply one standard deviation above the mean and is equivalent to a T score of 60 and to a z-score of 1. Each of these three standard scores indicates that the student is one standard deviation above the mean.

Under ordinary circumstances, a CEEB score of 500 would indicate that a student is exactly at the mean of the test. Yet, we know that as of the fall of 1993, the Educational Testing Service reported that the average score for college-bound seniors on the verbal test was 424 and the average score for the mathematics test was 478. How could this be? The answer is very simple. The CEEB standard score scale was established fifty years ago on the basis of the average performance of all students taking the test at that time. These students were primarily young men and women applying to prestigious and highly selective colleges, which required the test as part of the admissions requirement. Now many colleges require the test and a much broader segment of the population is taking the test. This is almost a classic case of a shift in the norm group. While the standard scores for the Scholastic Aptitude Tests are still reported on the 1941 scale, the percentile scores based on students tested during the current year is a much better indication of performance on the tests.

Normal Curve Equivalent

Normal Curve Equivalents, or NCE scores, are being reported by a number of test publishers. NCE scores are standard scores in which percentile scores are converted to a scale with a mean of 50 and a standard deviation of 21.06. This rather strange standard deviation was chosen because it leads to NCE scores in which one corresponds to a percentile of 1 and ninety-nine corresponds to a percentile of 99.

Anchoring the NCE scores to percentiles at these points may not have been worth the effort since the two scores can not be interpreted in the same way. Table 5.6 shows the relationship between normal curve equivalents and percentile ranks.

The relationships shown in table 5.6 hold for all normal curve equivalent scores, not just those from the Stanford Achievement Tests. Normal curve equivalents are an equal interval scale. In contrast to ordinary percentile scores, arithmetic is possible with normal curve equivalents, such as pooling data, calculating averages, and making comparisons. When it comes to interpreting scores to pupils, parents, and teachers, normal curve equivalents have no socially redeeming virtues.

IQ Scores

There is a mystique about **intelligence quotient** (IQ) scores that seems to put them in a class by themselves. Behind the mystique is the fact that IQ scores, like other scores, originate as raw scores on a set of test items. For the original Stanford-Binet, the items had already been tried out on groups of children and clustered by age levels. The logic of the IQ was that if a child performed like a typical eight year old, his "mental age" was 8. By comparing the mental age with the actual age, one could judge whether the child's mental development was on schedule. Later, the "mental age" was divided by chronological age and multiplied by 100 to get rid of decimals, and the IQ score was born.

Most modern intelligence tests bypass the conversion of the number to a mental age, the division of mental age by chronological age, and the multiplication of the ratio by 100. Instead, **deviation IQs** are obtained by

Table 5.6 *Normal Curve Equivalents Corresponding to Percentile Ranks*

Percentile Rank	NCE	Percentile Rank	NCE	Percentile Rank	NCE	Percentile Rank	NCE
1	1.0	26	36.5	51	50.5	76	64.9
2	6.7	27	37.1	52	51.1	77	65.6
3	10.4	28	37.7	53	51.6	78	66.3
4	13.1	29	38.3	54	52.1	79	67.0
5	15.4	30	39.0	55	52.6	80	67.7
6	17.3	31	39.6	56	53.2	81	68.5
7	18.9	32	40.1	57	53.7	82	69.3
8	20.4	33	40.7	58	54.2	83	70.1
9	21.8	34	41.3	59	54.8	84	70.9
10	23.0	35	41.9	60	55.3	85	71.8
11	24.2	36	42.5	61	55.9	86	72.8
12	25.3	37	43.0	62	56.4	87	73.7
13	26.3	38	43.6	63	57.0	88	74.7
14	27.2	39	44.1	64	57.5	89	75.8
15	28.2	40	44.7	65	58.1	90	77.0
16	29.1	41	45.2	66	58.7	91	78.2
17	29.9	42	45.8	67	59.3	92	79.6
18	30.7	43	46.3	68	59.9	93	81.1
19	31.5	44	46.8	69	60.4	94	82.7
20	32.3	45	47.4	70	61.0	95	84.6
21	33.0	46	47.9	71	61.7	96	86.9
22	33.7	47	48.4	72	62.3	97	89.6
23	34.4	48	48.9	73	62.9	98	93.3
24	35.1	49	49.5	74	63.5	99	99.0
25	35.8	50	50.0	75	64.2		

reference to a norm group. The average number of right responses at any given age level is set equal to 100, and the standard deviation is set equal to 15 or 16. By now, you will recognize the deviation IQ as just another standard score. An individual scoring at the mean of his age group will have a deviation IQ of 100. An individual scoring one standard deviation above the mean will have a deviation IQ of 115 or 116 depending on the scale adopted.

Relationships Among Derived Scores

Figure 5.8, developed by The Psychological Corporation and reproduced in all measurement books, helps show the relationships among the various derived scores.

We can summarize our discussion of norm-referenced tests by noting that all raw scores are converted into derived scores of some kind in order to make the raw scores interpretable. In a criterion-referenced test,

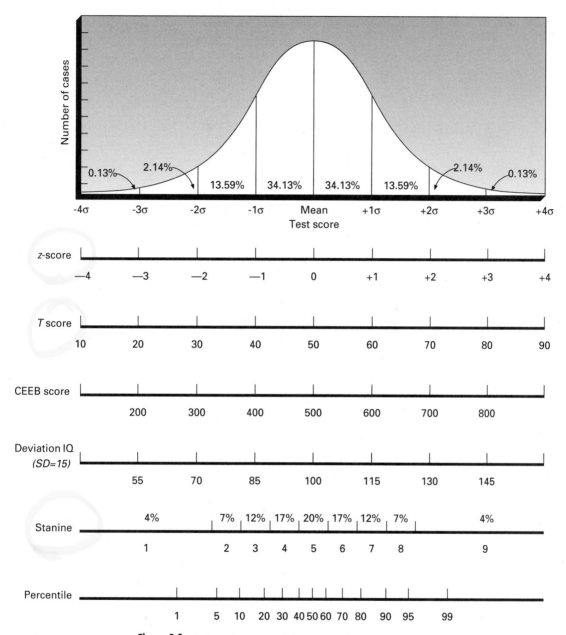

Figure 5.8 *Relationships among different types of test scores in a normal distribution.*
Source: Test Service Bulletin No. 48, The Psychological Corporation, San Antonio, Texas.

the test maker may have decided in advance how high the score should be in order to be acceptable, so no conversions are necessary. For most tests, however, the raw score is compared to the performance of a norm group to determine its meaning. It is essential that we know the characteristics of the norm group when we are interpreting the scores. The generalization holds true, no matter what kind of derived score is obtained—age equivalents, grade equivalents, percentiles, stanines, IQs, or standard scores. Knowing the composition of the norm group improves your ability to decide whether your interpretation of the score is on target.

Norms provide an excellent means of interpreting performance. For example, a teacher trying to determine whether to move a child from kindergarten to first grade despite evidence of immature behavior, may administer the Peabody Picture Vocabulary Test, a quick estimate of mental maturity. Scoring this test and converting the raw score to a percentile may reveal that the pupil is in the top five percent of children in her age group. The most relevant feature of this story is the powerful statement: " . . . in the top five percent of children in her age group," a statement that could not be made without reference to a norm group. In this case, the teacher has added precise information to the observations and other facts that she will consider in making a decision.

Expectancy Tables—Better than Norms

We have illustrated that norms allow a precise interpretation of test performance. Useful as they are, however, there is one thing better: **expectancy tables.**

Let's return to our example of Brad, the Kentucky high school senior trying to decide about going to college. Your last comments to him probably discouraged his idea of going to Ohio State University. Considering cost and the proximity of the school, your conversation might come to focus on the local university. "How well do you think I would do there?" asks Brad.

The norm allows you to determine his general academic ability in comparison with other freshmen entering colleges and universities in the Southern region of the country. You remember that his score is a little above the 40th percentile on this norm group. It requires a big inferential leap from this score to a prediction of how well Brad is likely to do at the local university. But, as a high school counselor in the region, you have something better: an expectancy table.

Figure 5.9 shows the grade point average at the end of the first semester of male students entering the local university with various score levels on the College Qualification Test. Since Brad's score is in the 40–49

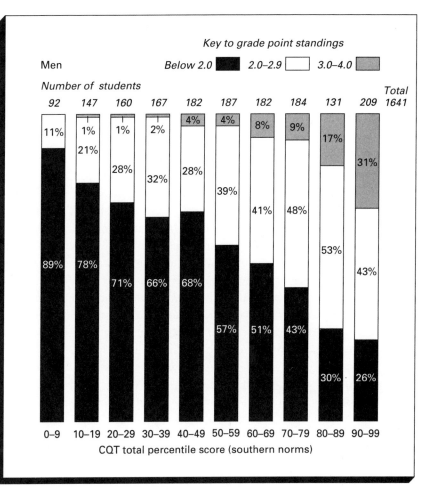

Figure 5.9 *First Semester Grade Averages of Male Freshmen as Related to Total Score on the College Qualification Tests.*

percentile range, examine this column carefully. You will notice that 68 percent of the men who entered the university with scores in this range ended the first semester with a grade average below 2.0, i.e., below a C average. This means that they were on probation. First semester grades tend to be the best predictors of later college success.

How would you interpret these results to Brad? Probably by turning the graph around so that he can see it. He might note that while 68 percent of the students with his scores end up on probation, another 28 percent earn a C average, and 4 percent even have B averages. He probably knows his own motivations and study habits, and with this new information can arrive at a decision. Note that the expectancy table has provided the most useful and relevant information thus far in interpreting Brad's test performance.

Table 5.7 *Sample Class Roster Showing Test Scores and Algebra Grades*

Total Mathematics Grade Equivalent Score	Grade in Algebra
12.0	A
8.2	B
10.1	A
9.6	C
7.2	F

Don't look for expectancy tables in the test manual. Expectancy tables have to be constructed to fit each local situation. Such tables help answer questions of importance to the teachers and counselors of a particular school. For example, how many children with low readiness test scores fail to adjust to first grade work? How are scores on a fourth grade reading test related to the teacher's judgement of "unable to benefit from the adopted text"? Are eighth grade math scores useful in predicting achievement in ninth grade algebra? Teachers in their own school situations can answer these questions without complicated statistical analyses.

An expectancy table, for example, could be constructed to see how many students at each score level passed algebra. We start with a collection of scores from the eighth grade achievement tests and the algebra grades earned by these same students during a subsequent semester. The first few cases might look like table 5.7.

We could tabulate the results on a chart with all possible grades across the top and all possible achievement scores along the left margin, but this would create so many cells that only a few cases would fall in each one. It is better to collapse the grades into two categories, pass and fail, with pass defined as a grade of C or above. It is also useful to collapse the grade equivalent scores into whole units. The empty expectancy table now looks like table 5.8, ready for the teacher to start tallying the results.

A tally mark is made for each student in the appropriate row and column. For example, if the first student had a test score of 12.0 and an algebra grade of A, a tally mark would be placed in the top row under the right column. When all tallies are placed, the total number of tallies on each row are recorded. The percentage of students at each score level passing algebra is obtained by dividing the number of tallies in the pass column by the total number of students on that row.

Table 5.8 *Empty Expectancy Table*

	Performance in Algebra		
	Failed (D or below)	**Passed (C or above)**	**Total**
Math Grade Equivalent			
12	_____	_____	_____
11	_____	_____	_____
10	_____	_____	_____
9	_____	_____	_____
8	_____	_____	_____
7	_____	_____	_____
6	_____	_____	_____
Below 6	_____	_____	_____

It is a simple matter to convert these percentages into a graphic display for students, parents, and teachers who may have an interest in your findings. A graph showing the percentage of students earning C or better in algebra at each level of the Stanford Achievement Tests is presented in figure 5.10. The white area of each bar indicates the proportion of students at that score level passing algebra as defined above.

Expectancy tables are best constructed on a large number of cases. There is no rule of thumb, but at least 100 cases will help iron out the irregularities that occur with small samples. Expectancy tables can be created quickly and easily using computer programs (such as the Crosstabs procedure in SPSS^X by SPSS, Inc.). Local expectancy tables will facilitate the use of test scores and they will prove to be better than norms when making many educational decisions.

Norms Are Not Normal

This chapter has demonstrated why adequate norms are the third leg of the tripod supporting a good test. Without norms, many tests are virtually uninterpretable. Yet, norms carry with them unspoken expectations that everyone must be at the norm or better. It is important for professionals working with tests to continue to communicate that norms do not represent benchmarks of progress that must be passed by everybody at the same time. While a grade equivalent of 6.2 may represent "normal" achievement for sixth graders in October, we must remember that this mark is the simple average of thousands of kids who took the test. Most of the children in the standardization program will have earned scores that are above or below this score.

Figure 5.10 *Percent of students at each score level earning algebra grades of "C" or better.*

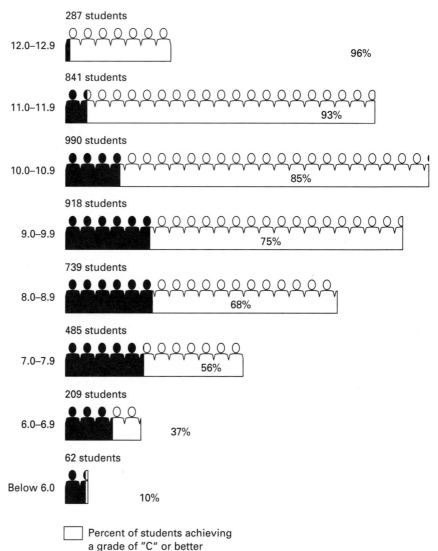

Grade equivalent score

287 students
12.0–12.9
96%

841 students
11.0–11.9
93%

990 students
10.0–10.9
85%

918 students
9.0–9.9
75%

739 students
8.0–8.9
68%

485 students
7.0–7.9
56%

209 students
6.0–6.9
37%

62 students
Below 6.0
10%

☐ Percent of students achieving a grade of "C" or better

It is also important to remember that even with the most representative sample, test norms represent a statistical abstraction. The situation is like a Hollywood film in which a philanthropist leaves one million dollars to be awarded to the "average American man." The statisticians construct specifications regarding height, weight, body build, eye color, hair type, and other characteristics. There is a long, extensive search for the typical specimen, but he is never found.

The search is for a statistical abstraction that does not exist. In a similar fashion, the norm group assembled by the test publisher usually provides a fair representation of the achievement of the typical student in a typical school in the U.S. But teachers interpret test scores for real children in specific school settings. A teacher may be interpreting the test for a Spanish speaking youth in a predominantly black, inner city school; or the school may be located in an affluent suburb or a university town where a score below the 85th percentile marks one as among the slower children in the class. Achievement test norms are based on Average Student, USA, but most students do not fit this statistical abstraction. Thus we have one of the paradoxes in testing. Norms provide carefully determined reference points by which to judge individual performance, yet many individuals have personal histories that depart significantly from the "average" person in the norm group. Test norms are an important and useful aspect of educational measurement, but in using norms we must guard against the assumption that "normality" can be defined by statistical operations rather than by the developmental history of a particular individual in a particular setting.

Summary

Scoring a test produces a raw score, the number of right answers earned by the test taker. From this point on, the teacher has the task of interpreting this score. Is it high, medium, or low? In making this decision, the teacher may fix an eye on the content and interpret the score in terms of the proportion of the content that has been learned; i.e., the teacher may make a criterion-referenced interpretation of the score. On the other hand, the teacher may examine the performance of the group as a whole and interpret a student's test score with respect to the rest of the group; i.e., the teacher makes a norm-referenced interpretation of the score.

Almost all commercially available tests are norm referenced. Tables are provided in the test manual to convert the raw scores into some more-interpretable form. No matter what this more-interpretable form is called—percentile, grade equivalent, or stanine—it is based on the performance of the individual compared to some larger group. The process of obtaining the norms of the test is called standardizing the test and the group on which the norms are based is called either the standardization sample or the norm group.

The characteristics of the norm group are the key features in determining the adequacy of the norms of the test. The essential requirement of the norm group is that it be **representative** of the population at large. If the norm group is entirely from the northeastern region of the United States, is drawn from the urban middle class, or is composed exclusively of Caucasians, then the norms will not reflect the performance of the "average person."

It is easy to recognize the importance of a representative norm group when considering achievement tests, but it should also be kept in mind that tests of intelligence, aptitude, perceptual ability, and other tests used for diagnostic purposes also depend on a norm group for the last step in generating an IQ score or a percentile score. It is essential to know the characteristics of the norm group in order to understand with whom the individual student is being compared when the score is being interpreted.

Perhaps the hardest lesson to learn is that while the norm is a useful reference point in making diagnostic decisions, it is a very poor standard of setting individual expectations. The great lesson of testing is that even in the best schools there will be a wide range of individual achievements existing in every class. Teachers and parents express much concern about students who are below the norm. It is important to remember that the norm represents a national average, and that for the nation as a whole, half the children are below the norm.

It is equally important to remember that many school communities represent major departures from the "typical school" for which the norms stand. The national norms may be perfectly representative if 84 percent of the norm group is white, but these norms may not be a good standard of comparison in Memphis where the population is 40 percent black, or in Laredo, Texas, which is 95 percent Hispanic, or in Honolulu with a 63 percent Asian population. School achievement typically reflects the demographic characteristics of the school neighborhood and little credit or blame can be assumed by local school personnel for being above or below the national norm.

In the last three chapters, we have stressed the importance of reliability, validity, and standardization procedures in defining a "good" test. In the next chapter, we will see how these principles come into play in the process of evaluating tests.

References

Brown, F. G. (1983). *Principles of educational and psychological testing*. New York: Holt, Rinehart & Winston.

Cunningham, G. K. (1986). *Educational and psychological measurements*. New York: Macmillan.

Peterson, N. S., Kolen, M. J., & Hoover, H. D. (1989). Scaling, norming, and equating. In R. L. Linn (ed.), *Educational measurement*. New York: American Council on Education/Macmillan.

Popham, W. J. (1978). *Criterion-referenced measurement*. Englewood Cliffs, NJ: Prentice-Hall.

Thorndike, R. M., Cunningham, G. K., Thorndike, R. L., & Hagen, E. P. (1991). *Measurement and evaluation in psychology and education*. (5th ed.) New York: Macmillan.

I started looking through the memos and announcements that had been stuffed in my mailbox during the morning. Here was a cryptic note scrawled on the familiar memo pad from the principal's desk: "I am asking you to represent our school on the district committee to select a new achievement test. The meeting is this Friday at 4:00 in the Board Room. I am attaching the manual of the test they are considering so that you can be prepared to represent us."

chapter six

Selecting and Critiquing Standardized Tests

Oscar Krisen Buros.
Courtesy of Barbara S.
Plake, Director, the
Buros Institute of
Mental Measurement.

The principles of reliability, validity, and standardization procedures come together in the act of evaluating and selecting tests. Confronted with an unfamiliar test, the potential user must evaluate the test and decide whether to use it. In this chapter, we introduce the **Mental Measurements Yearbooks,** the volumes most widely used by persons making decisions about a particular test. A brief review from this source is provided; note that the reviewer detects flaws in the test that might escape the casual reader of the test manual. You are then asked to assume the role of a teacher evaluating a test as a possible aid in judging readiness for first grade. As the chapter progresses, you will become increasingly aware that, in addition to knowing test principles, you must cultivate a critical stance.

The Mental Measurements Yearbooks

In the 1930s, educational leaders were convinced that scientific measurements could help teachers better understand pupil needs. At this time, a Rutgers University professor was concerned that tests might do more damage than good. Oscar Buros felt that "most standardized tests are poorly constructed, of questionable or unknown validity, pretentious in their claims, and likely to be misused more often than not." Buros perceived the

Mary Ellen Oliverio, Associate Professor of Education, Teachers College, Columbia University, New York, New York.

The traditionally measured abilities of prospective clerical workers are included in the six subsections of this test.

Section 3, Checking, would have been more appropriately set up if the lines on the two pages matched. In this section, the subject should be instructed to mark the errors and then count them for recording the number in the blank at the end of the line. In the actual clerical situation, the worker marks copy where errors are to be corrected.

The manual contains a brief but clear description of the manner in which the test was constructed and of the reliability and validity measures used. The authors caution the test user as to the interpretations of the various measures used. The cautions are appropriate. For example, although norms are provided, the statement is made that the "safest and best way is for each user to develop his own norms." This caution is exceedingly important since the reader is given no information concerning the 3,970 applicants for clerical positions at Purdue University and the 650 applicants in eight companies whose scores were used for the establishment of the norms. Inasmuch as the test, during the experimental stages, was found to be far too difficult for girls just leaving high school and was revised, some question must be raised about the use of the norms given for large groups of young workers entering their first jobs. The user is not given the age, level of education, or previous experience of the groups used for the establishment of norms. It would be helpful to know if these 4,620 applicants are representative of the group entering clerical occupations each year.

This test should prove helpful to those organizations that must choose large numbers of clerical workers and that have clearly identified that the job skills needed are those measured in this test.

References

1. Sinclair, Gordon Rogers. Standardization of the Purdue Clerical Adaptability Test. Master's thesis, Purdue University (Lafayette, Ind.), 1950.
2. Lawore, C. H., and Steinberg, Martin D. "Studies in Synthetic Validity: I, An Exploratory Investigation of Clerical Jobs." Personnel Psychology 8:291–301 au 55. (PA 30:7381)

----

need for a clearinghouse of information about tests to protect the unsuspecting test user from the hidden flaws of tests. He established a kind of consumer report that evaluated published tests, and these **critiques** were issued periodically as books. The most current of these books, the *Eleventh Mental Measurements Yearbook* (Kramer & Conoley, 1992) offers critical reviews of a wide array of educational and psychological tests. For both test experts and students of measurement, the first step in evaluating a test is to consult the reviews of the test in the Mental Measurements Yearbook.

To illustrate the reviews found in the Yearbooks, we have reprinted a review (Oliverio, 1959) of the *Purdue Clerical Adaptability Test*. A company that hires a large number of clerical workers might want to consider this test as a screening device for job applicants. The test provides six scores: spelling, computation, checking, word meaning, copying, and reasoning. Read the review of this test and then, drawing on your knowledge of validity, reliability, and standardization procedures, decide whether it would be a good choice for a company seeking to improve the selection and hiring of clerical personnel.

From this review of the test, did you notice anything either encouraging or alarming? Take a minute to make a few notes regarding any problems the reviewer detected that you consider serious. You will then be able to compare your observations with the comments that follow.

You certainly must have been disappointed that the reviewer did not provide the actual data regarding reliability and validity. It would have been most helpful in evaluating the test to see the correlation coefficients and descriptions of how these were obtained.

Assuming that the reliability and validity coefficients were satisfactory, how did you evaluate the standardization procedure? There are more than 4,000 people in this norm group, all applicants for clerical jobs. Using these norms, we can see how an applicant compares with the 4,000 other applicants. Do you believe that the norming procedure meets the criteria discussed in the last chapter?

In this review, Oliverio reminds us that the test authors suggest that we exercise caution in interpreting the scores. She states that we are given no information about the 3,970 applicants for clerical positions at Purdue University and the 650 applicants in eight companies who served as the norm group. Oliverio is being very tactful. She knows, and so do you after a little reflection, a great deal about the norm group. Who, indeed, applies for the many clerical positions at a large university? In general, the applicant pool will include a large number of student wives who are working temporarily. Typically, it is not the younger student who is married, but the graduate student. At this scientific and technical institution, a large number of the graduate students are majoring in tough programs such as mathematics, science, and engineering. They may have met and married their wives in undergraduate school. The wives may themselves have college degrees, but are putting their careers on hold while their husbands complete their advanced degrees.

Consider what will happen to high school graduates who are evaluated against this norm group when applying for their first clerical jobs. Consider also the consequences for the company that establishes a high cutoff score when selecting clerical workers based on this invisible norm group. The company will probably face a large turnover problem as their overqualified clerks move on to better positions with other companies. In short, for the unsuspecting test user, this test is likely to make very good applicants appear inadequate. Young applicants with only a high school education will be compared to a norm group with an over-representation of highly educated individuals. The third leg of the tripod just collapsed. Did you notice it?

A second review of the Purdue Clerical Adaptability Test appears right after Oliverio's review. The second reviewer, Donald Spearritt (1959), is not satisfied that only split-half reliability coefficients are reported in view of the fact that some of the tests on the battery are highly speeded tests; i.e., they have very short time limits. We remember that the split-half reliability is inappropriate for such tests. Additionally, "There is no mention of a standard error of measurement and no indication of the standard deviation of the scores of the group used for estimating reliabilities." On the matter of validity, Spearritt notes: "Expectancy charts based on a very small number of cases suggest that the subtests have satisfactory predictive validity for later job performance." Remarkable! He is using the same vocabulary and concepts we have been learning.

Evaluating Tests from Data in the Test Manual

It is relatively easy to evaluate tests with the help of experts to tell us what is right and what is wrong. But what happens when a new test is released, and there are no reviews available? Typically, the superintendent receives a flyer from the test publisher announcing a new or revised test. In our example, the superintendent is interested because the test seems to offer help in evaluating the skills and achievements of children leaving kindergarten and entering the first grade. It would be useful to have a diagnostic instrument since teachers seem concerned about children arriving in their classes with inadequate basic skills. The superintendent orders a specimen copy of the test and, when it arrives, pencils a brief request to your principal: "Please evaluate and let me know what you think of this test."

Your principal reads the message, leafs through the 91 page book of norms and technical material, and remembers that you are the only teacher in the school who has had a course in tests and measurements. It takes but a moment to scribble a note to you, "Please evaluate and report back to me by Friday."

You read the note twice, and turn to the enclosed test, the Stanford Early School Achievement Test, Third Edition (SESAT 2) published by The Psychological Corporation. This test is designed for use at the end of kindergarten and at the first grade level.

You start your review process by glancing through the test noting that it measures reading, mathematics, and listening skills in the basic battery with general knowledge about the environment added for the complete battery. You note that the items seem to be appropriate for children finishing kindergarten. For example:

Letters and Sounds

You see a picture of a sock. The other pictures are leg, horn, and saw. Mark under the one that starts with the same sound as sock.

The Environment

You see a car, a boat, and an airplane. Mark under the one that is used to carry large amounts of wheat across the ocean.

Turning to the Norm Booklet, you note that the test was normed as part of the 1991 standardization program of the Stanford Achievement Tests involving 120,000 students at various grade levels. You are pleased to observe that the norm group reflects appropriate representation for geographic regions. Tables are provided to demonstrate that the standardization group also matched the census data for city size, socioeconomic levels, and ethnic groups. Additional information was collected during the standardization program by administering the Otis–Lennon School Ability Test (OLSAT) to all pupils.

As you search for information about reliability and validity you find that the tests were constructed after reviewing curriculum guides, items were subjected to item analysis procedures and a special review panel of minority educators worked to eliminate biased items. You are encouraged to compare the test content with your curriculum to see if the test is valid for your purpose.

In the section under "Reliability" you find table 6.1 presenting Kuder-Richardson reliability coefficients, standard errors for each test, and related data.

You notice a heading, "Intercorrelations Among Stanford Tests" containing table 6.2 showing how the various sub-tests of the SESAT 2 are related to each other and to the Otis–Lennon School Ability Test. You examine this table with interest trying to determine how this information will help you judge the quality of the test.

Table 6.1 *Kuder-Richardson Formula #20 Reliability Coefficients, Standard Errors of Measurement, and Related Data for the SESAT 2 Spring Standardization Sample.*

Subtest/Total	Number of Items	Form J				
		N	Mean	S.D.	r	SE$_m$
Grade K						
Sounds and Letters	40	292	27.9	7.7	.89	2.5
Word Reading	40	221	23.2	9.6	.92	2.7
Sentence Reading	30	223	13.3	5.4	.78	2.5
Total Reading	110	221	64.3	20.2	.95	4.6
Mathematics	44	292	25.8	8.0	.88	2.8
Listening to Words and Stories	45	291	31.5	6.7	.83	2.8
Basic Battery	199	220	123.9	30.8	.96	6.1
Environment	40	222	28.3	5.2	.75	2.6
Complete Battery	239	219	152.2	34.4	.96	6.6

Table 6.2 *Intercorrelations Among Stanford Tests for SESAT 2 Form J and Otis-Lennon School Ability Test in the Spring of Kindergarten (N = 5967).*

Test/Total	Variable	2	3	4	5	6	7	8	9	10	11	12
Sounds and Letters	1	.79	.47	.89	.72	.63	.89	.58	.88	.64	.63	.68
Word Reading	2		.58	.94	.68	.54	.89	.49	.86	.57	.58	.62
Sentence Reading	3			.75	.46	.38	.68	.32	.65	.37	.35	.39
Total Reading	4				.73	.60	.95	.54	.93	.62	.61	.66
Mathematics	5					.69	.87	.65	.88	.72	.71	.76
Listening to Words and Stories	6						.78	.74	.81	.75	.66	.76
Basic Battery	7							.68	.99	.75	.72	.78
Environment	8								.76	.70	.62	.71
Complete Battery	9									.77	.73	.81
OLSAT Verbal	10										.74	.92
OLSAT Nonverbal	11											.94
OLSAT Total	12											

You also examine the tables provided for converting raw scores to percentile ranks, stanines, grade equivalents, and scaled scores. Table 6.3 presents the conversion tables for three of the major tests of the battery, Total Reading, Mathematics, and Listening to Words/Stories.

Table 6.3 *Percentile Ranks, Stanines, Grade Equivalents, and Scaled Scores Corresponding to SESAT 2 Form J Raw Scores for Students Tested at Midyear of Grade 1.* *

Total Reading

Raw Score	%-ile Rank	Sta-nine	Grade Equiv.	Scale Score	Raw Score	%-ile Rank	Sta-nine	Grade Equiv.	Scaled Score	Raw Score	%-ile Rank	Sta-nine
110	99	9	4.6	619	74	17	3	1.2	450	38	1	1
109	99	9	3.3	597	73	15	3	1.1	448	37	1	1
108	96	9	2.7	572	72	13	3	1.1	446	36	1	1
107	93	8	2.4	557	71	13	3	1.1	445	35	1	1
106	89	8	2.2	546	70	11	3	1.1	443	34	1	1
105	86	7	2.1	538	69	10	2	1.1	442	33	1	1
104	82	7	2.0	531	68	9	2	1.0	440	32	1	1
103	78	7	1.9	525	67	8	2	1.0	438	31	1	1
102	75	6	1.9	520	66	8	2	1.0	437	30	1	1
101	72	6	1.8	515	65	7	2	1.0	435	29	1	1
100	69	6	1.8	511	64	6	2	K.9	434	28	1	1
99	67	6	1.7	507	63	5	2	K.9	432	27	1	1
98	64	6	1.7	503	62	5	2	K.9	431	26	1	1
97	62	6	1.7	500	61	4	2	K.9	429	25	1	1
96	59	5	1.6	497	60	4	2	K.8	428	24	1	1
95	57	5	1.6	494	59	3	1	K.8	426	23	1	1
94	55	5	1.6	491	58	3	1	K.8	425	22	1	1
93	52	5	1.5	488	57	2	1	K.8	423	21	1	1
92	50	5	1.5	486	56	2	1	K.7	422	20	1	1
91	47	5	1.5	483	55	1	1	K.7	420	19	1	1
90	45	5	1.5	481	54	1	1	K.7	419	18	1	1
89	41	5	1.5	478	53	1	1	K.7	417	17	1	1
88	39	4	1.4	476	52	1	1	K.7	416	16	1	1
87	37	4	1.4	474	51	1	1	K.6	414	15	1	1
86	35	4	1.4	472	50	1	1	K.6	413	14	1	1
85	34	4	1.4	470	49	1	1	K.6	411	13	1	1
84	31	4	1.4	468	48	1	1	K.6	410	12	1	1
83	29	4	1.3	466	47	1	1	K.5	408	11	1	1
82	27	4	1.3	464	46	1	1	K.5	406	10	1	1
81	26	4	1.3	462	45	1	1	K.5	405	9	1	1
80	24	4	1.3	460	44	1	1	K.5	403	8	1	1
79	23	4	1.3	458	43	1	1	K.5	402	7	1	1
78	22	3	1.2	457	42	1	1	K.4	400	6	1	1
77	21	3	1.2	455	41	1	1	K.4	399	5	1	1
76	19	3	1.2	453	40	1	1	K.4	397	4	1	1
75	17	3	1.2	451	39	1	1	K.4	395	3	1	1
										2	1	1
										1	1	1

Grade Equiv.	Scaled Score	Mathematics					Listening to Wds/Stories				
		Raw Score	%-ile Rank	Sta-nine	Grade Equiv.	Scaled Score	Raw Score	%-ile Rank	Sta-nine	Grade Equiv.	Scaled Score
K.3	394	44	99	9	4.6	613	45	99	9	10.5	671
K.3	392	43	99	9	3.6	589	44	99	9	7.6	648
K.3	390	42	97	9	2.8	563	43	97	9	4.9	623
K.3	389	41	92	8	2.5	547	42	93	8	3.7	607
K.3	387	40	85	7	2.3	535	41	87	7	3.1	596
K.2	385	39	78	7	2.0	526	40	80	7	2.6	586
K.2	384	38	70	6	1.8	517	39	74	6	2.4	579
K.2	382	37	63	6	1.7	510	38	67	6	2.1	572
K.2	380	36	57	5	1.6	504	37	60	6	1.9	566
K.1	378	35	51	5	1.5	498	36	52	5	1.6	560
K.1	376	34	45	5	1.4	492	35	45	5	1.2	555
K.1	374	33	39	4	1.4	487	34	39	4	1.0	550
K.1	372	32	34	4	1.3	482	33	33	4	K.9	545
K.1	370	31	29	4	1.2	477	32	29	4	K.8	541
K.0	368	30	24	4	1.2	472	31	25	4	K.6	537
K.0	366	29	21	3	1.1	468	30	21	3	K.5	533
K.0	364	28	19	3	1.0	464	29	18	3	K.4	529
K.0	361	27	15	3	K.9	459	28	15	3	K.3	525
K.0	359	26	13	3	K.9	455	27	12	3	K.2	521
PK	357	25	10	2	K.8	451	26	9	2	K.1	517
PK	354	24	7	2	K.7	447	25	8	2	K.1	514
PK	352	23	5	2	K.6	443	24	6	2	K.0	510
PK	349	22	4	2	K.5	439	23	4	2	PK	506
PK	346	21	2	1	K.4	435	22	4	2	PK	503
PK	343	20	1	1	K.3	431	21	3	1	PK	499
PK	340	19	1	1	K.3	427	20	2	1	PK	495
PK	336	18	1	1	K.2	422	19	1	1	PK	492
PK	332	17	1	1	K.1	418	18	1	1	PK	488
PK	328	16	1	1	K.1	414	17	1	1	PK	484
PK	324	15	1	1	K.0	409	16	1	1	PK	480
PK	319	14	1	1	K.0	405	15	1	1	PK	476
PK	314	13	1	1	PK	400	14	1	1	PK	472
PK	308	12	1	1	PK	395	13	1	1	PK	467
PK	301	11	1	1	PK	390	12	1	1	PK	463
PK	293	10	1	1	PK	385	11	1	1	PK	458
PK	282	9	1	1	PK	379	10	1	1	PK	453
PK	267	8	1	1	PK	373	9	1	1	PK	448
PK	242	7	1	1	PK	366	8	1	1	PK	442
		6	1	1	PK	359	7	1	1	PK	436
		5	1	1	PK	351	6	1	1	PK	429
		4	1	1	PK	341	5	1	1	PK	421
		3	1	1	PK	329	4	1	1	PK	412
		2	1	1	PK	313	3	1	1	PK	400
		1	1	1	PK	286	2	1	1	PK	385
							1	1	1	PK	359

Well, there you have it. What kind of report will you write to the principal? As with all good puzzles, it is more interesting to try it yourself rather than to watch someone else do it. Remember, your report will go to the principal and then to the superintendent. Two reputations are at stake, yours and the principal's. More importantly, if your report is favorable, you and your fellow teachers may be using this test next year to make decisions about children and to interpret progress to parents. What do you say?

For this brief review, follow the outline:

1. Purpose
2. Standardization
3. Reliability
4. Validity
5. Recommendations

Since the following section provides feedback to you on your efforts to review the test, it is time to stop and write the review. Go ahead, write your report to the principal.

Have you done it? Let us examine your written report and see if you have covered all the bases.

Evaluation of the Stanford Early School Achievement Test, Third Edition

Purpose—The publisher suggests that this test will provide information for improving instruction and for determining strengths and weaknesses of pupils. Profile charts are provided to illustrate the use of the test scores to diagnose strengths and weaknesses. Do the areas covered by the test measure skills and abilities which the kindergarten teachers in your system consider important? Will the diagnostic information be useful to a first grade teacher if the test lives up to its promise?

Standardization—The publisher describes the basis for selecting the norm group, and it is clear that efforts were directed toward selecting a representative group of kindergarten and first grade students in the United States. The children are drawn from the nine census regions of the United States. The proper proportions of students from big cities and small towns are included. The average income and educational levels of the people in the norm group reflect the average income and educational levels of people in the country. The proportions of various minority children in the norm group reflects the proportions in the national school population.

Using the normative data, tables were developed which allow us to convert raw scores to percentile ranks, stanines, grade equivalents and scaled scores unique to the Stanford Achievement Series. The publisher provides a good description of each type of derived score along with advantages and cautions associated with each one.

Reliability—The Kuder-Richardson Formula 20 reliability coefficients for the sub-tests range from a low of .75 for Environment to a high of .92 for Word Reading. Scores constructed by adding various sub-tests together are higher: Total Reading .95, Basic Battery .96, and Complete Battery .96. These KR-20 values are high enough to inspire confidence. We will have more to say about the reliability of the scores a little later when we comment on the standard errors of measurement (SEm) presented in table 6.1. Did you mention them in your report?

Validity—In the section labeled "Validity," the publisher quite correctly points out that the critical aspect of validity in an achievement test is the correspondence between the test content and the instructional program. You are invited to compare the test content with the objectives of your curriculum.

As we scan the material accompanying the test, we feel the need for more information. No friendly reviewer from the Mental Measurement Yearbook is around to point out what to read and what to ignore. The eye naturally gravitates to a table of intercorrelations underneath a heading, "Intercorrelations Among the Stanford Tests." At first, we are not exactly sure what these intercorrelations may mean, but we note that they are all reasonably high. Isn't this what we want to see, high correlation coefficients?

The publisher was quite right by not labeling this section "validity." If we chose to interpret these high correlations as evidence of validity, we would have projected meaning into the tables which isn't there. Let us examine the intercorrelations in table 6.2 more closely. Down the left side of this table are listed the names of each part of the test plus the Otis-Lennon School Ability Test. Across the top is the same list, but because there is not enough room to print out the names, only the numbers corresponding to each variable are printed. The tabled values show the correlation of each test score with all other test scores.

On the first row, we see the correlations between Sounds and Letters and all other parts of the test. We can readily observe that the highest correlations in that row are .89 with variable 4, .89 with variable 7, and .88 with variable 9. Now these are really high. But wait a minute. Let us see what these variables are. They are Total Reading, Basic Battery, and

Complete Battery. All of these composite scores contain Sounds and Letters as part of them. We would expect a sub-test to be highly correlated with a composite score of which it is a part. Thus, the high correlation coefficients under columns 4, 7, and 9 do not have much meaning. These part-total correlation coefficients have nothing to do with the validity of the test.

Still examining the first row of the table, we see a correlation of .72 between Sounds and Letters and variable 5, Mathematics. This correlation seems relatively high. That's good, isn't it? No, that's bad. Let's think about it a minute. The author claims to have two scores, one measuring sounds and letters, the other measuring mathematics. One ordinarily thinks of these as two separate and independent abilities. Yet, the two scores are highly correlated. Whatever is driving up one is driving up the other. The scores are not independent of each other. If they were independent measures of separate abilities, the correlations would be much lower. We have here an interesting rule of thumb: When looking at intercorrelations among parts of the same test, the higher the correlations the more we must doubt the author's claim that each part score is measuring a different, independent ability. The high intercorrelations in table 6.2 actually subtract from the author's claim that separate areas of knowledge and skill are being measured.

Before leaving table 6.2, you may want to note that the correlations shown in columns 10, 11, and 12 are not intercorrelations among parts of the same test, but (with the exception of where they cross with rows 10, 11, and 12) correlations between each part of the Stanford Early School Achievement Test and the Otis-Lennon School Ability Test. These correlations tend to be relatively high. What do these relatively high correlations with a mental ability test suggest to you about the Stanford Early School Achievement Test?

Exploring Further—Before attempting to summarize the evaluation of this test, let us revisit table 6.1 presenting reliability information. The Kuder-Richardson reliability coefficients are high enough to inspire confidence, yet they may not tell the entire story. What other data in the table might be useful?

The standard error of measurement for each of the sub-tests and the composite scores will prove to be most interesting and helpful. The standard error for each of the sub-tests is between 2.5 and 2.8; we might round these to 3. If students were tested repeatedly on these sub-tests, about two thirds of the scores would fall between plus or minus 3 points of their original score. Rounding the composite scores to the nearest raw score value we get standard errors of 5 for Total Reading, 3 for Mathematics, and 3 for Listening to Words and Stories.

It is worthwhile to see what these standard errors mean when we are interpreting the score to a parent. Suppose that John is a first grade student and John's mother wants to know how well her child did on the test. John's scores for the major tests of the Basic Battery are shown below.

Total Reading	92
Mathematics	34
Listening to Wds/Stories	37

So as not to mislead the parent, you decide to add and subtract the standard error for each raw score and tell the mother that John, if retested, would fall within a particular percentile range.

Adding and subtracting one standard error to each of the above scores, we get the following raw score range for John. Can you enter the appropriate percentile scores after consulting table 6.3?

	Raw Score Range	**Percentile Range**
Total Reading	87–97	_____ to _____
Mathematics	31–37	_____ to _____
Listening to Wds/Stories	34–40	_____ to _____

Are you ready to interpret John's scores to his mother?

> "Mrs. Jones, first of all, I want to tell you what a delight it is to have John in my class. In our unit on insects last week, he was the only child who let the walking stick crawl all the way up his arm.
>
> As you know, the test we administered to the class is designed to help us learn more about the knowledge and skills of the children. In reading skills, John's score would place him between the 37th and 62nd percentile compared to other pupils finishing kindergarten across the country. With a score of 34 in Math, his performance is somewhere between the 29th and the 63rd percentile. On listening to words and stories, he falls between the 39th and 80th percentile."

The percentile bands are wide enough to be almost ridiculous. We wonder what John can actually do. In reading, for example he may be about average (62nd percentile) or below average (37th percentile). Indeed, the Norms Booklet suggests that you analyze student strengths and weaknesses in terms of three broad stanine groups: Stanines 1–3 below average, stanines 4–6 average, and stanines 7–9 above average. Did you detect this imprecision and describe it in your report to the principal?

In view of the evidence which we have reviewed, what is the test probably measuring? The high intercorrelations among the parts of the test considered along with the high correlation among the achievement scores and the Otis-Lennon School Ability Test strongly suggest that the test may be measuring general mental maturity. If so, the Stanford Early School Achievement Test may well be suited for screening purposes. The test might indicate which students are sufficiently low across the board to be at risk for first grade placement, but it is highly unlikely that the test can provide useful diagnostic information regarding strengths or weaknesses of a given child.

In completing this exercise, we found that evaluating tests involves more than a mechanical search for obvious evidence. In fact, we had to tease out some of the significant information and perform some paper and pencil experiments to discover problems with the test. We saw that the standard error provides a very powerful way for examining the reliability of test scores. We also discovered that it was necessary to think carefully about the meaning of the data presented by the test publisher.

Summary

Test reviews and test manuals provide essential information in deciding whether to use a particular test. This information also helps the user interpret the scores with better understanding of what the scores probably can or cannot indicate.

The authors of test reviews do not, however, shake you by the shoulders and announce "Wait a minute, only a fool would use this test." Test reviewers are hesitant to directly attack a test author. Rather than stating that the low reliability and questionable validity of a test make it dangerous to use in a practical setting, the reviewer is more likely to say "test scores should be interpreted with caution" or "the test may be useful as a research instrument." In test manuals, we may find such phrases as "this reliability is quite high for a test of this length." The unwary reader will feel reassured by such statements, but the smarter reader will know that unreliability means wobbly test scores leading to shaky interpretations.

In this chapter we saw how a thoughtful consideration of the standardization population warned us that a particular clerical aptitude test would probably make many competent job applicants look bad. We also discovered that a test designed to help teachers identify areas of strength and weakness among kindergarten and first grade students promised more than it could deliver, although the total score might well serve a useful purpose in making placement decisions.

Applying the principles of reliability, validity, and standardization procedures to actual examples of published tests should reinforce the feeling that these principles are powerful tools for prying apart the claims of test publishers and for revealing the strengths and limitations of a particular test.

In the next section, we turn to the task of measuring educational achievements. We shall see that test planning, item writing, and item revision help teachers meet the requirements of test reliability and validity. We shall note that difficulty in meeting the single criteria of reliability is a continuing problem with essay tests. Performance assessments and instruments to measure thinking are also examined, with a view to adequacy in meeting the criteria for good measuring instruments.

In the last section of the book we examine some of the major tests in the areas of intelligence, aptitude, interests, and personality. In all cases, the principles of measurement provide a firm foundation for evaluating the instruments and interpreting the scores.

References

Kramer, J. J., & Conoley, J. C. (1992). *The eleventh mental measurements yearbook.* Lincoln, NE: Buros Institute of Mental Measurements, The University of Nebraska–Lincoln.

Oliverio, M. E. (1959). Review of Purdue Clerical Adaptability Test. In O. K. Buros (ed.), *The fifth mental measurements yearbook.* Highland Park, NJ: The Gryphon Press.

Spearritt, D. (1959). Review of Purdue Clerical Adaptability Test. In O. K. Buros (ed.), *The fifth mental measurements yearbook.* Highland Park, NJ: The Gryphon Press.

Stanford Early School Achievement Tests, Third Edition, SESAT 2 1991 National Norms Booklet (1992). San Antonio: The Psychological Corporation/Harcourt Brace & Company.

"He who creates the test creates the learning situation." This anonymous quotation reminds us that tests play a large role in determining how students approach learning. Objective tests can be designed to engage students' higher mental processes. Essay tests open the way for unique organization of ideas and extension of information. Performance assessments go a step further in allowing students to show what they can do with information. Thinking processes are the most general outcome of education and new approaches to measuring thinking reveal the way students perceive and interpret information in new situations.

part two
Measuring Educational Achievement

Jefferson

When it comes to classroom testing, I generally use the items supplied by the book publisher. They should know the material better than anyone else. It's true that most of the questions just require the students to remember what they read, but I'm no expert on measuring higher thinking skills; I'm not even sure where to start.

chapter seven

Constructing Classroom Tests

1776

By far the largest number of tests administered in schools are teacher-made tests. These tests reflect the teachers' views of education and send signals to students about the content and the thinking processes that the teacher values. Students appreciate tests that are clearly written, focus on main ideas, and require more than memorization.

Many teachers rely heavily on items provided by the textbook publisher. Such items, however, are typically written by professional item writers who are not educators and who tend to trivialize the material. Teachers need to develop confidence in their own abilities to construct classroom tests. Good test design, item writing, and item revision are the keys to constructing superior classroom tests.

In this chapter, we focus on test design and item writing. The Bloom Taxonomy is introduced as a framework for designing tests that include higher order thinking and we illustrate how the taxonomy becomes part of the table of specifications, the blueprint of the test. We then turn to the process of writing test items and provide general rules and examples of items measuring higher cognitive processes.

In the next chapter we describe the process of item analysis and item revision.

Tests Reflect Teachers' Objectives

A case can be made that education is largely a process of acquiring broad concepts that restructure the ways we perceive and interpret events. Restructuring often depends on acquiring broad concepts from specialized fields of study. Thus, before a study of health, students may believe that heart attacks "just happen." During their study, students may come to see that heart attacks are frequently associated with high blood cholesterol, which in turn may be controlled through exercise and diet.

Unfortunately, some students never quite grasp the fact that concepts provide tools for organizing and interpreting experience. The encyclopedic nature of most texts tends to overburden both teacher and student with isolated bits and pieces of information. Content is likely to be tested as separate facts with little concern for the way such facts support or elucidate larger concepts.

The tests we construct will be a reflection of our beliefs about teaching and learning. Schwab (1974) suggests that we need to communicate the pattern of thinking that best organizes our knowledge about a particular aspect of living. This is another way of stating that students learning history, economics, or chemistry are learning to think more like historians, economists, or chemists. In all fields, large organizing ideas provide ways of approaching particular problems and good teaching helps students relate details to the large ideas and their uses. No set of rules about test construction will be nearly as important as a thoughtful consideration of how we expect the student to benefit from the material at hand.

Certainly, factual content is essential in all teaching, but tests limited to factual recall encourage students to concentrate on remembering rather than on developing larger meanings and seeing relationships. Whitehead (1929), the mathematician and philosopher, noted: "In training a child to activity of thought, above all things we must beware of what I will call 'inert ideas'—that is to say, ideas that are merely received into the mind without being utilized, or tested, or thrown into fresh combinations" (p. 13). Some teachers justify emphasis on facts by observing that students need the facts in order to think. But Whitehead does not support this simple generalization: "If you have much to do with the young as they emerge from the school and from the university, you soon note the dulled minds of those whose education has consisted in the acquirement of inert knowledge" (pp. 41–42).

Concern about the active use of information in classrooms continues to be a contemporary theme. Nash and Ducharme (1983) note: "What the schools are not doing is using the curriculum to develop student's ability to reason critically, to detect error, to evaluate the worth of content, and to learn independently of authority." Obviously, if schools are to help students become more thoughtful about subject matter, then tests made by teachers must reflect an emphasis on higher order thinking processes. Perhaps no one has done more to focus the attention of educators on higher cognitive processes than Benjamin Bloom.

The Bloom *Taxonomy of Educational Objectives*

Bloom was the university examiner at the University of Chicago. For many years, the university was led by a pioneering president, Robert Hutchins, who believed that students should come into college when they are ready and leave college when they are broadly educated. Thus, Hutchins championed early admissions to the university and advocated comprehensive examinations to help determine when students were ready for graduation. Bloom was the individual who met with the professors to help them design and construct the examinations.

At the national conventions of the American Psychological Association, Bloom and others in comparable positions would meet and discuss the objectives of general education and ways to build tests that reflected these objectives. It was as chairman of a committee to study such problems that Bloom and his associates published the classic *Taxonomy of Educational Objectives* (Bloom, 1956).

A **taxonomy** is a hierarchical classification such that the first level is necessary in order to have the second. The Bloom Taxonomy is a classification of educational objectives arranged in an increasing order of cognitive processes from memory to evaluation. The higher cognitive processes are assumed to be built on and make use of the behaviors described in the preceding levels.

Almost every book on education contains a summary of the taxonomy. These summaries correctly present the taxonomy as a scheme for thinking about educational objectives. Few of the summaries, however, point out that the book is also a manual for writing test items at the various cognitive levels. We shall examine each of these aspects of the Bloom Taxonomy in turn.

The Taxonomy as an Organization of Educational Objectives

In bare outline, the taxonomy organizes educational objectives on six levels:

1. Knowledge
2. Comprehension
3. Application
4. Analysis
5. Synthesis
6. Evaluation

Each of these levels is further defined and elaborated.

Knowledge

Knowledge involves the recall of specific facts, terminology, and pieces of information. This category also includes knowledge of much more abstract components of subject matter: knowledge of the ways and means of dealing with information, methodology, procedures, and methods of inquiry. This level also includes knowledge of criteria by which facts and findings in a field are judged, knowledge of principles and generalizations, and knowledge of theories and other abstract formulations that help organize and integrate specific information.

Comprehension

Comprehension represents the lowest level of understanding and is concerned with whether the learner has grasped the meaning of the material as opposed to simply acquiring a new set of verbal statements. Comprehension can be demonstrated by the ability to accurately paraphrase the information, interpret it, or extrapolate trends and suggest consequences that can be inferred from the information.

Application

Application refers to the ability to transfer the learnings acquired into a future situation. Application is demonstrated when a learner will bring forward an appropriate rule, generalization, or principle to help solve a problem without being prompted or reminded to do so.

Analysis

Analysis involves the breakdown of a communication or situation into its component parts so that the various elements are clearly recognized and the relationships among the elements are made explicit. Analysis may focus on the connections and interactions between elements and on the organizational principles that help explain how the system works as a whole.

Synthesis

Synthesis involves putting together the elements and parts so that they form a whole. Synthesis includes combining parts in such a way that they form a pattern not there before. Examples of synthesis include organization of ideas in a piece of writing, production of a plan or a proposed set of operations, and generating a conceptual scheme that might be used to organize observations in a particular area of study.

Evaluation

Evaluation involves making judgements about the value of methods, works, solutions, or ideas. It involves the use of criteria and standards for appraising. Evaluation is distinguished from quick opinion by reference to both internal evidence and external criteria.

Evaluative judgements will reflect the internal consistency, accuracy, and carefulness that the product or communication exhibits. Evaluative judgements will also reflect detailed knowledge of the phenomena under consideration and familiarity with the criteria customarily employed in judging such works or ideas.

The Bloom Taxonomy plays an important part in the development of the table of specifications for achievement tests.

The Table of Specifications

The **table of specifications** is actually the blueprint that guides the construction of the test. The test blueprint performs two important functions: (1) it ensures balance and proper emphasis across the content covered by the teacher and (2) it assures inclusion of items that require the use of higher cognitive processes as well as items measuring recall of specific materials.

Perhaps no task is more difficult, or more essential, for the teacher than deciding what material to include and what to omit in the course of instruction. Additionally, teachers tend to emphasize different features of the same course. One science teacher may emphasize laboratory methods while another teacher may concentrate on general theorems and principles. In a unit on the Civil War, one teacher may spend considerable time analyzing the factors leading to the war while another teacher may be most interested in the major battles. Such special emphases will not be reflected in the test if the teacher simply leafs through the text, page by page, looking for sentences that may be quickly converted into true-false or multiple-choice items. A better procedure is to decide in advance the number of items for each topic that will best reflect the teaching emphasis of the unit.

A unit on the Civil War might reflect the following balance:

Background Causes	Campaigns & Battles	Reconstruction
50%	20%	30%

Certainly, the full table of specifications would show a more detailed breakdown, including the social, economic, and political factors leading to the war, the proportion of items dealing with Gettysburg versus the Battle of Shiloh, the role of the carpetbaggers during the reconstruction period, etc.

With the unit divided into the important topics and a decision made about the proportion of the test to be devoted to each topic, it is now time to consider representation of cognitive levels that will be built into the test. To assist in this planning, the levels of the Bloom Taxonomy may be added to the blueprint so that the table of specifications now appears as shown in table 7.1. This test will contain 50 test items.

The teacher makes a judgement about the number of test items desired on the knowledge level and the number of items that will require comprehension, application, analysis, synthesis, and evaluation. In our example, thirty of the fifty items are on the knowledge level, but this leaves a considerable proportion of the items requiring higher cognitive processes. In most cases, the majority of the items will be at the knowledge level, and this may be appropriate. We would, however, be concerned if no test items call for use of the higher cognitive processes. Ebel (1972) argues strongly for the important role of knowledge in thinking, but adds: "Any test which can be prepared for most effectively by

Table 7.1 *Table of Specifications for Test over Civil War Unit*

	Background (50%)	Battles (20%)	Reconstruction (30%)	Total
Evaluation			1	1
Synthesis				0
Analysis	2		2	4
Application	3		2	5
Comprehension	5	3	2	10
Knowledge	15	7	8	30
Total	25	10	15	50

concentration on rote learning and which therefore encourages students to neglect meaning and understanding in their pursuit of knowledge is a bad test" (p. 72).

In the same publication, Ebel helps us maintain a valuable perspective in considering the Bloom Taxonomy as the second dimension of the test blueprint. Ebel doubts that we can distinguish clearly between different mental abilities and processes. He observes that the mind does not consist of separate faculties which behave differently for different tasks, and advises us to avoid this "mentalistic approach" whenever possible. Ebel would be happy if the vertical axis of our table of specifications specified four types of questions and let it go at that:

1. Ask what a particular term means.
2. Ask for a particular fact or principle.
3. Ask the explanation of something.
4. Ask the solution of a problem.

Certainly, following Ebel's advice would provide much more dimensionality to our tests than we typically achieve.

Thorndike, Cunningham, Thorndike, and Hagen (1991) provide a table of specifications for a final examination in health for the eighth grade (table 7.2).

Table 7.2 *Table of Specifications for a Final Examination in Health*

Process Objectives	Content Areas
	A. Nutrition, 40%
1. Recognizes terms and vocabulary 20%	Nutrients Incomplete protein Vitamins Complete protein Enzymes Amino Acids Metabolism Glycogen Oxidation Carbohydrate 4 or 5 items
2. Identifies specific facts 30%	Nutrients essential to health Good sources of food nutrients Parts of digestive system Process of digestion of each nutrient Sources of information about foods and nutrition 7 or 8 items
3. Identifies principles, concepts, and generalizations 30%	Bases of well-balanced diet Enzyme reactions Transfer of materials between cells Cell metabolism Functions of nutrients in body 7 or 8 items
4. Evaluates health information and advertisements 10%	Analyzes food and diet advertisements Interprets labels on foods Identifies good sources of information about foods and diets 2 or 3 items
5. Applies principles and generalizations to novel situations 10%	Identifies well-balanced diet Computes calories needed for weight-gaining or weight- losing diet Predicts consequences of changes in enzymes on digestive system Identifies services and protection provided by the Federal Food and Drug Act 2 or 3 items
Number of items	24

Total time for test—90 minutes

Reprinted with the permission of Macmillan Publishing Company from Measurement and Evaluation in Psychology, Fifth Edition, by Robert M. Thorndike, George K. Cunningham, Robert L. Thornkide, and Elizabeth Hagen. Copyright © 1991 by Macmillan Publishing Company.

B. Communicable Diseases, 40%		C. Noncommunicable Diseases, 20%	Number of Items
Immunity	Epidemic	Goiter	
Virus	Pathogenic	Deficiency diseases	
Carrier	Endemic	Diabetes	
Antibodies	Protozoa	Cardiovascular diseases	
Incubation period		Caries	
4 or 5 items		2 or 3 items	12
Common communicable diseases		Specific diseases caused by lack of vitamins	
Incidence of various diseases		Specific disorders resulting from imbalance in hormones	
Methods of spreading disease		Incidence of noncommunicable diseases	
Types of immunization		Common noncommunicable diseases of adolescents and	
Symptoms of common communicable diseases		young adults	
7 of 8 items		3 or 4 items	18
Basic principles underlying control of disease		Pressure within cardiovascular system	
Actions of antibiotics		Control of diabetes	
Body defenses against disease		Inheritance of abnormal conditions	
Immune reactions in body		Abnormal growth of cells	
7 or 8 items		3 or 4 items	18
Distinguishes between adequate and inadequate evidence for medicines		Identifies errors or misleading information in health material	
Identifies misleading advertisements for medications		Identifies appropriate source of information for health problems	
2 or 3 items		1 or 2 items	6
Recognizes conditions that are likely to result in increase of communicable disease		Predicts consequences of changes in secretion of certain hormones	
Identifies appropriate methods for sterilizing objects		Predicts probability of inheriting abnormal conditions	
Gives appropriate reasons for regulations, processes, or treatments			
2 or 3 items		1 or 2 items	6
24		12	60

Total number of items—60

The cognitive processes on the vertical axis of table 7.2 illustrate still another approach to the mental operations required of students. At the various levels, students are asked to recognize terms, identify facts, identify principles, evaluate information, and apply principles to novel situations. We can see how each of these cognitive processes is brought into play by following a single topic under the area of nutrition: Enzymes. At level 1, the term must be defined. At level 2, enzymes are related to the process of digestion. At level 3, more general principles regarding enzyme reactions must be identified. At level 4, knowledge of enzymes does not appear in evaluating food and diet advertisement. At level 5, the student is asked to predict consequences of changes in enzymes on the digestive system.

Examination of this table of specifications inspires confidence that the student's knowledge of eighth grade health will go well beyond a superficial acquaintance with the terminology of the field and will include an understanding of the more important generalizations and applications. The test contents suggest that the teacher has worked hard to bring out relationships and to cultivate habits of thinking.

It should be clear from these examples that the table of specifications is the critical first step toward good test construction. With a carefully developed plan, the items in the test should exhibit an appropriate balance across the subject matter taught, and an appropriate representation of items reflecting higher cognitive processes.

Writing Test Items

An experienced teacher of measurement and evaluation observed, "In our measurement classes, the most difficult job is to teach the student to write a measurable objective. Once that is done, few students have much trouble with writing items that measure their objectives, constructing a lesson to teach to those objectives, and processing data from their pre- and post-instruction assessments."

Indeed, translating general educational goals into measurable objectives is frequently a formidable task. The teacher who asserts, "I want my students to understand the causes of the Civil War" will need to specify the components of this goal and identify the kind of performance the student can be expected to demonstrate. Gronlund (1991) provides a practical guide that describes and illustrates how to write instructional objectives in terms of student performance.

Ideally, formulation of objectives precedes work on the table of specifications. Our Civil War example reflects a teacher who wants students to see that the war developed out of a pattern of conflicting desires and agendas of the North and the South. The task is to translate this rather global goal into a series of specific objectives. One approach to doing this is to pay particular attention to the verbs that specify the desired behavior of the students; for example, "When presented with four consequences of the agricultural structure of the South, the student will identify the demand for cheap labor as a relevant difference between the North and the South." It is easy to see that objectives stated in this form lead easily and naturally to the construction of a test item.

Perhaps most tests fail as satisfactory measurement instruments because of indiscriminate inclusion of material simply because it occurs in the text. Whitehead, whom we mentioned earlier in this chapter, observed: "I am sure that one secret of a successful teacher is that he has formulated quite clearly in his mind what the pupil has got to know in precise fashion. He will then cease from half-hearted attempts to worry his pupils with memorizing a lot of irrelevant stuff of inferior importance" (1929, p. 46). It follows that a first step in writing test items is to examine the material for its worth. If it is factual information, how does the information support or exemplify larger concepts? If the material deals with an important concept, the item should reveal that the student really understands the concept (comprehension) or can apply it to new situations.

We return to Bloom for more specific recommendations for writing test items that measure comprehension and application.

Writing Comprehension Items

Bloom states: "Probably the largest general class of intellectual abilities and skills emphasized in schools and colleges are those which involve comprehension. That is, when students are confronted with a communication, they are expected to know what is being communicated and to be able to make some use of the material or ideas contained in it" (p. 89).

Bloom identifies three behaviors that provide evidence that a communication has been comprehended or understood. Each of these behaviors defines tasks, which can take the form of test items. Thus, we can measure comprehension by asking students to perform any of the activities described below:

Translation

Translation involves the ability to restate the communication in other terms. Thus, a test item may require recognizing a concept originally learned in technical terms when it is restated in everyday words.

A. Paul Paré, a teacher in Culver, Indiana, provides the example in figure 7.1 in which the item expresses an idea in a mode of communication that is different from that in which it was originally learned. Students

BILL GARNER—*MEMPHIS COMMERCIAL APPEAL*

1. The idea illustrated in the cartoon above is best expressed by saying:
   (a) State governments have taken on too much responsibility in the past.
   (b) The federal government has assumed too much responsibility.
   (c) Federal and state governments should be obliged as usual.
   (d) New Federalism means more responsibilities for the federal bureaucracy.

Figure 7.1 *Example of a comprehension item involving translation from graphic to verbal information.* Cartoon copyright © 1983, *The Commercial Appeal.* Used with permission.

who have studied social and political proposals are presented with a cartoon summarizing the ideas to see if they actually comprehend the trends presented in class.

Paré (1983-84) notes: "Almost every day in our reading we encounter cartoons, graphs, editorials, and news story paragraphs which relate to our workday classroom lessons. These finds are often visually attractive and provocative. When clipped and pasted to the top of a blank piece of paper, they provide a base of information for the development of interesting and contemporary test items" (p. 9).

Interpretation

Interpretation involves the ability to recognize the essentials and to differentiate them from the minor aspects of the communication. It involves going beyond merely rephrasing the material and gets at the more general ideas contained in it.

Making your judgments only in terms of the information given in the graph, classify each of the following items by blackening space

A. if the item is *definitely* true;
B. if the item is *probably* true;
C. if the information given is not sufficient to indicate any degree of truth or falsity in the item;
D. if the item is *probably* false;
E. if the item is *definitely* false;

13. People were better off in 1932 than in 1949.
14. Since 1918 to the present, the dollar was most valuable in 1933.
15. More prices went up than went down between 1932 and 1940.
16. Men in the age group of 30–40 made the most income gains in the past decade.
17. In 1940–46 some loss in real income was most probably incurred by people living on interest from bonds.
18. More prices went down than went up between 1926 and 1929.
19. Anyone living on a fixed income was much worse off in 1949 than in 1940.

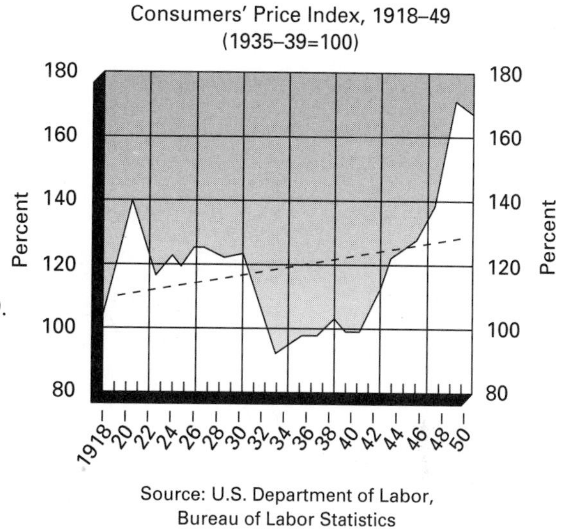

Consumers' Price Index, 1918–49
(1935–39=100)
180
160
140
120
100
80
Percent
1918
20
22
24
26
28
30
32
34
36
38
40
42
44
46
48
50
Source: U.S. Department of Labor, Bureau of Labor Statistics

Figure 7.2 *Example of an item requiring interpretation.* Reprinted with the permission of Longman Publishing Group from *Taxonomy of Educational Objectives (Handbook 1: Cognitive Domain)* by Benjamin S. Bloom. Copyright © 1956 and renewed 1984 by Longman Publishing Group.

In testing for interpretation, the student may be presented with a passage or a set of scientific data and asked to recognize inferences drawn from it. Alternatively, the student may be asked to judge whether the data are sufficient to establish the truth or falsity of a series of judgements. Bloom provides the example in figure 7.2.

Extrapolation

Extrapolation involves the ability to extend the trends or tendencies beyond the data and findings of the original document. Extrapolation requires the student to see implications and consequences when projected into future or hypothetical situations. Bloom includes the following behaviors under extrapolation:

Formulating hypotheses, inferences, and conclusions.
Predicting continuation of trends.
Interpolating where there are gaps in the data.
Estimating or predicting consequences.

Recognizing factors that make predictions inaccurate.
Recognizing consequences that are probable.
Differentiating predictions from value judgements.

It should be evident that we have three major devices available to measure comprehension. We can ask students to translate the original information into new terms, to interpret information, and to extrapolate trends.

Writing Application Items

In support of the educational value of application, Bloom wrote: "The fact that most of what we learn is intended for application to problem situations in real life is indicative of the importance of application objectives in the general curriculum. The effectiveness of a large part of the school program is therefore dependent upon how well the students carry over into situations applications which the students never faced in the learning processes" (p. 122).

Application means transferring knowledge and principles learned in one situation into a new situation. Application requires the student to apply the appropriate concepts without being prompted or cued. Comprehension shows that a student *can* use knowledge when requested. Application shows that a student *will* use knowledge when the situation calls for it.

The crucial feature in testing for application is constructing situations that the student has not previously encountered, but that may be understood by applying appropriate procedures, concepts, or ideas. Figure 7.3 presents an example by Bloom.

The key to writing application items is presenting the student with new situations that require interpretation. Bloom offers three approaches for constructing application items:

1. Present a fictional situation.
2. Use material from other texts or simplify complex material that the student has not yet covered.
3. Take a new slant on material that has been presented.

It should be obvious that taking an example out of the covered material or working an example from the test into your lecture immediately converts an application item into a simple memory item. The essential characteristic of an application item is that the students have not been previously confronted with the situation.

Problem VI from PEA Test 1.3, Application of Principles

2. An electric iron (110 volts, 1000 watts) has been used for some time and the plug contacts have become burned, thus introducing additional resistance. How will this affect the amount of heat which the iron produces?

Directions: Choose the conclusion which you believe is most consistent with the facts given above and most reasonable in the light of whatever knowledge you may have, and mark the appropriate space on the Answer Sheet under Problem VI.

Conclusions:
   A. The iron will produce more heat than when new.
   B. The iron will produce the same heat as when new.
   C. The iron will produce less heat than when new.

Directions: Choose the reasons you would use to explain or support your conclusion and fill in the appropriate spaces on your Answer Sheet. Be sure that your marks are in one column only—the same column in which you marked the conclusion.

Reasons:
   1. The heat produced by an electrical device is always measured by its power rating. It is independent of any contact resistance.
   2. Electric currents of the same voltage always produce the same amount of heat, and burned contacts do not decrease the amount of electricity entering the iron.
   3. The current which flows through the iron is reduced when the resistance is increased.
   4. Increasing the resistance in an electrical circuit increases the current.
   5. An increase in electrical resistance increases the heat developed.
   6. Manufacturers of electric irons urge that the contacts be kept clean to maintain maximum efficiency.
   7. An increase in the temperature of a wire usually results in an increase in its resistance.
   8. Burned contacts increase the heat developed in an electric iron just as increasing the friction in automobile brakes develops more heat.
   9. The heat developed by an electric iron when connected to 110 volts is independent of the flow of current.

Figure 7.3 *Example of an application item.*
Reprinted with the permission of Longman Publishing Group from *Taxonomy of Educational Objectives (Handbook 1: Cognitive Domain)* by Benjamin S. Bloom. Copyright © 1956 and renewed 1984 by Longman Publishing Group.

Measuring Analysis, Synthesis, and Evaluation

Testing analysis, synthesis, and evaluation by objective test items generally requires relatively complex displays followed by a series of response choices. The material may be a literary passage, a set of data, or a scientific experiment. The student may be asked to infer the author's purpose, produce a plan or a proposed set of operations, or compare the work with known standards in the field. As with application items, the stimulus material must be new; otherwise the student may be using statements remembered from earlier discussions of the situation, thus reducing the exercise to a memory level activity.

Bloom provides additional illustrations of test exercises that reach the higher levels of the cognitive domain. Synthesis usually requires the actual development of a product—a piece of writing, a work of art, a musical composition—that was not there before.

Beyond a thoughtful consideration of the subject matter and its important ideas, the quality of a test item depends on several characteristics of the item itself.

Objective Test Items

The sample table of specifications shown in table 7.2 assumes the construction of an **objective test.** Objective test items require students to recognize best answers or to complete a sentence with a word or phrase. Objective tests can sample a wide range of information in a short time and can be scored very efficiently. As the number of students to be tested increases, the attractiveness of objective tests goes up. In any setting involving a large number of students, or involving opportunities to use the test on subsequent occasions, a strong case can be made for the use of objective tests.

The test maker may choose among the following types of objective test items: true-false, matching, completion, or multiple-choice items. Each item type has both advantages and disadvantages.

True-False Items

True–false items are efficient and relatively easy to construct. A minimum amount of reading is required for each item and they provide a direct test of the students' knowledge. A serious disadvantage is that they are susceptible to guessing, with a chance score of 50 being possible on 100 items. Additionally, there is an unfortunate tendency to rely on sentences from the text in creating true–false items. This practice can produce tests that measure relatively unimportant aspects of knowledge and encourage rote learning.

The most general problem associated with true–false items is that they require an absolute standard of truth. A statement that seems obviously true to the teacher at the time the test item is written may be open to doubt by students considering other conditions or shades of meaning in the statement. True–false items probably cause more arguments and quibbling about correct answers than any other form of test item. The multiple-choice item does not require a student to pick a response that must be absolutely true, but simply the response that represents the best answer in comparison to the other alternatives available.

If, after reading thus far, you still feel compelled to use true–false items, your items will be improved if you keep the following suggestions in mind:

1. Express a single idea in the item; avoid complex statements.
2. The difference between true and false statements should be sufficiently wide that they are not spoiled by minor imperfections.
3. Word the statements so that sheer memory for words and phrases does not lead to the answer.
4. Avoid such sweeping terms as "all," "always," and "inevitable," which clue the student that the answer is false. Also, avoid "usually," "sometimes," and "often," which clue the student that the answer is true.

Matching Items

Matching items are exercises in which the student is asked to pair the related items in two or more sets of material. Matching items are well-suited to identification exercises in which pictured parts are associated with technical names or functions as illustrated in figure 7.4.

Guides for writing good matching items include the following rules:

1. Keep the list of statements relatively short.
2. Use lists of unequal numbers of statements to reduce guessing.
3. Arrange statements in a logical order if possible. For example, if one list contains historical dates and the other list contains historical events, list the dates in chronological order so the student is not constantly scanning the list to locate a single date.

Short-Answer or Completion Items

Short-answer (or completion) **items** are particularly useful when it is important to test over definitions, facts, nomenclature, relationships, or simple interpretations. Examples of completion items are:

How many states are in the Union? _____.
The capital of Montana is _____.
An instrument that will diffuse light into a
spectrum of colors is a _____.

Figure 7.4 *Example of a matching item.* Drawing of eye adapted from L. Dodge Fernald and Peter S. Fernald, *Introduction to Psychology,* Fifth Edition. Copyright © 1985 Wm. C. Brown Communications, Inc., Dubuque, Iowa. All Rights Reserved. Reprinted by permission.

Directions: For the next items, match each phrase in the list with the appropriate part of the eye. Blacken the space on the answer sheet for the correct label. A label may be used more than once.

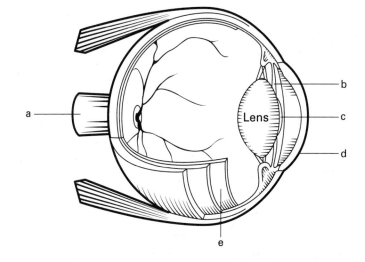

8. layer of light-sensitive nerve cells
9. controls the amount of light entering the eye
10. transmits nerve impulses to the brain
11. focuses light rays on the retina
12. provides protective covering for the eye
13. shape can be adjusted by muscles to see near and far

As the temperature of a gas increases, its volume will _____.
The labor-intensive cultivation of cotton made this practice attractive to Southern plantation owners. _____.

Completion items are easy to write, can be scored quickly, and appear to have the advantage of requiring the student to construct an answer rather than merely recognize it. Not only is guessing reduced, but some research (McDaniel & Mason, 1985) suggests that longer retention is obtained by the very act of recalling information rather than simply recognizing it.

In writing completion items, three good rules are:

1. Work backwards. Jot down the answer you want, then write a direct question that will elicit that answer.

2. Facilitate easy scoring by lining up all response blanks on the right side of the page.
3. Avoid using sentences right out of the book to discourage rote memorization.

Multiple-Choice Items

Because of their flexibility, clarity, and reduced opportunity for guessing, **multiple-choice items** have become the most common type of test item. Whereas a true–false item must be judged apart from any context, a multiple-choice item asks whether one of the alternative answers is more true than the others. As in other test items, the quality of multiple-choice items resides less in the form than in the care with which they are written.

While more than a dozen rules could be assembled to assist you in writing multiple-choice items, we prefer to offer only five. Then we will turn to the application of multiple-choice items in measuring higher cognitive processes.

The five essential rules to keep in mind while constructing multiple-choice items are:

1. *Avoid trivia. Test over important concepts.* This is the cardinal rule in all item writing, yet it is the rule most frequently broken. Students are inundated by factual material in texts. A high school biology text will have as many new terms as the total vocabulary learned in a semester of a foreign language. Items that indiscriminately sample from all available material will not encourage students to make judgements, identify concepts, or seek understanding.

2. *Pack the important material into the stem of the question. Keep the alternatives sharp and crisp.* Following this rule will help keep the reading load to a minimum and allows efficient comparison of the **alternatives.** Observe the difference in the following items:

Item A: Benjamin Franklin was the man who
a. commanded the continental army and rose to the rank of presidency.
b. is remembered as an important secretary of the treasury.
c. became both a man of science and an international statesman.
d. is often considered the father of the American constitution.

Item B: A colonist known both as a man of science and as an international statesman was
a. George Washington.
b. Alexander Hamilton.
c. Benjamin Franklin.
d. Thomas Jefferson.

3. ***Make all of your distractors work for you.*** This rule will help in constructing items that reduce guessing and improve the discrimination power of the items. Suppose you are making up an item requiring identification of the first astronaut to circle the globe. You name four astronauts and for the fifth choice offer Mickey Mouse, considering that a little humor might add a nice touch to the examination. In fact, since students can readily eliminate the last alternative, they have a better chance of guessing the right answer from the remaining alternatives. Finding attractive alternatives is the most difficult part of writing multiple-choice items. It is also one of the most important. The alternative answers, or **distractors,** must seem plausible to students who have not learned the material if the item is to discriminate between well-prepared and poorly prepared students.

4. ***Use novel situations to test applications.*** Much of the important material in every field consists of concepts and principles that apply to a wide variety of situations. For example, if students in psychology learn that "frustration leads to aggression," it is good testing practice to see if students use this principle as an explanation for behavior in a novel situation that has not been presented in the textbook or lecture.

5. ***Avoid trick items.*** There is occasionally a temptation to construct a test item that turns on an obscure point made in a footnote or on a rare and unimportant exception to a general rule. Such items destroy students' confidence that the teacher can be relied on as a guide to the important concepts in the subject matter and create a feeling that the tests are used to exploit weakness rather than measure achievement.

Multiple-Choice Items with Three Alternatives

There is a general pattern of constructing four or five responses for multiple-choice items. The reason for this is that guessing the right answer is harder if there are more choices. There is, however, an assumption that all choices will be attractive. Most item writers run out of good ideas quickly and are soon reaching to find incorrect responses that look plausible. Several investigators (Owen & Froman, 1987; Trevisan, Sax, & Michael, 1991) offer evidence that multiple-choice tests made up of items with only three alternatives have better psychometric properties than tests composed of traditional multiple-choice formats. Items with only three responses are significantly shorter and require less reading time.

In writing test items, we are striving for parsimony. Shorter items offer two advantages. First, the test writer can include more items per test period, thus increasing the sample of content covered. Second, with fewer words the influence of reading skill, often a problem associated with ethnic, socio-economic, and gender bias, is reduced. Concise multiple-choice items can be achieved both by keeping the alternatives short and by writing only three of them.

Summary

In this chapter, we noted that tests send important signals to students. Tests highlight specific content and emphasize the kinds of thinking desired.

The table of specifications is the blueprint that guides the construction of a classroom test. The table of specifications helps the teacher plan a test that: (1) reflects the emphasis given to each section of the subject and (2) contains items that require the student to use higher cognitive processes.

Bloom provides specific advice for writing items that measure higher cognitive processes:

Comprehension: Ask students to translate the material into different words, to interpret material, or to extrapolate trends.

Application: Ask students to apply knowledge or principles to new situations.

Analysis: Ask students to identify significant components of a situation and their relationships to each other.

Synthesis: Ask students to use relevant components to construct a larger product.

Evaluation: Ask students to make value judgements using the criteria that are customarily applied to such products.

We offered suggestions for improving true–false, matching, and short-answer items, but we concentrated on multiple-choice items. Good multiple-choice items can be written by following a few simple rules:

1. Avoid trivia; test over important concepts.
2. Pack important material into the stem; keep alternatives sharp and crisp.
3. Make all your distractors work for you.
4. Use novel situations to test applications.
5. Avoid trick items.

In addition, writing multiple-choice items with only three alternatives can reduce reading time, increase content coverage, and help students who may have language difficulties.

Armed with a table of specifications, item writing rules, and a commitment to include higher cognitive processes, teachers can markedly improve their classroom tests. In the next chapter, we will see how test items can be further studied and improved through the processes of item analysis and item revision.

References

Bloom, B.S. (ed.) (1956). *Taxonomy of educational objectives, the classification of educational goals. Handbook I: Cognitive domain.* White Plains, NY: Longman Publishing Group.

Ebel, R.L. (1972). *Essentials of educational measurement.* Englewood Cliffs, NJ: Prentice-Hall.

Gronlund, N.E. (1991). *How to write and use instructional objectives* (4th ed.). New York: Macmillan.

McDaniel, M.A., & Masson, M.E.J. (1985). Altering memory representation through retrieval. *Journal of Experimental Psychology: Learning, Memory and Cognition, 11,* 371–385.

Nash, R., & Ducharme, E. (1983). Where there is no vision, the people perish: A nation at risk. *Journal of Teacher Education, 34*(4), 38–46.

Owen, S. V., & Froman, R. D. (1987). What's wrong with three-option multiple-choice items? *Educational and Psychological Measurement, 47*(2), 513–522.

Paré, A. P. (1983–84). Developing students' higher-level reasoning skills through better social studies test questions. *Viewpoints—The Indiana Council for the Social Studies Newsletter, 11* (1), 9–11.

Schwab, J. J. (1974). The concept of the structure of a discipline. In E. W. Eisner & E. Vallance (eds.), *Conflicting conceptions of curriculum*. Berkley, CA: McCutchan.

Thorndike, R. M., Cunningham, G. K., Thorndike, R. L., & Hagen, E. P. (1991). *Measurement and evaluation in psychology & education* (5th ed.). New York: Macmillan.

Trevisan, M. S., Sax, G., & Michael, W. B. (1991). The effects of the number of options per item and student ability on test validity and reliability. *Educational and Psychological Measurement, 51,* 829–837.

Whitehead, A. N. (1929). *The aims of education*. New York: Macmillan. Paperback edition published as a *Mentor Book* by The New American Library of World Literature, Inc., New York.

While grading the test I had made, I noticed a pattern. Almost all the students were getting most of the items right. I wanted to believe that the children had learned the material, but a small voice inside kept saying that the questions were too easy. How hard should the questions be . . . and is difficulty the most important aspect of a test item?

chapter eight
Item Analysis and Item Revision

% Passing
Good Students 80%
Poor Students 50%

EST

Good classroom tests originate with thoughtfully constructed test blue-prints and are moved forward through careful item writing. Yet, after the test is administered, we observe that not all items performed as well as we had hoped. Some items, it turns out, were too easy, others too hard. Without more refined analysis, it may escape our attention that some items do not discriminate between students who have a good grasp on the subject matter and those who are apparently just sliding by. Item analysis, the systematic study of item performance, is a powerful procedure for revealing the difficulty level and discriminating value of each item in our tests. Given good test planning and careful item writing, item analysis provides the next step in constructing improved classroom tests. We shall examine the rationale for item analysis and describe item analysis procedures. In addition, we will offer suggestions for modifying and revising test items in the light of the information provided by item analysis.

The Rationale of Item Analysis

Item analysis is a procedure for determining two important aspects of a test item: the difficulty of the item and its discriminatory power. Difficulty is readily understood and is expressed as the percent of students answering the item correctly. If a test item is too difficult or too easy, it will not help the teacher discriminate between good and poor students.

Notice the phrase "discriminate between good and poor students." The ability to discriminate between these two groups is one of the key characteristics of a good test item. Let us see in a different context why this is so.

Suppose that you have been retained by a local insurance company to develop a test to help them select job applicants who will be good salespersons. Your fee for this consultation is quite high, but the company views it as a good investment considering the cost of training and keeping on the payroll an agent who must ultimately be released for lack of sales.

You set to work writing a pool of items to which the applicants can respond true or false. Your first five items are:

1. I like meeting and working with people.
2. I have traveled extensively and met many people.
3. I have experience in other kinds of sales.
4. Most of my recreation involves other people.
5. I can plan and organize my own work.

Armed with a pool of 150 such items, you approach the company in search of a group of salespeople on whom to try out your items. This is the point at which your training in measurement shows itself. Rather than

Table 8.1 *Percent of Each Group Getting Item Right*

Item	Good Salespersons	Poor Salespersons
1. Likes People	100	100
2. Extensive Travel	5	5
3. Sales Experience	85	80
4. Recreation	40	55
5. Plan & Organize	90	60

asking for a group of salespersons, you request two groups, a group of high performers and a group of low performers. The company obliges by arranging for you to test twenty good salespeople and twenty poor salespeople as indicated by their annual sales records. You test these two groups and organize your data as shown in table 8.1.

Visual inspection of these data provides some very interesting information. Item 1 will not be useful in the final test since it does not discriminate between people with good and poor sales records. Apparently anyone applying for a sales job is going to say that he or she likes meeting and working with people. Item 2 also appears to be of no help. Item 3, on which we had counted, shows a little difference, but not enough to be of any practical significance. Item 4 revealed a surprise: more poor than good salespeople reported enjoying recreation with others. This item may still be included in the final test, if we change the key. Item 5 is satisfactory. Substantially more good salespersons answer true to this item than do the poor salespersons. Item 5 discriminates between these two groups.

In revising our hypothetical test, the decisions are obvious. Only one of the original five items clearly discriminates between good and poor salespersons. If we change the key, we may also add a second item. All the others should be discarded. They occupy space, take up time, and contribute nothing to the task of helping the company decide on the best applicants.

It seems much easier to accept the rationale of item analysis when building a test to select salespeople than when building a classroom test. To many teachers, it seems heartless and unnecessary to put so much emphasis on items that discriminate among students. Advocates of criterion-referenced tests are quick to point out that there are other points of view about test construction. Criterion-referenced tests focus on the domain of knowledge and skills needed by students and are more concerned with describing what a student knows or can do rather than how a student ranks in a group. The point here is that the item analysis procedures we discuss fall within the traditional framework of norm-referenced tests, i.e., tests designed to reveal individual differences in attainment exhibited within a particular group of students.

There is much to justify efforts to make test items discriminating. As schools are currently organized, testing and grading are a way of life. Since this is so, the basis for evaluation should be as stable and objective as possible. Filling a test with nondiscriminating items means that the burden of the decision about grades will fall on those few items that do, in fact, discriminate. Since the stability of a small number of items will be low, assigning grades based on a test with few discriminating items is hard to justify. It seems far better to work toward a test that covers important aspects of instruction and contains items that clearly differentiate between those who have attained these objectives and those who have not.

Item Analysis of Classroom Tests

It may be noted in the example above that we had two criterion groups, good and poor salespeople. We examined the responses of each group to determine if an item discriminated between these two groups. When we turn to the analysis of items from an achievement test, how do we establish the criterion groups? To obtain these groups of students, we make an assumption that our test, with all its imperfections, provides the best readily available index of how much the students know about the material, i.e., how good they are. Thus, the criterion groups are formed by taking the top and bottom scorers on the test we are about to analyze. But how many students should we take off the top and bottom of the list?

For item analysis, the upper and lower 27 percent of the students is widely accepted as the best proportion of students to use. Why 27 percent rather than some other proportion? Considering that we want two distinctly different criterion groups for the item analysis, we could choose the top and bottom 10 percent, but then we would have very few students in each group. On the other hand, we could split the group into the upper and lower half. This would mean that our analysis could be based on more students, but the groups would not be very different from each other. Kelley (1939) demonstrated that the optimal proportion of students to take in forming the upper and lower groups is 27 percent. This percent is a good trade-off between the requirements that the groups be different from each other and that they still be large enough to provide reasonably stable results. For most class size groups (between twenty and forty students), selecting the top ten and bottom ten answer sheets provides a good approximation of the 27 percent rule and makes computations easy.

Table 8.2   *Example of an Item Analysis Work Sheet Using the Top and Bottom 10*
Answer Sheets from a Test

Number of Students in Each Group Answering Item Correctly

Item	Top 10 Papers		Bottom 10 Papers		Difficulty (p)	Discrimination (D)
1	卌 卌	10	卌 卌	10	1.0	0
2	卌 //	7	卌	5	.6	.2
3	卌	5	/	1	.3	.4
4	///	3	卌	5	.4	−.2

To provide an example of an item analysis procedure that a teacher can perform, let us suppose that you have selected the ten highest and ten lowest answer sheets from an American history test that you have administered to your class. Here are the steps you would go through to perform an item analysis that will yield information about the difficulty of each item and how well each item discriminates between the students who know the material and those who do not.

1. For each item, tally the number of students in each group who answered the item correctly.
2. For each item, obtain a **difficulty index** (p) by adding the number of students responding correctly in the high and low groups and dividing by the total number of papers analyzed (20 in this example).
3. For each item, obtain a **discrimination index** (D) by subtracting the number responding correctly in the low group from the number responding correctly in the high group and dividing by the number in one group (10 in this example).

The results of these three steps are shown in table 8.2.

Difficulty and Discrimination of Each Item

You can observe that, for the first item on the test, the difficulty level is 1.0. This difficulty level can be interpreted to mean that 100 percent of the students passed the item. This is an estimate. We are assuming that the middle students, whom we have ignored, are represented by the average of the high and the low students.

The discrimination index for the first item is zero. This index can be interpreted as showing there is no difference between the percent of top students and the percent of bottom students who answered the item correctly.

The discrimination index will ordinarily range from zero (no difference between the two groups) to 1.0 (all upper students passed, no lower students passed). You may, however, observe some negative discrimination values, as we will see in a moment.

From these two indices, you can conclude that item 1 of the history test is very easy and not discriminating. From a purely psychometric point of view, this item should be eliminated from the test as it contributes nothing to your knowledge of the relative learning of the students in your classes. From an educational point of view, however, item 1 may represent an essential piece of knowledge that you expect all students to know and you may want to retain it on the test.

Using the difficulty index and the discrimination index, let us examine the next three items.

Item 2 is moderately difficult (60 percent of the students passed it) and barely discriminating (20 percent more of the top students got the item right than did the bottom students).

Item 3 is both a difficult and a discriminating item. Only about a third of the class answered this item correctly, but 40 percent more of the top students got it right than did the bottom students.

Item 4 is also difficult; only 40 percent of the class answered it correctly. When we turn to the discrimination index, we see a red flag: a negative discrimination value. This means that more of the poorer students passed the item than did the better students. When negative discrimination values are observed, check the key. Usually, one of the alternatives is actually a better answer than the "right" answer.

In computing discrimination and difficulty levels, it is important to remember that the size of the top and bottom groups helps determine how strongly we can rely on the data. In a situation where the top and bottom groups are composed of ten students each, a discrimination value of .2 means that only two more students in the top group got the answer. The next time the test is administered, chance factors alone may change these values.

What levels of difficulty and discrimination should you look for in making decisions about test items?

How Difficult?

There is a direct relationship between the difficulty level of an item and how discriminating it can be. Most classroom tests are too easy. Items that are passed by everybody give you no information about any given student. On the other hand, if everyone misses an item, we learn nothing about any individual student. A general rule of thumb is that items become more discriminating as they approach the 50 percent difficulty level.

Some teachers feel that they should have a group of easy items and a group of difficult items to accommodate the individual differences in their classes. Empirical studies, however, do not support this view. In contrast to tests made of hard-easy items, tests with most items around the 50 percent difficulty level are more reliable. Additionally, the hard-easy tests do not do as good a job of spreading out the students. When examining item difficulties, a good rule of thumb is to favor items that are in the difficulty range of 30 to 70.

Are there exceptions to this rule? Of course. Some aspects of the unit of study are so important that the teacher can and should expect mastery on items measuring these ideas. Including items covering these critical ideas is justified even though 100 percent of the class get the items right. An unspoken contract has been fulfilled. The teacher stressed the knowledge, the students learned the knowledge, and the examination tested for the knowledge. Such items belong on the test even though they have no psychometric value. In such cases, the items testing for essential and obvious knowledge can be supplemented by more difficult items requiring the student to use essential ideas in new combinations and in applications involving analysis, synthesis, and evaluation.

How Discriminating?

Discrimination is the principle function of test items. Items that fail to discriminate make no contribution to the total score of a test. Suppose, in an extreme example, that a thirty-item test has twenty-two items that, for one reason or another, have a discriminating value near zero. Perhaps they are so easy that 90 percent or more of the students get these items right. Almost all the variation in the scores on the test is caused by the remaining eight items. In effect, the teacher has an eight-item test rather than a thirty-item test. Very few teachers have an accurate idea of the number of nondiscriminating items on a typical classroom test. Examination of the discrimination values of test items is an essential first step in improving tests through item selection and revision. In making judgements about items, a general rule of thumb is to look for and retain items with D values of .30 and higher. Items with D values below this level are good candidates for revision and improvement.

As a reminder, the item analysis statistics have nothing in them that helps determine the educational significance of the item. Educational significance is a value judgement made at the time the table of specifications is developed and the item written. The item analysis does, however, tell the teacher whether a particular item is making a contribution to assessing the differences in achievement among the students in the class.

Item Revision

For most test authors, item analysis is the necessary precursor to the important task of item revision. Items that fail to discriminate should be scrutinized and a decision made about whether to omit them from the next edition of the test. Nondiscriminating items may be retained for the reasons discussed, but a better strategy is to examine such items for ways they might be improved. Generally, it is much easier to revise an existing item than to write a new item.

A useful approach to test revision is to tabulate the number of students choosing each of the alternatives to the test item. In the following example, from a fifth grade test over a unit on the Native Americans, the number of students from a class of twenty-six marking each response is shown.

Many Americans lived in the south and had little need for warm clothing and shelter. If Native Americans from South America were forced to move north, how do you think they would survive?

	Percent of Students Choosing Each Alternative
a. Adapt to the New Environment	100
b. Die from Extreme Temperature	0
c. Would Not Be Affected by the Change in Environment	0

The item analysis data revealed that the difficulty level of this item was 100; i.e., all the students got the item right and the discrimination value was zero. None of the students found either of the wrong alternatives attractive.

Before assuming that these results indicate mastery of the concept of adaptation, let us examine the item more closely. The stem asks students to identify behavior that would lead to survival. Alternative b states that the Native Americans would not survive so it does not fit the requirements of the stem. Alternative c states that they would not be affected by the change in environment, an unlikely response since the stem relates geographic region to the need for clothing and shelter.

In analyzing the item, we note that the teacher wants the pupils to recognize that Native Americans moving from south to north would have to adapt to new conditions. In behavioral terms, the teacher wants the students to recognize an example of adaptation. This objective seems to be captured by reworking the stem of the item into the following revision.

> Native Americans moving from the south to the cold climates of North America would have to learn to make warm clothing and construct comfortable shelters. This is an example of
>
> a. adaptation to changing conditions.
> b. migration stimulated by changing climate.
> c. re-settlement around a new food source.

Machine Generated Item Statistics

The exercise of computing indices of item difficulty and discrimination by hand may be useful in grasping the logic of item analysis, and, of course, can be employed by classroom teachers who do not have the benefits of machine scoring of answer sheets. College instructors and teachers in school systems where tests are machine scored have the advantage of item analysis reports that usually accompany the scoring report. Additionally, item analysis software is available for personal computers. The printout shown in figure 8.1 illustrates the ease with which the performance of items can be studied.

In figure 8.1, the letters and symbols have these meanings:

★   The correct alternative (right answer) for the item.

N   The number of students choosing each alternative.

P   The percent of students choosing each alternative.

D   A discrimination value for each alternative. These values can be interpreted as follows:

Below − 10   Students who chose this response tend to be below class average on the test. We want high negative values for the wrong answers.

Between − 10 and +10   Students who chose this response tend to be near the class average. If the right answer is in this range, it is not discriminating.

Above 10   Students who chose this response tend to be above the class average. The higher this number, associated with the right answer, the more discriminating the item.

Figure 8.1

Computer printout illustrating item analysis.

ITEM		A	B	C	D	E	OMIT
1	N	1	1	30*	0	0	0
	P	3	3	94*	0	0	0
	D	7	-30	17*	0	0	0
2	N	32*	0	0	0	0	0
	P	100*	0	0	0	0	0
	D	0*	0	0	0	0	0
3	N	2	28*	2	0	0	0
	P	6	88*	6	0	0	0
	D	-46	50*	-23	0	0	0
4	N	1	1	0	30*	0	0
	P	3	3	0	94*	0	0
	D	-22	-42	0	46*	0	0

ALTERNATIVE

Figure 8.1 shows the item statistics for the first four items of a fifty-item multiple-choice test. Each item contains four distractors, A through D. Thirty-two students took this test. Let us examine the response pattern for item 1.

Looking at row N, the number of cases choosing each alternative, we see that one student chose option A, one chose option B, thirty chose option C, the correct answer, and no one chose option D.

Looking at the next row, P, we see the percent of students who selected each option and we note that 93 percent marked the correct answer. This is the difficulty index for this item.

We examine row D with interest because this provides the discrimination value. We are somewhat disappointed to find a discrimination value of only 17, suggesting that the item is contributing relatively little to our test.

A quick glance at item 2 tells us it is too easy, and we mark this item for further study. Is the knowledge required by this item so basic that we expect everyone to know it and we want to reinforce learning, or were the alternative answers obviously wrong even to individuals who had not prepared?

We are satisfied with the discrimination values for items 3 and 4. Do not be concerned with negative discrimination values associated with wrong answers. The negative sign means more poorly prepared students are selecting this option.

A negative discrimination value associated with a correct answer, however, is a red flag. Most often this means that a clerical error has been made in constructing the key for the test. If a check of the key reveals no error, then this item must be examined carefully. After all, poor students are marking your answer, but good students are avoiding it. When the scoring key is not in error, a negative discrimination value associated with the "right" answer is a clear call for item revision.

Perhaps these examples will suffice to show the important role played by item analysis in revision and improvement of classroom tests. From the simple step of counting the number of correct responses made by good and poor students to each item, we derive useful indices of the item's difficulty and discrimination. Study of the pattern of responses to each alternative helps us focus in on the aspects of the test item that needs revision.

Building an Item File

Good tests evolve over a period of time as good items are retained and poor items are discarded. More and more, such item files are being built and retained on computers, and tests can be assembled rapidly by specifying the topics, cognitive processes, and difficulty levels desired.

Many teachers find it convenient to keep this information on a file card. In table 8.3, the code identifies the first topic on the table of specifications and the Bloom level of cognitive processing required. The number of students responding to each alternative is shown and the item analysis data appear at the bottom.

Over several semesters, a record of the performance of test items can be obtained. These records help in building tests in which the majority of the items have difficulty levels in the 30 to 70 range and discrimination values of .30 or more. An item file composed of such cards will prove to be a great help in building better tests over the years. With widespread use of personal computers, these item files can be easily maintained and retrieved for tests that meet changing course emphasis.

Item Analysis of Criterion-Referenced Tests

In criterion-referenced tests, we are not particularly concerned with discriminating between high and low achievers. In fact, there is an expectation that most students will achieve the instructional objectives. The concern is that items should reflect the effects of instruction rather than some artifact of poor item construction. The item should discriminate between students who have had the instruction and those who have not.

In order to obtain criterion groups for item analysis of criterion-referenced tests, the test is administered both before and after instruction. An item discrimination value can be computed by subtracting the percent of students who obtained a correct answer before instruction from

Table 8.3 *Example of an Item File Card*

Unit: The Early Americans Code: 1-1

The civilization that grew up in South America was the . . .

	Number Choosing Each Option		
	1992	**1993**	**1994**
a. Pueblos	2	2	
b. Mayans	3	2	
c. Aztecs	5	3	
*d. Incas	20	15	
Date	10/92	2/93	
No. of students	30	22	
Difficulty	66	68	
Discrimination	.70	.50	

the percent of students who obtained a correct answer after instruction. In our earlier example of a flawed item written to measure the knowledge of the concept of adaptation, a pretest would probably show that 100 percent of the students would be able to find the right answer before instruction. We might also expect 100 percent of the students to answer the item correctly after instruction. The discrimination value would be zero and the teacher would be alerted to restudy the item in terms of appropriateness and construction.

Item Response Theory

Before leaving the topic of item analysis, it is necessary to say a word about newer item analysis procedures gaining acceptance in large-scale testing programs and in computerized adaptive testing (discussed more fully in chapter 17). **Item response theory** (IRT) refers to a family of mathematical procedures for calibrating test items. Item calibration gives the probability that an individual of a given ability level will get a right answer on that or similar items. Ability is typically defined by the total score on the test. Some approaches make use of only one characteristic of the item, difficulty, while others include item difficulty, discrimination, and a guessing parameter. In figure 8.2, Anastasi (1988) provides **item characteristic curves** for three hypothetical items.

With the ability scale along the bottom and the vertical axis indicating the probability of a person at any ability level getting an item right, we can examine the various item characteristic curves. A horizontal line has been drawn through the graph to mark the points on the item characteristic curves where the probability of a correct answer is 50 percent.

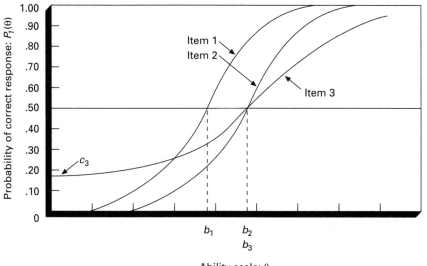

Figure 8.2

Hypothetical item characteristic curves for three items. Reprinted with the permission of Macmillan Publishing Company from *Psychological Testing,* Sixth Edition, by Anne Anastasi. Copyright © 1988 by Anne Anastasi.

Dropping a perpendicular from the point where this horizontal line crosses an item characteristic curve shows the ability level for which this item will be maximally useful. Note on the graph that item 1 is easier than items 2 and 3, and will be most useful for students at ability level b_1. Items 2 and 3 are equally difficult, but item 2 is more discriminating as indicated by its steeper slope. The item characteristic curve for item 3 never shows a zero probability of being answered correctly since it is a multiple-choice item and the formula used to calculate these functions includes a parameter for guessing.

While the item characteristic curves are mathematically generated, item response calibrations have to start with some empirical data. Wainer and Mislevy (1990, p. 82) report:

> A key question that is always asked during the course of item calibration is "How many examinees do we need for accurate item parameter estimates?" This question does not admit to a unique answer—it depends on the situation. However, experience has shown that with 1,000 suitably chosen examinees an item's parameters would be estimated accurately enough for most practical purposes.

With a thousand cases and sophisticated mathematical models needed to calibrate items, we can see that these procedures are well beyond the working capacity of classroom teachers. Even so, with test publishers announcing computerized adaptive testing based on item response theory, it is good to have a general idea of what they are talking about.

Summary

Item analysis is a way of examining the performance of a test item. Was the item too hard or too easy? Did the item help you identify students who knew the material as opposed to students who did not? More technically, item analysis reveals

(1) the difficulty level of the item, and
(2) the discrimination power of the item.

Item analysis is the key to revising your test so that the next time around, your test will be improved. This is accomplished by examining the items that have low discrimination values, and revising those items.

In most cases, items fail to discriminate because they are too easy: almost everyone will have answered them correctly. If these items reflect essential learnings, then the fact that all students got the items right might be interpreted as evidence of good teaching and good learning.

On the other hand, all students succeeding on an item may be due to the way the item was written. If the correct answer is a verbatim statement from the text, perhaps little understanding is required to recognize the statement. If the distractors were not plausible, very little knowledge is required to find the correct answer. Aiken (1987), reviewing twenty years of research on multiple-choice tests, emphasizes, ". . . the primary factor in determining the effectiveness of multiple-choice items as measures of ability is selection of the distractors . . ." (p. 46).

Since most of us teach the same course semester after semester, item analysis and item revision are powerful procedures for helping us weed out poor test items and improve existing items. Central scoring services are available to many teachers, and item analysis statistics can usually be requested at the time the answer sheets are submitted for scoring.

Item response theory (IRT) is a new approach to examining item characteristics; it is useful in large-scale testing programs and in developing computer administered tests that adapt to the knowledge level of students as they proceed through the test. While classroom teachers will have no need for detailed knowledge of item response theory, some understanding of this approach contributes to the ability to read test manuals and to see the role IRT plays in selecting items for computer applications of testing.

References

Aiken, L. R. (1987). Testing with multiple-choice items. *Journal of Research and Development in Education.* 20 (4), 44–58.

Anastasi, A. (1988). *Psychological testing* (6th ed.). New York: Macmillan.

Kelley, T. L. (1939). The selection of upper and lower groups for the validation of test items. *Journal of Educational Psychology, 30,* 17–24.

Wainer, H., & Mislevy, R. J. (1990). Item response theory, item calibration, and proficiency estimation. In H. Wainer, *Computerized adaptive testing: A primer.* Hillsdale, NJ: Erlbaum.

Looking out the window, I thought about the conversation in the teachers' lounge. Pat had been arguing the advantages of essay tests. "Nowadays, students don't know how to write, and they certainly don't think about the material ... why should they if they know we don't expect them to?" I could give more essay tests, but scoring seems so subjective.

chapter nine

Interpretive Exercises and Essay Tests

We have been examining ways of writing and analyzing objective test items that reflect behavioral objectives. In a moment, we will see that some educators have suggested that we broaden our consideration of educational goals to include "expressive objectives," educational outcomes that cannot be completely specified before instruction. There is a suggestion that when learning emphasizes convergent thinking or the finding of right answers, objective tests may well be the best kind of test to use. When instruction encourages divergent thinking or the formulation of several unique but workable solutions, we may have to turn to essays or other measurement approaches.

Even within a fairly structured framework, teachers are often searching for ways to assess the ability to analyze and interpret problem situations. For these teachers, both **interpretive exercises** and **essay tests** are available. The interpretive exercise offers complex material with interpretive possibilities presented in an objective test format. The essay test can offer opportunities for analysis and interpretation within either narrow or broad limits. We shall examine each of these approaches separately.

In discussing the essay test, we shall see that failure to obtain consistent scores upon rescoring has been one of its major shortcomings. On the other hand, essay tests can measure divergent thought processes and integration of information. There is also some evidence that essay tests motivate better study habits and a more thoughtful approach to subject matter. Given these advantages of essay tests, it is worthwhile to look into ways of writing better essay questions and ways of evaluating responses that are more objective and stable.

Expressive Objectives and Convergent Thinking

Eisner (1985), in a series of refreshing essays, points out that some subject matter areas—science and mathematics, for example—are more compatible with behavioral objectives than others. In art, literature, and social studies there is an emergent quality about the educational experience. The teacher does not always know in advance what may be produced or thought, and the final product may surprise both the student and the teacher.

Eisner would like to see us add expressive objectives to our educational lexicon.

> Expressive objectives differ considerably from instructional objectives. An expressive objective does not specify the behavior the student is to acquire after having engaged in one or more learning activities. An expressive objective describes an educational encounter: It identifies a situation in which children are to work, a problem with which they are to cope, a task in which they are to engage; but it does not specify what from that

encounter, situation, problem, or task they are to learn. An expressive objective provides both the teacher and the student with an invitation to explore, defer, or focus on issues that are of peculiar interest or import to the enquirer. An expressive objective is evocative rather than prescriptive (pp. 54–55).

Evaluating outcomes of instruction guided by expressive objectives does not involve applying a common standard, but noting the way meanings have become personalized, elaborated, and unique. Students are moving toward greater autonomy and confidence in their ability to figure things out on their own.

In considering interpretive exercises, we shall see that the student is analyzing and interpreting information, but within a convergent framework. The right answers have been determined in advance and students reason their way to these answers. Essay tests, on the other hand, have the potential for measuring expressive objectives and divergent thinking.

The Interpretive Exercise

The interpretive exercise consists of one or more paragraphs of material followed by a series of questions calling for various interpretations. Such exercises typically present a description of a situation followed by a set of multiple-choice or true-false items that ask pupils to identify relationships, assumptions, inferences, hypotheses, or conclusions. Since the content is provided in the first part of the exercise, the items do not measure memory, but rather the ability to interpret and draw inferences from the information. Of course, in interpreting a paragraph, other relevant knowledge and principles from the subject matter are likely to come into play. Wesman (1971) was so convinced that test items should reflect higher cognitive processes that he felt compelled to write:

> . . . the writer who prepares items for use in tests of educational achievement must possess a rational and well-developed set of educational values (aims or objectives) that are not mere pedagogical ornaments but that so permeate and direct his thinking that he tends continually to seek these values in all his educational efforts.

Wesman points out that interpretive exercises provide opportunities to measure understanding rather than recall details. More specifically, interpretive exercises allow the student to:

- interpret and evaluate printed material.
- answer questions on relatively complex topics.
- show a general ability to interpret information as well as use specific background knowledge and principles related to the material.

Illustration I.

It has been stated that "like Hellas, the Swiss Land was born divided," and also that "political solidarity had a hard, slow birth in the mountains." Certainly the physical features of the Swiss lands in serving sharply to confine movement and widely to separate settled areas did not facilitate intercourse and thus political cooperation. In mountainous Switzerland, at any rate, village communes tended to occupy the narrow lateral valleys of the Alps, where they engaged in agricultural and pastoral pursuits in a state of almost complete political and economic isolation and self-sufficiency. On the other hand, the geographical position of the Swiss lands was such as to induce a continual current of traffic *en route* for the passes of the Central Alps, whilst the major valleys of the principal rivers formed the main highways of communications. Moreover, the Swiss plateau stretching between Lake Constance and Geneva and cupped between the mountain ranges formed a broad belt of well-watered and relatively low-lying land that was capable of supporting a population much denser than that of the mountains. Actually, it was not the more-favored plateau lands, but certain cantons of the mountains that provided both the leadership in the wars for independence and the nuclear region around which the state grew. The reason seems to be that in the mountain valleys the peasant and shepherd population tenaciously defended its freedom from the encroachment of the feudal powers and largely escaped being reduced to serfdom, as were the inhabitants of the central plateau.

1. What is meant by "the Swiss Land was born divided"?
   1. There were many different religious sects.
   2. Different languages were spoken in different parts of the country.
   3. The mountains isolated the people in different parts of the country.
   4. The people fought among themselves.   *3*

2. With which of the following does the writer compare Switzerland?
   1. Ancient Rome
   2. Ancient Greece
   3. Medieval Italy
   4. Medieval France   *2*

3. Who took the lead in making Switzerland into a united nation?
   1. The traders
   2. The mountain people
   3. The farmers of the plains
   4. The serfs   *2*

4. What does the writer try to do in this paragraph?
   1. To describe the factors in the early commercial development of Switzerland
   2. To point out why Switzerland can never become a united country
   3. To explain how trade changed the character of the Swiss nation
   4. To show how geographical conditions affected the political unification of Switzerland   *4*

5. Which of the following is the most appropriate heading for this paragraph?
   1. Early Swiss Commerce
   2. Trade Routes and Their Effect on Switzerland
   3. Geography and Swiss Freedom
   4. Agriculture on the Swiss Plateau   *3*

Wesman offers the illustration of an interpretive exercise shown in figure 9.1. In figure 9.2, Gronlund and Linn (1990) provide another example of an interpretive exercise, taken from a publication of the Educational Testing Service.

Interpretive exercises are developed by selecting or writing a passage to provide the raw materials for analysis and constructing a series of questions that allow for the various interpretations. The questions may relate exclusively to the material presented or may require background information that the student is expected to have learned during instruction. Teachers interested in developing interpretive exercises will find help in the *Forty-fifth Yearbook of the National Society for the Study of Education* (Brownell, 1946), a volume devoted entirely to the measurement of understanding in the various subject matter areas.

Figure 9.1 *(facing page) Example of an interpretive exercise.* Adapted with the permission of the American Council on Education from an example by A. G. Wesman in *Educational Measurement,* Second Edition, by R. L. Thorndike (ed.). Copyright © 1971 by American Council on Education.

Essay Tests versus Multiple-Choice Tests

One of the major arguments for employing essay tests is that they provide a better measure of thinking processes than multiple-choice examinations. Ebel and Frisbie (1986) however, argue that many of the thinking processes presumably measured in essay tests can be equally well captured in a multiple-choice format. They offer the following example from a test in the area of dental prosthetics.
Essay Question:

> Sometimes a bridge will not go in place properly when being tried in the mouth after being soldered. If the operator should consider it admissible or necessary to unsolder, reassemble, and resolder the bridge, describe how this would be done.

The initial section of the "ideal answer" comprising the scoring guide is shown below:

> The operator should first determine which joint or joints are to be unsoldered. The parts of the bridge should never be separated with a saw or disc, as this leaves a wide space to be filled in with solder. Instead, the bridge should be held in a blow-torch flame in such a way that the flame is directed on the joint to be unsoldered. Only enough heat must be used to melt the solder, and care must be used not to melt or distort an abutment piece.

From Robert L. Ebel and David A. Frisbie, *Esstentials of Educational Measurement,* Fourth Edition. Copyright © 1986. Reprinted by permission of Allyn and Bacon.

This question is based on the following situation:

A piece of mineral is placed in a bottle half-filled with a colorless liquid. A two-holed rubber stopper is then placed in the bottle. The system is then sealed by inserting a thermometer and connecting a glass tube in the stoppered bottle and a beaker of limewater as shown in the accompanying diagram:

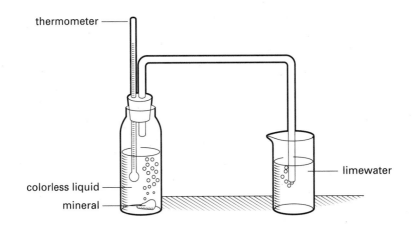

The following series of observations is recorded:

I. Observations during the first few minutes:

1. Bubbles of a colorless gas rise to the top of the stoppered bottle from the mineral.
2. Bubbles of colorless gas begin to come out of the glass tube and rise to the surface of the limewater.
3. The limewater remains colorless throughout this period of time.
4. The thermometer reads 20° C.

II. Observations at the end of thirty minutes:

1. Bubbles of colorless gas continue to rise in the stoppered bottle.
2. The piece of mineral has become noticeably smaller.
3. There is no apparent change in the level of the liquid in the bottle.
4. The colorless liquid in the bottle remains colorless.
5. The thermometer reads 24° C.
6. The limewater is cloudy.

Which one of the following is the best explanation for the appearance of gas bubbles at the end of the tube in the beaker of limewater?

A The pressure exerted by the colorless liquid is greater than that exerted by the limewater.

B The bubbles coming from the mineral cause an increased gas pressure in the stoppered bottle.

C The temperature increase at the end of thirty minutes causes an expansion of gas in the stoppered bottle.

D The decrease in the size of the piece of mineral causes reduced pressure in the stoppered bottle.

Figure 9.2 *Example of an interpretive exercise in science.*

Reprinted with the permission of Educational Testing Service from *Multiple Choice Questions: A Close Look.* Copyright © 1973 by Educational Testing Service.

The corresponding multiple-choice items follow directions establishing the context of separating, reassembling, and resoldering a bridge that will not go in place.

1. Which joint or joints should be separated?
    a. The joint between pontics and smallest abutment piece.
    b. Any single joint (the faulty joint must be located by trial and error).
    c. All that were originally soldered.
    d. Only the one or ones which appear responsible for the failure to fit.

2. Should the joints be separated using a saw or disc rather than heat?
    a. No, because a saw might damage the original castings.
    b. No, because the saw will leave too large a gap to be filled with solder.
    c. Yes, because the use of heat might damage the original castings.
    d. Yes, because the saw leaves a clean joint ready for resoldering.

This example suggests that essentially the same educational achievement can be tested by either essay or multiple-choice tests. Given the greater objectivity and stability of scores from objective tests, Chase (1978) is quite definite in his recommendation: "To the extent that the learning outcome can be measured by an objective test item, the objective test is to be preferred for its ease and reliability of scoring" (p. 147).

Chase goes on to recognize that not all objectives can be measured by objective tests. Indeed, Ebel and Frisbie's demonstration that multiple-choice items can be constructed to replace essay questions is based on material describing a set procedure to disassemble and resolder a dental bridge. The student is to arrive at the correct answer, which is predetermined and fixed. In such cases of convergent thinking, essay tests may have little advantage, and some definite perils, compared to multiple-choice items.

Rowntree (1977) identifies multiple-choice questions as the "ultimate in convergent assessment." When we turn to divergent thinking, however, the essay tests hold the most promise for allowing students to exhibit their unique perceptions or interpretations.

Realization of this promise is not automatic. It seems likely that most essay tests continue to seek the predetermined "right answers" the teacher has in mind. Rowntree elaborates on this point.

Indeed, one of the inherent weaknesses of formal assessment is the difficulty the teacher tends to have in generating situations or questions that allow students to express their own kinds of understanding in their own way. The teacher finds it much easier to think up the sort of questions that would enable him to display his kind of understanding. As long as the teacher honestly believes that his kind is the only kind worth having, he can justify asking students the sort of questions he would relish being asked himself. But as soon as he begins to admit that students may find other legitimate ways of construing reality, ways whose validity he may recognize once they are deployed but which he cannot anticipate, his faith in such convergent assessments can no longer be so easily maintained (pp. 153–154).

It should be clear that the term "essay test" is far too broad to allow generalizations about their value. Essay tests can fall anywhere along a divergent-convergent continuum. Some essay tests ask students to simply reproduce lists of facts, relationships, or interpretations that have been supplied during the course of instruction. Such essay tests are highly convergent, tap mostly memory, and require no original thinking. At an intermediate level, essay tests can reveal how a student is organizing and personalizing information. At the divergent end of the continuum, essay tests can reveal the extent to which students have developed unique perceptions and original interpretations.

Investigators who have studied thought processes in continuing programs of research have stated categorically that multiple-choice tests are simply inadequate for revealing the unique constructions that individuals bring to a problem (McDaniel, 1988; Peel, 1971; Schroder, Driver & Streufert, 1967). There is simply too much difference between *constructing* an interpretive position to an open problem situation and *recognizing* an appropriate position when it is presented. These studies, coupled with the discussion above, suggest that essay tests will be most appropriate when instructional objectives include genuine opportunities for diverse outcomes and unique understandings.

We turn now to examine the rise and fall of the essay test.

A Bit of History

Essay tests were in general use throughout the country until they came under attack in the 1920s by advocates of the "new-type" objective tests. It is interesting to remember that essay tests were once the "new tests," which were replacing the oral tests commonly used in educational settings. Written tests were being used at the University of Bologna by A.D. 1219, and we can imagine a number of professors expressing outrage that anything could replace the oral give-and-take that provided a gauge of what a student knew and did not know. To this day, the final orals are the last step before a university committee recommends that a candidate receive a Ph.D. degree.

Oral tests were the common procedure for formal examinations of school students in Boston until 1845 when school committees could no longer keep up with the increasing enrollments. Horace Mann praised written tests and summarized the faults of oral tests (Gerberich, Greene & Jorgensen, 1962). According to Mann, oral tests were:

- not equally fair to all students
- neither extensive nor efficient
- open to favoritism
- extremely time-consuming
- not recorded
- inadequate for evaluating difficult questions

In the end, essay tests won out, and it was not until around 1900 that the first objective tests appeared. The advocates of objective tests did not find it difficult to demonstrate that the essay tests lacked an essential characteristic in a measurement instrument, reliability. There was no assurance that a student would get the same score if the answer booklet were scored a second time.

Unreliability of Essay Tests

The demonstrations of unreliability among essay tests took several forms. Essay tests administered and scored by one teacher were collected, the scores removed, and the papers submitted to another for grading. There would frequently be little relationship between the two sets of grades. In one study summarized by Stalnaker (1951), almost 7,000 English composition tests given as part of the College Entrance Examination Board were scored twice by trained graders. The correlation between the two sets of scores was only .55, a very modest level of agreement. One would think there would be consistency in the scoring of the best and worst papers, but this was not the case. Among seventy-four papers initially graded as bad failures, worse than failing, only twenty-six received the same rating when scored again and ten actually got a rating of pass or better.

Another technique used to demonstrate the subjective scoring standards and unreliability of essay tests was to distribute the same essay among a number of teachers and then tally the marks assigned to this single paper. Typically, the same English paper would receive scores ranging from A to F. Surprisingly, the same range of scores was obtained when a single mathematics examination was scored by a large number of mathematics teachers.

One professor at Columbia University had a favorite means of driving home the subjective nature of the scoring standards. After tallying the marks assigned the same English composition, he would fix the class with a twinkle in his eye and observe, "It is interesting to see that among the future teachers of English composition in America, fewer than half would assign Mark Twain a passing grade."

Another method for studying the reliability of essay examinations was to return the essays to the original teacher for regrading after an interval of time, sometimes as little as one week. These studies also revealed changes in scores assigned the same papers. If the essay test in question asked for thinking and interpretation, the scores were even more unreliable than when the tests asked for listing of information.

Ashburn's (1938) findings based on the reading of essays by three qualified professors of humanities are frequently quoted to summarize the problem of unreliability in essay examinations. Ashburn concluded that passing or failing the examination of about 40 percent of the students depends not on what they know or do not know, but on who reads the paper. The passing of 10 percent of the students depends on when the paper is read.

The excellent discussion of essay tests by Hopkins, Stanley, and Hopkins (1990) makes an additional point about the reliability of essay tests. The studies mentioned thus far discuss the agreement among raters scoring the same essay. These correlations fall within the .5 to .7 range. But what happens when the underlying content is represented by two different questions? With two different questions scored independently by two raters, the reliability drops into the .3 to .5 range, a very low level of reliability.

The grade assigned to an essay examination is influenced by a number of artifacts that enter into the ratings. Research evidence indicates that teachers are influenced by such factors as the length of response and the quality of handwriting, spelling, and grammar in the essays, even when they are told to ignore such factors.

But the situation is even more complicated. Chase (1986) has demonstrated that when teachers expect students to do well, the effects of poor penmanship are reversed. Under expectations of high achievement, essays with poor handwriting get higher grades than the same essays written in a more legible hand.

Another disturbing research finding is the effect of the placement of an essay in a group of essays. An average essay read after two poor essays looks good and is assigned a higher grade than it deserves. If the average essay is read after two good essays, it will be assigned a lower grade than it deserves. Hughes and Keeling (1984) tried to block this carryover effect by providing teachers with a model essay to use when scoring, but ratings were still influenced by the quality of the papers preceding the "test" essay.

Problems of Sampling and Setting Adequate Questions

A further disadvantage of the essay test has been the difficulty of sampling a wide range of information with a small number of essay questions. A multiple-choice test of fifty items can test more material than an essay test of six questions. Teachers may feel this problem is offset by essay questions that ask for integration of material and the application of broad concepts and principles. Yet, if the student is weak in one particular area, the total score will suffer. Additionally, many essay tests do not elicit thinking about important themes, but test over knowledge of specific information. Where the intent of the teacher is to sample broadly from the material covered, the arguments favor use of an objective test.

Advantages of Essay Tests

There is some evidence that well-constructed essay tests motivate better study habits. In one study involving an introductory psychology class, students in separate sections were told to study for different kinds of tests: true-false, multiple choice, completion, and essay. Later, the students were given all four types of tests. One might expect the students would have done better on the type of test for which they had prepared, but this was not the case. Students who had prepared for the essay test did better, no matter what kind of test they took.

In determining why essay tests lead to better learning, the investigators interviewed the students about their study procedures. They found that students who had studied for the true-false, multiple-choice, or completion tests had fragmented the material into little pieces and tried to remember each piece. There was a tendency to underline material and rehearse it. Students who had studied for the essay test, on the other hand, reported looking for big ideas and major themes and trying to establish a position with respect to these themes. These students reported looking for data that supported or disconfirmed larger generalizations. It should come as no surprise that studying for essay tests produced better learning since the best way to remember material is to understand it.

Unfortunately, not all research supports these findings. Hakstian (1971), for example, found no difference between essay and objective tests in preparation time, organization of material, or study techniques. More recently, Speth and Brown (1990) separated 383 educational psychology students by gender and by four orientations toward learning. Each group was administered a fifty-five item questionnaire to determine what study strategies they would employ when preparing for an essay and a multiple-choice test. The results revealed complex interactions among the variables. For example, female students who had a meaningful orientation to learning (intend to understand and personalize information) indicated that they would use more study strategies directed toward integration of material for an essay test than for a multiple-choice test. Males in the meaningful orientation to learning group, however, indicated that they would use more integration strategies when preparing for a multiple-choice test. Evidently when we talk about the impact of essay versus objective tests on student study strategies, we need to ask "what kind of students?"

In summary, essay tests seem appropriate when we are working toward diverse instructional objectives and when we are interested in observing organization of information and higher thought processes. While the evidence is inconclusive, essay tests may motivate students to seek and integrate the major ideas in a body of material. We turn now to some suggestions for writing essay questions and for scoring responses.

Writing Essay Questions

Given the time required to formulate and write answers, only a limited number of essay questions can be asked. Decisions about what to sample are aided by reference to the table of specifications. Essay questions are suggested by the major ideas in a unit of study and the kinds of understanding and applications desired. A larger sample of concepts can be measured by asking questions requiring short responses and by asking more of them.

When formulating an essay question, indicate clearly the students' task and the boundaries within which the question should be answered. For example, a question asking the students to discuss the characteristics of various kinds of wood is almost too open-ended. The students may have difficulty knowing what to include and when to stop. A related question that makes clear the scope of the response is: "Which is better wood to use for fence posts, cedar or maple? Why?" Good essay questions ask the student to perform specific tasks such as comparing and contrasting, stating causes, explaining meanings, identifying intentions of authors, criticizing policies, and suggesting procedures.

Avoid giving students a choice among several essay questions. While this option is appealing to some teachers, it should be recognized that under these conditions, students are not all required to run the same race. This complicates the process of evaluating all students on the same scale and contributes to the unreliability of scoring essay tests.

Scoring Essay Tests

Essay tests have been most criticized for the unreliability of scoring. Yet, there are scoring procedures that markedly improve grading of essay tests:

1. **Develop a scoring rationale for each answer.** There are actually two approaches for doing this: global and analytic.

   The global approach starts with the construction of an ideal answer to the essay question. With this answer in mind, the grader reads the essay, gaining an overall impression of its quality. The grader may then place the answers in three piles reflecting a judgement of high, medium, or low. Each pile may then be read again, and the essays sorted with greater precision.

   The analytic approach also starts with an ideal answer. In this case, however, the major elements of the ideal answer are identified and given a separate numerical value. For example, if the question asks students to identify three major factors contributing to differences between the North and the South just prior to the Civil War, the teacher may decide to give three points each for identification of social, economic, and political factors plus three points for any example of how these factors were interrelated.

   Global scoring may be quicker and more appropriate where the essay question admits to greater diversity in student responses. Where expected responses can be well-defined in advance, analytic scoring has the advantage of applying the same explicit gauge to each essay and provides a clear justification for grades and discussion of student performance. In addition, analytic scoring is less likely to suffer from shifting subjective standards as the grader progresses through the papers.

2. **Grade each essay anonymously.** Preserving the anonymity of the essay writer while grading can be accomplished by asking students to put their names on the back of the examination or by using an identification number in place of their names. If the teacher knows the name of the student at the time of grading, there is a tendency to read between the lines, ascribing to good students more understanding than is communicated and

downplaying adequate responses from students who have a history of poor work. Not knowing who wrote a particular essay helps the grader focus on the content of the essay rather than the student.

3. **Grade the answers question by question rather than student by student.** For example, on a six-question essay test, all the responses to the first question would be read and graded before going on to the second question. This procedure makes it easier for the grader to make comparisons from one response to the next, and to develop a sense of the poor, typical, and good responses.

4. **Counterbalance the order in which the papers are scored.** This means if you scored question 1 by starting at the top of the stack of papers and working your way to the bottom, you should score question 2 by starting at the bottom of the stack and working your way to the top. Even in analytic scoring, there is a tendency for the scoring standard to erode in the process of scoring many responses. The first response scored may appear fresh, complete, and on target. By the time the scorer has reached the last essay booklets, the same answer appears common, ordinary, and stale. In addition, scorer fatigue and boredom tend to depress the scores assigned to answers near the bottom of the pile. By starting the scoring of the second question at the bottom of the pile, these students now have a chance to appear fresh and innovative in their answers. Moreover, counterbalanced scoring distributes the effects of fatigue and boredom more equally over all test papers.

5. **Avoid allowing mechanics of English to enter into evaluation of responses.** Some teachers rightly feel English language skills should be reinforced in all school activities. From a psychometric point of view, however, anything entering into the measurement of a specific skill or knowledge (i.e., understanding of science principles) that is not related to the construct tends to contaminate the score. If a teacher wants to recognize good English usage on an essay test, then a separate score for this ability can be provided. As a general rule, teachers should try to avoid being influenced by spelling, punctuation, penmanship, and other aspects of English usage when grading essay tests.

While we have discussed the advantages and disadvantages of the essay test with some confidence, it should be clear that many of the claims represent conventional wisdom more than well-established research findings. No form of measurement is more in need of research than the essay test. As written by the average classroom teacher, do essay tests fulfill their promise of measuring higher order thinking skills? Are we attempting to measure cognitive processes that are only partially defined and not well understood? Can we generate evidence that students who respond to essay tests over long periods of time, a semester or more, do develop a different stance with respect to their subject matter? These are important questions that still remain unanswered. In the meantime, teachers will be challenged to develop interpretive exercises and essay examinations that focus on the integration of knowledge and the use of knowledge in analyzing problems.

Summary

The continuing search for testing procedures that slant the evaluation process toward higher cognitive processes leads to interpretive exercises and essay tests, two procedures that emphasize meaningful interpretation of material.

Interpretive exercises are relatively complex problem situations requiring interpretations, inferences, deductions, and application of relevant information. Since the essential information is provided, emphasis is on higher cognitive processes rather than memory. Because the response format is usually multiple choice, the interpretive exercise preserves the advantages of the objective test while at the same time focusing on making meaning of the material.

Essay tests have the highest potential for encouraging students to organize and interpret information. The key word in this statement is "potential." Essay questions can ask for memory level responses or for analysis and interpretation. It seems likely that well-formulated essay tests can motivate students to take a reflective stance toward subject matter. Research on the effects of essay tests on study procedures will benefit from specifying the nature of the essay questions employed in the research.

The unreliability of essay test scoring and the effect of such factors as handwriting and position in the stack of tests continue to be problems with essay tests. There are, however, five steps that can make scoring more objective and reliable:

1. Develop and use an explicit scoring rationale for each question. Match each paper to the scoring criteria to minimize changing scoring standards as scoring proceeds.
2. Use an identification number rather than names so that scoring focuses on quality of responses rather than student personalities.
3. Grade a single question for the entire class before going on to the next question. This procedure helps you apply the scoring rationale for a single question consistently as you move from paper to paper.
4. If you scored the first question by working from top to bottom of the stack of essays, turn the stack over and grade the second question from bottom to top. This tends to distribute the effects of fatigue more equally over all test papers, and to reduce any detrimental effects due to the location of the paper in the stack.
5. Avoid letting handwriting, spelling, and grammar distract your attention from the way the student is using and interpreting the ideas in the material. If mechanics of English are a concern, these can be assigned a separate score.

With these aids in scoring essay tests, teachers can be encouraged to continue their efforts to use this measurement approach in determining the extent to which their students are organizing details into larger concepts, and generating unique and personal meanings from the material.

References

Ashburn, R.R. (1938). An experiment in the essay-type question. *Journal of Experimental Education, 7,* 1–3.

Brownell, W.A. (1946). *The measurement of understanding. Forty-fifth yearbook of the National Society for the Study of Education, Part I.* Chicago: University of Chicago Press.

Chase, C.I. (1978). *Measurement for educational evaluation.* Reading, MA: Addison-Wesley.

Chase, C.I. (1986). Essay test scoring: Interaction of relevant variables. *Journal of Educational Measurements, 23*(1), 33–41.

Ebel, R.L., & Frisbie, D.A. (1986). *Essentials of educational measurement (4th ed.).* Englewood Cliffs, NJ: Prentice-Hall.

Educational Testing Service (1973). *Multiple-choice questions: A close look.* Princeton, NJ: Author.

Eisner, E. (1985). *The art of educational evaluation.* Philadelphia, PA: Falmer Press.

Gerberich, J.R., Greene, H.A., & Jorgensen, A. N. (1962). *Measurement and evaluation in the modern school.* New York: David McKay.

Gronlund, N.E., & Linn, R.L. (1990). *Measurement and evaluation in teaching* (6th ed.). New York: Macmillan.

Hakstian, A.R. (1971). The effects of type of examination anticipated on test preparation and performance. *Journal of Educational Research, 64*(7), 319–324.

Hopkins, K.D., Stanley, J.E., & Hopkins, B. R. (1990). *Educational and psychological measurement and evaluation.* Englewood Cliffs, NJ: Prentice-Hall.

Hughes, D.C., & Keeling, B. (1984). The use of model essays to reduce context effects in essay scoring. *Journal of Educational Measurements, 21*(3), 277–281.

McDaniel, E.D. (1988). (Development of a multiple-choice test to measure cognitive complexity.) Unpublished raw data.

Peel, E.A. (1971). *The nature of adolescent judgment.* New York: Wiley-Interscience.

Rowntree, D. (1977). *Assessing students: How shall we know them?* London: Harper & Row.

Schroder, H.M., Driver, M.J., & Streufert, S. (1967). *Human information processing: Individuals and groups functioning in complex social situations.* New York: Holt, Rinehart & Winston.

Speth, C., & Brown, R. (1990). Effects of college students' learning styles and gender on their test preparation strategies. *Applied Cognitive Psychology, 4,* 189–202.

Stalnaker, J.L. (1951). The essay type of examination. In E. Lindquist (ed.), *Educational measurement.* Washington, DC: American Council on Education.

Wesman, A.G. (1971). Writing the test item. In R.L. Thorndike (ed.), *Educational measurement.* Washington, DC: American Council on Education.

My sister told me that the New York State testing program includes five performance tests in science. They set up testing stations in one room, and each fourth grade student in the school circulates through these stations. They are like learning centers. One has a battery, wires, and a little light bulb; one has paper towels, water, a medicine dropper; another has a homemade balance where they weigh a crayon with paper clips. The kids write down what they have discovered at each station.

chapter ten

Performance Assessment

Looking back over the chapters on teacher-constructed tests, we note a progression from multiple-choice tests through interpretive exercises to essay tests. At each step of the way, the student becomes more active, shifting from recognizing good answers to manipulating concepts and interpreting information. We applaud this transition from memory and recognition to analysis and interpretation, but there remains concern that our teaching and testing center on words. It is conceivable that a student can learn to write an explanation of how a lever works, but still be unable to use a crowbar to pry the lid off a packing crate. Performance assessment goes beyond multiple-choice and essay tests by evaluating student behavior in lifelike situations designed to elicit the knowledge and skills of interest. Mitchell (1992) provides the following example of a fourth grade boy participating in the New York State Elementary Science Program Evaluation Test.

> The boy with blond hair modishly short on top and long in back quietly exclaims, "Wow" as he begins the electrical test. He has no trouble making the bulb light by bringing the two alligator clips together. The instructions tell him to test the objects in the plastic bag to see if they make the bulb light. He takes the wire from the plastic bag and places it on one of the alligator clips. No light. He puts a check in the "bulb does not light" column on his answer sheet. Then he tries the same thing with a toothpick, also in the bag. Same results, same answer. He repeats the pattern for all five objects.
>
> Then he comes to the next question, which asks him to explain what happened, based on the results he noted in the columns. He looks again at the instructions and the questions, puzzled. Then he brings the clips together again-and the bulb lights. He lets out a soft "ohhh" and then puts one end of the wire in one clip and the other in the second clip. Bingo. Rapidly he goes through the four other objects, connecting them to both the terminals, with the expected results. Then he furiously erases the checks for the wire and the other metal objects and checks the column marked "bulb lights." He spends the last few minutes of the allotted time emphatically scribbling his explanation.

(Reprinted with the permission of the Free Press, a Division of Macmillan, Inc., from *Testing for Learning: How New Approaches to Evaluation Can Improve American Schools* by Ruth Mitchell. Copyright © 1992 by Ruth Mitchell.)

This account illustrates the latest trend in assessing achievement. From Connecticut to California and from Arizona to Wisconsin, states around the nation are now planning or actually using performance assessments as part of their statewide testing. England, Wales, and the Netherlands have substantial performance assessment programs in place. In addition, professional groups in curricular areas such as English, mathematics, science, and social studies are urging sharper definition of the general intellectual skills associated with their disciplines and the development of performance assessments that will help teachers determine student progress toward these goals.

Reasons Behind Performance Assessments

Performance assessments present students with a standard task and systematically evaluate behaviors as the student works through the task. Most commonly, the problem solving behaviors are inferred from notes, diagrams, and explanations accompanying the solution of a problem. Analytic examination of artwork or essays produced by the student provides insights about how well various components of the production process have been handled. Performance criteria are established so that all students are evaluated in the same way. One of the ideal outcomes of performance assessment, in contrast to more conventional tests, is a profile of the student's strategy and tactics as the student copes with a problem. While an ordinary test will tell whether the answer is right or wrong, a major emphasis of performance assessment is the cognitive processes employed in arriving at solutions.

Much of the impetus for performance testing has come from a reaction against multiple-choice formats. There is evidence that the "bubble tests," requiring students to shade in a machine readable bubble to indicate an answer, influence teachers who must prepare students for statewide assessments. Nolen, Haladyna, and Hass (1992) surveyed nearly 2,500 Arizona teachers and found that 60 percent of elementary and 40 percent of high school teachers said administrators pressured them to raise scores, and the main way they did it was by focusing on the skills that the test demanded. Proponents of performance assessment say that if tests are going to pull curriculum and teaching emphasis in a particular direction, then the tests should reflect worthwhile knowledge and skills. The argument is that performance tests are tests worth teaching to (Mitchell, 1992). Wiggins (1989) put it nicely: "Do we judge our students to be deficient in writing, speaking, listening, artistic creation, research, thoughtful analysis, problem posing and problem solving? Let the test ask them to write, speak, listen, create, do original research, analyze, pose, and solve problems" (p. 42).

The conceptual grounding that supports performance assessment has been reviewed in a report by the Center for Children and Technology at the Bank Street College of Education (1990). From this report, it is clear that currents are flowing from cognitive science and learning theory suggesting that students learn best in situations marked by problem sensing, problem finding, problem formulation, and problem solving. Students are stimulated by situations in which they can construct meanings during the processes of representing problems, managing parts of complex tasks, revising problem subcomponents, and working toward solutions.

Instructional practices consistent with this view of learning are illustrated by the work of John Bransford and his group at Vanderbilt University. The Cognition and Technology Group at Vanderbilt (in press) has developed videotaped situations in which mathematical problems are embedded in narrative situations. In one example from their Jasper adventure series, a wounded eagle is found in an isolated mountain meadow and the question arises whether an ultralight plane can be used to get the bird out for medical aid. Information concerning such variables as distance to the bird, load carrying capacity of the plane, miles obtained per gallon of gas, and other data is embedded in the narrative. Students must identify subproblems, find relevant data, perform calculations, and make decisions about feasible means of rescuing the wounded eagle. This kind of "situated cognition" allows the emergence of concepts from the situations in which they have relevance.

A major argument for performance assessment is that the behaviors tested are much more closely aligned to the behaviors desired at the conclusion of instruction than are paper and pencil tests. If one of the outcomes of mathematics and science instruction is to develop habits of formulating and testing hypotheses, then the test situation ought to afford opportunities for the student to exhibit these behaviors.

Performance Tasks as Realistic Work Samples

It may be observed that students learning mathematics in the context of the Jasper adventure series can use all the processes that people in real-life situations use: calculators, insights of other group members, ability to go back and check basic data, and opportunities to revise and reformulate earlier ideas. A powerful argument supporting both situated cognition and performance assessment is that learning and testing should reflect real-life behaviors. Thus, an important aspect of performance assessments is their "authentic" quality. There is an interest in designing performance tests so that they reflect the out-of-school world.

The Arizona Student Assessment Program provides a fascinating attempt to move assessment in the direction of realistic performances. The Arizona planners considered the typical essay test artificial. How many times during one's life must a polished essay be composed on the spot with a forty-five minute time limit? To bring the testing procedure more in line with a typical writing situation, the Arizona testing procedure covers a two-day span. The first day, students read a brief scenario that sets a situation, describes an audience, and states the purpose for the essay. Students then go through guided procedures to facilitate idea generation and development, followed by thirty minutes in which they develop a rough draft. On the second day, the draft is revised and polished. A checklist is provided to help students focus on significant aspects of the essay during the revision process. Before the essays are sent away for scoring, students are encouraged to read them to each other. "Contrast this with the emphasis on secrecy and security in administering norm-referenced, multiple-choice tests" (Mitchell, 1992, p. 45).

From a measurement viewpoint, we can find much to make us uncomfortable in this situation, including opportunities for coaching, if not indeed "ghostwriting" by overly involved parents during the overnight incubation period. On the other hand, consider the impact on the student of learning the sequence of idea generation, rough drafting, and final production. As Mitchell notes, "It gets writing out of the domain of inspiration and natural talent and into the sphere of effort . . ." (p. 45). If the mode of testing reinforces the role of the various steps in constructing clear communication, perhaps the aims of education are well served.

Performance assessment in mathematics is illustrated by Mitchell's (1992) review of California's statewide testing program. At the twelfth grade level, for example, students respond to the following question:

> James knows that half of the students from his school are accepted at the public university nearby. Also half are accepted at the local private college. James thinks this adds up to 100 percent, so he will surely be accepted at one or the other institution. Explain why James may be wrong. If possible, use a diagram in your explanation.

It should be recognized that selection of a problem is not the most difficult part of performance assessments. The development of scoring criteria is, perhaps, the most challenging aspect of designing performance tests. Ebel and Frisbie (1991) comment:

> For the problem test there is the additional element of subjectivity in scoring that is not present in the objective test. How much credit to give for an imperfect answer and which elements to consider in judging degree of perfection are often spur-of-the-moment, subjective decisions. In considering the relative merits of essay, problem, and objective tests, it is important to remember that *the only useful component of any test score is the objectively verifiable component of it*. To the degree that a test score reflects the private, subjective, unverifiable impressions and values of one particular scorer, it is deficient in meaning, and hence in usefulness, to the student who received it or to anyone else who is interested in using it (p. 116).

The concerns expressed by Ebel and Frisbie reflect the concern raised in the discussion of essay test scoring, i.e., concerns about the reliability of a test. If a measurement procedure does not yield consistent scores from one occasion to the next, or from one rater to the next, then the meaning and usefulness of the score is seriously jeopardized.

Much effort has gone into the development of explicit scoring guides to reduce the element of subjectivity in performance assessment. In addition, training of scorers and the adoption of quality control procedures have contributed to a high degree of inter-rater reliability in scoring performance tasks.

Scoring of Performance Tasks

Whether scoring is done by outside agencies or by teachers working as scoring teams, the essential tool is a scoring guide. Teachers working on scoring guides in California developed a six-point scale for scoring eighth grade essays supporting a judgement (figure 10.1) and a general guide for twelfth grade open-ended mathematics problems (figure 10.2).

In addition to the general scoring guide, scoring **rubrics** were developed for each specific mathematics problem in the statewide program. For example, the problem in which James tries to decide on his chances of being admitted to at least one college was evaluated with the help of the rubric shown in figure 10.3.

Groups of teachers use these rubrics to assess the level of student performance. A critical part of the scoring is the development of consensus among the scoring group about the kinds of responses that meet the listed criteria. Mitchell reports that sometimes half the time allocated for scoring (measured in days) is spent arriving at consensus on the meaning of the scoring rubrics and studying exemplary answer sheets at each level. Additionally, checks and balances are worked into the system by recirculating papers that have already been scored or by check scoring a sample of answer sheets by a lead scorer.

When teachers participate in training and work on scoring performance tasks, an added benefit is almost invariably noted in the professional growth of the teachers and in renewed commitment to instructional goals stressing broad generalizable knowledge and skills.

Psychometric Properties of Performance Tests

Shavelson, Baxter, and Pine (1992) subjected performance assessment to a rigorous study in order to answer a series of questions: How consistent would the scores be when rated by different raters? How stable would

Achievement in Evaluation

Score Point	Description of Achievement
6 Exceptional Achievement	The student produces convincingly argued evaluation; identifies a subject, describes it appropriately, and asserts a judgment of it; gives reasons and specific evidence to support the argument; engages the reader immediately, moves along logically and coherently and provides closure; reflects awareness of reader's questions or alternative evaluations.
5 Commendable Achievement	The student produces well-argued evaluation; identifies, describes, and judges its subject; gives reasons and evidence to support the argument; is engaging, logical, attentive to reader's concerns; is more conventional or predictable than the writer of a 6.
4 Adequate Achievement	The student produces adequately argued evaluation; identifies and judges its subject; gives at least one moderately developed reason to support the argument; lacks the authority and polish of the writer of a 5 or 6; produces writing that, although focused and coherent, may be uneven; usually describes the subject more than necessary and argues a judgment less than necessary.
3 Some Evidence of Achievement	The student states a judgment and gives one or more reasons to support it; either lists reasons without providing evidence or fails to argue even one reason logically or coherently.
2 Limited Evidence of Achievement	The student states a judgment but may describe the subject without evaluating it or may list irrelevant reasons or develop a reason in a rambling, illogical way.
1 Minimal Evidence of Achievement	The student usually states a judgment but may describe the subject without stating a judgment; either gives no reasons or lists only one or two reasons without providing evidence, usually relies on weak and general personal evaluation.

No Response

Off Topic

Figure 10.1 *Six-point scale for essays.*
Source: California Learning and Assessment System. Reprinted by permission.

Demonstrated Competence

Exemplary Response (Rating = 6)

Gives a complete response with a clear, coherent, unambiguous, and elegant explanation; includes a clear and simplified diagram; communicates effectively to the identified audience; shows understanding of the open-ended problem's mathematical ideas and processes; identifies all the important elements of the problem; may include examples and counterexamples; presents strong supporting arguments.

Competent Response (Rating = 5)

Gives a fairly complete response with reasonably clear explanations; may include an appropriate diagram; communicates effectively to the identified audience; shows understanding of the problem's mathematical ideas and processes; identifies the most important elements of the problems; presents solid supporting arguments.

Satisfactory Response

Minor Flaws But Satisfactory (Rating = 4)

Completes the problem satisfactorily, but the explanation may be muddled; argumentation may be incomplete; diagram may be inappropriate or unclear; understands the underlying mathematical ideas; uses mathematical ideas effectively.

Serious Flaws But Nearly Satisfactory (Rating = 3)

Begins the problem appropriately but may fail to complete or may omit significant parts of the problem; may fail to show full understanding of mathematical ideas and processes; may make major computational errors; may misuse or fail to use mathematical terms; response may reflect an inappropriate strategy for solving the problem.

Inadequate Response

Begins, But Fails to Complete Problem (Rating = 2)

Explanation is not understandable; diagram may be unclear; shows no understanding of the problem situation; may make major computational errors.

Unable to Begin Effectively (Rating = 1)

Words do not reflect the problem; drawings misrepresent the problem situation; copies parts of the problem but without attempting a solution; fails to indicate which information is appropriate to problem.

No Attempt (Rating = 0)

Figure 10.2 *Generalized rubric for open-ended mathematics questions.*
Source: California Learning and Assessment System. Reprinted by permission.

Students are given an example of a logic problem that involves college acceptance. The student must give a clear and mathematically correct explanation of the faulty reasoning involving the assumption of nonoverlapping sets in the problem. For the highest score, responses must be complete, contain examples and/or counterexamples of overlapping sets, or have elegantly expressed mathematics. A diagram is expected.

Demonstrated Competence

For 6 points: The response is exemplary. It goes beyond the criteria for 5 points. For example, the response may include:
• Example(s) and/or counterexample(s)
• Mathematics expressed elegantly
• An explanation that is complete

For 5 points: The response is correct and the explanation is clear. It may be expressed in words, with a diagram, or both.

Satisfactory Response

For 4 points: The response is generally correct, but the explanation lacks clarity.

For 3 points: The response indicates a *partial* solution (e.g., the same 50 percent are accepted by both colleges); or the response indicates that the student *may* understand the solution but the explanation is incoherent.

Inadequate Response

For 2 points: The response is incorrect, but it shows evidence of mathematical reasoning. A mathematical explanation is developed. However, the explanation does not address the crux of the problem or the essence of the solution. The paper may include a mathematical misconception.

For 1 point: The response is incorrect. It is not a sensible mathematical solution of the problem. The justification may use irrelevant arguments, such as:
• Whether a student is qualified for college
• Where a student attends college
• Whether a student desires to attend college
• Whether a student has applied to college

Off Track: The student leaves a blank page or writes: "I don't know."

Figure 10.3 *Scoring rubric for James problem.*
Source: California Learning and Assessment System. Reprinted by permission.

scores be across different tasks? Would less expensive testing and scoring procedures provide about the same score as assessments done by skilled observers watching the children at work? Finally, would performance assessments show more learning for children taught in "hands-on" science classes compared to "textbook" classes?

To answer these questions, the investigators used three performance activities that were appropriate for upper elementary school children.

In the first activity, "Paper Towels," students determined which of three kinds of paper towels soaked up the most water. To assist them, they had a water supply, trays, a scale, a timer, and beakers.

In the second activity, "Electric Mysteries," students determined the circuit components hidden in each of six mystery boxes shown in figure 10.4.

In the third activity, "Bugs," students tried to find out which conditions sow bugs liked better, dark or light, dry or damp, or a particular combination of these two variables.

More than 300 fifth-and sixth-grade children from two school districts (one stressing hands-on science, the other using a health book) were observed performing the three investigative activities.

The findings revealed that the raters agreed almost perfectly on the procedures students used in conducting their investigations. However, in examining the stability of scores from task to task, the investigators noted considerable variation in performance. Some students who did well on the mystery box or bug experiment did not do well on the paper towel experiment and vice versa.

Several less expensive measurement procedures were compared to the ratings provided by the skilled observers: grading of student notebooks kept while the investigations were going on; computer simulations of the same activities (electric mysteries and bugs experiment only); and short answer and multiple-choice questions covering the content and procedures of the investigations.

The results of these comparisons revealed a high degree of correspondence between the ratings of the students' notebooks and the observation of actual performance. The agreement between actual performance and performance on computer simulations was less high. Some students who did well in the investigative activity did poorly on the computer simulation and vice versa. The reliability of the short answer test proved to be lower than the reliability of the performance observations, and neither the short answer nor multiple-choice tests reflected any special learning that the hands-on science approach may have produced.

Find out what is in the six mystery boxes A, B, C, D, E and F. They have five different things inside, shown below. Two of the boxes will have the same thing. All of the others will have something different inside.

Two batteries:

A wire:

A bulb:

A battery and a bulb:

Nothing at all:

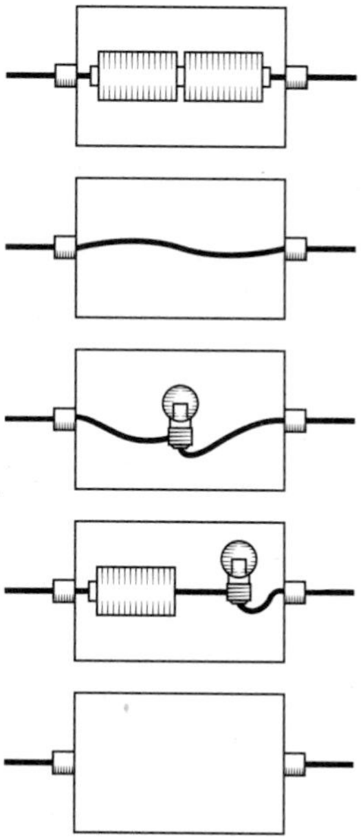

For each box, connect it in a circuit to help you figure out what is inside. You can use your bulbs, batteries and wires any way you like.

Figure 10.4 *Electric mysteries investigation.* Reprinted with the permission of the American Educational Research Association from "Performance assessments, political rhetoric and measurement reality" by R. J. Shavelson, G. P. Baxter, and J. Pine, 1992, *Educational Researcher, 21*(4), p. 23. Copyright © 1992 by American Educational Research Association.

The performance assessment appeared to live up to expectations in one important way: Children going through the hands-on science program showed higher scores on the performance assessments than children going through a textbook program. Part of the reason for this is that at least one of the tasks (electric mysteries) required some knowledge of how circuits work. Still, the short answer tests and multiple-choice tests did not distinguish between hands-on and textbook approaches.

How shall we summarize this complex experiment with performance testing? First, it is important to note that the performance assessments did show the effects of the hands-on curriculum while the paper and pencil tests did not. This finding reinforces the contention that if we teach with process goals in mind, it is important to measure outcomes with tests that are sensitive to the behaviors emphasized during instruction. A key observation, however, is the variability across performance tasks revealed by this study. If investigative processes are indeed being learned, these processes should be exhibited with some degree of consistency as the student turns from one task to the next. Yet, the study revealed lack of consistency across tasks.

How serious is this lack of consistency in student performance from one task to the other? If a student demonstrates good science procedures when investigating absorbency of paper towels but poor science procedures when exploring electric circuits, won't we be at a loss in judging the students' actual science skills? Does this mean that performance assessments should be abandoned? The answers to these questions depend on the purpose of the testing. More specifically, what kinds of inferences do we want to draw from the test behavior and to what other situations do we plan to generalize our findings?

Haertel (1991) discusses the problem of generalizability by examining three possible testing situations: (1) a middle school teacher wanting to know if a seventh grade student understands why maple leaves turn red in the fall while elm leaves turn yellow, (2) a high school physics teacher preparing a final examination, and (3) a state department of education considering performance tests as part of their annual educational assessment program.

In the first example, the teacher is not concerned with generalizing to any larger body of content but wants to know if a specific teaching transaction has been successful. Lack of consistency from one performance task to another would be of no concern to this teacher.

The physics teacher, on the other hand, needs a sufficiently broad sample of behavior to represent the major themes of the course and to support a grade reflecting each individual's competencies in physics. There should be sufficient consistency from task to task so that the physics teacher can generalize from the sample of behavior to overall competency in the underlying domain of physics.

The state department may be less interested in an individual's competency than in the level of achievement for the school as a whole. In this case, the variation of students from task to task will not be a problem, since averaging will provide a stable estimate of the achievement for the school. In fact, the state may employ "matrix sampling" in which different students take different tests. In this procedure, for example, six performance tasks may be included in the statewide program. Within any given class, five students may work only on task 1, five on task 2, and so on. The report sent back to the school will show the average achievement of the school on each of the six tasks but no scores for individual students. Where performance of the school as a whole is the focus of attention, lack of individual consistency from one task to another is not a problem.

The studies of Shavelson and his colleagues raise serious concerns about performance assessments when scores on a limited number of tasks are used to generalize to a broad class of knowledge and skills as, for instance, to a student's knowledge of scientific methodology. Performance assessment, however, is unlikely to survive or perish on the basis of psychometric characteristics. The movement toward performance assessments will continue to grow as educators feel that the gains in educational reform outweigh the shortcomings that performance assessments may display. There seems to be a willingness to accept some psychometric slippage in order to bring testing in line with curriculum reforms.

In Great Britain, considerable experience with performance testing has indeed led to a closer integration of testing and instruction. Spokespeople for the movement feel that the benefits in focusing curriculum and teaching on worthwhile goals are sufficient to outweigh problems of lower reliability. Bell, Burkhardt, and Swan (1992), for example, have taken a rather strong position on this issue: "We have already stated our view that (i) this conception of 'reliability' is an artifact, statistically sophisticated but educationally naive, and (ii) the valid assessment of mathematical performance in a balanced way is a fairly rough-and-ready matter whose genuine reliability is fairly low, as far as details of performance by individuals is concerned" (p. 180). These authors feel that averaging scores over tasks, subject areas, and individuals smooths out the irregularities. In any event, the deficiencies are seen as being outweighed by the formative and diagnostic information that performance assessment provides.

Certainly the impact of testing on teaching and learning is a major consideration, and we will soon turn our attention to steps that teachers can take within their classrooms to move toward performance assessments. At the same time, it is essential that teachers not expect more of performance testing than can be delivered. Ebel and Frisbie (1991) observe:

> The scoring of performance tests tends to be quite subjective, even when an explicit grading guide is prepared. Identification tests and simulations are time-consuming to prepare and administer, especially to large groups. On the whole, performance tests tend to be less efficient than objective tests. In many situations the validity of simulations is highly questionable; the most realistic simulations tend to be more costly to develop and administer. Even

when simulation scores yield high reliability, their cost is likely to be greater than their benefit. Despite these shortcomings, there are many circumstances under which performance testing is the only reasonable means of measurement (p. 117).

It is hoped that teachers will enter into performance assessments with an understanding of some of the difficulties accompanying these procedures, but at the same time, that they will appreciate the opportunities to rethink their own instructional and evaluation programs. What can teachers do to gain some experience with performance assessment?

Performance Assessment Applied by the Teacher

Initiating performance assessment as part of an evaluation procedure will require three steps: (1) analyzing the course for significant cognitive processes and understandings, (2) deciding on tasks, problems, or situations that will elicit behaviors reflecting these processes, and (3) constructing an observational checklist or scoring guide that allows systematic recording and evaluation of the conceptual models brought into play.

It would be a mistake to see performance assessment as simply a new approach to educational measurement. Performance assessment is deeply imbedded in the larger movement of educational reform. Further, it is important to see that educational reform itself is not a matter of finding new techniques for engaging students in the laborious processes of learning all the facts and methods that make up the semester's content. The reforming ideas reach to the very nature of learning and its definition. There is an emerging consensus that through learning, individuals acquire mental models of the way things work. In new situations, information is filtered, organized, and interpreted through the mental models, and the individual "makes sense" of the situation. ". . . the goal of instruction is not simply to get students to master more factual and procedural rules, but rather to help them construct powerful models that provide conceptual/procedural amplifiers in priority types of problem solving and decision-making situations" (Lesh and Lamon, 1992, p. 31). Lesh and Lamon go on:

> Therefore, when models are important cognitive objectives of instruction, one of the main goals of assessment is to probe the nature of the interpreting models that individual students have constructed to determine their accuracy, complexity, completeness, flexibility, and stability when they are used to generate descriptions, explanations, and predictions in a variety of problem-solving settings and for a variety of purposes under differing conditions. For example, when explanations are generated, the quality of response depends on the following kinds of criteria: (i) How much

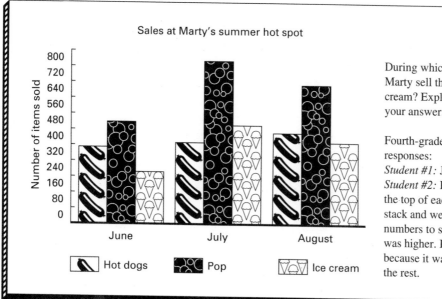

During which month did Marty sell the most ice cream? Explain how you got your answer.

Fourth-grade student responses:
Student #1: July. I looked.
Student #2: I put my finger at the top of each ice cream stack and went over to the numbers to see which one was higher. I picked July because it was higher than the rest.

Figure 10.5 *A graph-reading exercise and two typical fourth-grade student responses.* Adapted with the permission of the American Association for the Advancement of Science from *Assessment of Authentic Performance in School Mathematics* by R. Lesh and S. J. Lamon (eds.). Copyright © 1992 by the American Association for the Advancement of Science.

information was noticed? (ii) How well (and how flexibly) was the perceived information organized? (iii) How sophisticated, or complex, or rich were the relationships that were noticed? (iv) Were observations and subjective relationships perceived that were not objectively given? (p. 31).

Teachers initiating performance assessments are helped by keeping an eye on the concepts and models associated with their subject matter. Lamon and Lesh (1992) observe that ". . . merely providing an invitation for a student to expose a solution is not a sufficient condition for creating good assessment items" (p. 320). They provide an example of an item created by a fourth grade teacher to measure thinking while reading graphs (figure 10.5).

Lamon and Lesh point out: "Merely adopting an open-ended format was not enough; attaching the command 'Explain how you got your answer' failed to elicit students' thinking because the original question was procedural. The teacher gained no insight into the students' thinking because there was no need to reason, predict, describe, experiment, connect or interpret" (p. 321). The key element in performance assessment is the formulation of tasks, observations, and scoring procedures that allow the teacher to track the cognitive processes the student brings into play while coping with the problem.

Lamon and Lesh go on to suggest that performance items are more likely to evolve rather than simply be written. The evolution of an item is a consequence of three processes already mentioned: analysis of the domain to determine the particular concepts and processes of interest, development of tasks that seem to elicit the thinking required, and the experience of students with the item to reveal the variety of approaches and the nature of thinking that students bring to bear on the item. The following example illustrates these steps. The task was constructed to elicit students' cognitive models of change to see if they include the idea that quantities may be changing while the relationships among them may remain invariant. We also see the way student responses contributed to the development of a scoring guide. Lamon and Lesh presented this task to sixth grade students.

> Candy Bars: In Mr. Trent's science lab, there are three people to each table. For mid-morning break, Mr. Trent put two candy bars on each table and told the students to split them fairly. "Before you start your snacks, though, I would like you to push all four tables together," he said. Presuming that you like candy, if you had your choice, would you rather get your share of the candy before the tables are pushed together, or after?

The various approaches taken to this problem and the reasoning employed are illustrated from the student protocols in figure 10.6.

The various student responses provide clues to the scoring. Nancy's response, for example, avoided looking at the situation as one in which mathematical approaches would be relevant. Missy and Paul did not attend to all the relevant information, and Kari arrived at the answer but did not grasp the invariant relationship between two candy bars and three people. From such responses, Lamon and Lesh (1992, p. 338) developed the following scoring rubric, which represents varying degrees of student progress toward acquiring a mental model in which quantities may change while relationships within the situation remain unchanged.

0 = Student fails to focus on the mathematical nature of the situation.
1 = Student fails to incorporate all the relevant information.
2 = Student is hampered in attempts to reach the desired goal because of insufficient prior knowledge.
3 = Student reaches a correct answer in this situation, but has not actually built a model of the relationships.
4 = Student understands the invariant nature of the relationships between pairs of changing quantities.

In this example, we see all three aspects of teacher-made performance assessment: Identification of cognitive processes of interest, development of a problem situation that makes possible the observation of the relevant cognitions, and formulation of a scoring guide that focuses attention on the extent to which the desired cognitive processes were brought into play.

Nancy: There is no way I would ever cheat my friends. I just wouldn't do it. You couldn't get me to split up those candy bars. Most of them are too hard to split up. They never split just right. There's no way I would take a chance on cheating a friend of mine.

Missy: If there are two candy bars per table, splitting with 3 people you would get more than splitting with 12 people. You get a lot less if you have more people.

Ted: Well, they're really the same, 'cause if you reduce 12 and 8 down to its lowest thing, you get three and two. It doesn't matter where the tables are.

Interviewer: Can you tell how much each person would get?

Ted: Yeah. Let's see. That would be three for two people. No, that would be too much. It is less than a candy bar for each person. It would be two thirds.

Kari: Either way, 4 people won't get a candy bar.

Interviewer: What about splitting the candy bars so that everyone gets some?

Kari: (Long pause. Kari draws picture A.) Each person would get a half and a sixth, however much that is. Before, each would get 2/3. I would say you would get more before because I don't think 1/2 and 1/6 will be that much.

Picture A. Kari shows how to split two candy bars among three people.

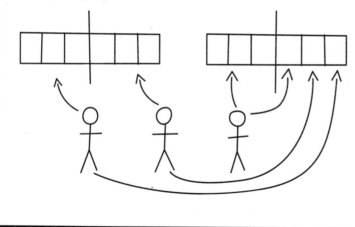

Interviewer: Can you figure out how much a half and a sixth is—exactly?

Kari: (Draws picture B.) Oh, I get it. You would get the same amount either way.

Interviewer: You're right. You would. Now suppose you had 20 people and 30 candy bars. Would those 20 people get the same amount of candy?

Figure 10.6 *Student responses to candy bars problem.*

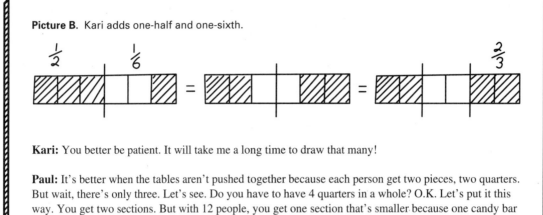

Picture B. Kari adds one-half and one-sixth.

$$\frac{1}{2} \qquad \frac{1}{6} \qquad \qquad \qquad \qquad \frac{2}{3}$$

Kari: You better be patient. It will take me a long time to draw that many!

Paul: It's better when the tables aren't pushed together because each person get two pieces, two quarters. But wait, there's only three. Let's see. Do you have to have 4 quarters in a whole? O.K. Let's put it this way. You get two sections. But with 12 people, you get one section that's smaller because one candy bar is divided into 12 sections.

Figure 10.6 *(continued) Picture B—Kari adds one-half and one-sixth.* Reprinted with the permission of the American Association for the Advancement of Science from *Assessment of Authentic Performance in School Mathematics* by R. Lesh and S. J. Lamon (eds.). Copyright © 1992 by the American Association for the Advancement of Science.

Getting Started in Performance Assessment

Getting started in performance assessment need not be a big step. Most subjects have specific problem areas that serve to illustrate or demonstrate application of general ideas. Performance assessment opportunities can be generated out of such specific events by shifting from their illustrative or demonstrative use in instruction to investigative occasions. De Vito (1989) provides a wealth of experiences for elementary science teachers that can serve as investigative opportunities. In the "Wandering Spool" example shown in figure 10.7, the activity of constructing the spool and experimenting with it is highly engaging for most students.

De Vito points out that this activity can be expanded by considering the many variables that can be manipulated (figure 10.8).

If investigation of the wandering spool is to be used for performance assessment, then the processes associated with the investigation must be identified and used to construct a scoring guide for recording and evaluating student performance. De Vito identifies the following processes:

- statement of a problem, usually in the form of a hypothesis
- identification of variables that have a bearing on the stated hypothesis
- formulation of strategies compatible with the stated hypothesis
- controlling the variables
- collecting and interpreting the data
- conclusions

A time-tested activity which has received wide acclaim in science instruction is the "Wandering Spool." A traditional description of this activity might appear thusly:

Topic Machines

Activity How to make a "Wandering Spool"

Materials Wooden spool
Two pieces of soda straw (one ten cm long and one straw shorter in length than the diameter of the spool)
Thumbtack
Plastic bead (from five mm to one cm in diameter)
Rubber band (the length of the rubber band should be shorter than the height of the spool)

Procedure Thread the rubber band through the spool and the bead. Tack the rubber band to the spool as shown. Insert the soda straw through the loop in the rubber band. Spin soda straw and release.

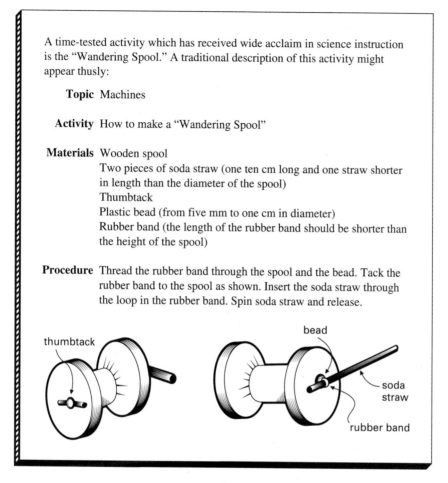

Figure 10.7 *Wandering spool activity.* Reprinted with the permission of Creative Ventures, Inc., from *Creative Wellsprings for Science Teaching* by A. DeVito. Copyright © 1989 by Creative Ventures, Inc.

Much of the creative work in converting the wandering spool activity into a performance assessment is deciding what behaviors will illustrate incomplete, marginal, acceptable, and excellent levels of performance in carrying out each of the six processes involved in moving from hypothesis to conclusions. Again, this scoring guide need not be set up in advance, but can grow out of observing children as they experiment with and talk about the wandering spool.

Using Simulations

One way of moving into performance assessment is to retrofit existing simulations. Karen Midden's (n.d.) Environmental Gaming Simulation involves middle school students in designing a housing development and building a three-dimensional model of the community on a large game

How and what components of the system can be manipulated or varied? Think of as many ways as possible to manipulate, change, vary, etc., each component on your list, permitting expansion on the basic activity. For example:

Spool
- size of the spool
- mass of the spool
- shape of the spool
- container (for example, plastic containers vs wooden spools)

Soda straw
- substitute wooden sticks (match stick devoid of the head), tongue depressors, swab sticks, doweling, etc.
- length of the straw
- number of straws

Plastic bead
- different materials, for example, wooden beads, metallic beads, etc.
- size of the bead
- number of beads
- beads with varying diameter holes drilled through the bead

Rubber band
- length of the rubber band
- thickness of the rubber band
- width of the rubber band
- number of rubber bands
- altering the rubber band to change the friction rate as it unwinds (for example, talc powder or some lubricant to reduce the friction of the rubber band)

Thumbtack
- substitute a small nail, map pin

Surface area
- alter the surface on which the spool travels; for example, waxed wood surface vs unwaxed surface, concrete, linoleum, various materials such as corduroy, silk, cotton (fastened down over wood or other material)
- change elevation (flat surface vs an inclined surface)

Figure 10.8 *Variables associated with the wandering spool.*

Reprinted with the permission of Creative Ventures, Inc., from *Creative Wellsprings for Science Teaching* by A. DeVito. Copyright © 1989 by Creative Ventures, Inc.

board representing a 150-acre site. The game board presents a number of "environmental features" that provide challenges and opportunities for the planners: a river, a floodplain, slopes, soil types, plants, wildlife, groundwater, and historical sites. Proximity to schools, shopping centers, woods, existing roads, and other housing and recreation areas can be considered. The students erect the community using wooden blocks for houses, green sponges for trees and vegetation, yarn for streets, thread for bike trails, a small rock for a historical site, and construction paper.

Students planning the community are assigned various roles that help make explicit the interlocking, and often conflicting, interests represented in any community development activity: real estate developer, contractor, banker, lawyer, merchant, neighbor, landscape architect, city planner, historic preservationist, and environmentalist. Role cards provide descriptions of the basic concerns and agendas motivating the actions of a particular player.

Decision-making processes are initiated by project cards that pose questions for the planners: How many houses should be built on the site? Where should the streets be located? Should there be a park on the site, a bicycle trail? Should the old orchard be preserved or plowed under? The project cards also list some of the cost-benefit and environmental impact arguments that can be mustered to support or oppose a particular building project. The discussions and development of the model can be carried out over a period of several days.

Using the simulation as a task for performance assessment would involve the development of a scoring guide reflecting the teacher's instructional goals. Individual performance might be evaluated in terms of how well the pupils understood and acted out their particular roles. The performance for the group as a whole might be evaluated in terms of housing density, convenience, attractiveness of the community, appropriateness of land use, and the impact of the development on soil erosion, wildlife, groundwater, and plants. Alternatively, participants might write summary essays describing their learnings as they progressed through the simulation. Scoring could recognize increased sensitivity to environmental issues, awareness of the various vested interests at work in community development, and the use of negotiations in resolving conflict.

Employing existing computer simulations offers another way to move into performance assessments. Chang and McDaniel (1993) made use of an existing program for a MacIntosh computer to present an electronic history book of the Vietnam War (Gabel, 1989). In this program, students can use a menu to go to any topic they choose or may branch from a topic directly to a related topic. The investigators asked a sample of college students to give the reasons why they made each choice as they worked through the program. From these responses, Chang and McDaniel classified students into four groups based on their search strategies: (1) aimless wanderers, (2) fact collectors, (3) emergent investigators, and (4) integrated analysts. This scoring guide for search behaviors separated students who appeared to wander through the program without a plan from those who developed an investigative theme. This kind of performance assessment would seem to have implications for helping students become more aware of the way they approach new material and how they use information to construct larger meanings.

Another example from the social studies is a series of computer simulations in American history. In one of these simulations, *1865: Should the Southern States Be Readmitted to the Union?* (Semonche, 1988), the student takes the role of a member of a Congressional committee who must decide whether to recommend readmitting the Southern states to the Union after the Civil War. The student can ask for additional background information, call on the various senators to elaborate on their viewpoints, and direct questions (selected from a list) to specific committee members. A "notepad" allows the student to take notes directly on the computer to assist in recalling important information. When ready, the student calls for a vote of the committee and adds his or her own vote. The computer reveals the vote that was actually cast by the committee of 1865.

The simulation provides a printout that shows how many times the player requested specific background information, how many times each committee member was called on to elaborate a position, how many times each committee member was questioned, and a record of the player's notepad. Also printed are the player's responses to eight questions such as "Did the deliberations of your committee change your mind?" "Which arguments did you find most convincing?"

The amount of information that must be assimilated and considered in this simulation is sufficiently large that it is appropriate only for able or gifted high school students and college classes. As far as we know, no scoring rubrics have been developed for use of this simulation as an indicator of ways students acquire and utilize information, but the challenge to develop scoring guides and to try this simulation in class settings is evident. More generally, computer simulations are appearing in a variety of subject areas, and the use of such simulations as part of performance assessments is well within the capabilities of classroom teachers who want to start working with performance assessments.

Summary

Performance assessment is developing great momentum both here and abroad. Instructional processes themselves are undergoing change in response to assertions from cognitive psychologists that teaching and learning should focus on the emerging cognitive structures of students, the mental models through which experience is screened and interpreted. Much performance testing aims at revealing the extent to which students are able to use relevant information and cognitive processes in solving science problems, writing essays, doing art, examining social problems, and applying mathematical concepts.

Performance assessments are developed by identifying relevant concepts and thinking strategies, designing problems for which such knowledge and skills are relevant, and formulating an explicit scoring guide to aid in evaluating the extent to which the relevant processes have been applied to the problem. Despite the care in constructing scoring guides, opportunities to introduce subjective judgements remain high, and there is evidence that performance may be sufficiently task-specific as to bring into question generalizing results from one task to another. In spite of such problems, performance assessments are likely to become increasingly widespread because they reflect deeper concerns for educational reform, and they bring evaluation procedures more closely in harmony with newer instructional goals.

The press to develop performance assessments has centered on large-scale testing programs and has developed most fully as a part of statewide or national assessment programs. Such programs have benefited from the developmental work of test specialists and teacher groups working together. There has been much less pressure for individual teachers to construct performance tests tied closely to their own instructional programs, but this seems to be a logical extension of the movement. Certainly as teachers move toward the development of broad understandings and competencies, they will want to measure the extent to which students can demonstrate these competencies. We have suggested several ways of getting started in performance assessment and believe that constructing scoring rubrics for existing simulations may be a promising way of proceeding.

In the next chapter, we will examine the possibility that thinking processes may be measured in a very general way, and we will describe a procedure for scoring students' written interpretations of a complex social problem.

References

Bell, A., Burkhardt, H., & Swan, M. (1992). Moving the system: the contributions of assessment. In R. Lesh & S.J. Lamon (eds.), *Assessment of authentic performance in school mathematics*. Washington, DC: American Association for the Advancement of Science.

California Learning and Assessment System (1989). *A question of thinking: A first look at students' performance on open-ended questions in mathematics*. Sacramento: California State Department of Education.

Center for Children and Technology (1990). *Applications in educational assessment: Future technologies*. Technical Report submitted to the Office of Technology Assessment. New York: Bank Street College of Education. (ED 340 773).

Chang, C.K., & McDaniel, E. (1993). *Information search strategies in a hypercard file*. Paper delivered at the Annual Meeting of the American Educational Research Association, Atlanta, GA.

The Cognition and Technology Group at Vanderbilt (in press). The Jasper series: A generative approach to improving mathematical thinking. In *This year in school science*. Washington, DC: American Association for the Advancement of Science.

De Vito, A. (1989). *Creative wellsprings for science teaching* (2nd ed.). West Lafayette, IN: Creative Ventures.

Ebel, R. L., & Frisbie, D. A. (1991). *Essentials of educational measurement* (5th ed.). Englewood Cliffs, NJ: Prentice Hall.

Gabel, P. (1989). *Vietnam War: A hypercard history book.* (Computer program). Scotts Valley, CA: Paul Gabel Regeneration Software.

Haertel, E. (1991). Form and function in assessing science education. In G. Kulm & S. M. Malcom (eds.), *Science assessment in the service of reform*. Washington, DC: American Association for the Advancement of Science.

Lamon, S. J., & Lesh, R. (1992). Interpreting responses to problems with several levels and types of correct answers. In R. Lesh & S. J. Lamon (eds.), *Assessment of authentic performance in school mathematics*. Washington, DC: American Association for the Advancement of Science.

Lesh, R., & Lamon, S. J. (1992). Assessing authentic mathematical performance. In R. Lesh & S. J. Lamon (eds.), *Assessment of authentic performance in school mathematics*. Washington, DC: American Association for the Advancement of Science.

Midden, K. S. (n.d.). *Environmental gaming simulation.* Carbondale, IL: Lands View Consulting.

Mitchell, R. (1992). *Testing for Learning.* New York: The Free Press.

Nolen, S. B., Haladyna, T., & Hass, N. (1992). Uses and abuses of achievement test scores. *Educational Measurement, 11*(2), 9–15.

Semonche, J. E. (1988). *Simulations in American history 1865: Should the Southern states be readmitted to the Union?* (Computer program). San Diego, CA: Harcourt Brace Jovanovich.

Shavelson, R. J., Baxter, G. P., & Pine, J. (1992). Performance assessments, political rhetoric, and measurement reality. *Educational Researcher, 21*(4), 22–27.

Wiggins, G. (1989). Teaching to the (authentic) test. *Educational Leadership, 46*(7), 41–47.

I had been reading about thinking skills when Austin brought in a model knight he had painted to show the class...this launched the whole thing. I bought plastic knights and glass jars of gloss enamel. Next came library books to see how the coats of arms might be colored. The rest unfolded naturally: the model castle protected by a moat, a study of why castles were needed, life in a medieval village, and the papers discussing whether it was better to grow up in the old days. There was no simple answer to that one. I could see the children growing by leaps and bounds during this unit. Kids were thinking, but I couldn't find a test of thinking skills that seemed to fit.

chapter eleven

Measuring Thinking Processes

Thinking in Education

Interest in teaching thinking skills goes back to and beyond Dewey's (1916) contention that the prime need of every person is the capacity to think. Certainly this emphasis on thinking continues to be an important aspect of schooling. Teachers and administrators must make intelligent decisions in a bewildering market offering workbook programs to teach thinking skills. They are also being pressured to demonstrate that their efforts are indeed increasing the thinking skills of their students. How can thinking be taught and measured? Polson and Jeffries (1985) examined four of the programs designed to teach thinking and problem-solving skills. These reviewers express strong reservations about exercises to develop thinking skills in content-free instructional settings. Apparently, thinking is best developed within subject matter contexts rather than in special thinking skills programs.

When it comes to measuring thinking, two widely recognized tests of critical thinking are available. It is important to know that even these state-of-the-art tests may not live up to their promise. We will see that in both tests students are asked to recognize good thinking, but are not required to construct perceptive answers. It seems probable that the problems with these tests go even deeper. Both tests are based on the assumption that thinking can be viewed as a series of logical thought processes. Ennis (1985, 1991) provides the most systematic description of this point of view.

There are, however, other ways to look at thinking. Some observers believe that "everyday thinking" proceeds from the way a person perceives, organizes, and interprets information. Viewing thinking in this way provides an entirely new approach to measuring thinking. Our own work along these lines has led to the development of a procedure in which students watch a videotape of a complex situation and write their responses to what they have seen. These responses are scored to provide a level of **cognitive complexity.** This chapter describes the procedure more fully and presents the essential background for understanding the logic of this approach. While the discussion of thinking may appear to digress somewhat from measurement issues, it is essential to see how approaches to the measurement of thinking grow out of the way thinking is conceptualized.

Standardized Tests of Critical Thinking

The emphasis in school for teaching thinking has been accompanied by demands for tests of thinking that are relatively independent of content. Do such tests exist and how good are they?

The two most commonly used thinking skills tests are the *Watson-Glaser Critical Thinking Appraisal* (Watson & Glaser, 1980) and the *Cornell Critical Thinking Tests* (Ennis, Millman, & Tomko, 1985).

The *Watson-Glaser Critical Thinking Appraisal* consists of a series of interpretive exercises designed for use at grade nine and higher. The test is divided into five parts: Inference, Recognition of Assumptions, Deduction, Interpretation, and Evaluation of Arguments.

In the following example of an Inference item, students are asked to read a brief passage about a student conference on social issues:

> Two hundred students in their early teens voluntarily attended a recent weekend student conference in a midwestern city. At this conference, the topics of race relations and means of achieving lasting world peace were discussed, since they were the problems the students selected as being most vital in today's world.

After reading this passage, students evaluate each of the following inferences using the key: true, probably true, insufficient data to decide, probably false, or false.

1. As a group, the students who attended this conference showed a keener interest in broad social problems than do most other students in their early teens.
2. The majority of the students had not previously discussed the conference topics in their schools.
3. The students came from all sections of the country.
4. The students discussed mainly labor relations problems.
5. Some teenage students felt it worthwhile to discuss problems of race relations and ways of achieving world peace.
   (From *Watson-Glaser Critical Thinking Appraisal,* Forms A & B, Copyright © 1980 by Harcourt Brace Jovanovich, Inc., Reproduced by permission. All rights reserved.)

While the Watson-Glaser is the oldest and best-established measure of critical thinking, the reliability is comparatively low, suggesting students would not necessarily get the same score if the test were readministered to them. The manual shows a number of relatively high correlations with school ability and school achievement, but no direct evidence that the test is measuring thinking processes rather than general ability. Most important of all, the student must simply recognize good answers rather than construct them. We have no way of knowing whether the inferences, interpretations, and evaluations marked on the answer sheet reflect thought processes that the student will actually use when confronted with a new problem situation.

The *Cornell Critical Thinking Tests* are similar in format and design to the Watson-Glaser. Level X is for use from grade four through the college sophomore level, and Level Z is for advanced high school students and college students.

Level X is both easier and more interesting. The items are connected by a story line that runs through all questions. The story describes the activities of a search party that has arrived on the planet of "Nicoma" to find out what has happened to a group of missing explorers who were sent to the planet earlier. Members of the second party make observations, hear reports from their experts, advance hypotheses, and interpret evidence. Students mark multiple-choice questions to indicate whether the information bears on the hypotheses, whether the information is reliable, whether the statements made by the explorers follow from the premises, and whether certain assumptions are made.

Support for the validity of the test is offered by presenting correlations with other measures of critical thinking and with school ability and achievement measures. Based on a study of 812 ninth grade students, correlations between Level X of the Cornell test and the subscores of the Watson-Glaser ranged from .41 to .49. Since both tests are designed to measure similar thinking processes, we would expect these correlations to be higher.

As with the Watson-Glaser, it is not clear that students confronted with real world problems would actually use the thought processes they exhibit when responding to the multiple-choice alternatives on the tests.

In summary, both tests of thinking processes ask students to recognize right answers rather than construct them. Both tests show moderately high correlations with measures of school ability and achievement, but little evidence that the tests are related to thinking processes rather than to general verbal ability. These observations suggest that further study and research is needed before we can use them with confidence.

Alternative Efforts to Measure Thinking Processes

Scholars who make a special study of thinking point to a distinction between "formal reasoning" and "everyday reasoning" (Galotti, 1989). In tests of formal reasoning, a well-defined problem is set before the learner and the essential premises and information are provided. If the learner follows logically sound rules of reasoning, the correct answer is obtained.

In everyday reasoning the problems are less well-defined, all the information one needs is rarely available, and there are a number of possible solutions rather than a single answer. In everyday reasoning, the way information is perceived, selected, and interpreted plays the major role in formulating solutions.

It may be observed that the tests of critical thinking that we have just reviewed are constructed within the formal reasoning framework. Students consider the arguments or statements presented in the test and decide whether these statements logically follow from the information given.

We turn now to three lines of research that conceptualize thinking in terms of the cognitive processes that come into play as individuals try to make sense out of everyday situations. These approaches focus on the way an individual perceives, selects, and organizes information.

The Describer-Explainer Continuum

Peel (1971) suggests that if you want to know how a person thinks, ask that person to explain a complex situation. Responses can be placed on a **describer-explainer continuum.** Low level thinkers remain on a descriptive level, reciting back the information provided. High level thinkers point out cause and effect relationships, apply general world knowledge, and construct possibilities that are not clearly indicated in the information given.

In a typical exercise used by Peel, students read about an Andean farmer who cut down the forest and planted a crop that produced a profitable harvest. Soon other farmers followed his example. Before long, floods eroded the soil and the land became barren. After reading the story, students respond to the question, "Why did the deep fertile soil cover disappear and make farming impossible?"

Low level thinkers respond to such stories with concrete descriptions limited to a recapitulation of the information given. Their explanations amount to little more than descriptions. They bring to the problem little in the way of abstract concepts, comparisons, evaluations, or analytic insights. High level thinkers see causal connections and draw on their knowledge of how things work to generate explanations.

Intellectual Development

Perry (1970) views the way students respond to problematic situations as an indication of their general moral and **intellectual development.** Perry's ideas are based on extensive interviews with students at Harvard University.

During the freshman year, students appear to view the world as divisible into simple "black-white" categories. Problematic situations are quickly broken into either-or compartments: we-they, right-wrong, good-bad. Authorities have answers and there is a feeling that everything will turn out all right if one relies on hard work and obedience.

By the senior year, most students have reached a more intellectually mature level. Students see knowledge and values as contingent on circumstances and relative from person to person and place to place. At a still higher level, students accept the necessity of living in a relativistic and uncertain world, but learn to make commitments that reflect their values and come to see these commitments as an ongoing activity that expresses their particular life-styles.

Perry's work helps us see a distinction in thinking processes between the relatively immature tendencies to simplify the world and the more mature tendencies to accept a complex world that is open to many interpretations and that guarantees few "right answers." This continuum from simple to complex is further elaborated on by cognitive psychologists who view thinking as contingent on information processing structures.

Information Processing Structures

Schroder, Driver, and Streufert (1967) contend that concepts, attitudes, needs, and norms are **information processing structures** that markedly influence our perceptions and the ways these perceptions are integrated into beliefs and actions. Individuals with more complex cognitive structures are able to see more dimensions and to make finer distinctions in situations they encounter. They are also able to combine and integrate these perceptions in more complex ways.

According to Schroder and his colleagues, individuals with low cognitive complexity exhibit thinking processes marked by (1) categorical, black-white thinking, (2) minimizing conflict, (3) seeking causes of behavior in external circumstances, and (4) compartmentalizing and abruptly shifting categories. With greater cognitive complexity, there is (1) movement away from absolutism, (2) perception of a less deterministic system, (3) tendency to see situations from more than one point of view, and (4) greater use of internal processes in generating possibilities.

The work of Schroder and his associates points to cognitive structures, rules, or habits for making meaning and generating knowledge from encounters with the environment. These information processing structures lie on a continuum ranging from simplistic categorization to the generation of theoretical frameworks that organize complex events.

Levels of Cognitive Complexity—An Approach to the Measurement of Thinking

McDaniel and Lawrence (1990) have built on these three lines of research to develop a new approach to the measurement of thinking. In this approach, students are confronted with a complex situation that is open to a variety of interpretations. Student written responses are scored using a **scoring rationale** that allows the grader to rate the level of cognitive complexity expressed in the response.

Much work with this approach has been done using as stimulus material the first fifteen minutes of a videotape originally broadcast as a television program. The ABC news presentation *The Bomb Factories* (1988) shows plants that make nuclear weapons and describes problems with plant safety and environmental pollution. After viewing the tape, students write summary statements of their reactions and interpretations of the situation.

In scoring the responses, the rater attends to three cognitive processes that help determine the level of complexity reflected in the students' reactions: (1) the way the student perceives and defines the situation, (2) the organizing structure the student uses to help make sense of the situation, and (3) the way the student analyzes the situation and supports a position. Let us examine each of these processes more closely.

Perception and Definition of the Situation

The student perceives and selects salient features to characterize the situation and give it meaning. These perceptions define the complexity seen in the issues presented. The student may simplify the situation and ignore information. On the other hand, the student may preserve the complexity in the situation and incorporate divergent information.

Imposition of an Organizing Structure

The organizing structure provides a frame of reference within which the events are interpreted. This frame of reference reflects the student's values, concerns, and world knowledge. The student may accept and simplify the framework of the problem situation adding no new ideas or perspectives. On the other hand, the student may extend the framework, bringing in world knowledge and value positions not implied by the situation.

Analysis, Support, and Elaboration

The student may either describe or analyze the situation. Describing is characterized by restatements of the given information coupled with assertions rather than reasons. The student paraphrases information and uses assertions, simple rules, and appeals to authority. Explaining is characterized by an integrated network of relationships. The student constructs networks of causal relationships, applies principles, uses analogies, generalizes, and extrapolates.

Assigning Ratings to Student Responses

Raters of student responses try to be sensitive to these cognitive processes when assigning a rating to the student's paper. The rater reads the papers to determine how the student defines the situation, organizes information, and supports a position. The rater assigns a value of one to five based on the level of cognitive complexity as defined by the scoring rationale.

Scoring Rationale for Levels of Cognitive Complexity

Level 1: Unilateral Descriptions

Simplifies the situation. Focuses on one idea or argument. Does not identify alternatives. Brings in no new information, meaning, or perspectives. Makes good-bad and either-or assertions. Appeals to authority or simple rules. Simply paraphrases, restates, or repeats information.

Level 2: Simplistic Alternatives

Identifies simple and obvious conflicts, but the conflicts are not pursued or analyzed. Develops a position by dismissing or ignoring one alternative and supporting the other with assertions and simple explanations rather than by making a deeper assessment of the situation.

Level 3: Emergent Complexity

Identifies more than one possible explanation or perspective. Establishes and preserves complexity. Introduces new elements. Supports position through comparisons and simple causal statements.

Level 4: Broad Interpretations

Uses broad ideas to help define and interpret the situation. Manipulates ideas within the perspective established. Has a clearly recognizable explanatory theme. Integrates ideas into "subassemblies," each supporting a component of the explanation.

Level 5: Integrated Analysis

Restructures or reconceptualizes the situation and approaches the problem from a new point of view. Constructs a network of cause and effect relationships. Integrates and extrapolates ideas. Arrives at new interpretations by analogy, application of principles, generalizations, and world knowledge. Constructs organizing framework, sketches connections, and predicts consequences.

(Slightly abridged from *Levels of Cognitive Complexity: An Approach to the Measurement of Thinking* by E. McDaniel and C. Lawrence, 1990, New York: Springer-Verlag. Copyright © 1990 by Springer-Verlag. Reprinted by permission.)

Discussion of Levels of Cognitive Complexity

Scoring is labor-intensive and in spite of the detailed scoring rationale, classification of a student's response is open to subjective judgements. An inter-rater reliability of .80 was obtained for 39 eleventh-grade students, a moderately high level of reliability.

There is a consistent pattern of moderately high correlations between *The Bomb Factories* and learning style tests that measure favorable attitudes toward thinking and problem solving. These correlations range from .33 at the eighth grade level to .41 at the college level and suggest that students who like thinking and problem solving receive higher ratings on *The Bomb Factories* exercise.

Of more importance were correlations ranging from .54 to .65 obtained with other exercises requiring students to construct interpretations of complex situations. These relatively high correlations suggest that *The Bomb Factories* measures cognitive processes that are brought into play when students are confronted with new, open-ended situations.

Why Is All of This Important?

The discussion of thinking skills in this chapter is important as a means of gaining an orientation to a field in which there are pressures for quick answers. There is a tendency to believe prepackaged programs can teach thinking skills, and the results can be assessed with readily available instruments.

We have suggested that neither of these assumptions is true. Teachers can best teach thinking processes within the context of the subject at hand and can measure thinking by the quality of student interpretations of complex events.

The levels of cognitive complexity framework will enable teachers to note how students perceive and define problems and how they organize and interpret information. The teacher can construct stimulus situations closely tied to the topics taught and can ask for written interpretations of these situations. Applying the scoring rationale will help detect tendencies to simplify situations, to describe rather than explain, and to think within very narrow limits. The scoring rationale will also help teachers identify tendencies to preserve complexity, seek causal explanations, and use broad concepts in arriving at interpretations.

Summary

Research evidence is rather clear that thinking is most likely to be developed within content areas rather than by stand-alone exercises purporting to teach thinking skills. How we think is affected by what we are thinking about, and there appears to be no substitute for expert knowledge in any given subject matter field. This point of view has implications for the way thinking processes are measured. Within a specific content area, term papers, projects, special reports, essays, interpretive exercises and laboratory performance provide excellent opportunities for assessing thinking processes.

We have described at length a special exercise scored for levels of cognitive complexity. Students are confronted with a situation that is open to a variety of interpretations. Responses are scored on a five-point continuum on which the low end is marked by tendencies to simplify the situation into right-wrong categories and describe rather than explain. Responses at the high end of the continuum tend to identify the complexity in the situation and build explanatory networks.

Teaching in ways that enhance cognitive growth as we have been defining it is completely consistent with the broadest goals of education. More complex cognitive structures are marked by less egocentric and less ethnocentric ways of viewing the world. Thus, one of the more general aims of education is the development of people who are able to view events of the world in all of their complexity without needing to simplify, distort, avoid issues, or think in stereotypical terms. Scoring student productions for levels of cognitive complexity provides a measure of thinking processes that is consistent with these educational goals. The procedure is also general enough to fit a variety of subject matter areas.

The measurement of thinking processes is an emerging field in educational measurement. New products purporting to measure thinking will be appearing in greater numbers. This discussion of alternative ways of conceptualizing thinking should furnish a useful perspective from which to judge new instruments and should provide a specific methodology that can be adapted to a variety of individual classrooms.

References

Dewey, J. (1916). *Democracy and education*. New York: Macmillan.

Ennis, R.H. (1985). A logical basis for measuring critical thinking skills. *Educational Leadership, 43*, 44–48.

Ennis, R.H. (1991, April). *Critical thinking: A streamlined conception*. Paper presented at the meeting of the American Educational Research Association, Chicago.

Ennis, R.H., Millman, J., & Tomko, T.N. (1985). *Cornell Critical Thinking Tests, Level X & Level Z Manual*. Pacific Grove, CA: Midwest Publications.

Galotti, K.M. (1989). Approaches to studying formal and everyday reasoning. *Psychological Bulletin, 105*(3), 331–351.

McDaniel, E., & Lawrence, C. (1990). *Levels of cognitive complexity: An approach to the measurement of thinking*. New York: Springer-Verlag.

Polson, P., & Jeffries, R. (1985). Instruction in general problem solving skills: An analysis of four programs. In J.W. Segal, S.F. Chipman & R. Glaser (eds.), *Thinking and learning skills (Vol. 1) Relating instruction to research*. Hillsdale, NJ: Erlbaum.

Peel, E.A. (1971). *The nature of adolescent judgment*. New York: Wiley-Interscience.

Perry, W.G. (1970). *Forms of intellectual and ethical development in the college years: A scheme*. New York: Holt, Rinehart & Winston.

The Bomb Factories (1988). An ABC News Close-up Special Report. ABC Distribution Company. Capital Cities/ABC Video Enterprises, 825 7th Avenue, New York, NY 10019–6001.

Schroder, H.M., Driver, M.J., & Streufert, S. (1967). *Human information processing: Individuals and groups functioning in complex social situations*. New York: Holt, Rinehart & Winston.

Watson, G., & Glaser, E.M. (1980). *The Watson-Glaser Critical Thinking Appraisal*. San Antonio, TX: The Psychological Corporation.

It is impossible to teach and counsel young people without thinking about their abilities, aptitudes, interests, and personal adjustment. Analysis of tests in these areas leads to deeper awareness of our uncertainty about the underlying constructs that the tests purport to measure. Binet struggled with the problems of measuring intelligence and provided us with a method that endures to this day, even though the nature of intelligence remains a topic of debate. Test development and theory about human behavior advance hand in hand. Need we comment that progress on both fronts is proceeding at a rapid rate?

part three

Measuring Human Behavior

I remember learning in Introductory Psychology that Alfred Binet had constructed the first
intelligence test sometime around 1900, but
Binet was just a name. What kind of man was
he and how did he go about deciding what to
put in his test?

chapter twelve

Binet and His Great Invention

Sometimes a single man takes a leading role in shaping our thinking about a particular phenomenon. Such a man was Alfred Binet. It is strange indeed that although Binet spent his life studying mental processes and wrote prodigiously about them, he is remembered not for his writings, but for a single contribution: the first intelligence test. It is also interesting that Binet did not create the test out of a well-developed theory of intelligence, and, as far as we know, he never defined intelligence. What he did do was assemble a wide assortment of mental tasks, which he slowly honed over the years by administering them to his daughters, to schoolchildren, and to adults. At some point he had a wonderful insight, perhaps spurred on by the French government's interest in identifying children who could not learn in a normal school situation. Binet and his colleague, Simon hit upon the idea of seeing which of these tasks could be performed by children of a given age who were making normal progress in school. Thus, he developed packages of tests that most six-year-olds could do, and similar packages of tests for other age groups. Using these packages of tests with a child of unknown capabilities, Binet could determine the child's "mental level" by seeing which packages of tests the child could accomplish. This was, and is, the fundamental rationale for the measurement of intelligence.

But let us not move so quickly over the interesting details of Binet's life and his groping attempts to bring a scientific approach to the study of mental processes.

The Early Scales

It was the year 1905 and Henry Ford was putting the finishing touches on a new four-wheeled contraption that would change the face of America. In France, another great invention was launched, which would change our thinking about human abilities—the intelligence test. Of course, no great invention takes place in a single year. Alfred Binet, the major author of the intelligence test, had been working on problems of measuring individual differences for at least fifteen years before the test was published.

Binet had a mind that was open, curious, searching. He seemed to enjoy lowering his lance and charging full gallop at investigators whom he perceived were working from misguided points of view, sterile methods, or unscientific approaches. He was a prodigious worker, counting 150 titles to his credit covering a broad range of topics in psychology. "One of my greatest pleasures," he told a friend, "is to have a piece of white paper to fill up. I work as naturally as a hen lays eggs" (Wolf, 1973, p. 34).

Binet and his daughters.
Courtesy of Theta Wolf,
Jupiter, FL.

Binet was the only child of a physician. As a young man, he successively earned a degree in law, entered medical school but withdrew, read psychology independently, and earned a doctorate in natural sciences with a dissertation entitled "A Contribution to the Study of the Subintestinal Nervous System of Insects." In the meantime, he spent a seven-year period working with Charcot on hypnotized patients at the Salpêtrière, the great hospital for the mentally ill in Paris.

In 1891, being without a university affiliation, he asked the Director of the Laboratory of Physiological Psychology at the Sorbonne in Paris to take him on as a member of the staff, a request that was easy for the director to grant since Binet was sufficiently well off to work without pay. Three years later, in 1894, Binet became the director.

Binet was interested in developing methods of measuring mental functioning. He had spent long hours finding out that bright children could not be distinguished from dull children on the basis of size of cranium, tactile discrimination, graphology, palmistry, phrenology, or the many other approaches in vogue during the time. He had done intensive studies of the thought processes of his two adolescent daughters. Further, he had accumulated a number of tasks involving memory, imagery, judgement, attention, comprehension, aesthetic appreciation, and motor skills, which he tried out with schoolchildren. Yet, by 1904, he had found no single mental faculty, with the possible exception of memory, that differentiated children judged by their teachers to be bright from those judged to be slow. Perhaps the search for a single test that would assess children's mental abilities was a fruitless quest.

In 1904, France established a commission to determine instructional procedures for mentally deficient children and called for screening so that special classes would not become the dumping grounds for problem children. Binet himself was a member of the commission. He and his colleague Simon went to work in earnest. They took to task the existing methods for evaluating and classifying mentally disabled children, noting that such methods were subjective, unreliable, and gave different results from one examining physician to another. They were not kind to their predecessors, who suggested that "imbeciles" could be detected by observing such symptoms as defective speech and limited language.

> . . . We are also ignorant of the value of the following symptoms which are noted in the definition of imbecility, "defective speech," "limited language." We admit that we have no idea what precise defect of articulation corresponds to "defective speech." There are people who stammer slightly, and others whose speech is scarcely intelligible. All have defective speech. The same remark is true for "limited language." Very many peasants have a limited language. What extent of vocabulary must one possess in order to have a "limited language?" (Binet & Simon, 1905/1916a, p. 23).

Binet and Simon declared that they would proceed in a scientific manner, and indeed, in their subsequent work on the intelligence test, they lived up to their definition of the scientific method: "prolonged meditation upon the facts gathered at first hand" (Binet & Simon, 1908/1916b, p. 182).

Simon had come to Binet from the Paris colony for mentally disabled children, where he had been serving an internship under a Dr. Blin. Blin was also working on ways to make a better diagnosis of mentally defective individuals. He and his student, Damaye, had developed a questionnaire and a set of tasks, including the ability to follow simple commands, indicate parts of one's own body, name objects, identify geographical features of France, copy designs, read, write, and calculate. Blin and his associate had combined the responses to their questions and activities into a single score. While they had no good data on which to decide how low a score should be in order to classify a person as mentally defective, at least they were combining a series of heterogeneous behaviors into a single index of performance. As Damaye put it in his thesis: ". . . The different faculties are thus no longer studied separately, in an experimental dissociation, we can even say dissection. . . ." Wolf (1973) identifies the Blin-Damaye approach as the "catalytic agent" that helped Binet shift his thinking from a search for individual mental faculties like memory, attention, and comprehension to the notion of combining a variety of tasks into a more global measure of performance.

Binet and Simon went to work in search of a collection of tasks and activities that would differentiate between the fast and the slow. For their tryouts, they supplemented judgements of teachers and principals by working with children who were placed in grades above their normal grade placement and children who were working in grades below the normal grade for their age. If the tasks did not discriminate between these two groups, the tasks were thrown out. Simon remembers:

> We moved along somewhat at random, always with the same preconceived idea of discovering how, intellectually speaking, one subject, appearing more developed, differed from another subject, older by one or more years, but no further advanced. We tried things that occurred to us, or reactions that one of our subjects had by chance revealed; or even some incident that the parents related to us, like the impossibility of their child's carrying out three requests that they had given him simultaneously. . . . (Wolf, 1973, p. 176).

Eventually, Binet and Simon had a collection of tasks that seemed to differentiate between more advanced and less advanced students of the same age. The Binet-Simon tests of 1905 consisted of thirty tasks administered orally in an individual interview. The tasks were arranged according to difficulty level and included such activities as finding and eating a square of chocolate wrapped in paper, pointing to objects represented in pictures, repeating a sentence of fifteen words, drawing a design from memory, placing five weights in order, telling how two common objects are alike, using three nouns in a sentence, and defining abstract terms. The order of difficulty was determined by trials with fifty normal children aged three to twelve and an unspecified number of mentally disabled children. The tests were offered as a way of obtaining an approximation of the level at which a child functioned.

The 1905 publication of the Binet-Simon Tests caused hardly a ripple in France and even the Commission seemed to have taken little note of it. In Brussels, it was recognized as a contribution and recommended for immediate use in screening schoolchildren for special training.

Like Ford's Model T, Binet's test was refined and improved. The 1908 edition had grown from thirty to fifty-seven items, each cluster of items grouped at a particular mental level, that is, the level at which most normal children of that age could pass the tests. The 1911 revision showed additional refinements. New items were added, some were eliminated, and others were moved to more appropriate age levels. The test was extended to include fifteen-year-olds and five tasks were added for adults.

While it is easy to fixate on the intelligence test as a set of items carefully selected to represent critical cognitive processes, Binet himself would be the first to point out the diversity in the nature of the items, which, when combined, provided a picture of mental development. "It matters very little what the tests are so long as they are numerous" (Binet & Simon, 1911/1916c, p. 329). Binet's large contribution was his perception that mental performance had to be calibrated against benchmarks of achievement of normal children at particular ages. His great invention was age-grading the tests, so that he could identify, for any given child, the mental level on which the child was functioning.

The final product of the Binet testing was establishment of a "mental level." If a twelve-year-old child could get no higher than the tests passed by ten-year-olds, then Binet would simply subtract the mental level from the actual age and point out that the mental level was two years below the accomplishments of normal children at that age. Binet never interpreted his measurements beyond this point. He never employed the term "mental age" or "intelligence quotient" in any of his writings. Yet, the organization of clusters of tests by age levels and the clear notion of describing performance by noting the mental level which the child could achieve, was firmly established in the 1908 revision of the scales. Writing in 1908, Binet summarized:

> Our principal conclusion is that we actually possess an instrument which allows us to measure the intellectual development of young children whose age is included between three and twelve. The method appears to us practical, convenient and rapid. If one wishes to know summarily whether a child has the intelligence of his age, or if he is advanced or retarded, it suffices to have him take the tests of his age; and the performance of these tests certainly does not require more than thirty minutes which should be interrupted by ten minutes rest if one thinks this necessary for the child (Binet & Simon, 1908/1916b, p. 261).

Henry Goddard, Director of the Vineland Training School in New Jersey, had been using the 1905 tests with children at the school. When Goddard read the article presenting the 1908 version with its clear delineation of performance as mental levels, he found it unbelievable:

> It seemed impossible to grade intelligence in that way. It was too easy, too simple. The article was laid aside for some weeks. One day while using the old tests, whose inadequacy was great, the new scale came to mind and I decided to give it a fair trial. . . .

> Our use of the scale was a surprise and a gratification. It met our needs. A classification of our children based on the scale agreed with the Institution experience (Goddard, 1916, p. 5).

It remained for the German psychologist, William Stern, to replace "mental levels" with the term "mental age" and to argue that it was more meaningful to divide the mental age by the chronological age than to subtract it, since a difference of two years meant a bigger proportion of mental ability at age six than, for example, at age twelve. Multiplying by 100 got rid of the decimal and the Intelligence Quotient (IQ) was born. Most people familiar with Binet's philosophy of measurement feel that, had he been alive, he would have opposed the notion of talking about an IQ as something that someone "has." He would have claimed that we had no more than a description of the level of intellectual performance that a child had achieved at a particular time. He would have argued, however, that the description was objective, based on observed behavior, and replicable from examiner to examiner.

The Stanford-Binet

In America, Binet's test was quickly translated into English and used at the Vineland Training School in New Jersey. But the real credit for widespread adoption and use in the United States goes to Lewis Terman.

Terman was born on a farm not far from Indianapolis, Indiana. A traveling salesman and self-styled phrenologist read the bumps on Terman's head, sold the family a book, and predicted great things for the boy. Indeed, Terman turned out to be a fast learner, grew up, got married, settled in an old farmhouse near the country high school where he taught, and started a family. Things seemed to be going well, when an attack of pleurisy took him to the country doctor. He was diagnosed as having tuberculosis.

Terman finished out the year at the high school and then resigned. On borrowed money he enrolled at Indiana University, studied psychology, and went on to get a Ph.D. at Clark University by administering a series of tests to a sample of "bright" and "stupid" boys.

With his dissertation completed, Terman, anxious about his health, pondered over a choice of jobs. Anticipating the benefit of the dry climate of southern California, he accepted the principalship of the high school in San Bernardino. The year was 1905. Binet had just released his test in France. Terman, arriving in California, was more concerned with his health than with intelligence tests.

> . . . Here, if anywhere, I should be able to rid my self of the threat that had been hanging over me. The people we met were so proud of their climate that I was constantly being told of this or that person who had come to San Bernardino twenty or thirty years ago as a 'one-lunger' and was soon restored to health. My new friends who told me these stories could not know what an eager listener I was! (Seagoe, 1975, p.31).

Five years later, Terman was a faculty member at Stanford University, working on a revision and standardization of the Binet scales. Terman added new items to the scales and worked tirelessly to place the Binet items at the appropriate age. If a test did not work well at one age level, he would modify it and try it at another. By the time he was done, Terman and his students had increased the 1911 Binet scale from fifty-four tasks to ninety and had extended the range of the tasks to include "superior adults." Terman had six tests at each age level above age six. This meant that each test was worth two months of mental age, thus simplifying the calculations of mental age. Terman also adopted Stern's idea of the "intelligence quotient." Finally, Terman standardized his revision on a sample of nearly one thousand American students. In 1916 Terman published the famous Stanford-Binet. Who knows . . . were it not for the warm, sunny climate of California, we might now be learning about the Indiana-Binet; but, then, that is all history.

The 1916 Stanford-Binet became instantly popular. Within a period of fifteen years, it was translated into approximately twenty languages and its use reached fifteen to twenty million annually. This is an impressive figure when one realizes that the test is a "one-on-one" interview using uniform materials and requiring about an hour to administer. The Stanford-Binet became the meter bar by which all other tests of general mental ability were measured. It was revised in 1937 and in 1960; renormed in 1972, and revised and renormed again in 1986.

In 1921 Terman initiated a longitudinal study of intellectually gifted children. Teachers were asked to identify the brightest children in their classes and these children were tested with the Stanford-Binet. The intention was to identify a large pool of children with IQ scores of 140 and above. Interestingly, Terman's workers learned to change their queries to "Send me the youngest child in your class." Ultimately, 1,528 students were selected for study, almost all of whom had IQ scores of 140 and above.

The initial analysis of the data did much to dispel the popular conception of the "genius" as an undersized wimp, peering at abstruse material through thick glasses, disinterested in games and sports, shunned by peers, and exercising a one-track mind fixed on a single narrow interest. The data revealed that this group of exceedingly bright youngsters in the top one percent of ability were, on the average, a little larger and healthier than children their age, had wide-ranging interests, possessed more knowledge of sports and games than their age mates, and were popular, even leaders, among their peers.

By 1936, the children were between twenty-nine and thirty years old, and again, the folklore about people with unusual mental ability was confronted with the facts. There was no pattern of early burnout, insanity, job failure, divorce, and other human calamities. In fact, the group appeared to be average or have more positive ratings in these areas than people in general. Students who had been accelerated in school showed good personality adjustment and went further educationally and vocationally than those who had not been accelerated.

A third follow-up was conducted in 1950 when the average age of the sample was forty-one years. Again, the ratings of personality and adjustment continued to be superior to that of the general population. Achievement was outstanding. Eighty-five percent had entered college and seventy percent of these had graduated. Of the graduates, more than sixty percent went on to graduate work.

Considering the traditional values of the time, maybe we should not be too surprised that most of the women in the sample became housewives. Those women who did enter the professions or the business world tended to be highly successful. Of the men, more than eighty-five percent went into the professions or semiprofessions or business.

The productivity of the 795 men in the sample can only be appreciated if one performs the mental experiment of going to the corner of Fifth and Main streets and stopping the first 800 men who pass by.

> Pardon me, sir. We are from the local university and we would like to take just a minute of your time to ask a few questions. First of all, are you the author of any books? Have you written any articles or papers that have been published? What about things for radio or television . . . or even the movies? Do you hold any patents for new inventions?

To make the comparison, go ahead and record your best guess of the productivity you might expect from your survey of approximately 800 men chosen at random from the street corner.

Scientific and technical papers	_____
Books and monographs	_____
Patents	_____
Other writings	_____

Terman and his co-worker, Melita Oden, summarized the productivity of the almost 800 men identified over thirty years earlier as having Stanford-Binet IQs of 140 or higher:

> Additional evidence of the productivity and versatility of the men is found in their publications and patents. Nearly 2000 scientific and technical papers and articles and some 60 books and monographs in the sciences, literature, arts, and humanities have been published. Patents granted amount to at least 230. Other writings include 33 novels, about 375 short stories, novelettes, and plays; 60 or more essays, critiques, and sketches; and 265 miscellaneous articles on a variety of subjects. The figures on publications do not include the hundreds of publications by journalists that classify as news stories, editorials, or newspaper columns, nor do they include the hundreds, if not thousands, of radio, television, or motion picture scripts. Neither does the list include the contributions of editors or members of editorial boards of scientific, professional, or literary magazines (Terman & Oden, 1959).

Looking Back

In the CBS documentary-commentary film *The IQ Myth,* Dan Rather parades the misuses and abuses of IQ testing, leaving the audience with the feeling that the resources of modern science should be mobilized to help stamp out the plague of IQ testing. Would we really be better off without IQ tests?

We can return to the pre-IQ days of yesteryear by looking through the *Journal of Educational Psychology,* which was first published in 1910. In the first issue, sandwiched between "Abstracts and Reviews" and

"Publications Received" is a little section on "Notes and News," the bulletin board printed to keep readers up to date on the comings and goings of their colleagues across the country. In this section we note that Capt. John L. Shepard of the United States Army is investigating the feasibility of adding one or more mental tests to the usual physical and medical examination of applicants for enlistment. The present mental examination requires only the ability to read and write and to tell right from left.

We also note that a professor Huey is changing jobs:

> Dr. E. B. Huey, professor of psychology in the University of Pittsburgh, who has been spending the past year in Paris in the clinical study of mental defectives, has been placed in charge of the newly established department of clinical psychology at the Lincoln State School and Colony, the state institution for the feeble-minded, Lincoln, Ill. (Notes and News, p. 57).

Two issues later we find an article by Mary Macy (1910) describing the growth in New York City of special classes for defective children and detailing the method of selection for such classes. In 1905 there had been only eighteen such classes, but now there were approximately 100 classes and an "inspector," Miss Elizabeth E. Farrell. A physician, Dr. Isabelle Thompson Smart, had been appointed to help in the examination and assignment of children to the classes:

> (In) September and February, application forms are forwarded to the principals of the schools (Form A.) on which they are requested to report, to the city superintendent's department, furnishing for each laggard, who in their opinion or that of their teachers is a candidate for the Ungraded Class, the data asked for in the form. Following, as soon as possible, the receipts of these applications the school or district is visited by Dr. Smart, the children, as reported, are examined and the results of each examination recorded on the medical examination blank (Form F.) in duplicate. If in the judgment of Dr. Smart and Miss Farrell, who also examines these candidates on pedagogical lines, a child is considered mentally deficient or eligible for the classes, he is assigned to the nearest Ungraded Class in the district, in which there is a vacancy, or is placed in a new class as quickly as one can be organized and a teacher obtained (Macy, 1910, pp. 135–138).

In the eighth issue, we find Dr. Huey's name appearing again, this time as author of an interesting article, "The Binet scale for measuring intelligence and retardation." In this article, Huey prints the 1908 revision of the Binet scale in its entirety. In his introductory remarks, Huey states:

> It seems to be generally conceded, and I think correctly, that we have in this scale the most practical and promising means yet made available for determining the fact and for measuring the amount of mental retardation. . . . In the Binet scale, norms have been determined for each age from three to thirteen inclusive, and the tests and apparatus have been so simplified that

the testing psychologist may carry everything needed in a very small hand case, and may test a pupil and make the necessary record in from twenty minutes to an hour and a half.

. . . The present article is written to call the attention of psychologists and educators to the fact that we have here an immediately available means of measuring retardation which can be of immediate and extensive use in the schools and institutions of America. . . . What I would urge especially is first that we have here the most usable ready-made scale, and second that we have, in it, the right 'idea' for the construction of a still better scale (Huey, 1910, pp. 435–436).

Yes, in 1910 it seemed that this fellow, Binet, had the "right idea."

Summary

In the story of Binet and his test, we get a glimpse of the almost atheoretical beginnings of the concept of intelligence. There was an amazing amount of trial and error as Binet sought to find measures that would differentiate normal children from those judged mentally disabled. Further, it seems fair to say that Binet was essentially on the wrong track as he tried to identify specific faculties in the sensory psychology of the time that would separate the mentally disabled from the normal. Yet, out of these efforts, Binet hit upon the idea of calibrating the tests on groups of normal children at a single age and of expressing performance in a single, communicative unit: the mental level. Only after his death was the mental level translated into mental age and the term IQ coined.

Terman, the Indiana farm boy who ended up with a professorship at Stanford, refined the Binet, standardized it on American children, and turned to a lifetime of work on the gifted. By the way, I neglected to mention who it was that urged the young Terman to take up his work with the Binet. It was none other than E. B. Huey (Linden & Linden, 1968).

We shall see in the next chapters that the individual intelligence test is still one of the major instruments in diagnostic work with children, but a debate rages about whether we have one global intelligence or many kinds of intelligence.

References

Binet, A., & Simon, T. (1916a). Upon the necessity of establishing a scientific diagnosis of inferior states of intelligence. In A. Binet & T. Simon, *The development of intelligence in children* (E. S. Kite, Trans.). Publications of the Training School at Vineland, New Jersey, Department of Research, No. 11. Baltimore: Williams & Wilkins (Reprinted from *L'Annee Psychologique,* 1905, 163–191). Reprint edition 1973 by Arno Press, New York.

Binet, A., & Simon, T. (1916b). The development of intelligence in the child. In A. Binet & T. Simon, *The development of intelligence in children* (E. S. Kite, Trans.). Publications of the Training School at Vineland, New Jersey, Department of Research, No. 11. Baltimore: Williams & Wilkins (Reprinted from *L'Annee Psychologique,* 1908, 1–90). Reprint edition 1973 by Arno Press, New York.

Binet, A., & Simon, T. (1916c). New investigations upon the measure of the intellectual level among school children. In A. Binet & T. Simon, *The development of intelligence in children* (E. S. Kite, Trans.). Publications of the Training School at Vineland, New Jersey, Department of Research, No. 11. Baltimore: Williams & Wilkins (Reprinted from *L'Annee Psychologique,,* 1911, 145–201). Reprint edition 1973 by Arno Press, New York.

Goddard, H.H. (1916). Editor's introduction. In A. Binet & T. Simon, *The development of intelligence in children* (E. S. Kite, Trans.). Publications of the Training School at Vineland, New Jersey, Department of Research, No. 11. Baltimore: Williams & Wilkins. Reprint edition 1973 by Arno Press, New York.

Huey, E.B. (1910). The Binet scale for measuring intelligence and retardation. *Journal of Educational Psychology, 1,* 435–444.

Linden, K.W., & Linden, J.D. (1968). *Modern mental measurement: A historical perspective.* Boston: Houghton Mifflin.

Macy, M.S. (1910) The subnormal child in New York city schools. *Journal of Educational Psychology, 1,* 132–144.

Notes and News. (1910). *Journal of Educational Psychology, 1,* 55–57.

Seagoe, M.V. (1975). *Terman and the gifted.* Los Altos, CA: William Kaufmann.

Terman, L.M., & Oden, M.H. (1959). *Genetic studies of genius, Vol. V. The gifted group at mid-life: Thirty-five years follow-up of the superior child.* Stanford: Stanford University Press.

Wolf, T.H. (1973). *Alfred Binet.* Chicago: The University of Chicago Press.

Note: In 1991, I interviewed Dr. Theta Wolf, age 87, about her research on the life and work of Binet. An edited 27-minute videotape, *Wolf on Binet,* is available from the Undergraduate Film Library, Stewart Center, Purdue University, West Lafayette, IN 47907.

I looked at the report from the school psychologist, but there was no IQ score there, only Standard Age Scores, whatever they are. The report said that Ruth Ann did not qualify for the learning disabled class, but that she had difficulty recalling sequential information presented orally, and that I might want to pay special attention to that. I thought Ruth Ann was going to get an intelligence test.

Sequential reasoning

Memory for sound patterns

Word fluency

Ideation fluency

Language comprehension

Perceptual speed

Speed of reasoning

Sound discrimination

Spatial relations

Associative fluency

Memory span

Imagery

Meaningful memory

Mental comparison speed

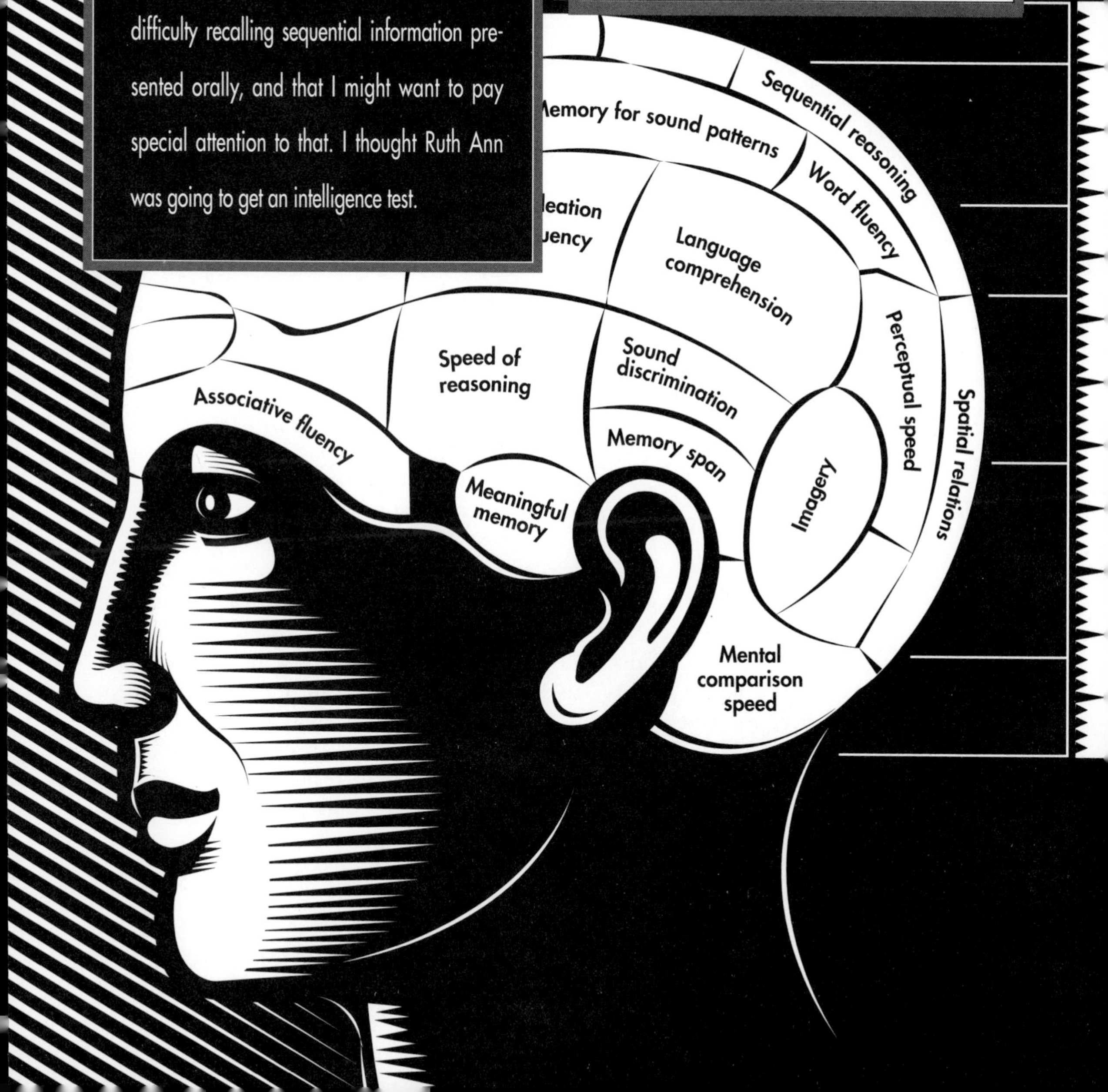

Intelligence. What is it? How is it measured? What use do teachers and other school personnel make of the scores? The last chapter gave us a view of the historical antecedents of intelligence tests. But each generation tends to redefine constructs to fit the needs of the time, and the times are changing. Intelligence, a concept welcomed in the twenties and thirties as a means of understanding and adapting education to individual differences, has come under attack by many professionals today. Most measurement texts have abandoned their chapter on intelligence and folded discussion of this topic into the more general discussion of academic aptitudes. Certainly, the notion of intelligence has carried with it unwanted connotations of a fixed and immutable capacity. Some say teachers give up on children labeled "low intelligence" and some point out that children from minority groups have been discriminated against by intelligence tests. As Locurto (1991) notes, debates over the nature of intelligence and the value of the intelligence test have been taken over by extremists, making it difficult to find a more rational middle ground.

On a more technical level, cognitive psychologists have turned their attention from consideration of innate abilities to the various cognitive processes that individuals use in acquiring information, solving problems, and adapting to life situations. Some psychologists claim that items on IQ tests have little relationship to real-life problems and that IQ tests encourage a simplified view of human abilities by suggesting that there is one overall general ability rather than many kinds of specific abilities.

Modern though these arguments may sound, they are in many ways a continuation of the debates that were launched by Charles Spearman's contention, back in 1904, that there is a general intellectual factor, a "g" factor underlying any specific mental test. Understanding the arguments for such a 'g' factor is the essential starting ground for thinking about intelligence.

In this chapter, we shall review the debate about single versus multiple mental abilities. We will then examine the two most widely used individual intelligence tests, the Stanford-Binet and the Wechsler Intelligence tests. We will see that both these instruments provide a measure of general ability, but in addition, these tests provide scores for more specific cognitive processes. These tests must be administered by trained psychologists. Even so, the teacher is the consumer of their efforts since it is the teacher who will read the report and make use of the test findings. Thus, it is important for teachers to have a clear idea of the nature of the tests and of the kinds of information that the tests provide.

Charles Spearman.
Courtesy of the Archives
of the History of
American Psychology,
University of Akron,
Akron, OH.

Charles Spearman and the Theory of Two Factors

Almost from the beginning of intelligence tests, there was controversy about the nature of human abilities and procedures for measuring them. Charles Spearman, a British psychologist, was the first to argue that within most measures of specific abilities is hidden a large g factor—a component of "general ability."

Charles Spearman was a big, rugged British army officer with an interest in philosophy and a passion for tennis. Spearman resigned his military commission in 1897 to study the new experimental psychology getting started in Germany under Wundt. Back in England, between periods of study, Spearman was following his own curiosities:

> One day, inspired by Galton's *Human Faculty,* I started experimenting with a little village school nearby. The aim was to find out whether, as Galton had indicated, the abilities commonly taken to be "intellectual" had any correlation either with each other or with sensory discrimination. The intellectual abilities I measured by the children's school marks in various subjects; the sensory discrimination by a musical "discord" of my own contrivance. The reply of the experiment was prompt and decisive; all the mental powers measured did obviously correlate with each other in considerable degree (Spearman, 1930, p. 322).

Observing that grades in different subjects are correlated with each other would not attract much attention—unless one had a philosophical frame of mind and unless one were wondering about the nature of human abilities. Folklore already offered one view of human abilities: "strong back but weak mind," "dumb but good looking." Nature was somehow fair. If you were deficient in one area, you had talents in another. You might not be very good in mathematics, but you were a good writer. But if human abilities were organized as separate, independent skills, there would not be any relationship between grades in one subject and grades in another. Spearman's data showed definite correlations. He reasoned that any measure of human ability would be made up of two factors, a g factor reflecting a common general ability that would appear to some degree on all tests, and an s factor that would capture the specific skill the test was designed to measure. If one had a whole battery of diverse tests, the total score would reflect the underlying g factor, i.e., general ability. Thus, g was indifferent to the tests used to measure it.

Spearman published his conception of general intelligence in 1904, one year before the Binet test came out. It seems ironic that Spearman had the theory, while Binet, working from totally different theoretical grounds, had the test.

Is all this irrelevant history? History, maybe, but hardly irrelevant. Contemporary critics of intelligence tests claim that there is no such thing as "general intelligence," but rather many separate abilities. This position has been most completely developed by Howard Gardner (1983) who postulates seven intelligences or ways of viewing the world: linguistic, logical-mathematical, spatial, musical, kinesthetic, interpersonal, and intrapersonal. While most of these intelligences can be readily understood by the titles, interpersonal and intrapersonal require further definition. Interpersonal involves understanding others; how they feel, what motivates them, and how they interact with one another. Intrapersonal intelligence centers on the individual's ability to be acquainted with himself or herself and to have developed a sense of identity. Gardner believes that highlighting these diverse abilities will help us focus on an individual's strengths rather than becoming overly concerned about a student's verbal and numerical abilities.

Arthur Jensen (1981) disagrees with Gardner and others who attack the concept of general ability. Jensen cites Spearman's classic work and points out that such diverse tests as vocabulary, number series, and block designs can be equally g-loaded, i.e., shown through factor analysis to be measuring something in common. **Factor analysis** is a family of mathematical procedures for establishing contributions that individual tests make to assessing a common underlying ability or trait. Jensen continues:

. . . if we arrange various tests, each composed of homogeneous item types, in the order of their g loadings, from highest to lowest, we notice that the g is related to the complexity of the cognitive activity demanded by the items. Test items are g-loaded to the degree that the mental activity they call forth involves seeing relationships between elements, grasping abstract concepts, reasoning, analysis, finding common features among superficially dissimilar things, inferring conclusions from given items of information. In the most general terms, the g factor shows up whenever a test item requires one to fill a gap, turn something over in one's mind, make comparisons, transform the input to arrive at the output. Spearman believed g was most clearly manifested in items calling for inductive and deductive reasoning and abstraction. He characterized g as inventive rather than reproductive.

Even more generally, g seems to be involved in items that require mental manipulation of images, symbols, words, numbers, or concepts. Tests that merely call for the recall or reproduction of previous learning or highly practical skills are poor measures of g. Tests depending on rote memory, for example, have relatively low g loadings.

Examples of tests with high g loadings:

Raven's Progressive Matrices (see figure 13.1), which call for perceiving key features and relationships among simple geometric figures and designs, and discovering the rules that govern the differences among the elements in the matrix.

Verbal similarities and differences. For example, in what ways are pairs of abstract words, such as triumph and victory, or defeat and vanquish, the same or different?

Verbal analogies. For example, "Cut is to sharp as burn is to (a) fire (b) flame (c) hot (d) hurt."

Series completion. For example, "1, 4, 2, 5, 3, ____, ____" and "81, 49, 64, 36, 49, 25, 36, ____, ____."

Paragraph comprehension. Drawing conclusions based on inferences that are logically implied but not explicit in the contents of the paragraph.

Figure analogies and figure classification. Seeing common elements, patterns, or systematic progressions in varieties of simple nonrepresentational figures consisting of lines, angles, circles, dots, etc.

Arithmetic reasoning. For example, "Bob is twice as old as his sister, who is now 7. How old will Bob be when his sister is 40?"

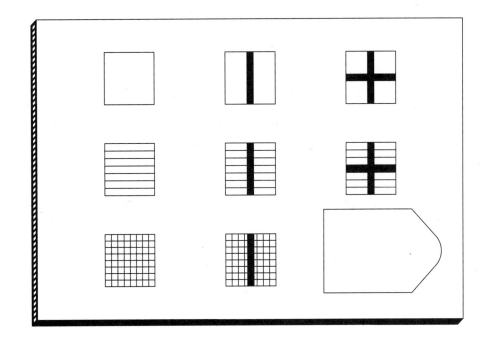

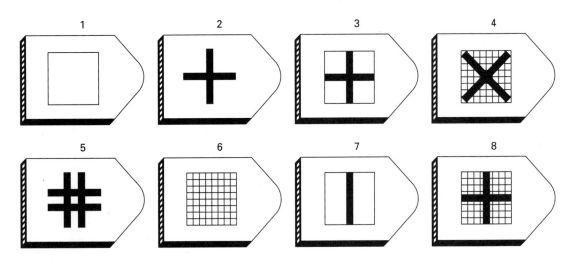

Figure 13.1 *Item excluded from the Raven Advanced* Progressive Matrices.
Reproduced by permission of the copyright owners, J. C. Rauen, Ltd.

When large numbers of psychological tests have been categorized into four groups strictly according to their g loadings, the groups of tests, from highest to lowest g loadings, can be characterized as involving primarily (1) relational, (2) associative, (3) perceptual, and (4) sensory motor processes.

Such evidence clearly contradicts the idea that what our best g-loaded IQ tests measure is merely some narrow ability that is only important in school.

(Abridged with the permission of the Free Press, a division of Macmillan, Inc., from *Straight Talk about Mental Tests* by Arthur R. Jensen. Copyright © 1981 by The Free Press.)

Becoming More Thoughtful About Intelligence Testing

These issues have direct relevance for the way we view tests of mental ability. If Spearman was right about g, tests that purport to measure independent abilities may be promising more than they can deliver. If Spearman was wrong about g, perhaps we should abandon attempts to measure general ability and concentrate on measures of specific mental abilities.

While the debates rage, teachers must still face the problems of student behavior and learning. In facing these problems, there is a need both for estimates of general intelligence and for information about specific cognitive functions. If the teacher has evidence that the mental abilities of a problem student are within the normal range, then further diagnostic study can be initiated to detect the reasons behind the behavior. On the other hand, if there is evidence that the child's ability is distinctly above or below average, the teacher can adjust educational expectations or instructional strategies. Additionally, teachers are called on to nominate children for special classes or for programs in gifted education. In all these cases an individual test of intelligence is of inestimable value.

Psychologists make an important distinction between individual intelligence tests and group intelligence tests. Individual tests, in the hands of a competent examiner, are among the best instruments available for the assessment of mental capability. Group intelligence tests, on the other hand, are more likely than individual tests to underestimate true ability because of language difficulties, poor reading skills, low motivation, and misunderstood instructions.

Even individual intelligence tests, however, can miss the mark. Intelligence test scores will not be valid for a child who has had little opportunity to learn the dominant culture because of linguistic, ethnic, or socioeconomic differences. Neither will the child be accurately measured if he or she is anxious, apprehensive, or defensive in the testing situation. Serious sensory defects may also contribute to scores that underestimate true ability.

In diagnostic practice, intelligence test scores are only one of many pieces of data to be integrated into a plan to help the student. Motivation, study habits, family support, personal adjustment, and other factors enter into a complete picture of the reasons behind academic performance. Full consideration of the total context helps prevent overinterpretation of the IQ scores.

Two giants, the Binet and the Wechsler series, dominate individual intelligence testing. Teachers benefit from a knowledge of each of these instruments because reports of evaluations by psychologists will almost always include a description of performance on one or the other of these instruments.

It is impossible to interpret intelligence test scores or decide on appropriate actions to follow up testing without coming to some belief about what the scores mean. We need to become better informed about the tasks that are used to generate IQ scores, and we need to become more thoughtful as we interpret test reports. As we shall see, the trend in reporting intelligence test results is to point out to the teacher the specific cognitive abilities in which the child may have strengths or weaknesses.

Crystallized and Fluid Intelligence

Before turning to the two major intelligence tests in use today, it is helpful to examine one other theory about the nature of intelligence. Raymond Cattell (Cattell, 1943; Horn & Cattell, 1966) proposed two types of intelligence, fluid intelligence and crystallized intelligence. **Fluid intelligence** is more like general problem solving and the ability to acquire new learnings. It is measured, for example, by tasks that require analysis of figures or of a series of numbers or letters. The Progressive Matrices is an excellent example of fluid intelligence. In this test, the student must analyze a matrix of designs and figure out the rules governing the systematic changes in the matrix (see figure 13.1).

Crystallized intelligence is more a product of what one has learned. Tests of crystallized intelligence tap the skills and knowledge that have been acquired through education and cultural assimilation. Good examples are measures of vocabulary and general information.

As we turn to the latest version of the well-known Stanford-Binet intelligence test, we will see that its contents reflect both fluid and crystallized intelligence and that the scoring and reporting procedures emphasize not just IQ, but also area scores designed to illuminate the information processing skills of the student.

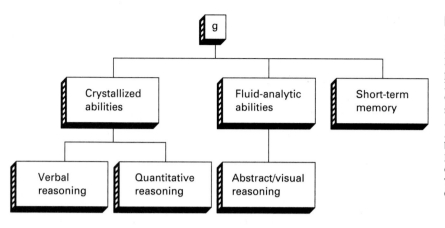

Figure 13.2 *Theoretical model of the Stanford-Binet, Fourth Edition.* Reprinted with the permisision of The Riverside Publishing Company, Chicago, IL, from the *Stanford-Binet Intelligence Scale: Fourth Edition, Technical Manual* by R. L. Thorndike, E. P. Hagen, and J. M. Sattler. Copyright © 1986 by The Riverside Publishing Company, Chicago, IL.

The Fourth Edition Stanford-Binet

The latest version of this classic test is the *Fourth Edition Stanford-Binet* (Hagen, Delaney, & Hopkins, 1987; Thorndike, Hagen, & Sattler, 1986a, 1986b). Much has changed in this revision. Whereas in earlier editions, each cluster of six tests was identified with an age level, the fifteen tests that now comprise the battery may be thought of as fifteen ladders that extend up through the age levels, with the child climbing each ladder as far as he or she can. The fifteen tests measure abilities in four broad areas: verbal reasoning, quantitative reasoning, abstract/visual reasoning, and short-term memory. As we can see from figure 13.2, the authors of the test see all these areas as contributing to g, the measure of general ability of the student. The verbal and quantitative tests measure crystallized abilities, the abstract/visual reasoning tests measure fluid abilities, and short-term memory stands alone.

The Fifteen Tests of the Stanford-Binet, Fourth Edition

The fifteen tests of the Stanford-Binet, Fourth Edition, are described below by showing how the child responds to items on each test.

Verbal Reasoning

> *Vocabulary*—defines a word.
> *Comprehension*—answers questions involving why, what, or where.
> *Absurdities*—identifies what is wrong or silly in a picture.
> *Verbal relations*—indicates how three words are related to each other without including an unrelated fourth word.

Quantitative Reasoning

Quantitative—answers arithmetic word problems.

Number series—determines what numbers would follow in a series of numbers.

Equation building—makes a correct equation given four or five numbers, an equal sign, and one or more operators, such as +, −, or ×.

Abstract/Visual Reasoning

Pattern analysis—uses blocks to recreate a pattern made by the examiner.

Copying—is given a one- or two-dimensional design and draws one like it.

Matrices—selects an image to fill a blank box in a matrix containing shapes, animate objects, or letters.

Paper folding and cutting—selects one of five options to show how a paper that has been folded and cut by the examiner will look when unfolded.

Short-Term Memory

Bead memory—places five objects on a vertical stick from memory after viewing for five seconds a picture of five variously colored objects on the stick.

Memory for sentences—repeats phrases and sentences from memory.

Memory for digits—repeats a series of three to nine digits read one second apart by the examiner.

Memory for objects—points to a series of objects (two to eight) on a picture containing five to thirteen objects to show the order in which examiner presented the pictures of the objects one second at a time.

A test profile sheet presents a picture of performance on each of the separate tests.

Standardization Procedure

More than 5,000 individuals aged two to twenty-three from various ethnic groups and geographical regions were tested to provide the norms for the tests. The test results from this sample were used to construct tables for converting raw scores to Standard Age Scores. The Standard Age Scores permit one to see how far any individual deviates from the mean of his or her age group and it can be readily converted to a percentile or to a deviation IQ. We will talk more about deviation IQs as we move to the Wechsler tests.

The Standard Age Scores for the fifteen tests have a mean of 50 and a standard deviation of 8. As we shift attention to the four broad area scores and the total composite score, the Standardized Age Scores change to a mean of 100 and a standard deviation of 16. This last set of means and standard deviations is identical with the older editions of the Stanford-Binet.

Reliability

Individual intelligence tests have tended to exhibit the highest reliability of any tests in the psychologist's kit of testing tools and the Fourth Revision is no exception. The Kuder-Richardson reliability coefficients for the composite score range from .95 to .99, depending on the age of the children tested. Test-retest reliability studies conducted on samples of about fifty-five children—one group of five-year-olds and another group of eight-year-olds—showed reliability coefficients of .90 to .91 with two to eight months elapsing between the test and the retest. The standard error for the composite score is 2.5. We remember that the standard error gives us the amount of variation (plus or minus 2.5) within which the true score is likely (68 percent of the time) to lie.

When we get to the four large area scores, the reliability drops somewhat, ranging from .80 to .97; and for any one of the fifteen tests making up the battery, the reliability figures are even lower.

Validity

The authors of the Fourth Edition of the Stanford-Binet place considerable emphasis on the construct validity of this revision and on statistical analysis to support their claims. Thus, the cognitive processes behind each of the fifteen tests making up the battery are defined, and item analysis techniques were used to be sure that the items of a test are all related to the total score of that test. High intercorrelations of tests within an area are used to support the contention that the tests do indeed define a larger cognitive process (verbal, spatial, quantitative, memory), and the factor loadings of all tests on a general factor support the notion that all tests represent, to some extent, part of a more global composite score.

Additional evidence for validity is offered through correlations between the Fourth Edition and other widely used and respected individual intelligence tests, including its immediate predecessor, Form L-M of the Stanford-Binet. The correlation between these two instruments is .81 for children making normal progress in school. Also, the Fourth Edition revealed significant differences among students in the standardization sample and known groups of gifted, learning disabled, and mentally retarded children.

In summary, the earlier editions of the Stanford-Binet provided an IQ score and nothing more. Now the test provides a Standard Age Score (SAS) for each of the fifteen tests, four cognitive areas, and the test composite. The following example shows how school psychologists make use of the composite score, the area scores, and the individual test scores in drawing a picture of a student's intellectual abilities.

Familiarity with the various tests of the Stanford-Binet Fourth Edition makes the psychological report understandable. For example, we do not have to guess what the "Verbal Reasoning SAS" is all about. We understand that this phrase describes the Standard Age Score for the area of Verbal Reasoning. Knowing that these SAS scores for the four broad areas have a mean of 100 and a standard deviation of 16 helps us understand why the psychologist considered the SAS score for Verbal Reasoning (95) and Abstract/Visual Reasoning (98) as falling within the normal range. We also understand why the psychologist expressed concern over the dramatic drop in scores for the next two broad cognitive areas, Quantitative Reasoning (73) and Short-Term Memory (73). Did you notice that the last two scores are more than one-and-a-half standard deviations below the mean?

It is also helpful to know which tests comprise the Short-Term Memory area score. We can glance back at the four tests defining Short-Term Memory and note the specific tasks on which Tim is far behind his age mates. We may want to pay particular attention to Tim's behavior

Statement of Referral and Background Information

Tim is five years and six months old. He was referred by his kindergarten teacher who was concerned over an apparent delay in the development of auditory and language skills. He is having difficulty learning the alphabet and identifying numerals. He has had individual help from his teacher and from an aide. He is in speech therapy and his speech teacher reports that such sentences as "the boy is jumping because it is fun" becomes "the boy jumping cause it fun." He wears glasses and hearing is noted as normal on his health record.

Test Results and Test Interpretations

1. Stanford-Binet Intelligence Scale: Fourth Edition

   Verbal Reasoning SAS = 95
   Abstract/Visual Reasoning SAS = 98
   Quantitative Reasoning SAS = 73
   Short-Term Memory SAS = 73
   Test Composite = 92

On the Stanford-Binet Intelligence Scale: Fourth Edition, Tim obtained a test composite score of 92, placing him overall within the average range of intellectual functioning and ranking him at the 31st percentile for children of his age. According to Sattler's factor scores, there was a significant discrepancy between Tim's verbal comprehension and nonverbal reasoning/visualization factor scores in favor of the latter. This suggests that Tim is significantly more successful with nonverbal, visual-perceptual types of tasks than with tasks requiring verbal knowledge and understanding acquired from experience and education. His verbal abilities were within the low average range, whereas his skills in nonverbal areas were average. Within the verbal comprehension factor, a relative strength was evidenced in Tim's ability to recognize absurdities and illogical situations in pictures. He demonstrated a relative weakness in his ability to recall sentences presented orally, reflecting his speech difficulties as well as deficient short-term auditory memory. Within the nonverbal reasoning/visualization factor, Tim's performance was relatively consistent, indicating evenly developed nonverbal problem-solving and reasoning skills, understanding of spatial relations, visual-motor coordination, and short-term visual memory.

Summary

Tim's current intellectual functioning is within the average range. Academically, although his performance is inconsistent, his overall basic skills appear to be significantly below expectancy when his ability level is taken into consideration. Tim's overall spoken language skills are measured to be below average for his age group. Relatively well developed visual-motor coordination and fine motor expression are noted. Projective testing suggests some feelings of insecurity. The Adaptive Behavior Rating Scale completed by his teacher indicates specific difficulties in the area of task-related behaviors.

Based on these test results, Tim qualifies for placement within the learning disabilities program. He has been referred for further diagnostic testing and observation to identify specific strengths and weaknesses.

I am indebted to Hee-sook Choi, School Psychologist, for the psychological report of Tim.

when class work requires keeping several objects in mind or remembering instructions to see if our observations are consistent with this aspect of the test report.

It is sometimes useful to view comments about a child's specific cognitive abilities based on test performance as hypotheses rather than prescriptions. Such comments provide promising leads to further observations and exercises with the child. The teacher, given his or her close contact with the child, is an essential participant in the long-term assessment of the child's capabilities.

The Wechsler Intelligence Tests

If the last generation thought of Alfred Binet when they heard intelligence testing, this generation thinks of David Wechsler. David Wechsler was born in Romania in 1896, a year when Binet was searching for correlations between physical measurements and mental functioning. At age six, Wechsler's family emigrated to New York City where David worked his way through the public schools, earned an undergraduate degree from the College of the City of New York, and a master's degree from Columbia, all by the time he was twenty-one. It was 1917 and Wechsler immediately entered the army, where he worked in the assessment of recruits.

Following military service, Wechsler's career moved through a series of psychology-related jobs and study to his appointment in 1932 as chief psychologist at Bellevue Psychiatric Hospital and a faculty appointment at New York University College of Medicine.

In his clinical work, Wechsler found that the Stanford-Binet was not well-suited to testing adults. Some of the items were inappropriate, and the procedure for calculating IQ made no provisions for the fact that the scores of older people declined on most of the Binet tasks. In addition, the Binet provided only a single global IQ score. Wechsler was impressed with the variety of abilities that seemed to make up adult performance in the real world and was concerned that the Binet did not provide a profile of these abilities.

Wechsler set about designing his own intelligence test for adults. The result was the 1939 Wechsler-Bellevue Scale. It differed from the Stanford-Binet of its day in three major ways:

1. Rather than relying almost exclusively on verbal material in testing adults, half the test involved performance tasks.
2. Rather than extrapolating into the adult years, it was normed on an adult sample.
3. Rather than being an *age scale* with tasks linked to specific age levels, it was a *point scale* with performance evaluated against the number of points earned by others of one's age group.

In addition to these changes, the Wechsler-Bellevue provided not one, but three, IQ scores: Verbal IQ, Performance IQ, and Full Scale IQ.

The Wechsler-Bellevue was later revised and its basic approach to testing intelligence was extended to school-age children and preschool children. Presently, the Wechsler series includes the *Wechsler Adult Intelligence Scale-Revised* (WAIS-R), the *Wechsler Intelligence Scale for Children-Revised* (WISC-R), the *Wechsler Intelligence Scale for Children-Third Edition* (WISC-III), and the *Wechsler Preschool and Primary Scale of Intelligence* (WPPSI). All share the same structure illustrated by the WISC-III published in 1991.

The Wechsler Intelligence Scale for Children-Third Edition (WISC-III)

The latest edition in this series is the *Wechsler Intelligence Scale for Children-Third Edition* (WISC-III) (Wechsler, 1991). The test provides a score for Verbal IQ, Performance IQ, and Full Scale IQ. In addition, four factor-based index scores are computed to show performance on four components of intellectual functioning. The new version offers new norms and a number of revised items that are more up to date and free from gender, ethnic, or regional bias. New colored artwork makes some of the tests more attractive and a new supplemental test, Symbol Search, has been added.

The thirteen tests comprising the WISC-III are described in table 13.1. The first five odd-numbered tests comprise the Performance Scale and the first five even-numbered tests comprise the Verbal Scale. The last

Table 13.1 *Descriptions of the WISC-III Subtests*

Subtest	Description
1. Picture Completion	A set of colorful pictures of common objects and scenes each of which is missing an important part which the child identifies.
2. Information	A series of orally presented questions that tap the child's knowledge about common events, objects, places, and people.
3. Coding	A series of simple shapes (Coding A) or numbers (Coding B), each paired with a simple symbol. The child draws the symbol in its corresponding shape (Coding A) or under its corresponding number (Coding B), according to a key. Coding A and B are included on a single perforated sheet in the Record Form.
4. Similarities	A series of orally presented pairs of words for which the child explains the similarity of the common objects or concepts they represent.
5. Picture Arrangement	A set of colorful pictures, presented in mixed-up order, which the child rearranges into a logical story sequence.
6. Arithmetic	A series of arithmetic problems which the child solves mentally and responds to orally.
7. Block Design	A set of modeled or printed two-dimensional geometric patterns which the child replicates using two-color cubes.
8. Vocabulary	A series of orally presented words which the child orally defines.
9. Object Assembly	A set of puzzles of common objects, each presented in a standardized configuration, which the child assembles to form a meaningful whole.
10. Comprehension	A series of orally presented questions that require the child's solving of everyday problems or understanding of social rules and concepts.
11. Symbol Search	A series of paired groups of symbols, each pair consisting of a target group and a search group. The child scans the two groups and indicates whether or not a target symbol appears in the search group. Both levels of the subtest are included in a single response booklet.
12. Digit Span	A series of orally presented number sequences which the child repeats verbatim for Digits Forward and in reverse order for Digits Backwards.
13. Mazes	A set of increasingly difficult mazes, printed in a response booklet, which the child solves with a pencil.

Table 13.2 *Scales Derived from Factor Analyses of the WISC-III Subtests*

Factor I Verbal Comprehension	Factor II Perceptual Organization	Factor III Freedom from Distractibility	Factor IV Processing Speed
Information Similarities Vocabulary Comprehension	Picture Completion Picture Arrangement Block Design Object Assembly	Arithmetic Digit Span	Coding Symbol Search

three tests are supplemental tests used in the event that an earlier test has been spoiled during administration, or administered in order to compute the four optional factor-based scores.

The four factor-based scales of the WISC-III are Verbal Comprehension, Perceptual Organization, Freedom from Distractibility, and Processing Speed. Factor analysis, you remember, is a mathematical procedure used to identify tests that cluster together, thus suggesting that they may be measuring a common underlying ability. Table 13.2 shows the tests entering into each of these index scores.

The first two factor scales, Verbal Comprehension and Perceptual Organization, are essentially the Verbal and Performance scales of the test battery and reflect the two major components of intelligence measured by the WISC-III.

The third factor-based score, Freedom from Distractibility, seems to involve numerical ability and attentional habits. This factor has often been identified with learning disabilities and investigators have noted that performance depends on sequential memory and short-term auditory memory. Wielkiewicz (1990), after reviewing the research, suggests this factor may reflect the ability to hold material in memory and use it in more complex cognitive operations. He concludes, however, that so little is known about what it actually measures that it should not be named; rather we should refer to it simply as the "third factor."

The fourth factor-based score, Processing Speed, as its name implies, is related to the speed of processing in visual search and matching tasks.

Standardization Procedure

The WISC-III was standardized on a national sample of 22,000 children selected to be representative of the population as described by data gathered in 1988 by the U.S. Bureau of the Census. There is almost an exact

Table 13.3 *Relation of IQ and Index Scores to Standard Deviations from the Mean and Percentile Rank Equivalents*

IQ/Index Score	Number of SDs from the Mean	Percentile Rank Equivalent[a]
145	+3	99.9
140	+2 2/3	99.6
135	+2 1/3	99
130	+2	98
125	+1 2/3	95
120	+1 1/3	91
115	+1	84
110	+2/3	75
105	+1/3	63
100	0 (Mean)	50
95	−1/3	37
90	−2/3	25
85	−1	16
80	−1 1/3	9
75	−1 2/3	5
70	−2	2
65	−2 1/3	1
60	−2 2/3	0.4
55	−3	0.1

[a] The percentile ranks are theoretical values for a normal distribution.

match between the normative sample and the U.S. population with regard to socioeconomic status, race/ethnicity, geographical region, and size of communities. Both public and private schools were included, and within schools, children in special programs were part of the sample. As a result, 7 percent of the sample were in learning disabled or similar special programs and 5 percent were in gifted and talented programs.

The data from the standardization program were grouped by eleven age levels (six to sixteen) and provide the basis for conversion of raw scores to scaled scores. These are standard scores with the mean and standard deviation of each age group set to the following values:

The thirteen subtests: mean = 10, standard deviation = 3.
The four index scales: mean = 100, standard deviation = 15.
The three IQ scales: mean = 100, standard deviation = 15.

The IQ scores obtained from the tables in the manual are deviation IQs. Table 13.3 illustrates the logic of the deviation IQ.

It can be seen in table 13.3 that when a student's performance is expressed in deviations from the mean the IQ can be read directly from a table. For example, a student scoring at the mean of the age group would have a zero deviation from the mean (middle column). This performance would translate to an IQ score of 100 (left column) and also indicate that he or she would have equaled or exceeded 50 percent of the students in the norm group (right column).

While the Full Scale IQ scores correlate .89 with the older edition, the scores for the older version were about five points higher than on the revised version.

Reliability

The reliability of the subtests, the factor-based scales, and the IQ scales were assessed for each age group using the split-half method corrected with the Spearman-Brown formula. The exceptions to this procedure were the two highly speeded tests, Coding and Symbol Search, which were evaluated using a test-retest method. The average reliability coefficients for the thirteen subtests ranged from a low of .69 for Object Assembly to highs of .87 for Vocabulary and Block Design.

The four factor-based scales had reliability coefficients of .94 for Verbal Comprehension, .90 for Perceptual Organization, .87 for Freedom from Distractibility, and .85 for Processing Speed.

The three IQ scales had reliabilities of .95 for Verbal, .91 for Performance, and .96 for the Full Scale.

The standard error of the three main IQ scales varies between 3 and 5 IQ points depending on the age of the child. The average standard errors for all ages (rounded) are Verbal IQ, 3.5; Performance IQ, 4.5; and Full Scale IQ, 3.2.

Test-retest stability was determined by a study of 353 children examined again twelve to sixty-three days after the initial test. A notable result of this testing showed that scores on the performance test improved on the average about thirteen IQ points as a consequence of having seen and worked with the items previously. The test-retest reliability coefficients over this period of time were Verbal IQ, .94; Performance IQ, .87; and Full Scale IQ, .94.

Validity

The validity of the WISC-III is supported by a number of studies done with the earlier edition, the WISC-R, showing correlations around .65 with reading tests and .58 with arithmetic tests.

Table 13.4 *Correlations of WISC-III with Other Measures of Ability and Achievement*

| WISC-III | Ability Test | | | Achievement Tests | | | School Grades | | |
	Verb	Num	Tot	Read	Math	Tot	Math	Read	Eng
Main Scales									
Verbal IQ	.69	.44	.64	.70	.63	.74	.35	.36	.44
Performance IQ	.59	.59	.65	.43	.58	.57	.35	.31	.39
Full Scale IQ	.73	.58	.73	.66	.68	.74	.41	.40	.48
Factor-Based Scales									
Verbal Comprehension	.65	.43	.61	.70	.56	.70	.32	.42	.35
Perceptual Organization	.51	.51	.56	.43	.56	.63	.32	.35	.28
Freedom from Distractibility	.60	.36	.55	.50	.63	.63	.29	.36	.32
Processing Speed	.47	.38	.48	.37	.50	.50	.32	.39	.35

Teachers will want to know how the scores on the WISC–III correlate with group measures of school ability and achievement. The manual reports a correlation of .73 between the Full Scale IQ and the Total School Ability Index of the *Otis-Lennon School Ability Test.* Sixty-five children aged six to sixteen years were included in this study and we must note that the extended age range will tend to produce an artificially high correlation coefficient.

Studies with widely used achievement tests for 358 children, but with the same extended age range, show average correlations with Full Scale IQ of .66 for reading and .68 for mathematics. School grades for 617 children, aged six to sixteen, correlated with the Full Scale IQ score .41 for mathematics, .40 for reading, and .48 for English. These findings, along with additional results, are shown in table 13.4.

The correlations presented in table 13.4 are consistent with other studies of intelligence and group measures of school ability and achievement. The WISC–III correlates most highly with a group test of school ability and with standardized achievement tests. Correlations with grades in specific subjects are substantially lower. Grades, of course, often reflect such nonachievement variables as effort, attitude, attendance, punctuality, neatness, and citizenship. More simply, the WISC–III is a good predictor of school achievement as measured by tests, but only a moderate predictor of school grades.

The data summarized in table 13.4 show the Full Scale IQ and the Verbal IQ to be somewhat more predictive of achievement than is the Performance IQ or the factor-based index scales. There is one additional

Table 13.5 *Qualitative Descriptions of WISC-III Full Scale IQ Scores*

| IQ | Classification | Percent Included | |
		Theoretical Normal Curve	Actual Sample
130 and above	Very Superior	2.2	2.1
120–129	Superior	6.7	8.3
110–119	High Average	16.1	16.1
90–109	Average	50.0	50.3
80–89	Low Average	16.1	14.8
70–79	Borderline	6.7	6.5
69 and below	Intellectually Deficient	2.2	1.9

observation we will store away for later consideration. The Freedom from Distractibility scale, the mysterious "third factor," shows a surprisingly high (.63) correlation with mathematics achievement tests.

Applications of the WISC-III

Scores on the WISC-III are widely used as an aid in diagnostic and placement decisions. In making these decisions, it is important to regard intelligence test scores as one among many indicators of the student's abilities. Matarazzo in his preface to the WISC-III manual, reminds us that intelligent behavior is rarely captured by a single test score. Such behavior reflects social and educational background and a complex interplay of drive, motivation, and personality orientation. The test score is one source of information, but it is also imperative "to gather the **essential** extra-test information and background history with which to compose a psychological portrait that is unique and personally and socially meaningful for each individual" (Wechsler, 1991, p. iv).

In view of the role the WISC-III often plays in making decisions about educational placements, we have reproduced three tables showing the distribution of WISC-III scores for the general sample (table 13.5), a gifted and a mildly mentally disabled sample (table 13.6), and a learning disabled sample (table 13.7). We can see, for example, that the average Full Scale IQ for the gifted sample is about 129. This may seem to be a

Table 13.6 *Means and Standard Deviations of WISC-III IQ and Index Scores for Children Identified as Gifted or as Mildly Mentally Disabled*

Scale	Gifted (N = 38)		Mildly Mentally Retarded (N = 43)	
	Mean	SD	Mean	SD
Verbal IQ	128.0	12.2	59.2	8.0
Performance IQ	124.6	14.1	59.2	8.8
Full Scale IQ	128.7	10.5	55.8	7.8
Verbal Comprehension	126.9	12.7	61.3	8.0
Perceptual Organization	125.8	12.0	59.4	9.2
Freedom from Distractibility	123.0	13.2	62.5	10.9
Processing Speed	110.2	17.9	70.2	11.1

Table 13.7 *Means and Standard Deviations of WISC-III IQ and Index Scores for Children with Learning Disabilities, Reading Disorders, or Attention-Deficit Hyperactivity Disorder*

Scale	Learning-Disabled (N = 65)		Reading-Disordered (N = 34)		Attention-Deficit Hyperactivity Disorder (N = 68)	
	Mean	SD	Mean	SD	Mean	SD
Verbal IQ	92.1	15.6	98.0	9.3	98.0	16.0
Performance IQ	97.2	16.7	101.9	10.2	101.3	15.0
Full Scale IQ	93.8	15.9	99.6	8.1	99.4	15.6
Verbal Comprehension	93.8	15.3	100.4	10.0	98.8	15.8
Perceptual Organization	100.5	16.3	104.7	10.3	105.0	16.3
Freedom from Distractibility	87.1	15.4	93.2	9.3	93.4	15.0
Processing Speed	89.1	15.2	95.4	13.2	92.0	14.8
ACID total	**85.7**	**16.4**	**92.7**	**9.5**	**90.6**	**14.7**

relatively modest performance for students identified as gifted. Yet, table 13.5 shows us that only 2 percent of the 22,000 students in the norm group exceeded this score.

Turning to average scores earned by students exhibiting various learning problems (table 13.7), we note that a special ACID score has been computed. ACID is an acronym for Arithmetic, Coding, Information, and Digit Span, a cluster of subtests that frequently shows depressed performance among learning disabled students. Examination of table 13.7 reveals that the learning disabled children and the attention-deficit/hyperactive children exhibit fairly pronounced differences between their Verbal Comprehension Index and their Perceptual Organization Index. The learning disabled group also shows depressed scores on the Freedom from Distraction and Processing Speed scales. The ACID score for the learning disabled group is a full standard deviation below normal performance. These data suggest that the factor-based indices and the ACID scores merit close attention when inspecting the cognitive functioning of youngsters having difficulty with schoolwork.

Special Class Placement and IQ Scores

We have reviewed two individual intelligence tests in some detail and suggested that these instruments will provide essential information for decisions about educational placement. There seems to be an implication in this discussion that special placement is a desirable remedy for learning problems. No such message is intended.

Shepard's (1989) discussion of the risks and benefits of special placement reveals a continuing debate within the inner circle of practitioners and scholars. Some claim that the assumption of benefit from special education classes is not warranted and point to inconclusive evidence that children in such classes do better than comparable children who are accommodated within regular classes. Others claim the one-to-one attention that a teacher gives a student in a special class coupled with adjusted educational objectives facilitate student growth. Almost all participants in the debate recognize the stigma of special labeling, the threat to self-esteem, and the changed perceptions of peers accompanying placement in a special class.

Shepard is clear about where she stands: "My opinion is that children should not have to be labeled handicapped to receive remedial help" (p. 567). She also notes that a teacher's referral "is essentially a statement that the child's behavior is beyond the limits of tolerance and that learning will not take place without special help" (p. 567). Shepard points out that the national trend in special education is toward noncategorical placement and the use of assessment to determine the instructional needs of the child.

This trend toward remedial help within the context of the regular class leads naturally to the next question: How much help can the teacher expect from the testing report in suggesting instructional approaches for a particular child? We have presented some data suggesting that learning disabled children rather consistently show depressed scores in some areas. We also cited researchers who feel so little is known about the actual cognitive processes involved that we should not even name some of the scales. One thing should be kept clearly in mind: The surface characteristics of a test may not be a good guide to the cognitive process at work. For example, a depressed arithmetic score on an intelligence test should not signal the teacher to immediately assign more drill and practice. The ability to retain verbally presented information and hold in mind relevant features of the problem may be the critical deficit.

The promises for specific guidance implied by the numerous subtest scores of individual intelligence tests may be viewed within the perspective of the continuing debate about whether intelligence tests measure a large g factor or a number of more specific s factors. The evidence continues to suggest that intelligence tests are most defensible as measures of global or general ability. There are substantial intercorrelations among the large components of the intelligence tests we have examined. Moderate correlations among the smaller subtests, in combination with their lower reliabilities, suggest that they offer only limited guidance in pinpointing specific cognitive deficits.

Information Processing Approaches to the Measurement of Intelligence

We opened our discussion of intelligence testing with a description of Spearman's concept of g, a general factor underlying ability, and s, specific abilities that, in addition, partly reflect g. Jensen (1981) argues that intelligence is largely a matter of g and this is exactly what is captured in most good intelligence tests. Gardner (1983), on the other hand, argues that there is not one intelligence, but at least eight, ranging from linguistic ability to the abilities of understanding one's self and of getting along with others.

Table 13.8 *Means, Standard Deviations, and Intercorrelations for the SBIV and Achievement Measures*

SBIV	WRAT-R			WJTA			
Area Scores	Reading (102/11)[a]	Spelling (98/11)	Arithmetic (99/12)	Reading (104/11)	Math (104/13)	Written Language (104/10)	Knowledge (105/13)
Verbal Reasoning (107/10)	.52**	.38*	.25	.50**	.37*	.37*	.65***
Abstract/Visual Reasoning (104/13)	.46**	.32*	.42**	.41*	.57***	.41*	.34*
Quantitative Reasoning (103/10)	.16	.09	−.12	.27	.27	.28	.12
Short-Term Memory (104/11)	.48**	.32*	.21	.52**	.43**	.36*	.64***

[a](M/SD)
*p<.05, **p <.01, ***p<.001.
Adapted from Rothlisberg (1990). Reproduced by permission of *Psychology in the Schools.*

You may have breathed a sigh of relief to find that the new editions of the Stanford-Binet and the Wechsler seem to have solved this theoretical dilemma. After all, they provide a single global score, which should satisfy Jensen, and four broad area scores plus as many as fifteen subscores. This is moving in the direction advocated by Gardner. If we want a single score of general ability, we have it. If we want an area score for quantitative ability, we have it too. Or do we?

Consider a study conducted by Rothlisberg (1990) relating the Fourth Edition Stanford-Binet area scores with achievement for 31 first- and second-grade children in a normal class. Table 13.8 shows the correlations among the four area scores of the Stanford-Binet Fourth Edition (SBIV) and achievement scores from the Wide Range Achievement Test-Revised (WRAT-R) and the Woodcock-Johnson Psychoeducational Test of Achievement (WJTA).

We can see from table 13.8 that verbal reasoning correlates highly with reading as measured by both achievement tests. This is exactly what we would expect. Abstract/visual reasoning is also related to achievement in all areas and we are not too surprised. The next row of data contains a shocker. Quantitative reasoning has essentially no relationship to arithmetic achievement as measured by either achievement test. We are also in for another surprise. Short-term memory has a significant relationship with arithmetic achievement for the Woodcock-Johnson and with reading scores. Wheras one study does not establish a relationship, let us neverthe-less speculate about the finding that a relatively simple mental capability, short-term memory, is more highly correlated with arithmetic achieve-ment than is the heavyweight subscore, quantitative reasoning. Do you re-member the similar finding we reported earlier when the mysterious "third factor" of the WISC-III showed a surprisingly high relationship with arithmetic achievement?

How is it that short-term memory is related to arithmetic, reading, written language, and even knowledge?

Our perplexity may stem from an unspoken expectation that behind any given achievement area lies a specific mental ability. We assume that high arithmetic scores must be driven by high arithmetic ability.

Alternative views of the nature of human abilities are offered by cog-nitive psychologists who view mental functioning as a series of informa-tion processing operations that occur as individuals perceive, interpret, or-ganize, and make sense of their environment. Information processing models abound in psychology and most models specify a short-term working memory plus executive functions that interpret and utilize the information in the short-term store to make decisions and orient action. Some theorists hold that the more effective the limited-capacity processor is in holding information, the more "raw material" there is to work on. If short-term memory is too limited, then information arriving in sequence might not be retained long enough to make useful connections. An arith-metic problem presented orally may contain more parts than the student can "keep in mind," or a complex sentence may contain more meanings than can be integrated into a more complex thought.

Just and Carpenter (1992) summarize much of the work on reading comprehension and support the view that working memory capacity is critical to higher order cognitive activity. Thus, we may have an explana-tion of how measures of short-term sequential memory, an apparently sim-ple function, could be importantly related to more general achievement.

John Carroll (1993) takes this approach even further. He views men-tal functioning as a series of hierarchical layers or stratums. A wide variety of elemental cognitive functions at stratum I support higher-order cogni-tive functions at stratum II with a factor of general intelligence or g at the top stratum. Carroll's three-stratum organization of cognitive abilities is presented in figure 13.3. No mistake should be made about the support for Carroll's proposed structure of cognitive abilities. Behind this model lies a monumental survey and reanalysis of some 467 sets of data from pre-vious factor analytic studies of cognitive abilities.

In figure 13.3, we see clearly the large g factor originally postulated by Spearman and we also see eight broad abilities at stratum II. In the figure, the nearness of each of these eight boxed abilities to the box marked General Intelligence indicates the closeness of the association between that ability and g.

Where is "mathematical ability" in this model? Carroll points out that, as tested, there will certainly be different mathematical abilities at the elementary and secondary levels. At the secondary level, his studies show that mathematical tasks involve a variety of abilities including general ability, fluid ability, crystallized ability, induction, sequential reasoning, quantitative reasoning, and visualization as well as specialized mathematical knowledge. " 'Mathematical ability,' therefore, must be regarded as an inexact, unanalyzed popular concept that has no scientific meaning unless it is referred to the structure of abilities that compose it. It can not be expected to constitute a higher-level ability" (Carroll, 1993, p. 627).

More generally, the reasoning we have traced illustrates newer concepts and models of intelligence suggested by information processing theory. Robert Sternberg (1991) of Yale University is developing a new test based on information processing conceptions of intelligence. His Triarchic Abilities Tests will measure mental processing in three content areas: verbal, quantitative, and figural. Within each of these areas, four abilities or mental processes will be assessed: general ability, coping with novelty, automatization, and practical applications.

By now it should be clear that the evaluation of testing instruments in the area of intelligence is inseparably linked to theoretical ideas about the nature of intelligence. Further, it should be evident that the construct intelligence is undergoing piercing scrutiny by cognitive scientists. We sense that the old debates that have surrounded intelligence are giving way to attempts to formulate more sophisticated models of mental activity and to develop tests that reflect these models.

Binet would enjoy this new activity and would be dusting off his aged manuscripts to show that he was struggling with the same issues 100 years ago. We might also imagine him eagerly addressing a pad of blank paper to scribble in his agitated hand a provocative argument that whatever test is used to probe intellectual abilities, we will inevitably find large individual differences in the developmental rates at which these abilities mature and function.

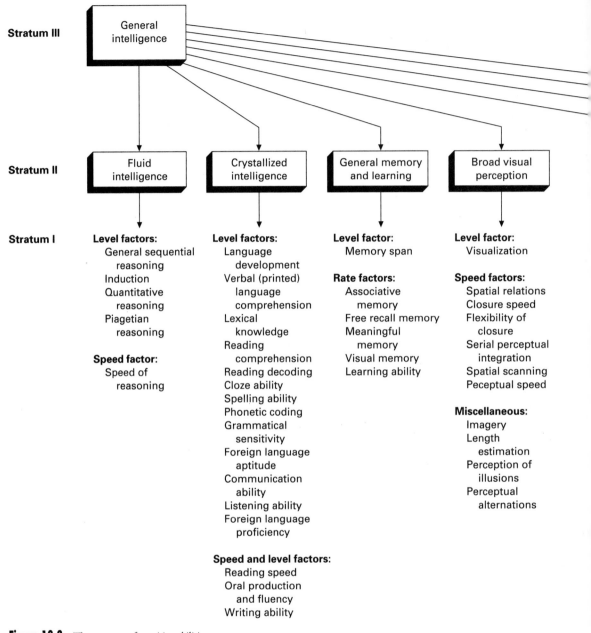

Figure 13.3 *The structure of cognitive abilities.*
Adapted with the permission of Cambridge University Press from *Human Cognitive Abilities* by John B. Carroll. Copyright © 1993 by Cambridge University Press.

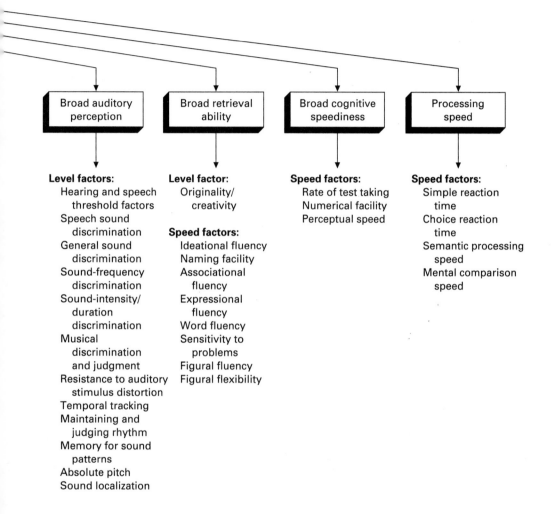

Broad auditory perception

Level factors:
Hearing and speech threshold factors
Speech sound discrimination
General sound discrimination
Sound-frequency discrimination
Sound-intensity/duration discrimination
Musical discrimination and judgment
Resistance to auditory stimulus distortion
Temporal tracking
Maintaining and judging rhythm
Memory for sound patterns
Absolute pitch
Sound localization

Broad retrieval ability

Level factor:
Originality/creativity

Speed factors:
Ideational fluency
Naming facility
Associational fluency
Expressional fluency
Word fluency
Sensitivity to problems
Figural fluency
Figural flexibility

Broad cognitive speediness

Speed factors:
Rate of test taking
Numerical facility
Perceptual speed

Processing speed

Speed factors:
Simple reaction time
Choice reaction time
Semantic processing speed
Mental comparison speed

Summary

The term intelligence seems to conjure up some mystical entity that determines a child's future from the moment it is born. No wonder there has been resistance to such a concept. We should recognize that this picture of intelligence exists more in the minds of the general public than in the minds of the professional psychologists who are continuing to refine their theories and tests.

We can maintain some orientation in this welter of information by returning to Binet's basic work. Remember that his test showed how a particular child was working compared to other children at various age levels. No matter what the actual age, if a child solved the problems like a typical six-year-old, then the child in question was working at a "mental level" equivalent to age six. There is nothing mysterious about this. Further studies have shown that children who tend to be substantially behind or advanced in their rate of cognitive development do not suddenly "bloom forth" or "burn out." These are empirically observed facts that are independent of theoretical concerns or social philosophy.

Certainly children can be mismeasured. Certainly the tests do not work well when the child's culture has not afforded opportunities to learn the processes contained in the test. Certainly there are cases where marked score changes are observed on a later test. These concerns must always be in the minds of those using intelligence test scores in making decisions about children. These concerns should not, however, be considered strong arguments against the underlying construct of general ability or that such ability eludes our attempts to measure it.

Jensen's (1981) description of the mental activities reflecting the g factor might be proposed as a working definition of intelligence: ". . . seeing relationships between elements, grasping abstract concepts, reasoning, analysis, finding common features among superficially dissimilar things, inferring conclusions from given items of information."

The strength of the Stanford-Binet and the Wechsler Intelligence tests has been their ability to provide an estimate of general ability based on relatively heterogeneous subtests. Wechsler led the trend in attempts to differentiate this single score into useful components: a verbal IQ and a performance IQ.

In the newest revisions of both these tests, we see this trend extended even further. In addition to a single score reflecting general cognitive ability, we see four area scores or factor-based scales representing verbal, quantitative, visual, and memory processes. We are also encouraged to interpret from ten to fifteen specific scores nested under these four large group scores. Since the ten to fifteen scores represent relatively short work samples, they suffer more from lower reliability than do the group or total scores. Since they also tend to be intercorrelated, their interpretation is clouded.

It is difficult to say whether the newest forms of these individual intelligence tests will prove to be more useful than the earlier editions. Reports from school psychologists will include descriptive comments about specific cognitive abilities and deficits. Teachers need to reflect on the work samples (subtests) that support these statements, and view them as valuable leads to further observation and study of the child. It should be evident that the individual intelligence test is likely to remain as a firmly established instrument for understanding the level of mental functioning of students.

At the same time, we have seen that new approaches to thinking about intelligence are emerging from work on human information processing. New tests and new programs of research based on information processing theory are likely to characterize the next steps in our continuing efforts to understand and measure cognitive abilities.

References

Carroll, J.B. (1993). *Human cognitive abilities*. Cambridge, England; New York: Cambridge University Press.

Cattell, R.B. (1943). The measurement of adult intelligence. *Psychological Bulletin, 40,* 153–193.

Gardner, H. (1983). *Frames of mind: The theory of multiple intelligences*. New York: Basic Books.

Hagen, E., Delaney, E., & Hopkins, T. (1987). *Stanford-Binet Intelligence Scale examiner's handbook: An expanded guide for fourth edition users*. Chicago: Riverside.

Horn, J.L., & Cattell, R.B. (1966). Refinement of the theory of fluid and crystallized general intelligences. *Journal of Educational Psychology, 57,* 253–270.

Jensen, A. R. (1981). *Straight talk about mental tests*. New York: Free Press.

Just, M.A., & Carpenter, P.A. (1992). A capacity theory of comprehension: Individual differences in working memory. *Psychological Review, 99,* 1, 122–149.

Locurto, C. (1991). *Sense and non-sense about IQ*. New York: Praeger.

Rothlisberg, B.A. (1990). The relationship of the Stanford-Binet: Fourth Edition to measurements of achievement: A concurrent validity study. *Psychology in the Schools, 27,* 2, 120–125.

Shepard, L.A. (1989). Identification of mild handicaps. In R.L. Linn (ed.), *Educational measurement*. New York: American Council on Education/Macmillan.

Spearman, C. (1930). Autobiography. In C. Murchison (ed.), *A history of psychology in autobiography,* Vol. 1 (pp. 299–334). Worcester, MA: Clark University Press.

Sternberg, R.J. (1991). Theory-based testing of intellectual abilities: Rationale for the Triarchic Abilities Test. In H. A. H. Rowe (ed.), *Intelligence: Reconceptualization and measurement*. Hillsdale, NJ: Erlbaum.

Thorndike, R.L., Hagen, E.P., & Sattler, J.M. (1986a). *The Stanford-Binet Intelligence Scale: Fourth Edition, Guide for administering and scoring*. Chicago: Riverside.

Thorndike, R.L., Hagen, E.P., & Sattler, J.M. (1986b). *The Stanford-Binet Intelligence Scale: Fourth Edition, Technical manual*. Chicago: Riverside.

Wechsler, D. (1991). *Wechsler Intelligence Scale for Children—Third Edition. Manual*. San Antonio, TX: The Psychological Corporation.

Wielkiewicz, R.M. (1990). Interpreting low scores on the WISC-R third factor: It's more than distractability. *Psychological Assessment, 2,* 1, 91–97.

I have always heard about students who are whizzes in math but can't write a complete sentence. But most of my kids who can do math can do about anything else. Are there such things as special aptitudes and can we identify them through tests?

chapter fourteen

Measuring Aptitudes

As we turn to the consideration of **aptitudes,** we must still be concerned with the question of how human abilities are organized. Do aptitude tests, as the name implies, sidestep the inclusion of g and provide pure measures of specific ability? We will continue to examine these questions as we turn to the study of aptitude tests. Two of the most commonly used tests of aptitudes will be examined in some detail. The *Differential Aptitude Tests* are widely used in high schools throughout the country. Do they actually help us decide whether a student will do better in an English course than in mathematics? The *General Aptitude Test Battery* is used by state employment offices throughout the nation. Do scores on the test actually assist employment counselors in predicting success as a computer programmer or a tool and die maker? We may be in for some surprises as we examine the nature and measurement of aptitudes.

The Nature of Human Abilities

There is ample evidence in music, art, literature, and science that some individuals seem to be endowed with special gifts and talents, which are recognized at an early age. Ball (1956) describes the feats of George Bidder, one of the well-documented calculating prodigies. Bidder was born in 1806 in England. At age seven he astonished two villagers who were arguing over the price of something being sold by the pound, by announcing that they were both wrong. Finding that his son had unusual abilities in calculating, his father took him on the road where he could charge for his son's exhibitions of mental arithmetic.

If you have pencil and paper handy, you may want to try some of the problems that Bidder solved during these performances. Ball tells us that Bidder did it all in his head, was less than 10 years old, and got the answer in less than a minute.

If the moon be distant from the earth 123,256 miles, and sound travels at the rate of 4 miles a minute, how long would it be before the inhabitants of the moon could hear of the Battle of Waterloo?

Answer: 21 days, 9 hours, and 34 minutes.

How many hogsheads of cider can be made from a million apples, if 30 apples make one quart?

Answer: 132 hogsheads, 17 gallons, 1 quart, and 10 apples left over.

If a coach wheel is 5 feet 10 inches in circumference, how many times will it revolve in running 8,000,000,000 miles?

Answer: 743,114,285,704 times and 20 inches remaining.

Bidder had a remarkable memory. At one performance, a number was read to him backward that he at once repeated in its normal form. An hour later, he was asked if he remembered it. He gave the number correctly: 2,563,721,987,653,461,598,746,231,905,607,541,128,975,231.

Bidder did not visualize numbers, but relied on auditory memory. In fact, if the figures were written on paper, it took him much longer to do the required calculations. In contrast, Bidder's eldest son, also an able mental calculator, reported: "If I perform a sum mentally it always proceeds in a visible form in my mind; indeed I can conceive no other way possible of doing mental arithmetic" (Ball, 1956, pp. 475–476).

Bidder, unlike many other calculating prodigies, graduated from the University of Edinburgh, receiving help from some of the faculty who had persuaded his father to let him enroll at the university. Bidder ultimately went on to a distinguished career in civil engineering.

As suggested earlier, most calculating prodigies either fizzle out or retain remarkable ability in one area while exhibiting an unbelievable incompetency in other areas. Treffert (1989) documents the story of Leslie Lemke, a blind, retarded, cerebral palsied child. As an adult, Leslie gives piano concerts around the world. He recently completed a concert tour that included twenty-six cities in Japan. Even so, a complete neuropsychological examination performed in 1986 revealed mental functioning in the moderately mentally disabled range in most areas and a complete absence of abstract ability. A CAT scan examination revealed brain damage in the left frontal area and in various regions of the left hemisphere.

Does the study of **idiot savants** teach us anything about aptitudes that lie more within the normal range? Treffert believes that the savant syndrome can be explained by three factors: (1) unique brain function and circuitry, (2) acquired and sometimes inherited abilities, and (3) motivation and reinforcement. The fact that unusual memory, math ability, and music ability are so frequently seen suggests that savants are marked by left brain damage and compensatory right brain dominance. In addition, there may be a genetic endowment that exists independently of general intelligence, i.e., music running in the family. Finally, the child receives rewards and reinforcements from showing off the special ability and, indeed, the sustained encouragement of parents plays a significant role in the continued development of the talent.

Benjamin Bloom, who gave us the Taxonomy of Educational Objectives, also has turned his attention to the development of unusual talent (Bloom, 1985). Examining the bibliographies of young people who excelled in such diverse areas as mathematics, music, and swimming,

Bloom found an interesting combination of innate ability and family encouragement among the high achievers. It was common for parents to recognize early that their child had unusual ability and go to great lengths to find appropriate teachers and coaches who could take their children into the realms of excellence.

These accounts indicate that individuals may show an early proclivity for a special field, which is developed through sustained encouragement and effort. Each of us might be advised to discover our aptitudes early in life and set to work developing them. But things may not be quite that simple. It is interesting to note that some psychologists, quite early, were questioning the entire notion of such special abilities. Take memory, for example. In 1816, Herbart wrote:

> Strength of memory is usually limited in every man to particular kinds of objects. . . . He who easily remembers the technical expressions of a Science that interests him has often a bad memory for the novelties of town (cited in Spearman & Jones, 1950).

Thus, there may not be a special ability called memory, only a set of interests that lead to remembering information of particular relevance or importance. Spearman advanced this line of reasoning through his empirical studies. His factor analyses of batteries containing many types of tests revealed that tasks involving arithmetic reasoning had high g loadings. As arithmetic tasks became more concrete, involving simple manipulation of numbers in known ways, the loadings on g dropped away quite rapidly. Spearman took this view to the limit: "Contrary to popular belief, even that of most mathematical teachers, there is *no general mathematical ability.* On eliminating g, the arithmetical and the geometrical processes have been found to have zero correlation" (Spearman, 1936, p. 253).

Aptitude Tests

As we shift from discussions of general ability to aptitude, there is a temptation to leave theory behind and move on. In fact, the problem of how human abilities are organized remains very much with us. When measuring intelligence, we seemed to be in danger of leaving out important specific abilities. Now that we turn to the measurement of specific abilities, we may be in danger of capturing too much g in the tests. We will be examining two widely used aptitude tests. We will be interested in what abilities are included in these batteries and in what light the validity data for these tests shed on the continuing debate over s and g.

The Differential Aptitude Tests

The Differential Aptitude Tests (DAT) were first published more than forty years ago as a tool for high school counselors helping young people make career decisions. The battery has undergone subsequent revisions and is now available at two levels: Level 1 for grades seven to nine and Level 2 for grades ten to twelve. The *Differential Aptitude Tests, Fifth Edition, Technical Manual* (1992) presents voluminous reliability and validity information. Norms were established on a representative sample of more than 100,000 students across the nation.

The DAT yields eight scores:

Verbal Reasoning (VR)
Numerical Reasoning (NR)
Abstract Reasoning (AR)
Perceptual Speed and Accuracy (PSA)
Mechanical Reasoning (MR)
Space Relations (SR)
Spelling (SP)
Language Usage (LU)

A Scholastic Aptitude Score can be generated by combining the verbal and numerical reasoning scores (VR + NR). This score provides a good index of general scholastic ability and norms are provided for this index.

The makeup of the Differential Aptitude Tests can be observed from the sample items of each test presented in figure 14.1.

After examining these sample items, do you have a good idea of the abilities measured by each of the eight scores? Suppose a high school student who has just taken this test battery comes to you for help in deciding whether to take an elective in English or in math. What scores will you examine in order to help the student make a decision? Take a minute to decide which test scores on the battery will be most relevant in making a choice between English and mathematics as an elective course.

Are your choices based on the assumption that verbal and numerical abilities are relatively independent of each other, i.e., that the student may be high in one and low in the other? Do we have any evidence that the DAT measures separate, independent abilities?

As a matter of fact, the DAT Technical Manual does provide information that helps answer that question. Table 14.1 shows the intercorrelations among the various tests in the battery.

Verbal reasoning* (25 min.)

Measures the ability to see relationships among words; may be useful in predicting success in business, law, education, journalism, and sciences.

Sample Item

Which answer contains the missing words to complete this sentence?

. . . . . is to fin as bird is to . . . . .

    A water—feather
    B shark—nest
★ C fish—wing
    D flipper—fly
    E fish—sky

Numerical reasoning* (30 min.)

Measures the ability to perform mathematical reasoning tasks; important in jobs such as bookkeeping, lab work, carpentry, and toolmaking.

Sample Item

Which number should replace R in this correct addition example?

```
  7R        ★ A 9
+ R           B 6
 ──           C 4
 88           D 3
              E None of these
```

Abstract reasoning (20 min.)

A nonverbal measure of the ability to reason using geometric shapes or designs; important in fields such as computer programming, drafting, and vehicle repair.

Sample Item

Choose the Answer Figure that should be the next figure (or fifth one) in the series.

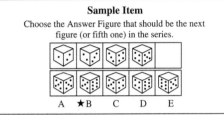

A ★B C D E

Perceptual speed and accuracy (6 min.)

Measuring the ability to compare and mark written lists quickly and accurately; helps predict success in performing routine clerical tasks.

Sample Item

Look at the underlined combination of letters or numbers and find the same one on the answer sheet. Then fill in the circle under it.

```
1 XY Xy XX YX Yy      XY Yy YX XX Xy      nn mn nv nm mm
2 6g 6G G6 Gg g6      ○ ○ ● ○ ○          ○ ○ ○ ● ○
3 nm mn mm nn nv
4 Db BD Bd Bb BB      g6 Gg 6g G6 6G      BD BB Bd Db Bb
                      ○ ○ ○ ○ ●          ● ○ ○ ○ ○
```

* Also available in the DAT <u>Partial Battery</u>

Figure 14.1 (Continued on facing page) *Typical items from differential aptitude tests, Fifth Edition.* Copyright © 1990, by The Psychological Corporation. Reproduced by permission. All rights reserved.

Based on the information in this table, would you expect to find many students with high numerical but low verbal scores? Check the first entry in the table where the first row (Verbal Reasoning) crosses the column labeled Variable 2 (Numerical Reasoning). Do you see the tabled value of .73? This is a rather high correlation coefficient. Notice that with the exception of Perceptual Speed and Accuracy, the Verbal Reasoning score is substantially correlated with all other tests on the aptitude battery. Is your confidence that the battery measures different aptitudes growing or diminishing?

Mechanical reasoning (25 min.)

Understanding basic mechanical principles of machinery, tools, and motion is important for occupations such as carpentry, mechanics, engineering, and machine operation.

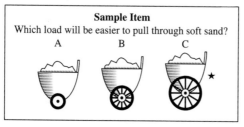

Sample Item

Which load will be easier to pull through soft sand?

A   B   C

Space relations (25 min.)

Measures the ability to visualize a three-dimensional object from a two-dimensional pattern, and to visualize how this object would look if rotated in space; important in drafting, architecture, design, carpentry, and dentistry.

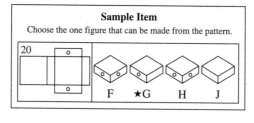

Sample Item

Choose the one figure that can be made from the pattern.

20

F   ★G   H   J

Spelling (10 min.)

Measures one's ability to spell common English words; a useful skill in many academic and vocational pursuits.

Sample Item

Decide which word is not spelled correctly in the group below.

  ★ A paragraf
     B dramatic
     C circular
     D audience

Language usage (15 min.)

Measures the ability to detect errors in grammar, punctuation, and capitalization; needed in most jobs requiring a college degree.

Sample Item

Decide which of the four parts of the sentence below contains an error. If there is no error, mark the space on your answer sheet for the letter next to No Error.

Jane and Tom / is going / to the office / this morning.
   A   ★B   C   D
E No Error

Table 14.1 *Intercorrelations Among the* Differential Aptitude Tests *for the Level 2 Grade 11 Sample, Spring Standardization Program. Male and Female Combined (N = 2790).*

Test/Total	Variable	Form C 2	3	4	5	6	7	8	9
Verbal Reasoning (VR)	1	.73	.66	.21	.48	.60	.60	.70	.93
Numerical Reasoning (NR)	2		.67	.28	.43	.58	.60	.66	.93
Abstract Reasoning	3			.23	.60	.71	.38	.51	.71
Perceptual Speed & Accuracy	4				.12	.18	.23	.26	.27
Mechanical Reasoning	5					.59	.16	.31	.49
Space Relations	6						.32	.45	.63
Spelling	7							.72	.64
Language Usage	8								.73
Scholastic Aptitude (VR + NR)	9								

Even if it seems improbable that you will find a student with big differences in scores on the various tests, maybe you can capitalize on the differences you do observe. The student is still hoping for help in selecting an elective. It seems logical that Verbal Reasoning will be the best predictor of grades in English and Numerical Reasoning the best predictor of grades in mathematics.

Again, the Technical Manual provides data that are helpful in checking the accuracy of this expectation. Figure 14.2 summarizes the results of hundreds of studies of the relationships among the DAT and grades earned in various subjects. The Psychological Corporation summarized studies conducted with both male and female students, but to simplify the display and make comparisons across subjects easier, figure 14.2 presents only the findings for male students.

As you look at the patterns in figure 14.2, are your expectations confirmed? Do most studies show Verbal Reasoning (VR) as the best predictor of grades in English and literature? Is Numerical Ability (NA) the best predictor of grades in mathematics?

You can observe that fifteen studies relating Verbal Reasoning to English grades showed correlations of .50 to .59. Twenty of the studies relating Numerical Ability to English grades showed correlations of .50 to .59. It seems that we can use either test equally to help the student make a decision. Adding the two tests together (VR + NA) does an even better job.

Observing the relationships between grades in mathematics and DAT scores, we do find that the Numerical Ability Test lives up to our expectations. This is satisfying. We also note that numerical ability does a surprisingly good job of predicting grades in social studies and history. This is puzzling. What does numerical ability have to do with history?

This exercise tends to confirm Spearman's contention that many tests of special ability are highly saturated with g. The exercise might also serve as a continuing warning about counseling from test labels without first consulting validity data.

The examples we have presented support Anastasi's (1988) conclusions regarding the role of multiple aptitude batteries in school testing programs:

> A common feature . . . is their disappointing performance with regard to *differential validity*. . . . In a counseling situation, the profile of test scores is utilized to aid the student in choosing among several possible fields. . . . In terms of available data, however, multifactor batteries have fallen short of their initial promise (p. 395).

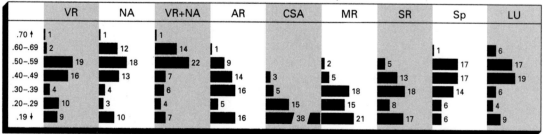

Figure 14.2 *Graphic summary of validity coefficients for the DAT for course grades.* Adapted from the Differential Aptitude Tests, Fifth Edition, Techical Manual. Copyright © 1990 by The Psychological Corporation. Reproduced by permission. All rights reserved.

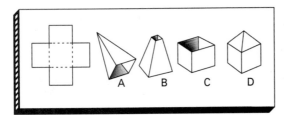

Figure 14.3 *Sample item of spatial aptitude.*

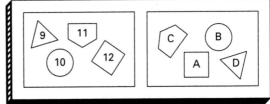

Figure 14.4 *Sample item of form perception.*

Anastasi goes on to point out that traditional tests of general intelligence, employing essentially the same skills as those assessed by VR + NA, have about the same validity for predicting a variety of educational achievements. These general tests are more cost efficient than the multiple aptitude batteries and may be sufficient for most educational planning.

A recent development is the availability of a computer administered version of the Differential Aptitude Tests. Since the computer version can detect when the student is working at problems that are too easy and can move at once to a more appropriate level of difficulty, working time is cut in half. In addition, instantaneous scoring and profiles are ready at the conclusion of the test. These new developments make the Differential Aptitude Tests more available to students embarking on a course of self-discovery. The same cautions against overinterpreting the score profile still hold, however, and we encourage counselors to remember the high intercorrelations among the separate tests and the power of the VR + NA score in predicting achievement in almost any school subject.

The General Aptitude Test Battery (GATB)

A second widely used multiple aptitude test battery is the General Aptitude Test Battery (GATB) developed by the United States Employment Service. This battery is used by all state employment offices as a tool in placing applicants for jobs. The test is much like the DAT with two important differences. First, the GATB has a series of three performance tests added to the usual verbal, numerical, and perceptual tasks. Second, the GATB has more strict time limits, making speed of work more important than in the DAT.

The GATB yields nine scores:

G. *General Learning Ability*: obtained by adding scores on Vocabulary, Arithmetic Reasoning, and Three Dimensional Space.

V. *Verbal Aptitude*: vocabulary test requiring recognition of words with same and opposite meanings.

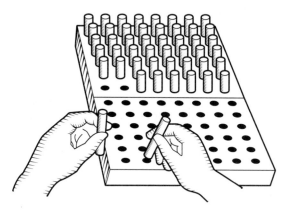

Figure 14.5 *Manual dexterity test of the GATB.*
Source: Doing Your Best on Aptitude Tests, U.S. Department of Labor.

N. *Numerical Aptitude*: computation and arithmetic reasoning.

S. *Spatial Aptitude*: ability to recognize forms from two dimensional drawings and to visualize effects of movement in three dimensions (see figure 14.3).

P. *Form Perception*: measured by two tests, one matching pictures of tools, the other matching forms (see figure 14.4).

Q. *Clerical Perception*: rapid matching of names.

K. *Motor Coordination*: rapid placement of three pencil marks in a page of small squares.

F. *Finger Dexterity*: rapid assembly and disassembly of rivets and washers.

M. *Manual Dexterity*: rapid transfer of pegs from one to another section of peg board. Part two requires that the pegs be turned end to end and then placed (see figure 14.5).

The most outstanding feature of the GATB is the extensive work that has been done relating aptitude scores to job placement and job performance. Thus, minimum cutoff scores on two to four of the most relevant GATB tests have been established for thousands of occupations.

The U.S. Department of Labor makes the GATB available to schools, hospitals, prisons, and colleges and stresses that it is part of a co-ordinated career counseling system to be used in connection with a measure of interest, the *Dictionary of Occupational Titles,* and the *Guide for Occupational Exploration,* all published by the Department of Labor.

Most of the subtests of the GATB exhibit the high intercorrelations that we observed in the DAT, an undesirable characteristic in a test designed to measure separate abilities. Anastasi (1988) reports that the GATB has been recently factor analyzed on more than 23,000 subjects, yielding three broad factors:

Cognitive—General Intelligence, Verbal Aptitude, Numerical Aptitude.
Perceptual—Spatial Aptitude, Form Perception, Clerical Perception.
Psychomotor—Motor Coordination, Finger Dexterity, Manual Dexterity.

In related studies, it was found that the broad cognitive factor yielded high validity coefficients with most jobs. The perceptual and motor factors added to the validity as the jobs became less complex.

Armed Services Vocational Aptitude Battery (ASVAB)

The Department of Defense, for the past twenty years, has made available to high schools a testing service designed to help students make career choices and to allow armed forces recruiters to talk with students who may be interested in a military career. The Department of Defense administers, scores, and reports the test results to the students without cost to the schools. More than 1.3 million students take this test each year.

The three-hour test battery yields seven scores: Academic Ability; Verbal; Math; Mechanical and Crafts; Business and Clerical; Electronics and Electrical; and Health, Social, and Technology. Scores are reported in terms of percentile scores based on a nationally representative sample of approximately 12,000 young men and women between the ages of sixteen and twenty-three.

This battery of tests has been reviewed by Jensen (1988) who notes that the battery has only two significant factors, a very general g factor and a relatively small speed factor. Jensen believes that there is a danger that many counselors will overinterpret the profile of scores:

Occupational choice should be thought of more in terms of *general ability* plus *interest* than in terms of differential aptitudes, which really boils down to g + interest (Jensen, 1988, p. 62).

While our study of aptitude testing has not extended to the areas of art, music, and other areas of talent in which important work has been done, we have seen that the popular conception of independent aptitudes for diverse school subjects is not supported by the accumulated evidence at hand. For teachers and counselors working within a school setting, it will be useful to remember that most tests claiming to measure specific cognitive skills are likely to have a large component of g. Further, the g score obtained by combining the verbal and arithmetic performance will generally be the most useful score available in helping students predict probable success in a wide variety of academic subjects.

Creativity as a Specific Ability

Since the early 1960s, there has been considerable interest among teachers and educators in the measurement and development of creativity. Nicholls (1972) presents a critical analysis of tests purporting to measure creativity and raises questions about the existence of creativity as a general trait.

In testing for creativity, attention has been fixed on the surface processes that apparently lead to creative products: unusual use of a common object or the recombination or application of existing elements. Thus, tests purporting to measure creativity call for such abilities as verbal fluency, ideational flexibility, and originality. These obvious features of the creative event, however, mask the essential element in all creative acts: a prolonged struggle to resolve a problem. There is general agreement that the creative process involves long, laborious work that precedes the creative breakthrough. Shekerjian (1990), sweeps away the "inspired moment" view of creativity as represented by the apple falling on Newton's head:

> . . . by failing to pay proper heed to the long dance with uncertainty that precedes most creative breakthroughs, these stories neglect the very soil from which the creative flower blooms. Cut short the floundering and you've cut short the possible creative outcomes. Cheat on the chaotic stumbling-about, and you've robbed yourself of the raw stuff that feeds the imagination (pp. 32–33).

The function of the "dance with uncertainty" is that it slowly defines the shape of the solution that will solve the problem. Searching for a missing piece of a jigsaw puzzle involves an image of the shape and, once you spot it, you know that it will fit. This process is illustrated by Shapiro's (1979) account of Horace Wells' encounter with laughing gas. Wells was a dentist who, with a partner, had developed a new way of fitting false teeth. Rather than the expected fame and wealth, however, Wells and his associate met with dismal failure. The new method required that all the old teeth be removed. The time period was 1840 and there was no anesthesia. While attending a demonstration of laughing gas offered as public entertainment, Wells observed a neighbor who had inhaled the gas and had crashed into a bench on the stage, severely injuring his leg. To Wells' astonishment, the neighbor felt no pain. Before the night was over, Wells was experimenting with the new gas and "the magic sleep" was born.

In this example, one may ask what role was played by verbal fluency, ideational flexibility, or originality. Wells' long-standing involvement with the problem of how to remove teeth without pain was the key to his recognition of a potential solution. Current tests of creativity miscarry because they fail in formulating a defensible construct of creativity.

Aside from research studies, creativity tests are likely to be used in schools as part of a battery for selecting students for gifted and talented programs. Our discussion should make clear that such applications are highly questionable. Other measurement specialists are even more emphatic.

> Creativity tests tend not to be reliable or valid; therefore, heavy reliance on them will result in the misidentification of students for gifted programs. Thus, some students are placed in such programs, despite not being gifted, while other students who could benefit from such programs may be ruled ineligible (Thorndike, Cunningham, Thorndike, & Hagen, 1991, p. 432).

In this limited survey of tests designed to measure special abilities, we have seen that most of the widely used tests fail to live up to their promises. We have also seen that interpreting test scores from their labels can result in inaccurate and misleading advice to students. There are some positive insights to be gained also. Learning to tease out the meanings from tables of correlation coefficients puts us in a powerful position to understand the strengths and weaknesses of the tests we are using.

Summary

We started our discussion of aptitude by noting the fascinating accomplishments of young George Bidder, who at age ten could do lightning calculations. It seems fair to say that he had an aptitude for numerical work. But Bidder was also bright, as suggested by his later success as a civil engineer. Was Bidder's calculating power mostly an expression of the underlying general ability?

Genetic endowment and early experience may tip the scales in favor of progression along certain lines of human endeavor, but do not guarantee an automatic development of expertise. Practice and effort are needed to bring out these abilities. Thus, it is not entirely clear whether one should think of aptitudes as specific latent abilities waiting to be discovered, or as expressions of general ability in an area where the individual has focused much concern and effort. Benjamin Bloom's studies of young people who excelled in a variety of fields revealed early signs of ability but stressed the development of these abilities through sustained training and effort.

We introduced the Differential Aptitude Tests as a widely used test battery claiming to measure different aptitudes. Examining a table of intercorrelations from the test manual, we found about half the coefficients to be .55 or higher, indicating considerable overlap among scores claiming to measure different abilities. This finding suggests that even tests designed to measure specific abilities may actually be reflecting a large component of general ability.

Examining a graphic summary of validity coefficients from the Differential Aptitude Test Battery, we found that it did not matter very much whether we used verbal scores or numerical scores to predict grades in English; both tests show a number of high correlations with grades in this subject, and with grades in other subjects as well. These observations suggest that specific aptitude scores may actually be reflecting general ability more than some specific ability. Counseling from test labels without consulting validity data is a dangerous practice.

A second aptitude battery, the General Aptitude Test Battery, was examined. This battery includes measures of motor performance and is widely used by the United States Employment Office. Based on extensive studies, minimum scores have been established for thousands of occupations. Such studies suggest that the battery may provide valid scores for occupational placement and may even offer support for those who believe we can measure specific abilities independently of general ability. On the other hand, factor analysis of the General Aptitude Test Battery reveals three broad factors: cognitive ability, perceptual ability, and psychomotor ability, and related studies found that the cognitive factor yielded high validity with most jobs.

Similar studies have led Jensen to conclude that aptitude may be reduced to general ability plus interest in a specific area. This conclusion would be consistent with our opening discussion emphasizing the development of special abilities over a long period of time with a large input of learning and effort.

This orientation to aptitudes may be extended to the construct, creativity. There is little research evidence suggesting that tests of verbal fluency, flexibility, or originality should be held forth as tests of creativity. In fact, creative acts are invariably preceded by long work and concentrated effort, which define the desired solutions and assemble the raw material from which new options are generated. At a minimum, such efforts prepare the individual for recognition of a solution when presented, as we saw in the case of Wells, the dentist who saw a unique application for laughing gas.

An alternative to the popular conception that aptitudes are innate is an idea we have hinted at all along. The special abilities we observe in others may be largely the consequence of highly focused efforts in an area of absorbing interest. In the next chapter we turn to a consideration of the measurement of interests.

References

Anastasi, A. (1988). *Psychological testing* (6th ed.). New York: Macmillan.

Ball, W. W. R. (1956). Calculating prodigies. In J. Newman (ed.), *The world of mathematics,* Vol. 1. New York: Simon & Schuster.

Bloom, B. S. (1985). *Developing talent in young people.* New York: Ballantine Books.

Differential Aptitude Tests, Fifth Edition, Technical Manual (1992). San Antonio: The Psychological Corporation.

Jensen, A. R. (1988). Review of the Armed Services Vocational Aptitude Battery. In J. Kapes & M. Mastie (eds.), *A counselor's guide to career assessment instruments.* Alexandria, VA: The National Career Development Association.

Nicholls, J. G. (1972). Creativity in the person who will never produce anything original or useful: The concept of creativity as a normally distributed trait. *American Psychologist, 27,* 717–727.

Shapiro, I. (1979). *The gift of magic sleep: Early experiments in anesthesia.* New York: Coward, McCann & Geoghegan.

Shekerjian, D. (1990). *Uncommon genius.* New York: Viking.

Spearman, C. (1937). *Psychology down the ages,* Vol. II. London: Macmillan.

Spearman, C., & Jones, L. L. W. (1950). *Human ability.* London: Macmillan.

Thorndike, R M., Cunningham, G. K., Thorndike, R. L., & Hagen, E. (1991). *Measurement and evaluation in psychology and education* (5th ed.). New York: Macmillan.

Treffert, D. A. (1989). *Extraordinary people.* New York: Harper & Row.

On the way home, I stopped at the supermarket, where I encountered an acquaintance who seemed pleased to see me. "Boy, I'm glad I ran into you. You're a teacher, maybe you can help. Leroy is going into high school this year and is totally clueless about what he wants to do. Are there any interest tests the school counselor could give him to see what he should go into? I think Leroy could really do something if he can find out what he is fitted for."

chapter fifteen

Measuring Interests

The *New York Times* of Monday, March 23, 1992, describes the case of a missing man. A publisher of a weekly newspaper and owner of a convenience store and gas station disappeared from a small town in Massachusetts without a word to his employees, bankers, customers, or newspaper readers. He did call a friend and offer her his furniture if she would come over and get it. Five months later, he was located fulfilling a long-time dream: he was dealing poker at the Poker Palace in North Las Vegas, Nevada. He didn't seem too concerned that he was working for minimum wage plus tips. He valued the freedom to do what he wanted.

Is there a time in life when freedom to pursue one's own interests is unimportant? If you mention **interests** to elementary teachers you will find that there is a constant concern with getting children interested in the material and in linking children's interest with study units and library reading.

At the high school level, the urge is to help students find out more about their emerging interests so that course selection and career exploration reflect these interests. In this chapter, we will see that two major interest inventories are readily available and widely used in career counseling with young adults. The elementary teacher, however, must fall back on informal inventories and observations to probe the interests of pupils. There are suggestions for making this effort more systematic and fruitful.

But first, who did the pioneering work in the measurement of interest, and what kind of person was he?

Edward Strong and His Vocational Interest Blank

Edward K. Strong, Jr., was the grandfather of the measurement of vocational interests. He published the *Strong Vocational Interest Blank* in 1927, an inventory still in use today although extensively revised and expanded.

Strong was born in Syracuse, New York, the son of a Presbyterian minister. He grew up mostly in Bloomington, Illinois, and in Bay City, Michigan. He enjoyed fishing, roaming the woods, and cataloging birds and flowers. After his family moved to California, he entered the University of California at Berkeley, earned a degree in biology, and went to work as a forest ranger. He returned to Berkeley to earn a master's degree in psychology after which he promptly applied for a teaching position in China. Instead of China, Strong ended up in New York City working for a Ph.D. in psychology at Columbia University. After graduation, he taught at George Peabody, Carnegie Institute of Technology, and Stanford, where he spent the major part of his professional career. He arrived at Stanford in 1923 and published the initial interest inventory four years later.

Table 15.1 *Form for Estimating Strong's Interests as a Young Man*

General Occupational Themes	Low	Medium	High
Realistic			
Investigative			
Artistic			
Social			
Enterprising			
Conventional			
Basic Interest Scales Nature			
Adventure			
Mechanical Activities			
Science			
Mathematics			

Table 15.1 gives you a chance to estimate how high Strong's scores might have been on a few of the scales of his interest inventory.

Let's round out the picture of Edward Strong. He certainly was interested in the development of students and one might believe that he was a warm and attentive counselor. But he had a private side which he protected. When a colleague was asked about Strong's personality, he replied: "He was like a grizzly bear. . . . He was not hesitant to express his opinions. He was in no way reluctant to say what the world was like. He would growl at you, look at you, and then tell you what the truth was" (Hansen, 1987).

Strong constructed his interest inventory by listing a wide variety of words describing school subjects, occupations, types of people, etc. Some examples were golf, tennis, biology, history, fat people, skinny people. Students taking the inventory indicated whether they liked, disliked, or were indifferent to each item.

Edward K. Strong, Jr.
Courtesy of the Archives
of the History of
American Psychology,
University of Akron,
Akron, OH.

Strong's approach to scoring the questionnaire was pure dust bowl empiricism. Rather than deciding in advance what responses should indicate an interest in medicine, Strong let the facts speak for themselves. He administered the inventories to groups of doctors, lawyers, merchants, and chiefs. He then compared responses of the doctor group with the responses of all the rest of the men, who were termed men in general. If he found, for example, that doctors liked golf, but men in general did not, then liking golf would earn a student a point on the physician's scale.

By developing a separate key for each occupation, Strong was able to report the vocational interest of students by such phrases as: "Your responses are very much like those of doctors." Of course, Strong knew better than to rely on a single high score. Looking for a common thread uniting a group of high scores provides the best basis for interpreting interest profiles.

The Strong Interest Inventory

Strong's original inventory has been revised several times, most notably in 1974 with publication of the Strong-Campbell Interest Inventory. The current version, the Strong Interest Inventory (Hansen & Campbell, 1985), has more than 300 items and the complex scoring can be handled

Table 15.2 *Samples of the More Than 200 Scales on the Strong Interest Inventory*

Six General Occupational Themes:

Realistic
Artistic
Social

Twenty-Three Basic Interest Scales:

Agriculture
Science
Music/Dramatics
Teaching

Two Hundred and Seven Occupational Scales:

Vocational Agriculture Teacher
Speech pathologist
Psychologists
Dietitian
Army Officer

only by a computer. The student receives a profile sheet with three kinds of scores. Table 15.2 shows the types of scores reported, along with a few representative samples.

Strong wanted to know about the stability of interests and the predictive power of interest inventories. To answer these questions, Strong followed up 663 students who had taken his interest inventory while in college. Eighteen years later, he asked them to take the inventory again and to supply information about their employment status (Strong, 1955).

What did Strong find? First, let us look at the permanence of interest scores. Table 15.3 provides the correlation between the original inventories and the inventories taken eighteen years later for a sample of the occupational scales. Data such as these stimulated Strong to assert that ". . . interest scores are more stable than scores on all other tests except intelligence tests" (p. 139).

What happened to the people who made an A on a particular scale? Did they, indeed, enter the occupations where they expressed high interest? Strong found that one third of the students who had an interest score of A for engineering actually went into engineering. Of the students with an interest score of less than A, only 5 percent went into engineering. Strong's inventory seems much better than flipping a coin to decide about one's vocational interest.

Table 15.3 *Test-Retest Correlations over an Average of 18 Years (N = 663)*

Scale	Test-Retest Correlation
Author	.69
Engineer	.79
Life ins. agent	.75
Chemist	.79
Sales manager	.68
Real estate agent	.69
Physician	.76
Farmer	.88
Lawyer	.73
Psychologist	.76
Office worker	.65

Adapted from Vocational Interest 18 Years After College by Edward K. Strong, Jr., University of Minnesota Press. Copyright © 1955 by the University of Minnesota. Reprinted by permission of the University of Minnesota Press.

A continuing research program has provided extensive data on the reliability and validity of this inventory. Anastasi (1988) reports median retest reliability for the occupational scales after 3 years as .87 and for periods extending up to 20 years as ranging between the .60s and .70s. Anastasi also reports substantial correspondence or validity between interest profiles and the occupations that the individuals actually pursued.

By the way, did you estimate Strong's own interest scores for him as a young man? Figure 15.1 shows his actual scores on his original inventory and then collected again after his retirement (Hansen, 1987).

The Strong Interest Inventory is widely used with adults, and a solid body of research and studies attest to its usefulness in a variety of vocational counseling settings. Among the more consistent, and surprising, findings of this research is the fact that measures of interest are not correlated with measures of ability. Put more simply, an expression of interest in a particular line of work is no guarantee that the student possesses the corresponding abilities required to perform in that vocational area.

The Kuder Preference Record

A second major interest inventory, developed by Frederick Kuder in 1932, indicates interest in ten broad occupational areas.

General occupational themes			
Theme	1927	1949	
R-Theme	44	49	X 0
I-Theme	61	61	
A-Theme	35	34	0X
S-Theme	37	33	0 X
E-Theme	41	37	0 X
C-Theme	56	54	0 X

(I-Theme scale: 35 40 45 50 55 60 65, marker at ~61)
(A/S-Theme scale: 35 40 45 50 55 60 65)

Basic interest scales			
Scale			
Nature	54	62	X 0
Adventure	39	55	X 0
Mechanical activities	55	53	0 X
Science	61	65	X 0
Mathematics	65	65	■
Medical service	45	43	0 X
Music/Dramatics	32	39	X 0
Art	41	38	0 X
Writing	36	36	■
Teaching	43	43	■
Social service	32	35	X 0
Athletics	34	34	■
Public speaking	45	36	0 X
Law/Politics	44	33	0 X
Merchandising	44	40	0 X
Sales	42	38	0 X
Business management	48	44	0 X
Office practices	47	47	■

(Mechanical activities scale: 35 40 45 50 55 60 65)
(Science scale: 35 40 45 50 55 60 65)
(Writing scale: 35 40 45 50 55 60 65)
(Public speaking scale: 35 40 45 50 55 60 65)

Figure 15.1 *Strong interest profiles for E. K. Strong, Jr. taken in 1927 (X) and 1949 (O).* Reprinted with the permission of the American Counseling Association from "Edward Kellog Strong, Jr.: First author of the Strong Interest Inventory" by Jo-Ida C. Hansen, 1987, *Journal of Counseling and Development, 66,* 119–125.

It may seem curious that an author of a vocational interest inventory designed to help young people find a career may have found his own profession through the chance meeting of a fellow student at college. As a young man, Kuder majored in English at the University of Arizona. There, he met a student from out East who had never spent a day in public schools and was amazed that no one in Arizona had heard of his famous father: James McKeen Cattell, professor of psychology at Columbia University and the first American to use the term "mental test" in a published article. The two students became fast friends and upon graduation the senior Cattell took both young men for a tour of the west as a graduation present. By the time the trip was over, Cattell offered young Kuder a job working on a massive compendium ranking the American men of science. From working with Cattell, Kuder went on to achieve his own special eminence in the area of measurement.

The vocational interest inventory developed by Kuder was based on a logical grouping of items that seemed to indicate interest in a particular field. Students taking the inventory were confronted with three activities, and within each group of three, they had to choose one activity they liked *most* and one activity they liked *least*. The items looked like this:

	Most	Least
Repair a broken clock	•	•
Sell books door to door	•	•
Read to an invalid	•	•

The items were grouped together on rational grounds, and items that did not intercorrelate with each other to provide a homogeneous scale were dropped. Scores were reported for ten broad areas: Outdoor, Mechanical, Computational, Scientific, Persuasive, Artistic, Literary, Musical, Social Service, and Clerical.

A green answer pad was used and students indicated their preference by punching a stylus through the proper position to indicate their likes and dislikes. Later, this answer pad was opened up and the number of "bull's eyes" were counted for each interest area. It was a clever device that made it easy for students to score their own inventory booklets.

These arrangements provided grist for the mill of a reviewer who offered an unusually critical view of the inventory. The reviewer noted that a green plague was sweeping through the schools of the land; that the Kuder Preference Record had not the slightest shred of evidence for its validity, but it would likely continue to be used widely. Not since kindergarten had children had so much fun with sharp objects and stiff paper. They seemed to enjoy the popping sound made as they punched their choices into the answer pad. Besides, the reviewer continued, English teachers had discovered that they could get out of an hour of class preparation by devoting a period to the interest inventory and then assigning a book review on a topic of the child's highest interest.

It is doubtful if Kuder was overly concerned about the criticism. Subsequent studies showed that the test differentiated between workers who were satisfied and those who were dissatisfied with their jobs. More than that, Kuder had designed an inventory that seemed to have a high degree of construct validity, was easily administered, easily scored, could be readily profiled, and opened the way for school students to begin to explore their own vocational interests. His inventory was even accompanied by a book list with the titles organized according to the ten areas of interest and grouped according to reading difficulty. What more could a teacher want?

Because of its applicability to younger students, its ease of administration and scoring, and its relatively low cost, the Kuder Preference Record—Vocational remains the most commonly used of the several interest inventories in the Kuder series (Shertzer & Linden, 1979). A revised edition of this scale, the Kuder General Interest Survey, offers simpler language and can be used as low as grade six.

In addition, a new form, the Kuder Occupational Interest Survey (Kuder & Diamond, 1979) provides scores for more than 100 specific occupations and 48 college majors. It is available only with computer scored answer sheets.

The Self-Directed Search

Another instrument that is gaining popularity is a self-scoring questionnaire designed to encourage vocational exploration and counseling.

The Self-Directed Search (Holland, 1990) is composed of two booklets, the Assessment Booklet and the Occupational Finder. These booklets are used to encourage students to explore their interests and to investigate jobs that match their expressions of interest.

Students are encouraged to obtain additional information about jobs from such sources as the *Occupational Outlook Handbook* published every two years by the Bureau of Labor Statistics. Indeed, it is instructive to note from figure 15.2 the projections of the U.S. Bureau of the Census regarding the ten fastest growing occupations.

As might be expected, medical assistants and medical health aides lead the list, followed by radiologists and medical secretaries. It may be a commentary on our times that among the fastest growing occupations are

Figure 15.2 *10 Fastest Growing Occupations: 1988 to 2000.* *Source:* Statistical Abstract of the United States, 1991.

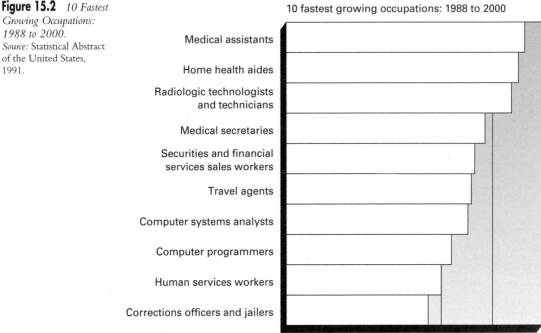

10 fastest growing occupations: 1988 to 2000

- Medical assistants
- Home health aides
- Radiologic technologists and technicians
- Medical secretaries
- Securities and financial services sales workers
- Travel agents
- Computer systems analysts
- Computer programmers
- Human services workers
- Corrections officers and jailers

corrections officers and jailers. As young people begin to think about their own futures, current occupational information and fuller job descriptions become a necessary adjunct of vocational interests inventories.

Measuring Interests at the Elementary Level

Our discussion has focused on vocational choice at the secondary school level. In working with students at all levels, our task is to assist students in the gradual emergence of a career orientation, a reflective stance on the kind of person one is becoming, and the work activities that might bring satisfaction. In elementary school such orientations are developing, and attention to the process can broaden the range of possibilities children consider.

Baldauf (1990) has compiled an annotated bibliography of 1,066 titles of children's books related to the world of work.

The books are classified according to major occupational fields: animal care, arts and entertainment, business and office, communication, construction, education, farming and fishing, forestry and natural resources, health care, law, manufacturing and industry, public service and government, religion, sales, science, mathematics and technology, service, space and exploration, sports and recreation, and transportation. The grade range for which each book is appropriate is identified.

The annotations of this volume can be used by the teacher to formulate descriptive phrases for a reading interest questionnaire. Six such phrases are shown below, along with the item number linking the phrase to a specific book in Baldauf's volume. All these books would be appropriate for children in grades four through six.

Books I Would Like to Read

Yes	Maybe	No	Eight women who have won the Nobel Prize	58
Yes	Maybe	No	A day in the life of a veterinarian	83
Yes	Maybe	No	Behind-the-scenes work of a ballet company	121
Yes	Maybe	No	Spielberg—began making movies as a child	198
Yes	Maybe	No	Einstein, a simply told story of his life	905
Yes	Maybe	No	What does an airplane pilot do	1055

The list could be as long as the teacher chose to make it. The code number to the right provides immediate access to the annotations in the Baldauf volume. For example, the complete annotation for item 58 is shown below.

Shiels, Barbara. *Winners: Women and the Nobel Prize*. Minneapolis: Dillon, 1985. 254 pages. Gr. 5–9. Devotes one chapter to each of eight Nobel Prize winners: Nellie Sachs (literature), Rosalyn Yalow (medicine), Alva Myrdal (peace), Maria Goeppert Mayer (physics), Pearl S. Buck (literature), Dorothy Crowfoot Hodgkin (chemistry), Mother Teresa (peace), Barbara McClintock (medicine).

While the example here draws on a published list of books, it seems best to construct reading interest inventories in cooperation with the school librarian and the youth librarian of the nearby public library. This step assures that books identified by individual children will be available.

Librarians can frequently provide updated lists of their holdings in a particular topic area. Shown in the Appendix is a list of books written to help children appreciate and accept various handicaps.

Similar lists can be used by teachers to draw the attention of pupils to particular areas of interest. Conversion of such lists to reading interest inventories allows the teacher to quickly ascertain which titles will be of particular interest to each of the pupils.

Interpreting Interest Inventory Scores

How much should we rely on measurements of interest in helping young people move toward a career? We started our discussion with a brief review of Strong's life. Perhaps we can do no better than to end with his view of the role of interest inventory scores in working with young adults.

> Tests are useful in this period in that they provide students with additional information about themselves; this is especially true if the scores are explained so that the youths thoroughly understand their significance. But it seems wrong for counselors to go further and attempt to force young people to decide their future careers. Many parents, mostly fathers, have complained to the writer that their boys just would not settle down and decide. The writer was that kind of boy and he was not dead sure he wanted to be a psychologist until his second year of graduate work, four years after graduation from college.
>
> . . . For years he mulled things over with no feeling of hurry, which must have exasperated his elders, and from time to time said to himself, "I am not going to do this all my life."
>
> Instead of trying to force adolescents to decide upon a vocational career, we should remember that 'vocational choice is a process, not an event'.[1] For most, if not for all, it is a process of trying out this and that. . . .
>
> Test scores are a valuable aid but the process of choosing a vocation continues over many years and cannot be made on the basis of such scores alone (Strong, 1955, pp. 197–198).

---

[1] Thompson, A. S. (1954). A rationale for vocational guidance. *Personnel and Guidance, 32,* 399–402.

Summary

Everyone sooner or later enters a profession or field of work. Frequently, this step is preceded by a long period of education and preparation, so tentative decisions are made well in advance of actual entry into the job. In the area of testing vocational interest, two giants stand out: the Strong Interest Inventory and the Kuder series of inventories.

For adults, the Strong Interest Inventory is the most widely used interest inventory in the world. A large body of research on this instrument points to the stability of interest scores and to the relationship between expressions of interest on the inventory and entry into interest-related jobs. The Strong Interest Inventory provides a comprehensive report of scores that allows individuals to first look at what kind of person they are (for example, social); then determine what basic interests they have (for example, teaching, social service); and finally, to look at what occupational groups their interests actually match (for example, guidance counselor, elementary teacher).

For students in grades six through twelve, the Kuder General Interest Survey provides scores for ten broad interest areas ranging from interest in outdoor endeavors to clerical activities. A later version in the Kuder series provides scores for 126 specific occupations and 48 college majors. This version requires computer scoring.

The Self-Directed Search is an attractive questionnaire that provides occupational codes rather than scores. These codes lead directly into job descriptions that should be relevant to individual students.

Strong pointed out that vocational choice is a process, not an event. Interest inventories may serve to initiate and broaden the processes of self-examination and exploration of the world of work.

While our discussion has centered on the use of well-known vocational interest instruments for use at the secondary level, informal measures of interest can be constructed by elementary teachers. When such measures are keyed to the holdings of school and public libraries, the immediate consequence is the ready identification of books that appeal to individual curiosities and broaden the student's emerging perceptions of career options.

References

Anastasi, A. (1988). *Psychological testing* (6th ed.). New York: Macmillan.

Baldauf, G. S. (1990). *Career index: A selective bibliography for elementary schools.* New York: Greenwood Press.

Hansen, J. C. (1987). Edward Kellog Strong, Jr.: First author of the Strong Interest Inventory. *Journal of Counseling and Development, 66,* 119–125.

Hansen, J. C., & Campbell, D. (1985). *Manual for the SVIB-SCII* (4th ed.). Stanford, CA: Stanford University Press.

Holland, J. L. (1990). *The self-directed search* (1990 Revision). Odessa, FL: Psychological Assessment Resources.

Kuder, G. F., & Diamond, E. E. (1979). *Kuder Occupational Interest Survey. General Manual.* Chicago: Science Research Associates.

Shertzer, B., & Linden, J. D. (1979). *Fundamentals of individual appraisal.* Boston: Houghton Mifflin.

Strong, E. K., Jr. (1955). *Vocational interests 18 years after college.* Minneapolis: University of Minnesota Press.

I watched the children trooping into the classroom promptly at 8:00. Some came in laughing with friends, others moved purposefully to their seats. And then came Jacob, all alone, hesitant, taking his seat without greeting or being greeted by any of his classmates. A socially isolated child? I made a mental note to dig below the surface and understand Jacob better before the semester went too much further.

chapter sixteen

Measuring Affective Aspects of Schooling

What develops during life in school? Achievements? Abilities? Interests? Feelings? All of these, of course, but our tendencies to put feelings last is, perhaps, an occupational hazard of our role as teachers. Ask parents to talk about their hopes for their children's schooling and they will tell you they want their children to like school and to feel comfortable there. They want their child to be accepted, to fit into the social life of the class, and to work at a level that is neither too easy nor too hard. Parents count on teachers to help their children with any special problems. The hope is for a personalized and individualized relationship between the teacher and the student. Realizing this hope requires sensitivity on the part of teachers to the attitudes, perceptions, and feelings of students. Measuring these **affective** aspects of students' lives in school can bring broader insights into students' behavior.

Curriculum guides, textbooks, and classroom routine conspire to focus attention on cognitive development. But there are often unintended consequences of our emphasis on subject matter. **Attitudes** about content, school, and one's own abilities are also being learned. The feelings that a student is developing toward science may be as important as the knowledge being acquired. More generally, attitudes toward learning, perceptions of one's abilities, and patterns of coping with academic and social demands are important aspects of schooling.

Emphasis on a common core of subjects for all students coupled with a push for high standards has made it more difficult for teachers to attend to these noncognitive developments among students. In some situations, it is becoming increasingly difficult for nonacademically oriented students to feel that schools are places where they are nurtured. Problems of alienation and disengagement from learning continue to plague many students.

While these problems of school adjustment can be most extreme among nonacademically oriented students, even students who are doing well might be working hard for the wrong reasons. Students who work hard in school may be motivated to enhance their own feelings of adequacy rather than responding to any appeal within the subject matter. Such behaviors run counter to the educational ideal that students become more autonomous and inner-directed in their learning and come to view school as a means for increasing their own understanding and ability to contribute to society.

In this chapter we shall see that teachers can draw on a number of published instruments to measure such affective aspects of students' lives as attitudes and feelings. Teachers can also construct instruments to obtain useful information and consult the research literature for additional devices. We will end with the suggestion that sensitive observation of a child's behavior is a useful tool in understanding the psychological processes underlying overt actions.

Self-Report and Projective Techniques

Measures of perceptions and personal adjustment are typically divided into two categories, self-report instruments and projective techniques. In **self-report inventories,** students respond to direct questions about themselves, usually by marking yes or no on an answer sheet. One example might be: "Do you enjoy working on difficult problems?" Such questionnaires develop a great deal of information in a short period of time, and this chapter provides examples of useful instruments constructed in this way. At the same time, it is important to caution you that these questionnaires are open to possible inaccuracies. Self-report inventories assume that students know themselves well enough to provide accurate answers. In addition, self-report devices frequently reflect a **social desirability bias,** a tendency to respond in ways that would be viewed favorably by most people. Students may believe it is desirable to feel challenged by difficult problems and indicate that they enjoy working on them when in reality they try to avoid them. This tendency to answer in socially desirable ways has been noted, for example, in surveys of reading habits in which respondents claim they have read books that have never been published.

A second approach to measuring personality, which is less dependent on conscious awareness and less open to social desirability bias, is the **projective technique.** In these procedures, individuals appear to be describing an objective stimulus when in reality they are revealing much about themselves. In the Rorschach test, individuals describe what they see in ten "ink blots." In the Thematic Apperception Test (TAT), individuals are shown a series of pictures about people in loosely structured situations. Individuals taking the test tell stories about each picture including what is happening, what led up to the situation, and how the story will unfold. Recurring themes of problems with authority figures, depression, frustrated ambitions, etc., suggest to the clinician concerns that may belong to the storyteller.

As interesting as projective tests are, the research evidence provides little support for their validity. In any event, these are tools that are used in clinical settings and are introduced here as a way of showing the full range of devices used to get at affective dimensions of personal adjustment. Our major concern will be with self-report instruments that can be constructed or obtained from other sources.

Using Existing Tests or Designing Your Own

Teachers and administrators who want to measure some aspect of their students' attitudes and feelings can decide between using an existing test or constructing one of their own. For example, a school system may have adopted a new approach to science teaching, and teachers and administrators want to know if the new system makes a difference in the way students view science.

Deciding whether to buy or construct one's own instrument generally involves some trade-offs. The questions on existing instruments may have been carefully developed and refined through item analysis. Reliability and validity data will ordinarily be available and perhaps even some normative data showing how students in other settings have responded. On the other hand, the off-the-shelf test may not zero in on the exact features of the program you want to evaluate: Did students like the ecology unit better than the unit on electricity? Was this year's computer simulation on genetics better received than last year's work sheets on the same material? In general, what is gained by using an existing instrument is offset by losses in measuring exactly what you want to measure. Still, it is prudent to see what is available before embarking on developing your own instrument.

Finding Existing Instruments

The Buros Mental Measurements Yearbooks were mentioned in chapter 6. In *The Eleventh Mental Measurements Yearbook* (Kramer & Conoley, 1992), the largest single group of tests reviewed, 28 percent, are tests of personality. The personality category is used rather broadly and includes such diverse instruments as measures of learning style and job attitudes. The Yearbook is available on CD-ROM, which allows rapid search of its contents, and most university libraries will have this disk available. *Tests in Print* IV (available in 1994) indexes all previous Mental Measurements Yearbooks.

Another source of tests in the affective area is *The ETS Test Collection Catalog* series. Volume 5 of this series, Attitude Tests (Test Collection, 1991), lists 1,275 attitude tests, and Volume 6, Affective Measures and Personality Tests (Test Collection,1992), lists more than 1,500 tests measuring everything from locus of control to shyness and alienation.

If these sources and a check of the research literature fail to provide a test that can be used or adapted, then the only option is constructing an instrument of your own.

Constructing Measures of Perceptions and Attitudes

A clearly written guide to the construction of affective measures is available as a small paperback book by Henerson, Morris, and Fitz-Gibbon (1978). Teachers constructing tests of attitudes and perceptions have a choice between asking open-ended questions and constructing questionnaires that can be scored objectively. Open-ended formats can range from direct questions ("Describe a school situation in which you felt particularly good") to sentence completion items ("I feel good in school when . . . "). Open-ended questions have the advantage of eliciting perceptions that might not be anticipated in advance. Additionally, open-ended questions elicit nuances of feeling that might not otherwise be observed. Note the range of responses obtained from middle school students to the incomplete sentence "When I study history. . . ."

> I just try to get through the dumb stuff.
> I try to remember all of the dates and people so I will have it for the tests.
> I think of how hard it was in the old days and how far we have come.

An alternative to open-ended questionnaires is a closed response format with limited response options. Closed response questionnaires present a series of statements to which students answer yes or no or indicate their level of agreement on a five-point scale ranging from strongly agree to strongly disagree. Such five-point response scales are referred to as **Likert scales,** after R. A. Likert who originated this format in 1934 and coupled it with item analysis procedures for retaining effective items from a larger pool.

At the elementary level, a three-point scale—agree, uncertain, and disagree—is more common. Smiling, straight, and frowning faces are sometimes substituted for the words. A typical stem for a closed format questionnaire would be "I feel good when my teacher stands near me." Closed format questionnaires have a major advantage in the ease with which large amounts of data can be collected, scored, analyzed, and summarized.

Attitudes Toward Subjects and School

A number of scales are available to measure attitudes toward specific subject areas. Perhaps more work has been done in mathematics (Fennema & Sherman, 1976) and science than in most other areas. In the 1986 National Assessment program, students were asked to convey their attitudes

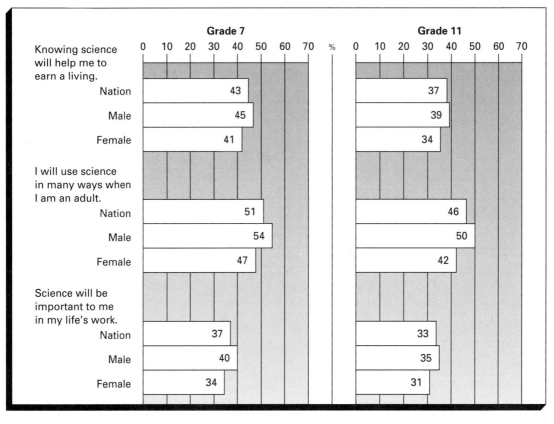

Figure 16.1

Perceptions of the personal relevance of science knowledge for the nation and demographic subgroups, 1986. From *The Science Report Card* by I. V. S. Mullis and L. B. Jenkins, 1988, Princeton: Educational Testing Service. Adapted by permission.

toward learning science. Figure 16.1 shows the percent of boys and girls in grades seven and eleven agreeing with three statements about how they might use scientific knowledge.

From figure 16.1, it is evident that females show slightly less favorable attitudes toward science than do males. Mullis and Jenkins (1988) go on to comment: "What is perhaps more salient in these responses than difference in the attitudes between males and females is the fact that so few students overall reportedly believe that science knowledge will be useful or relevant in their lives. Less than half of the seventh graders—and even fewer eleventh graders—perceived that science would help them earn a living, be important to them in life, or be used in many ways during adulthood" (p. 126).

Ehrlich (1968) measured attitude toward school with 120 Likert items administered in grades 3 through 6 and concluded that school attitude consists of a number of components that vary from grade to grade and between sexes. Using a research version of 45 items drawn largely from the Ehrlich study, McDaniel et al. (1973) found attitude toward school correlated with reading achievement .40, mathematics .38, and self-concept .34 for 169 fourth grade students. Browne and Rife (1991) found that these 45 items differentiated between at-risk and not-at-risk sixth grade students.

Surveys of attitudes about courses and school in general can be a first step in self-studies conducted by school faculties. Where new teaching strategies and innovative curricula changes are in progress, such measures can help evaluate the new programs. Additionally, school counselors and teachers can monitor school attitudes and use the surveys as possible indicators of difficult adjustment to the school setting.

Why Students Work: Motivational Orientation Scales

A related aspect of schooling is the **motivation orientation,** or the various kinds of motives that appear to drive efforts to perform in school. Nicholls (1989) discusses student orientations to schoolwork and makes a distinction between **task-orientation** and **ego-orientation.** Task-orientation implies a tendency to work on a task because of the intrinsic satisfaction gained from understanding or mastering new techniques. Ego-orientation, on the other hand, is a tendency to engage or persist in a task because of opportunities to enhance one's own ego by demonstrating superiority over others. Table 16.1 shows items measuring the two orientations from Nicholls' *Motivational Orientation Scales.* Students respond on a Likert scale indicating their agreement or disagreement with statements describing feelings of success in school.

Additional clusters of items on the complete Nicholls scales measure tendencies to avoid work ("I don't have to do any homework") and academic alienation ("I do almost no work and get away with it"). With small variations in wording and items, the scales can be used from second grade through high school. Reliability, as indicated by coefficient alpha, is in the mid to high .80s at the high school level but drops to the .70s at the second grade level.

These motivational orientation scales may reflect deep-seated ways of perceiving and interpreting the school environment and one's relationship to it. The orientation scales are importantly related to satisfaction with learning and to student beliefs about what leads to success in high school. High Task-Orientation is linked to beliefs that academic success is

Table 16.1 *Items Measuring Task-Orientation and Ego-Orientation*

Items follow the stem "I feel most successful if . . .".

Task-Orientation (does not appear on questionnaire)

Something I learn makes me want to find out more.

I get a new idea about how things work.

I learn something interesting.

I solve a tricky problem by working hard.

I finally understand a really complicated idea.

Something I learn really makes sense to me.

A class makes me think about things.

I keep busy.

I work hard all day.

Ego-Orientation (does not appear on questionnaire)

I do work better than other students.

I show people I'm good at something.

I show people I'm smart.

I score higher than other students.

I am the only one who can answer the teacher's questions.

Reprinted by permission of the publishers from *The Competitive Ethos and Democratic Education* by John G. Nicholls, Cambridge, MA: Harvard University Press. Copyright © 1989 by the President and Fellows of the Harvard College.

helped by wanting to learn, being interested, working hard, working co-operatively, and trying to understand rather than memorize. On the other hand, Ego-Orientation is linked with beliefs that school success is related to intelligence, trying to do better than others, having teachers who expect one to do well, knowing how to impress the right people, and acting as if one likes the teacher (Nicholls, 1989, p. 98). Similar patterns are found as early as the second grade, all of which raises scary questions about the unintended consequences of stressing high achievement per se without equally persuasive emphasis on the intrinsic benefits of seeking understanding and the private and personal pleasures of accomplishments.

Learning Styles and Learning Strategies

Our discussion of orientations toward learning leads naturally to considerations of **learning strategies** and **learning styles.** Although there have been many articles written for teachers about pupils' learning styles, they have unfortunately centered on popular conceptions of cerebral hemispheric specialization (right-brain versus left-brain learners) and superficial aspects of learning preferences (i.e., preference for working in warm versus cool temperatures, noisy versus quiet environments, alone versus in groups, etc.). The popular literature omits the fact that hemispheric specialization is most dramatically demonstrated when the large bundle of nerves connecting the two hemispheres is severed by surgical means, or under stringent experimental conditions that feed stimuli to one hemisphere while denying it to the other. The most significant fact of human cognitive functioning is the complex interactive involvement of both hemispheres in even the simplest acts of perception and learning (Gazzaniga & LeDoux, 1978). While there may indeed be learners who favor one or another of the visual-verbal modalities, of far greater importance is the way pupils make use of the information they are acquiring.

Similarly, the claims for useful interaction between learning conditions and learning preferences as measured by such widely used instruments as the Dunn, Dunn, and Price *Learning Style Inventory* outstrip the research evidence for such interactions. Hughes' (1992) review of this instrument found the manual presenting a "confused" use of factor analysis in supporting the scales, an "appalling" lack of test-retest reliability data, so little information about the norm group as to render the norms "meaningless," and essentially no empirical evidence to support the contention that students will learn better when learning conditions are adjusted to students' learning styles. Hughes concludes that the *Learning Style Inventory* has no redeeming values and extends this conclusion to many other measures of individual learning styles.

Schmeck's Conceptualization of Learning Styles

The construct *learning style* takes on a radically different connotation as defined by Ronald Schmeck at the University of Southern Illinois in Carbondale. Schmeck and his colleagues(1988) focus on the cognitive processes that students bring to bear at the time they encounter information. They see student approaches to learning as a continuum ranging from "surface" to "deep." A **surface approach** to learning leads to a faithful reproduction of the words of the textbook and of the teacher with attention to disconnected bits and pieces of information that are memorized. A **deep approach** to learning reflects an intention to extract meaning from the material, to seek interrelationships and organizing structures, and to interpret material in personally meaningful ways.

Schmeck, Ribich, and Ramanaiah (1977) wrote questionnaire items asking students about their study tactics. Factor analysis of responses to the questionnaire revealed four major clusters of items subsequently named Deep Processing, Elaborative Processing, Fact Retention, and Methodological Study. Items measuring Deep Processing and Elaborative Processing are

Table 16.2 *Items Measuring Deep Processing and Elaborative Processing*

D	I have trouble making inferences.	F
E	New concepts rarely make me think of many other similar concepts.	F
D	I have trouble organizing the information that I remember.	F
D	Even when I know I have carefully learned the material, I have trouble remembering it for an exam.	F
E	I do not try to convert facts into "rules of thumb."	F
D	I try to resolve conflicts between the information obtained from different sources.	T
E	I learned new words or ideas by visualizing a situation in which they occur.	T
E	I learn new concepts by expressing them in my own words.	T
D	I often memorize material that I don't understand.	F
D	I have difficulty planning work when confronted with a complex task.	F
E	I remember new words and ideas by associating them with words and ideas I already know.	T
D	I often have difficulty finding the right words for expressing my ideas.	F
D	I can easily handle questions requiring comparison of different concepts.	T
D	I have difficulty learning how to study for a course.	F
E	I rarely sit and think about a unit of material which I have just read.	F
D	I read critically.	T
E	I "daydream" about things I've studied.	T
E	I learn new ideas by relating them to similar ideas.	T
E	When learning a unit of material, I usually summarize it in my own words.	T
D	I think fast.	T
E	While learning new concepts their practical applications don't usually come to my mind.	F
D	I get good grades on term papers.	T
D	I can usually formulate a good guess even when I don't know the answer.	T
E	While studying, I attempt to find answers to questions I have in mind.	T
D	I can usually state the underlying message of films and readings.	T
D	I find it difficult to handle questions requiring critical evaluation.	F
D	Most of my instructors lecture too fast.	F
E	I rarely look for reasons behind the facts.	F
E	When I study something, I devise a system for recalling it later.	T
D	I have trouble seeing the difference between apparently similar ideas.	F
E	I am rarely able to design procedures for solving problems.	F
D	I do well on essay tests.	T

Reproduced from "Development of a Self Report Inventory for Assessing Individual Differences in Learning Processes" by R. R. Schmeck, F. D. Ribich, and N. Ramanaiah, *Applied Psychological Measurement*, 1, 1977. Reproduced by permission of Applied Psychological Measurement, Inc. Copyright © 1977.

shown in table 16.2. Students answer each item true or false. The letters *D* and *E,* designating items from the Deep Processing Scale and the Elaborative Processing Scale, and the key, shown to the right of each item, do not appear in the actual questionnaire.

The orientations to learning measured by the scales of Schmeck and his colleagues have great importance. Students who habitually engage in surface learning are unlikely to realize the full potential of the information they may be working so hard to get. Missing the relationships among ideas, failing to integrate details into larger structures, and not seeing the implications of the larger ideas for their own lives, these students find that the fruits of "education" become barren, sterile, and unsatisfying.

It is easy to see a close relationship between the learning styles of Schmeck's inventory and the motivational orientations described by Nicholls. It seems obvious that students who are working to please the teacher or to excel over their classmates (ego-orientation) are more likely to see learning as a memory activity (surface approach) than are students who are exploring information and developing understanding for their own sakes.

The story may even go deeper than that. Schmeck and his colleagues suggest that learning styles may be importantly related to self-concepts. Students with poor perceptions of their own abilities to do schoolwork may become dependent on the exact words of teachers and texts because of the apparent safety of explicitly stated knowledge. Learners who have developed a surface orientation to learning may have adopted this stance because they don't feel secure enough to risk making their own interpretations and arriving at their own understandings.

Considering the role that self-concept may play in the student's learning stance as well as the student's overall adjustment, let us now turn to the measurement of self-concept.

Self-Concept Scales

The idea of the **self-concept** has been around since the early sociologist, Charles Horton Cooley (1902), suggested that our interactions with others leave us with a sense of ourselves. Cooley believed that the responses that other people make to an individual provide a basis for self-perceptions. Social interactions thus provide a mirror through which we develop our "looking-glass self," our self-concept.

Jersild (1952), a professor at Columbia University, collected essays from a large sample of pupils at various grade levels written in response to the topics "What I like about myself" and "What I dislike about myself." These responses ultimately served as the basis for a series of items assembled by Piers and Harris into what is now the Piers-Harris Self-Concept Scale (Piers & Harris,1969–84) suitable for students in grades four through twelve. Students responding to this scale answer yes or no to eighty items such as the following:

I have a nice-looking face.
I do many bad things.
I am good in my schoolwork.

Factor analysis was used to identify six clusters of items and a score can be obtained for each of these scales:

Behavior
Intellectual and school status

Physical appearance and attributes
Anxiety
Popularity
Happiness and satisfaction

The manual cautions against overinterpretation of these scores. The total score of the scale has yielded internal consistency coefficients ranging from .88 to .93. Research with the Piers-Harris, extensively reported in the manual, suggests that this scale correlates moderately well with other measures of self-concept and personality. The company distributing the scale requires a "User Qualification Form" as a guard against use by individuals who may not be qualified to interpret the findings. Jeske (1985) concludes his review of this scale with the following observations:

> Even though caution should be exercised in interpreting specific cluster scales for individual children, the Piers-Harris appears to be the best children's self-concept measure currently available. It is highly recommended for use as a classroom screening device, as an aid to clinical assessment, and as a research tool (p.1170).

Young Children's Self-Concept

A downward extension of the Piers-Harris was developed by McDaniel as part of a larger study (McDaniel et al., 1973). The downward extension is designed for use with children in grades one through three. This scale contains forty items and yields three scores:

My feeling self.
My behaving self.
My school self.

The reliability for the subscales is too low for use in individual diagnostic work, but the internal consistency coefficient for the total scale (KR–20 = .86), established on 459 pupils in grades one through four, is sufficiently high to provide relatively consistent estimates of the child's self-concept.

Working with 138 first grade urban students with a large proportion of disadvantaged children, McDaniel and his colleagues (1973) found correlations of .23 with reading achievement and .42 with mathematics achievement. While it is difficult to know whether low achievement causes low self-concept or vice versa, Shavelson, Bolus, and Keesling (1980) advance the tentative conclusion that low self-concept contributes to low achievement.

For three randomly selected pupils in each class in the study described above, the teacher completed twenty-seven Likert items describing each pupil's behavior. These items were scored to indicate three characteristics for the sixteen children selected: Independence, Cooperativeness, and Social. Self-concept was significantly related to two of these scales, Independence (.45) and Social (.59).

In a study of twenty-one elementary teachers in grades one through four, McDaniel and Leddick (1978) found correlations between self-concept scores and teacher ratings of their children's self-concepts that ranged from zero to .58 with a median of .32.

More recently, Coder (1990) found a correlation of −.44 between scores on the downward extension and anxiety as measured by the Revised Children's Manifest Anxiety Scale (Reynolds & Richmond, 1987). The relationship between self-concept and anxiety for third grade pupils was −.52. Thus, a high self-concept was related to low anxiety.

A scholarly review of self-concept research, including programs designed to enhance self-concept, is presented by Hattie (1992). It is clear from this book that much work is ahead of us in understanding how students integrate information about self and how self-concept affects behavior. Even so, measures of self-concept may be one of the most promising tools for helping teachers and counselors identify children who merit a closer look. Additionally, self-concept measures will be an important research tool as we continue to search for patterns among abilities, school attitudes, motivations to learn, learning styles, and self-concepts.

Measures of Individual Adjustment

We have been discussing some relatively global measures of school attitudes, learning orientations, and self-concepts and have suggested there may be interactive patterns among these three characteristics of students. On a more personal level, do negative attitudes, alienation from learning, or low self-concepts signal temporary difficulties or more deep-seated adjustment problems? Are there measures of adjustment that can be used to help teachers decide whether a child should be referred to the school counselor?

Problem Check Lists

A quite different approach to gathering information about children and adolescents is the use of problem check lists. The *Mooney Problem Check List* (Mooney & Gordon, 1950) lists more than 200 problems that might be of concern to students. Here are some representative items from this check list:

Often have headaches
Afraid of failing in schoolwork
Never having fun with mother or dad

Wanting to earn some of my own money
Not knowing how to make a date
Wishing people liked me better
Being nervous

Students read through the list, underlining all problems that apply to them. Later they look back over the problems that are underlined and circle problems that are bothering them most. Questions at the end of the check list request additional comments about the most troublesome problems and ask if the students would like to talk over their problems with someone.

It is not necessary to generate scores from the check lists. The items are grouped in such a way as to facilitate quick identification of problem areas: health and physical development, school, social relations, home and family, money and work, and boy-girl relationships.

Variations of these check lists are published for use at the elementary grade levels by Science Research Associates (SRA). The SRA inventory places a small box, a middle-size box, a large box, and the word "no" by each problem statement. Children are instructed to check the appropriate box to indicate whether the problem is a little, middle-size, or big problem, or no problem at all.

Problem check lists have the advantage of not providing scores that may be used to stigmatize a child. They also provide a convenient way for a child to refer himself or herself to a counselor. Additionally, problem check lists allow school counselors to quickly identify areas of concern and invite children to talk more about specific problem areas. Finally, tallies of problems checked by all students can sensitize teachers to some of the common concerns that may face large numbers of students at a particular school.

For example, table 16.3 shows the ten top problems indicated by sophomore students in two different high schools in the same community. From these lists of problems, would you say that the general concerns of students at School A are different from those at School B? If a faculty group at each school were making recommendations about programs to help students, what might be some of the recommendations?

Problem check lists have much to recommend them. They do not provide scores that can be used to label individuals, they identify specific problems that can serve as a basis for discussions with counselors, and they provide opportunities for self-nomination for counseling interviews. In school settings where counseling time is limited and students with serious concerns can go undetected, problem check lists can help identify children who need special attention.

Table 16.3 *High Frequency Problems from Two High Schools in the Same Community*

Problem	Percent of Students Marking Problem
School A (n = 121)	
Wanting to earn some of my own money	64
Not spending enough time in study	60
Wanting to buy more of my own things	60
Hurting people's feelings	59
Worrying	58
Being nervous	56
Not interested in some subjects	56
Worrying about grades	56
Wanting to improve my appearance	55
Being talked about	54
School B (n = 131)	
Don't like to study	73
Worrying about grades	65
Worrying about examinations	61
Wanting to earn some of my own money	53
Needing to know my vocational abilities	52
Worried about a member of the family	51
Parents not understanding me	51
Parents not trusting me	51
Choosing best subjects to take next term	50
Just can't get some subjects	50

Nominating Techniques, Sociograms, and Direct Observations

The procedures we have discussed thus far depend on the pupil's self-appraisal or self-report. Sometimes the perceptions of a student's peers provide additional perspectives that are important in the total picture. Nominating techniques and sociometric procedures can reveal aspects of the student's patterns of interaction with other students. Direct observations by teachers are also an essential source of information about a student's affective development and the causes that may lie behind particular behaviors.

Nominating Techniques

While teachers frequently have a good sense of the social interactions within their classes, there are subtle perceptions among peers that may go undetected. One way of learning more about the way children perceive and respond to each other is to use **nominating techniques;** ask for nominations for particular roles. In "Casting Characters," the teacher solicits nominations for a class play and asks children to put down names of

Figure 16.2

*Illustrative Guess Who
form for evaluating pupils'
"concern for others."*
Reprinted with the
permission of Macmillan
Publishing Company
from *Measurement and
Evaluation in Teaching,*
Sixth Edition, by Norman
E. Gronlund and Robert
L. Linn. Copyright ©
1990 by Macmillan
Publishing Company.

Directions

Listed below are descriptions of what some pupils in this room are like. Read the descriptions and write the names of the pupils who *best fit* each description. You may write the names of anyone in this room, including those who are absent. Your choices will not be seen by anyone else. Give first name and initial of last name.

Remember!

1. Write the names of pupils in this room who best fit each description.
2. Write as many names as you wish for each description.
3. The same person may fit more than one description.
4. You should write the first name and initial of last name.
5. Your choices will *not be seen* by anyone else.

Write the names below each description.

1. Here is someone who enjoys working and playing with others.

2. Here is someone who is willing to share materials with others.

3. Here is someone who is willing to help others with their schoolwork.

4. Here is someone who makes sure others are not left out of games.

5. Here is someone who encourages others to do well.

6. Here is someone who is kind to others who have a problem.

---

people who would be good for particular roles. These roles could include a villain who likes to hurt others, someone who is quiet and shy, an individual always ready to help, and so on.

In a related procedure, "Guess Who," characteristics are described and students guess who among their classmates fits the description. Gronlund and Linn (1990) provide the example in figure 16.2, designed to evaluate pupils' concern for others.

Teachers and researchers are frequently reluctant to use such nominating techniques for fear that children's feelings will be hurt if they are cast in negative roles and, in addition, parents might object. A case can be made on the other side that the measuring device does not create the attitudes, and that recognition of the problem and timely intervention may be more desirable than leaving the attitudes undetected.

Table 16.4   *Sociometric Choice Matrix: Five-member Group, Two-Choice Question[a]*

		a	b	*j* c	d	e
	a	0	1	0	0	1
	b	1	0	0	0	1
i	c	0	0	0	1	1
	d	0	1	0	0	1
	e	1	1	0	0	0
	Σ:	2	3	0	1	4

[a]Individual *i chooses* individual *j.* That is, the table can be read by rows: *b* chooses *a* and *e.* It can also be read by columns: *b is chosen* by *a, d,* and *e.* The sums at the bottom indicate the number of choices each individual receives.
Reprinted with the permission of Holt, Rinehart, and Winston from *Foundations of Educational Research*, Third Edition, by Fred N. Kerlinger. Copyright © 1986 by Holt, Rinehart, and Winston, Inc.

Sociometric Procedures

An easy device for seeing rather quickly who are leaders and who are left out of a group is to ask for names of children with whom an individual would like to share an activity. Children may be asked whom they would like to play with, sit next to at lunch, work with on a committee, have as their companion on a field trip, or perhaps, give a birthday present. Kerlinger (1986) suggests that the data be organized in a **sociometric matrix** for easy scanning, and provides the example in table 16.4.

Examining the bottom row of the matrix, the sum (Σ) of the choices, we see that student e, who was chosen four times, is the most popular and student c has received no choices.

The pattern of relationships can be more readily visualized by constructing a **sociogram.** In a sociogram, each student is represented by a dot and lines are drawn to show the direction of each student's choice. In figure 16.3, Kerlinger (1986) provides a graphic representation of the choices tabulated in the matrix.

Again, we see that student e is very popular, but we can readily observe something more. Students a, b, and e form a clique, a small group of students who mutually choose each other. Additionally, student c stands out as socially isolated, having been chosen by no one. In most schools, there will be from two to three isolates in each classroom. These isolates can be considered private tragedies played out in the teacher's presence, but frequently without his or her knowledge.

Asher and Dodge (1986) make an important distinction between children who are sociometrically *neglected* by their peer group and those who are sociometrically *rejected.* The child who is neglected by the peer

Figure 16.3

Sociogram. Reprinted with the permission of Holt, Rinehart, and Winston from *Foundations of Educational Research,* Third Edition, by Fred N. Kerlinger. Copyright © 1986 by Holt, Rinehart & Winston, Inc.

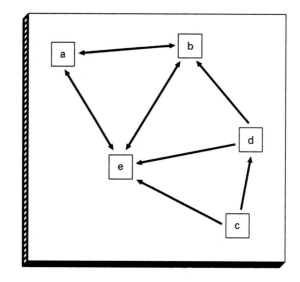

group may have no friends but is not actively disliked by other children. On the other hand, the rejected child is overtly disliked by others. There may be reasons for the dislike. The rejected child is more likely to be aggressive and disruptive.

Of the two kinds of socially isolated children, the sociometrically rejected child appears to be most at risk. Unlike the neglected child, a change of situation does not often bring a fresh start. Patterns of rejection are observed in the new situation. Rejected children report more depression and loneliness than neglected children and are more likely to experience serious adjustment problems in later life.

It is important to note that the sociogram, by itself, does not differentiate between sociometrically neglected and rejected children. From the sociogram pictured above, it is impossible to tell whether child c, who was chosen by no one, is simply neglected or is actively rejected by the other children. In general, the rejected child would be the child who receives a high number of nominations for negative behavior using the nominating techniques described above. Since many teachers do not like to use these techniques, Asher and Dodge (1986) offer a method for making a distinction between neglected and rejected children. This method involves providing each child with a class roster and asking children to rate each classmate on a scale of one (low) to five (high) according to some criteria, i.e., liking to play with the classmate. Each rating of one is considered equivalent to a negative nomination and, generally, students with a high number of one ratings are likely to be actively rejected by their peers.

Table 16.5   *Loneliness and Social Dissatisfaction Questionnaire*

1. It's easy for me to make new friends at school.
2. I like to read. (ns)
3. I have nobody to talk to in class.
4. I'm good at working with other children in my class.
5. I watch TV a lot. (ns)
6. It's hard for me to make friends at school.*
7. I like school. (ns)
8. I have lots of friends in my class.
9. I feel alone at school.*
10. I can find a friend in my class when I need one.
11. I play sports a lot. (ns)
12. It's hard to get kids in school to like me.*
13. I like science. (ns)
14. I don't have anyone to play with at school.*
15. I like music. (ns)
16. I get along with my classmates.
17. I feel left out of things at school.*
18. There's no other kids I can go to when I need help in school.*
19. I like to paint and draw. (ns)
20. I don't get along with other children in school.*
21. I'm lonely at school.*
22. I am well liked by the kids in my class.
23. I like playing board games a lot. (ns)
24. I don't have any friends in class.*

Asterisks identify those items for which scoring is reversed.

As mentioned earlier, rejected children tend to feel more lonely than socially isolated children who are simply ignored, but not actively disliked. A direct measure of loneliness can be obtained by using a sixteen-item scale discussed by Asher and associates (1990). This scale is shown in table 16.5, along with eight items that are not scored, but have been added to disguise the nature of the questionnaire. These items are indicated with the notation (ns) following the item.

Children respond to the items in the loneliness questionnaire using a five-point scale:

1. That's always true about me.
2. That's true about me most of the time.
3. That's sometimes true about me.
4. That's hardly ever true about me.
5. That's not true at all about me.

For children below the third grade, a three-point scale is more appropriate, sometimes accompanied with smiling and frowning faces to help convey the meaning.

Coie and Koeppl (1990) contend that rejected children lack critical skills for making friends and suggest that we help them by teaching social skills. It is a mistake, however, to believe that all rejected children can profit from the same social skills training strategies. Aggressive, disruptive, low-achieving students may need help in handling hostile feelings. Parents may need help in making aggressive behavior at home less rewarding. Lochman (1985) developed an eighteen-session program for direct teaching of self-control of anger ("I'm getting angry. Don't let him make me lose it now."). Intervention programs have been developed by Patterson (1971) to change the parenting behaviors that may inadvertently reward aggressive behaviors. Additionally, skill training in achievement can help increase the rewards students gain by staying on-task in class with a consequent improvement in image among the students' peers.

It should be evident that sociometric devices followed by questionnaires help identify children who are at risk of establishing and maintaining maladaptive patterns of social behavior. Intervention activities for peer-rejected children should become an increasingly important part of our programs for the psychological welfare of children in our schools.

Direct Observations of Behavior

Anastasi (1988) notes that tests of personality are brief observations of behavior occurring under standard conditions. "But against the obvious advantages of such standardized procedures, we must balance the advantages of a much more extensive sampling of behavior available through observational techniques in natural settings" (p. 643). Teachers, observing and monitoring students over a long time span, are in a unique position to make judgements about students' behaviors and to modify some of the pressures that may be at work.

We introduce this section with a brief glimpse at an episode from a play therapy session where the therapist's sole concern is on recognizing and helping the child express the feelings behind the behavior.

Play Therapy

In play therapy children use a variety of play materials, and in the process frequently recreate life situations and express deep-seated feelings. The child, or children, are closely observed to see what feelings are expressed and what kinds of human relations are played out. In this session, two brothers, ages 8 and 7, express their feelings toward their mother through their behavior with a doll (Axline, 1947, pp. 238–239). The mother and father have separated and the children have been placed in a foster home.

> Timmy (pounding the doll): I'm beating her up. I'm pounding her to pieces.
> Therapist: You're pounding the mother to pieces.
> Timmy (trying to tear her in half): I'll pull her apart. I'll jerk her to pieces.
> Therapist: You want to destroy the mother.
> Timmy: I'll show her. I'll get even.
> Therapist: You'll get even with the mother.
> Timmy (pulling off the doll's removeable arms): See there? I pulled off her arms.
> Therapist: You pulled off her arms.
> Timmy (throwing the doll down on the floor): I'll slam her around good. I'll fix her.
> Therapist: You'll fix her.
> Bobby (picking up the doll and throwing it down): That'll fix the mean thing.
> Therapist: You want to get even with the mean old thing, too.

In this dramatic instance, we note that the therapist is not concerned with stopping behavior or whether the feelings are socially acceptable. The energy is focused on close observation of what is occurring and on recognizing the feelings behind the behavior.

Teachers' Observations

Some teachers may feel that the therapist's job is less complex than their own. Emotional problems are frequently expressed in antisocial and disruptive ways, which interfere with class routine and may even threaten other students. The immediate need is frequently to stop the disruptive behavior. The crucial feature of the teacher's involvement is that, while stopping the behavior and redirecting the feeling, the teacher constantly scans for underlying causes.

It is important to take this stance, for with all our formal instruments to measure pupil adjustment, it is likely that teachers will continue to be the first line of defense against the possibilities that children with severe problems will go unnoticed and unhelped. The key is to search for the underlying problems that lie behind the immediate behavior.

In all the educational literature, no one has talked more directly to teachers about children's behavior than James Hymes. We have abridged the following pages from his small pamphlet, *Teacher Listen . . . The*

Children Speak (Copyright © 1949 by the State Charities Aid Association, New York. Abridged by premission). In the first passage, we will see that our immediate impulses in reacting to the overly aggressive child are open to a number of productive alternatives.

"I'll hit you. . . . I'll hurt you"

The youngster who hits and bullies can make you angry. It is very easy to feel angry BUT . . . you have to feel some sympathy for the bully too. He is an unhappy child. Often he is a frightened child, a worried child. He too needs your help.

People—his parents, neighbors, children, his other teachers—have told him over and over again: "You mustn't hit, you mustn't push, you mustn't hurt." He knows. He has probably been punished a thousand times in a thousand ways, and yet he goes ahead and does it anyhow. He hits even though he knows that it gets him into trouble.

Usually it takes a long time to make a child a bully. Something happens in his life, not once but over and over, to make him act this way. There have been some pressures on him. Things have gone wrong in the way he has been treated.

Don't look for wonders. It took a long time to build up the problem or it took some very major event. You are entitled to a long time to help overcome it.

Don't expect the child to know why he is acting the way he is. You can understand that there are some basic causes but the child cannot.

Don't pile on more pressure. You know that some worry is causing the behavior. Don't add fuel to the fire.

Don't listen when people say: "We've tried everything and nothing works." The people who say this have not tried everything at all. In fact, they probably have tried only one thing: punishment.

Even when you have to stop the youngster, don't be angry with him or blame him or give him the feeling that now you, too, are through with him. Be firm, but be as sympathetic as you can.

Sometimes you can even put this into words: "I know you feel like hitting something but you can't hit other children. That hurts them. I wouldn't want anyone to hurt you."

Keep looking for causes. Visit his home, if you can. Talk with his parents. See the youngster in all the places you can: in the lunchroom, on the playground, on the street, in clubs, at home. The more you know about him the more surely you will be able to help.

The biggest thing: Give him ways to get back at the world . . . ways that are safe and possible. You know how sometimes you would like to bang the table when you are mad . . . how you could kick something when you are feeling angry? These children need opportunities—acceptable, safe, and possible—to do this too. It makes them feel better inside and they need to hit children less. A punching bag that the child can sock? More clay to pound? Games where roughhouse is O.K.? Dolls the child can boss around in play? More top-of-the-voice singing of lively songs? Or perhaps the child can make puppets. Then the puppet is the bossy bully one.

Don't let people talk you out of what you are doing. You have your understanding to back you up. You know that you are dealing with an unhappy child. You know that there are reasons now why he has to act the way he does. But you are bringing nearer the day when he will feel safe with people and safe with the world.

Hymes introduces four other patterns of behavior that communicate important feelings and suggest hidden causes. In each case, Hymes recommends that the teacher look behind the behavior to the underlying needs, then find ways to help the child meet these needs in more acceptable ways.

"look at me . . . look at me . . . look at me"

The minute your back is turned he starts acting up. He clowns. He makes faces. He throws something. He starts everyone giggling at him. Always he wants attention. Always he wants people to look at him. Always he wants to be the center of the stage. What can you do about this?

Maybe you feel like wringing his neck. He spoils your work. With that grin and his antics, those queer noises he makes, he can ruin all the interest you have been building up.

"I want you . . . I need you . . . I love you"

Do you have a youngster who clutches your hand? He holds you so tight that it hurts.

Do you have a youngster you can't shake off? He is your shadow every minute of the time.

Do you have a youngster who doesn't know when to stop? He hangs on you and demands . . . demands . . . demands.

In most classrooms there are some children like this. Boys and girls who drain you dry because they want you to give so much.

"Don't see me . . . Don't hear me"

You can't forget some children. Some are bright and they know all the answers . . . or some raise their hands and always have something to say.

Other youngsters need bells on them. Something should tinkle when they walk.

They blend in so well. They sit quietly and say nothing. They hand in their work. These children are no trouble to you BUT some of them may be real trouble to themselves. Some of them may be unhappy, uncomfortable . . . lost!

"I chew my nails . . . I twist my hair"

Are any of these youngsters in your classroom? A child who chews his nails . . . a girl who pulls and twists her hair . . . a youngster who sucks his fingers . . . a boy who picks his nose . . . one who bites his lips . . . another who bites a pencil?

Little mannerisms! And a great many children in a great many classrooms have them.

When you see it you often have a strong urge to STOP it.

Sometimes it even makes you angry when you see a big child doing such a silly little-child thing. Why do they do it anyhow?

Watch these youngsters and you will see why. Their behavior will tell you.

Teachers who observe such behaviors and seek a better understanding of the conditions that motivate them are making personality assessments. These assessments may be noted in anecdotal records, or may become part of the understanding that serves to guide the teacher's interaction with the child.

Teachers can meet some of the underlying needs in more healthy ways; for example, needs for attention can be met by helping a child get the spotlight by working a special talent into the curriculum. The teacher can notice the dependent child more during class and arrange special jobs: erasing the board, carrying messages, watering plants. A sociogram can help determine a quiet child's status in the group and confidence can be developed by encouraging special skills and by bringing together youngsters who are good for each other. For the nervous child, the teacher can watch for those situations that bring strain and stress, and can look for ways to build confidence and to demonstrate friendship. Perhaps more than anything else, viewing behavior as expressions of underlying needs means a greater acceptance of the child and a more positive attitude.

Summary

Search the heart of any parent of a school-age child or adolescent and you will find a fervent wish that the child "be happy." This translates to a desire that the child make an adjustment to the demands of school and to the social context in which schooling takes place. It also expresses a hope that the teacher understands the child and tries to adapt to any special difficulties that the child exhibits.

In meeting these expectations, teachers are alert to disparity between abilities and expectations, or other situational factors that may contribute to a student's unhappiness. At other times, it seems that the student may be bringing into the situation attitudes and behaviors that are dysfunctional. But each attitude and behavior has a history. No matter how many problems the behavior may be causing now, at one time this behavior was a solution, of sorts, to similar situations in the past.

As teachers, we need to cultivate a tendency to look beneath the surface of behavior in search of explanations. Attempts to assess personal adjustment are essentially efforts to determine the habitual perceptions and reactions that individuals bring to situations and to understand why these perceptions and reactions make sense to the individual concerned. When we say "make sense" we don't mean that the individual can supply reasons for the behavior. We mean that the actions and attitudes are the best resolution of forces available to the individual at that time in meeting his or her emotional needs.

We noted that teachers can construct self-report inventories to learn about the attitudes and perceptions of their students. Additionally, a variety of instruments are available to measure a wide range of student responses to schooling. An enormous amount of information about learning strategies, self-concept, personal problems, and social adjustment can be obtained and used to help understand individual students. We have also tried to reinforce the use of direct observation in appraising the adjustment of children. As teachers, we can frequently adjust classroom routines, social groupings, and our own patterns of interactions to facilitate the affective adjustment of students. We can also serve as referral sources when we detect problems that require more long-term, systematic attention.

References

Anastasi, A. (1988). *Psychological testing* (6th ed.). New York: Macmillan.

Asher, S. R., & Dodge, K. A. (1986). Identifying children who are rejected by their peers. *Developmental Psychology, 22*(4), 444–449.

Asher, S. R., Parkhurst, J. T., Hymel, S., & Williams, G. A. (1990). Peer rejection and loneliness in childhood. In S. R. Asher & J. D. Coie (eds.), *Peer rejection in childhood*. Cambridge, England; New York: Cambridge University Press.

Asher, S. R., & Wheeler, V. A. (1985). Children's loneliness: A comparison of rejected and neglected peer status. *Journal of Consulting and Clinical Psychology, 53,* 500–505.

Axline, V. M. (1947). *Play therapy*. New York: Houghton Mifflin.

Brown, C.S., & Rife, J.C. (1991). Social, personality, and gender differences in at-risk and not-at-risk sixth grade students. *Journal of Early Adolescence, 11,* 482–485.

Coder, K. (1990). *Relationships between self-concept and anxiety among elementary school children.* Unpublished Ed.S. dissertation. Purdue University.

Coie, J. D., & Koeppl, G. K. (1990). Adapting intervention to the problems of aggressive and disruptive rejected children. In S. R. Asher & J. D. Coie (eds.), *Peer rejection in childhood*. Cambridge, England; New York: Cambridge University Press.

Cooley, C. H. (1902). *Human nature and the social order.* New York: Scribner's.

Ehrlich, V. (1968). *The dimensions of attitude toward school of elementary school children and grades three to six.* Unpublished doctoral dissertation, Columbia University, New York.

Fennema, E., & Sherman, J. A. (1976). Fennema-Sherman mathematics attitude scale: Instruments designed to measure attitudes toward the learning of mathematics by females and males. *JSAS Catalog of Selected Documents in Psychology, 6* (31), Ms. No. 1225.

Gazzaniga, M. S., & LeDoux, J. E. (1978). *The integrated mind*. New York: Plenum Press.

Gronlund, N. E., & Linn, R. L. (1990). *Measurement and evaluation in teaching* (6th ed.). New York: Macmillan.

Hattie, J. (1992). *Self-concept*. Hillsdale, NJ: Erlbaum.

Henerson, M. E., Morris, L. L., & Fitz-Gibbon, C. T. (1978). *How to measure attitudes*. Beverly Hills, CA: Sage Publications.

Hughes, J. N. (1992). Review of Learning Style Inventory (Price Systems, Inc.). In J. J. Kramer & J. C. Conoley (eds.), *The eleventh mental measurements yearbook*. Lincoln, NE: Buros Institute of Mental Measurements.

Hymes, J. L., Jr. (1949). *Teacher listen, the children speak . . .* New York: New York Committee on Mental Health of the State Charities Aid Association, 105 E. 22 Street, New York, New York.

Jersild, A. T. (1952). *In search of self*. New York: Columbia University Press.

Jeske, R. J. (1985). Review of Piers-Harris Children's Self-Concept Scale (The Way I Feel About Myself). In James V. Mitchell, Jr. (ed.), *The ninth mental measurements yearbook*. Lincoln, NE: Buros Institute of Mental Measurements.

Kerlinger, F. N. (1986). *Foundations of educational research* (3rd ed.). New York: Holt, Rinehart & Winston.

Kramer, J. J., & Conoley, J. C. (1992). *The eleventh mental measurements yearbook*. Lincoln, NE: Buros Institute of Mental Measurements.

Lochman, J. E. (1985). Effects of different treatment lengths in cognitive behavioral interventions with aggressive boys. *Child Psychiatry and Human Development, 16*, 45–56.

McDaniel, E., Ames, C., Anderson, J., Cicirelli, V., Feldhusen, J., Felsenthal, H., Kane, R., Lohmann, J., Moe, A., & Wheatley, G. (1973). *Longitudinal study of elementary school effects: Design, instruments and specifications for a field test*. Final report submitted to the U.S. Office of Education. West Lafayette, IN: Purdue Research Foundation. (ERIC No. ED100945).

McDaniel, E., & Leddick, G. (1978, August). *Elementary children's self-concepts, factor structures, and teacher ratings*. Paper presented at the meeting of the American Psychological Association, Toronto.

Mooney, R. L., & Gordon, L. V. (1950). Manual. *Mooney Problem Checklists*. San Antonio, TX: The Psychological Corporation.

Mullis, I. V. S., & Jenkins, L. B. (1988). *The science report card*. Princeton, NJ: Educational Testing Service.

Nicholls, J. G. (1989). *The competitive ethos and democratic education*. Cambridge, MA: Harvard University Press.

Patterson, G. R. (1971). *Living with children*. Champaign, IL: Research Press.

Piers, E. V., & Harris, D. B. (1969–84). *Manual of the Piers-Harris Children's Self-Concept Scale*. Los Angeles: Western Psychological Services.

Reynolds, C. R., & Richmond, B. O. (1987). *Revised Children's Manifest Anxiety Scale*. Los Angeles: Western Psychological Services.

Schmeck, R. (1988). *Learning strategies and learning styles*. New York: Plenum.

Schmeck, R. R., Ribich, F. D., & Ramanaiah, N. (1977). Development of a self-report inventory for assessing individual differences in learning processes. *Applied Psychological Measurement, 1*, 413–431.

Shavelson, R. J., Bolus, R., & Keesling, J. W. (1980). Self-concept: Recent developments in theory and method. In D. A. Payne (ed.), *New directions for testing and measurements: Recent developments in affective measurements*. San Francisco: Jossey-Bass.

Test Collection, Educational Testing Service. (1991). *The ETS test collection catalog, Volume 5: Attitude tests*. Phoenix, AZ: Oryx Press.

Test Collection, Educational Testing Service. (1992). *The ETS test collection catalog, Volume 6: Affective measures and personality tests*. Phoenix, AZ: Oryx Press.

Tests in Print IV (in press). Lincoln, NE: Buros Institute of Mental Measurements.

I think I understand educational measurement. When I learned that the three things needed for a good test were reliability, validity, and adequate standardization, the mysteries of test jargon were solved. But now so many new things are appearing. Some states are using portfolios in their testing programs and there is talk of doing it here. They have ordered a computer administered test for the counseling office and the special ed teacher is talking about "dynamic assessment." At least I feel I have the background to think about these new trends.

chapter seventeen

New Trends in Testing

Student portfolios, dynamic assessment, and computer applications to testing are new trends appearing on the testing scene. In some cases, these trends represent shifts in philosophy about testing, while in other cases they reflect applications of new technology. We shall examine each of these new trends in turn, focusing on the way each approach broadens and extends our thinking about measurement.

Portfolio Assessment

"A **portfolio** is a file or folder containing a variety of information that documents a student's experience and accomplishments. The portfolio can contain summary descriptions of accomplishments, official records and diary items" (Archbald & Newmann, 1988, p. 29). Use of portfolios in evaluating student achievement reflects a larger move away from standardized tests toward "authentic" evaluations that stress the productive uses of knowledge rather than the reproduction of knowledge. Archbald and Newmann (p. 3) continue, "When people write letters, news articles, insurance claims, poems; when they speak a foreign language; when they develop blueprints; when they create a painting, a piece of music, or build a stereo cabinet, they demonstrate achievements that have a special value missing in tasks contrived only for the purpose of assessing knowledge (such as spelling quizzes, laboratory exercises, or typical final exams)."

Portfolios as records of student achievement make sense to teachers who realize, perhaps more than anyone else, that educational achievement is recorded in the personal stories of individual pupils. This point is illustrated by this slightly abridged account of a fifth grade inner-city pupil taught by Brenda Church of Akron, Ohio (Vacca & Rasinski, 1992).

> Gaddis, a lean and gangling eleven-year-old whose body impatiently waits for manhood, spent the first couple of weeks in Brenda's class stomping around the room. Angry. Defiant. Unwilling. He railed against most activities involving literacy, especially writing. His outward demeanor masked an inner fear that conveyed the message: "If I don't try, then I can't fail."

> With the first parents' night of the year approaching, the students decided to illustrate and then write thumbnail sketches of the main characters in Jean Georges's *My Side of the Mountain*. Although Gaddis worked painstakingly on his character's picture, he could not bring a written description to completion. According to Brenda, "He proceeded to crumple his drafts, stomp across the room and dispose of them in the wastepaper basket, maybe eight or nine times."

Brenda could easily have been intimidated by Gaddis's behavior, given up on him, accepted his drawing as the best he could do, and not have him follow through on the character description. But she knew that he had something to say. A crumpled draft, which she retrieved from the wastepaper basket, indicated the same, although it was riddled with spelling and other mechanical errors. So they talked. Gaddis, it turns out, had not written anything of any length or substance in previous grades, other than fill-in-blanks or one sentence responses. Putting ideas on a blank sheet of paper frightened him.

Brenda worked with Gaddis, supporting him in the writing process. He stuck with it and completed a two-paragraph description. His mother, who worked nights, had never been to a parents' night, and she didn't attend on this occasion either. But it didn't matter. His contribution was proudly displayed with the work of his classmates. Gaddis, the writer, visited the display every so often over the course of the next several days, reading his piece and other character descriptions. Something unexpected then happened. Brenda invited his mother to visit the class during the day to see Gaddis's work and discuss his progress. She did. As the year progressed, Gaddis maintained his familiar stomp, but continued to make significant strides in his literacy development.

In figure 17.1 we see Gaddis's two paragraphs describing the main character of the story, along with his drawing of this character with a falcon perched on his shoulder. Absorbing the paragraphs and viewing this drawing, we suddenly find ourselves with a new and surprising appreciation of Gaddis and his potentialities for further growth. We sense that Gaddis, too, has attained a new perception of himself. This is the power of portfolios in the evaluation process.

Portfolio assessment is an extension of an educational philosophy recognizing the highly personal directions that growth and development might take at any particular time. Vacca and Rasinski (pp. 241–242) describe the role of portfolios in Brenda's assessment procedures:

> Far more important to Brenda than assigning grades is the ongoing assessment she conducts of each student's progress as readers and writers. She keeps portfolios of students' work. Portfolio assessment, as the name implies, represents a collection of many indicators of student progress. She maintains a portfolio folder for each child: "I keep oral reading samples, writing pieces, samples of work from the thematic units, lists of books that they have read, and observation notes on 3×5 index cards." These cards describe how the students are doing, the interest they are showing in reading, and the kinds of reading they are doing.

Brenda uses portfolios to assess students' progress for instructional purposes. She examines the portfolios periodically to determine where each child is as a reader and writer. She asks herself, "What is the child doing well?

Sam Gribley is the wildboy. He weighs 109 pounds and is thirteen years old. He lives in the Catskill Mountains and is missing from home for about one year. Sam has dreamed about living in the wilderness. Now it has come true. He wanted to prove to his father that he could live out there in the mountains.

He made a tree for his home. He was proud of himself. This boy even found himself a falcon so he could have company through the winter days. He named his bird Frightful. Frightful helped him find his food. He was a great help to Sam.

Figure 17.1 *Gaddis's character sketch*

Figure and excerpts from *Case Studies in Whole Language* by R. T. Vacca and T. V. Rasinski. Copyright © 1992 by Holt, Rinehart, and Winston, Inc. Reprinted by permission of the publisher.

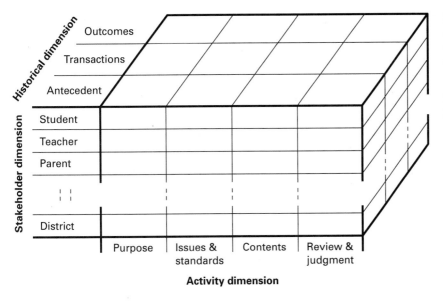

Figure 17.2 *The cognitive model for assessing portfolios showing the activity, historical, and stakeholder dimensions.* Reprinted with the permission of F. L. Paulson and P. R. Paulson from *The Making of a Portfolio* by F. L. Paulson and P.R. Paulson. Copyright © 1991 by F. L. Paulson and P. R. Paulson.

What does the child need help in?" When she holds the evaluation conferences at the end of the grading period, Brenda uses the work samples in the portfolio as the basis for her comments. She makes sure that the children know what they are doing well and what they may need to work on to continue growing as readers and writers.

Paulson and Paulson (1991) lodge portfolios firmly within the teaching procedure itself and assert that the processes involved in creating the portfolio are more important than the products they contain. As an aid in systematizing thinking about portfolios, they have constructed a cognitive model (see figure 17.2) that directs attention to the stakeholders who have an interest in portfolios, to the activities involved in initiating portfolios, and to the historical dimensions that preserve developmental trends in the record.

We will use Paulson and Paulson's framework and follow their discussion as we examine the elements that enter into portfolio assessments.

The Stakeholder Dimension

The placement of students at the head of the list of stakeholders reflects an explicit value judgement by Paulson and Paulson. They see the student as the primary stakeholder in portfolios, playing a major role in deciding the purpose of the portfolio, what goes into it, and how the contents will be used. "The role of the students as portfolio owners, creators and reviewers is our central concern" (p. 1). Teachers, as instructional leaders, also play an important role, but students benefit from entering into their own educational planning and reflecting on progress toward standards that have been cooperatively established.

The Activity Dimension

The activity dimension refers to efforts devoted to developing reasons for the portfolios and making decisions about curricular objectives, the kinds of content that will be relevant, standards for selecting them, and opportunities for interpreting and evaluating the contents.

As illustrated in the Paulson and Paulson model, these activities are not the exclusive domain of the teacher, but involve the other stakeholders as well. In fact, it is while the student is participating in all phases of the portfolio program that metacognitive skills such as the use of standards in self-evaluation can develop.

The comments of a high school student illustrate this kind of self-evaluation (Paulson & Paulson, 1991, p. 6):

> One of the goals I set for myself and didn't reach is finding a voice, a way of writing that is comfortable for me and doesn't sound silly or unreal to others. I think I am going to have to experiment a little (or lots more) before I find it. I like to keep a sense of humor in all my pieces—a person, or place, or event that is a little off the wall. Sometimes I think I take it a little far: it doesn't always work. But I keep trying anyway.

An exhibit from Hampton (1989) provides another example of self-evaluation and allows us to observe the sense of achievement expressed by a third-grade student finishing a year of work on writing (see figure 17.3). Arter (1990) emphasizes the benefits of portfolios in shifting evaluations from the hands of the teachers to the hands of the students.

Paulson and Paulson point out that stakeholders do not perform evaluations in isolation. "They talk about what has been learned and why it is important. This communication among stakeholders may be the single most powerful contribution of portfolios to education"(p. 8).

The role of communication in the portfolio process is illustrated by Romano (1991), working at the college level. Interestingly, his solicitation for portfolio contents included a request for comments, in a cover letter and in a "reflective interview," on pieces that the student elected to omit from the portfolio. Through these communications, he found that Meg, a student completing a senior project, had exercised rigorous editorial standards in deciding to exclude certain pieces on which she had spent extensive labor.

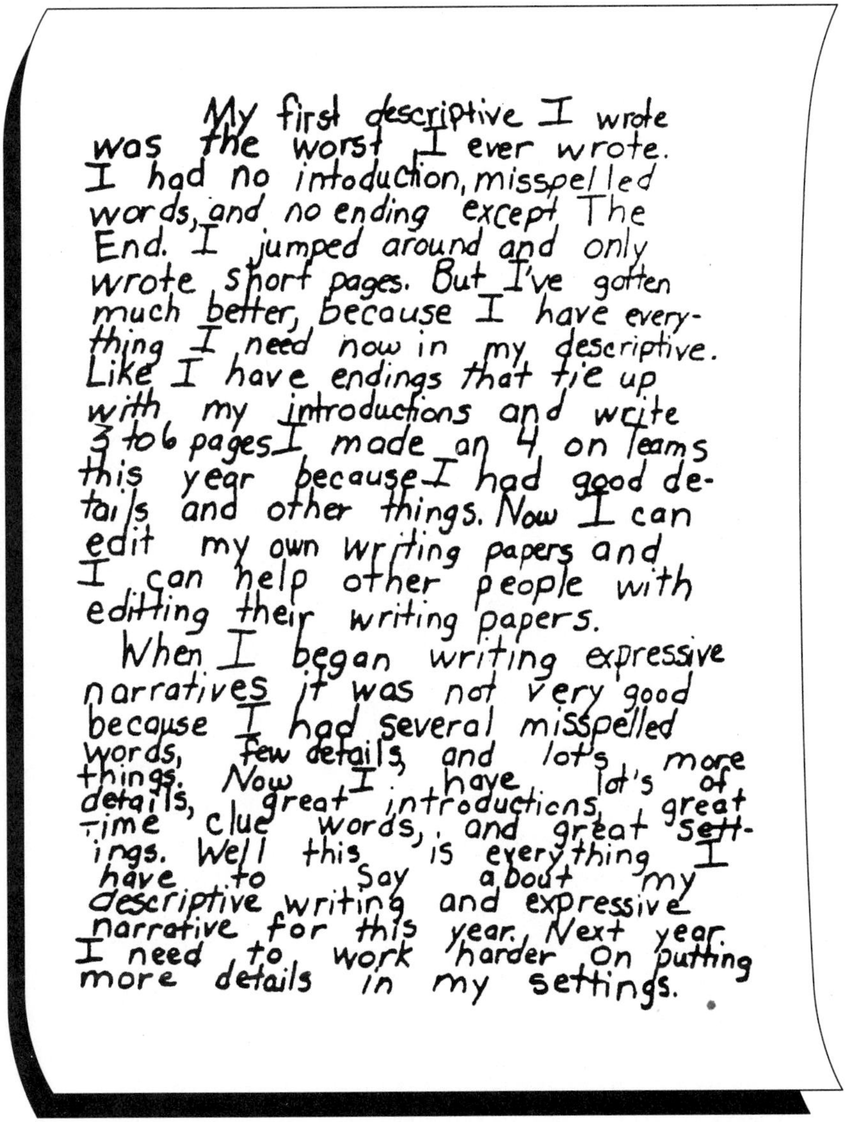

Figure 17.3 *Student's self-evaluation of progress in descriptive writing.* Reprinted with the permission of Sally Hampton from *A Further Word: The Teaching of Writing* by Sally Hampton. Paper presented at the annual meeting of the Association of Supervision and Curriculum Development, Orlando, Florida, March 1989.

> My first descriptive I wrote was the worst I ever wrote. I had no intoduction, misspelled words, and no ending except The End. I jumped around and only wrote short pages. But I've gotten much better, because I have everything I need now in my descriptive. Like I have endings that tie up with my introductions and write 3 to 6 pages I made an 4 on teams this year because I had good details and other things. Now I can edit my own writing papers and I can help other people with editing their writing papers.
> When I began writing expressive narratives it was not very good because I had several misspelled words, few details and lot's more things. Now I have lot's of details, great introductions, great time clue words, and great settings. Well this is everything I have to say about my descriptive writing and expressive narrative for this year. Next year, I need to work harder on putting more details in my settings.

Meg didn't mind sharing what she considered her failed writing with me, as long as she had the opportunity to point out that she'd had trouble with them. The stories of these "failed" pieces revealed so much about Meg as a thinker and writer that in the future I will ask students to include unsatisfactory pieces or failures, in their portfolios.

. . . Had I merely evaluated her final product, stamped a grade on it, and written a succinct note to Meg, had I not asked her to gather her significant work together and to reflect upon it through cover letter and interview, I would have missed learning about Meg's critical skills and writing standards (pp. 19–22).

The Historical Dimension

The historical dimension recognizes that portfolios represent a longitudinal record of individual growth. Baseline data and antecedent work, together with chronicles of instructional transactions, provide a context for interpreting current work and reflecting on progress. In a revised and expanded draft of their earlier work, Paulson and Paulson (August, 1992) present four scoring rubrics for evaluating various dimensions of the portfolios: the holistic, stakeholders, activity, and historical dimensions. We have reproduced the Holistic Scoring Rubric in figure 17.4.

The effort of Paulson and Paulson to develop scoring rubrics that preserve and make explicit the values inherent in portfolios is an important step in moving toward an understanding of how portfolios may be most profitably viewed and used.

Comments on Portfolio Assessments

While our examples of portfolio assessment have been drawn largely from whole language reading programs and courses in writing and composition, this approach is applicable throughout the curriculum areas. Arter's (1990) discussion of portfolio assessment includes an annotated bibliography of almost 100 articles. Portfolio assessment appears to be a rapidly growing supplement to more formal testing. Portfolios capture and preserve useful information about the growth and development of individual students that could readily slip by. Adoption of a policy of portfolio assessment can send important signals to teachers, parents, and students. The message says that school efforts are focused on student growth; that school achievement is defined by the next developmental step the individual student needs to take. Portfolios can encourage individualization of goals and engage students in the planning and reflective evaluation of their own learning.

These observations may sound more like persuasive commentary than critiques of a new approach to measuring school achievement. Yet Linn, Baker, and Dunbar (1991) suggest that we need to take note of evolving concepts of validity as we evaluate "authentic assessments." A broadened concept of validity includes the consequences of using a particular assessment procedure. "High priority needs to be given to the collection of evidence about the intended and unintended effects of assessments on the ways teachers and students spend their time and think about the goals of education" (p. 17). We have offered anecdotal evidence that portfolios can broaden the perceptions of both students and teachers about educational processes. Linn, Baker, and Dunbar suggest that such procedures could also narrow perceptions. We await more definitive research studies.

CMAP Holistic Scoring Rubric

Definition of Portfolio

A portfolio addresses the question "who am I" and tells a coherent story of the student as learner. It is a purposeful, integrated collection of student work that shows student effort, progress, or achievement in one or more areas. The collection includes evidence of student self-reflection and student participation in setting the focus, developing the standards, selecting contents, and judging merit. A portfolio communicates what is learned and why it is important.

An <u>Outstanding</u> Portfolio

An **outstanding** portfolio is a coherent story of the student as a reflective learner where all the parts of the portfolio bear a clear relationship to each other and to a central purpose. Moreover, a reviewer can look at the portfolio and easily understand how the judgments about the learner came to be made and the degree to which other stakeholders would agree. When reviewing the portfolio, outsiders get the feeling they really know the person whose achievement is depicted there, and have a fair understanding of how the learning came about.

An <u>On-Track</u> Portfolio

An **on-track** portfolio is in the process of becoming a story of the student as an independent learner. While self-reflection is evident, a reviewer may have to infer the relationships of some parts of the portfolio to other parts. The role of other stakeholders in the development of the portfolio may be uncertain. While there is evidence of reflection on the overall portfolio, the basis of judgments may be poorly documented. The portfolio requires a reviewer to make inferences about the nature and extent of learning and the characteristics of the learner.

An <u>Emerging</u> Portfolio

In an **emerging** portfolio exhibits of student work bear some relationship to each other. Choices seem to be made intuitively and then followed with reflections on the student's learning. However, at this point in the development of the portfolio there is insufficient information or organization to characterize the portfolio as either a story of learning or a portrait of the learner. There is evidence of self-reflection that adds information to the presentation. The portfolio appears to be evolving toward becoming **on-track**, given time.

An <u>Off-Track</u> Portfolio

An **off-track** portfolio is simply a container of student work or assessments, without an attempt on the part of the learner to provide organization. There is no attempt by the learner to make a coherent statement about what learning has taken place. The child's understanding of the task is minimal—the portfolio is about "collecting of stuff that the teacher wants." Someone other than the student, some *secondary stakeholder*, is calling the shots. To the child, building a portfolio is done by following instructions. An off-track portfolio is static, giving little indication of evolving toward becoming on-track. Self-reflective statements if present add little to clarify organization or explain learning.

Figure 17.4 *CMAP Holistic Scoring Rubric*

Reprinted with the permission of F.L. Paulson and P.R. Paulson from *The Making of a Portfolio* by F.L. Paulson and P.R. Paulson. Copyright © 1992 by F.R. Paulson and P.R. Paulson.

In addition to the instructional consequences of particular assessment procedures, Linn, Baker, and Dunbar discuss other criteria that must be met by new evaluation approaches, including content quality, breadth of coverage, and transfer and generalizability. "Whether conclusions about educational quality are based on scores on fixed-response tests or ratings of performance on written essays, laboratory experiments, or portfolios of student work, the generalization from the specific assessment task to the broader domain of achievement needs to be justified" (p. 19).

These are fair requirements and, as experience with portfolio assessment accumulates, we may come to understand their adequacy in relationship to the key phrase "conclusions about educational quality." But for now, portfolios are likely to play a useful role in the more modest goal of engaging students in thoughtful reflection about their own development and in linking evaluation with personal and tangible products of their efforts.

Dynamic Assessment

It may seem strange to talk about new trends in testing by looking back to the works of Vygotsky, a Russian psychologist who lived between 1896 and 1934. Vygotsky saw the child as always emerging and identified social interactions with other people as the primary mechanism for facilitating the next developmental step. Since Vygotsky was frequently working with retarded children or children raised in remote and isolated regions of the Soviet Union, he came to distrust assessment of what children knew, and focused his attention on how well they could handle new learning with outside help. Just any learning would not do. The new tasks had to be at the threshold of the child's competencies. The crucial observation was not whether the child could or could not perform the task, but how the child responded to hints and prompts offered by the tester-teacher. Showing the child how to do the task, then presenting additional problems of a similar nature revealed, not what the child had learned, but what the child could learn. The difference between what the child could do independently and the heights the child could reach with help was the "zone of proximal development," the key phrase linked with Vygotsky's name.

Perhaps only professional examiners trained in the strict discipline of administering individual intelligence tests can fully appreciate the radical departure from standardized test procedures represented by this new **dynamic assessment** in which the helpful interaction of the examiner is not only permitted but, indeed, required. Teaching appropriate perceptions and strategies is an absolutely essential feature of the testing process. The end product of these diagnostic teaching probes is not a score, but an understanding of what the child might be capable of doing and where to start remedial teaching. Finally, it should be a matter of interest that Vygotsky never assembled a package of tasks. His contribution was the *idea* that the zone of proximal development would be a better source for predicting future school achievement and of more use in educational planning than would a static assessment of what a child had achieved.

Even at this level of understanding of dynamic assessment, we can readily appreciate some of the problems facing this procedure. First, it is very time-consuming. When the procedure was used in Russia for the identification of retarded children who might be educable, the process usually extended over several weeks in quasi-instructional settings, and when used in East Germany for admission to special education classes, children were observed for one week in natural school settings (Guthke & Wingenfeld, 1992). Secondly, since the prompting and training that enters into the testing situation is highly dependent on the individual examiner, the amount of help any given child will receive will depend on who is doing the assessment and the level of rapport between the examiner and child. In addition, the evaluation itself can become very subjective in the absence of standards and norms.

The leading figure among contemporary psychologists working in the area of dynamic assessment is Reuven Feuerstein. He and his colleagues have produced the *Learning Potential Assessment Device* (Feuerstein et al., 1986) and a companion program for improving intellectual functioning, the *Instrumental Enrichment* program (Feuerstein, et al., 1980). Although the tasks used by Feuerstein include such conventional measures of intelligence as the *Raven Progressive Matrices,* a training phase precedes the testing phase. Additionally, the examiner seeks to determine whether difficulties in accomplishing the tasks are associated with the input, elaboration, or output phase of mental performance. The examiner also tries to identify deficient cognitive functions and the kinds of mediation that help remedy them. Tzuriel and Haywood (1992, pp. 12–13) describe some of the deficient cognitive functions Feuerstein expects the *Learning Potential Assessment Device* to reveal:

> Examples of deficient cognitive functions at the input phase are blurred and sweeping perception, impaired systematic exploratory behavior, impaired verbal tools for processing of information, impaired need for precision and accuracy, impulsivity in gathering of information, and difficulty in simultaneous consideration of two or more sources of information. Deficient cognitive functions at the elaboration level include episodic grasp of reality, "narrowness" of the mental field, and impairments in spontaneous comparative behavior, need for pursuing logical evidence, hypothetical thinking, planning, and interiorization. At the output phase some deficient cognitive

functions are egocentric modality of communication, trial-and-error responses, blocking behavior, deficient projection of virtual (implied or projected) relationships, impulsivity, and impaired precision and accuracy in communication.

Dynamic assessment has been of greatest interest to those working with individuals who have not, for one reason or another, had the advantage of ordinary opportunities for learning, such as culturally deprived or mentally impaired people. Haywood and Tzuriel's (1992) book contains a collection of studies and reports on dynamic assessment with such diverse populations as mentally disabled adults, profoundly deaf adults, penitentiary inmates, and other populations where a single IQ score or achievement test would generally provide a very pessimistic prediction without revealing any potentials for learning. While more research is needed to establish the psychometric properties (reliability, validity, normative data) of dynamic assessment, this approach seems to be ushering in a change in perception of human abilities. There is still a residue of feeling among test users that IQ reveals something fixed and immutable. In contrast, dynamic assessment finds—at any level of ability—opportunities for growth and development.

Comments on Dynamic Assessments

The most general idea in dynamic assessment is that students' responses to instruction may tell us more about learning capabilities than do "static" tests of ability or knowledge. An essential feature is the alternating process of testing-teaching-testing, with the examiner's attention focused on the behaviors that facilitate or impede acquisition of new learning. This approach shifts our attention from what has been learned to what might be learned under optimal conditions. This orientation to assessment appears to hold large potentialities for the evaluation of culturally deprived or mentally disabled individuals who have not had normal developmental opportunities.

The most critical questions that arise relate to reliability and validity. Will evaluations by two different examiners paint essentially the same picture of the learner, and do dynamic assessments predict future learning better than do existing instruments? Tzuriel and Haywood (1992) cite work by Samuels, Tzuriel, and Malloy-Miller (1989) showing about 88 to 92 percent agreement among three examiners completing a rating scale for type of deficient cognitive functions, remediation required, and nonintellective variables for twelve-to fourteen-year-old children previously identified as learning disabled, educable mentally disabled, or normal. The rating scales were marked after testing sessions using the *Learning Potentials Assessment Device.* Tzuriel and Haywood note that these percentages of agreement were much higher than those reported in a similar study by Vaught

(1989). Tzuriel and Haywood also report that, in some cases, assessments with the *Learning Potentials Assessment Device* are more predictive of school learning than traditional IQ test scores. We might note that a large body of evidence from well-controlled studies is not yet available to document the claims by proponents of dynamic interactive testing.

An associated issue remains unresolved: does testing and remediation of basic cognitive processes transfer to more school-like settings? Campione and Brown (1990) argue that evaluation and teaching of skills is most productive when done in a domain-specific content. That is, evaluating the planning and self-monitoring skills of students while they are solving mathematics problems will be more informative than observing the same student behaviors in a content-free context. "Knowing something about sources of difficulties associated with doing subtraction problems provides information that can be used to design instruction, whereas knowing that someone has an auditory sequencing problem does not" (p. 149). We turn now to consider some of the advances in computer adaptive instruction, advances that in some ways can be considered an extension of Vygotsky's early thinking about the zone of proximal development.

Computerized Adaptive Testing

The key concept in **computerized adaptive testing** is that the test administrator—in this case the computer—is constantly adapting the flow of questions to the performance history of the student. If the student is experiencing difficulty, the computer adapts by supplying easier questions. If the student is sailing along with no problems, the computer adapts by supplying harder questions. Since the student is being tested at the threshold of competency, little time is wasted with items that are too hard or too easy. This means that testing time can be reduced to as much as one third of the time required for comparable paper and pencil testing.

A moment's thought will make it clear that with computerized adaptive testing, no two students will work the same items, or even the same number of items. Thus the score on the test cannot be the number of items answered correctly. Rather, the student's score becomes more dependent on which items were answered correctly.

Wainer (1990) states that item response theory (IRT) is the "theoretical glue" that holds the computerized adaptive testing together. We touched briefly on item response theory in chapter 8. You may remember that item response theory provides the procedures for generating item characteristic curves. These curves show the probabilities of producing a correct answer for students at various proficiency levels. A proficiency level is defined as the amount of proficiency in the ability or knowledge being tested and, when calibrating items, is usually indicated by the total score on the test. At each step of adaptive testing, the next item is drawn from a pool of calibrated items so that it is best fitted for the proficiency of the individual student. The estimate of proficiency for an individual student is revised after each response on the test. Optimum items are selected and presented until some stopping rule is satisfied. The usual stopping rule is that a desired level of precision has been reached in estimating the student's proficiency. Thus, the test is stopped when the standard error of measurement for the last computed proficiency estimate meets a preestablished criterion. Notice that the final score on the test is not the number of items answered correctly, but the final estimate of the student's proficiency.

The flowchart in figure 17.5, constructed by Thissen and Mislevy (1990), shows the various steps in starting, continuing, and stopping an adaptive test.

Thissen and Mislevy point out that it may be easier to construct clusters of items or "testlets" rather than a large pool of items, and that these prepackaged testlets might help prevent one item from supplying information needed by the next in a computer selected sequence. Most interestingly, they suggest that the computer may not need to adapt its presentation after each response; a test that adapts from three to five times between testlets could provide the precision and advantages of fully adaptive testing. While consideration of these issues may take us further than we want to go in adaptive testing, they point the way to future developments in this area.

Research indicates that reliability and validity of computer adaptive testing is comparable to that of more conventional tests, but with a savings in number of items administered and in testing time (Anastasi, 1988). The *Differential Aptitude Tests* is available in a computerized adaptive edition that requires about half the usual time and can print a complete individualized score report as soon as the test is over. A computerized adaptive edition of the *Armed Services Vocational Aptitude Battery* is also in use.

On the horizon are developments that may lead to a closer integration between assessment and instructional programs. Collins (1990) visualizes an integrated learning and testing environment in which there is no clear distinction between teaching and testing. Collins points to computer programs that keep track of specific errors students make in solving problems and give prompts or advice accordingly.

Campione and Brown (1990) take this process one step further. They argue that as students take advantage of hints in the program, this should help them acquire more general metacognitive processes. The critical consideration is whether the student can use the acquired procedures

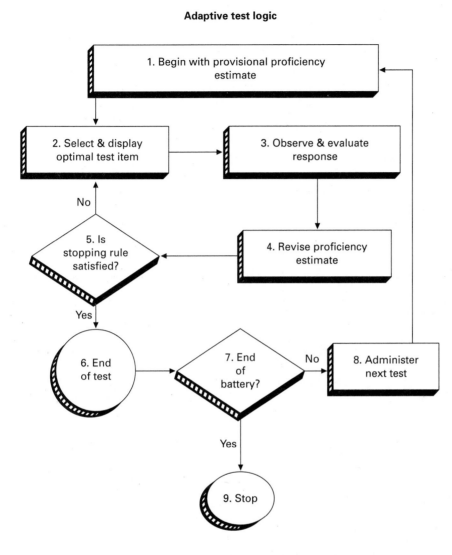

Adaptive test logic

1. Begin with provisional proficiency estimate

2. Select & display optimal test item

3. Observe & evaluate response

4. Revise proficiency estimate

5. Is stopping rule satisfied? — No / Yes

6. End of test

7. End of battery? — No / Yes

8. Administer next test

9. Stop

Figure 17.5

A flowchart describing an adaptive test.
Reprinted with the permission of Lawrence Erlbaum Associates, Inc., from *Computerized Adaptive Testing: A Primer* by H. Wainer. Copyright © 1990 by Lawrence Erlbaum Associates, Inc.

in solving novel problems. Such "transfer propensity" is regarded as the best index that a student has understood principles and is the best indicator of how well a student will progress in learning a domain of knowledge. Emphasizing transfer phenomena in learning helps keep the attention of the teacher on metacognitive processes that assist transfer. Campione and Brown observed that students who were efficient learners and good at transferring principles spent more time planning, analyzing, checking reasoning, and applying "fix-up strategies" when they got off track as compared to poorer performers. Hints and prompts built into adaptive testing-teaching programs can help students develop the self-monitoring and self-regulatory behavior important in problem solving and transfer.

Comments on Computerized Adaptive Testing

Computerized adaptive testing is a procedure that gains great efficiency by administering items in the 50 to 60 percent difficulty range for a particular student. The extensive work required in the calibration of items means that such tests will be produced by agencies with large technical staffs. Teachers and counselors will benefit, as testing for diagnostic and guidance purposes can be done in considerably less time and on an individual basis as needed.

Computerized adaptive testing opens the way for a blending of testing-teaching programs into a single continuous routine. Since the computer, in effect, is constantly studying the responses of the student, it can estimate dysfunctional cognitive processes and supply cues, hints, prompts, and direct teaching to move students through difficult stages while simultaneously encouraging students to be more reflective about the mental processes they are using.

Summary

In this final chapter, we have pointed to three emerging trends on the measurement scene: portfolio assessment, dynamic assessment, and computerized adaptive testing. Interest in portfolio assessment represents an attitude and a belief. The attitude is that we have defined educational achievement too narrowly; that an individual learner is inadequately characterized by a test score. This attitude is accompanied by a belief that evaluation plays its most productive role in education as students review their own progress, grasp a glimpse of future developments, and formulate the next steps in realizing their potentialities.

Dynamic assessment is also reflective of an attitude as much as a technique. This attitude brushes aside the search for a single score reflecting ability and sets in its place a search for cognitive and affective processes the learner brings into play, or fails to bring into play, during the act of learning itself.

Computerized adaptive testing, employing item response theory, moves the student quickly to problems lying in that zone of difficulty that is most likely to challenge existing competencies. Such testing can be interspersed with computer-based teaching programs that direct students to examine their own planning, analyzing, checking, and reasoning processes.

Other trends in the field of measurement might have been described, but these three will serve as examples to illustrate that knowledge in the field of measurement, as in all disciplines, is emergent rather than fixed. Concepts of test validity are being broadened, better explanations of cognitive processes are appearing, more adequate theories of human abilities are being formulated, and new tests are being developed. Even at this moment, in the chalk-stained seat of an overheated classroom of some community college, or in the lecture-auditorium of some great and noble university, a student stirs to the challenge and history may later find that student's name added to those of Galton, Binet, Cattell, Strong, Buros, Wechsler, and others who have contributed to understanding human behavior through measurement.

References

Anastasi, A. (1988). *Psychological testing* (6th ed.). New York: Macmillan.

Archbald, D. A., & Newmann, F. M. (1988). *Beyond standardized testing. Assessing authentic academic achievement in the secondary school.* Reston, VA: National Association of Secondary School Principals.

Arter, J. A. (1990). *Curriculum-referenced test development workshop series, addendum to workshops two and three: Using portfolios in instruction and assessment.* Portland, OR: Northwest Regional Educational Lab. (ERIC No. ED335364).

Campione, J. C., & Brown, A. L. (1990). Guided learning and transfer: Implications for approaches to assessment. In N. Frederiksen, R. Glaser, A. Lesgold, & M. G. Shafto (eds.), *Diagnostic monitoring of skill and knowledge acquisition* (pp. 141–172). Hillsdale, NJ: Erlbaum.

Collins, A. (1990). Reformulating testing to measure learning and thinking. In N. Frederiksen, R. Glaser, A. Lesgold, & M. G. Shafto (eds.), *Diagnostic monitoring of skill and knowledge acquisition* (pp. 75–88). Hillsdale, NJ: Erlbaum.

Feuerstein, R., Haywood, H. C., Rand, Y., Hoffman, M. B., & Jensen, M. R. (1986). *Learning Potential Assessment Device Manual.* Jerusalem: Hadassah-WIZO-Canada Research Institute.

Feuerstein, R., Rand, Y., Hoffman, M., & Miller, R. (1980). *Instructional enrichment.* Baltimore: University Park Press.

Guthke, J., & Wingenfeld, S. (1992). In H. C. Haywood & D. Tzuriel (eds.), *Interactive assessment* (pp. 64–93). New York: Springer-Verlag.

Hampton, S. (1989, March). *A further word: The teaching of writing. Grades K–5.* Paper presented at the meeting of the Association for Supervision and Curriculum Development, Orlando, FL. (ERIC No. ED312648).

Haywood, H. C., & Tzuriel, D. (eds.). (1992). *Interactive assessment.* New York: Springer-Verlag.

Linn, R. L., Baker, E. L., & Dunbar, S. B. (1991). Complex, performance-based assessment: Expectations and validation criteria. *Educational Researcher, 20* (5), p. 15–21.

Paulson, F. L., & Paulson, P. R. (1991). *The making of a portfolio.* Unpublished manuscript available from the authors, 6800 Gable Parkway, Portland, OR 97225. (ERIC No. ED334251).

Paulson, F. L., & Paulson, P. R. (1992, August). *The making of a portfolio.* Revised and expanded draft.

Romano, T. (1991). *A time for immersion, a time for reflection: The multigenre research project and portfolio assessment.* Paper presented at the 1991 National Council of Teachers of English Spring Conference, Indianapolis. (ERIC No. ED333428).

Samuels, M., Tzuriel, C., & Malloy-Miller, T. (1989). Dynamic assessment of children with learning difficulties. In R. T. Brown & M. Chazan (eds.), *Learning difficulties and emotional problems* (pp. 145–165). Calgary: Detselig Enterprises.

Thissen, D., & Mislevy, R. J. (1990). Testing algorithms. In H. Wainer, *Computerized adaptive testing: A primer* (pp. 103–136). Hillsdale, NJ: Erlbaum.

Tzuriel, D., & Haywood, H. C. (1992). The development of interactive-dynamic approaches to assessment of learning potential. In H. C. Haywood & D. Tzuriel (eds.), *Interactive assessment* (pp. 3–37). New York: Springer-Verlag.

Vacca, R. T., & Rasinski, T. V. (1992). *Case studies in whole language.* Fort Worth: Harcourt Brace Jovanovich.

Vaught, S. (1989). *Interjudge agreement in dynamic assessment: Two instruments from the Learning Potential Assessment Device.* Unpublished master's thesis, Vanderbilt University, Nashville, TN.

Wainer, H. (1990). *Computerized adaptive testing: A primer.* Hillsdale, NJ: Erlbaum.

> Often people with disabilities feel misunderstood by their families and friends. Books can help bring about better understanding as we learn to appreciate and accept the differences among ourselves.

Appendix

Fiction

Albert   *But I'm Ready To Go*

Learning disabled, Judy has a hard time handling the way her family and friends behave toward her.

Carrick   *Stay Away From Simon!*

Lucy learns that there is no need to fear Simon, a boy who does not go to school.

Clifton   *My Friend Jacob*

Sam and Jacob are two good friends who help one another.

Fanshawe   *Rachel*

Rachel uses a wheelchair, but this inconvenience does not lessen her enjoyment of life, her participation in school, and the fun she has with friends and family.

Gilson   *Do Bananas Chew Gum?*

Since sixth-grader Sam is able to read and write at only a second grade level, he considers himself dumb, until it is discovered that something can be done to help him with his learning difficulties.

Greenwald   *Will The Real Gertrude Hollings Stand Up?*

Gertude, who is learning disabled, is finally able to discard her label and be herself after spending three weeks with her overachieving cousin, who has problems of her own.

Heide   *Secret Dreamer, Secret Dreams*

The inner world of a handicapped thirteen-year-old girl is revealed.

Hermes   *Who Will Take Care Of Me?*

Twelve-year-old Mark realizes that caring for his handicapped brother is not solely his responsibility.

Laird   *Loving Ben*

Teenage Anna changes and matures as she cares for her hydrocephalic brother and experiences the pleasures and problems of relationships with family and friends.

Litchfield   *Making Room For Uncle Joe*

When Uncle Joe has to move in with Dan and his family, everyone is uncertain about having a retarded adult living with them.

Marek   *Different, Not Dumb*

Because he gets some letters mixed up or reversed, Mike is assigned to a special class in which he learns the basic reading skills he later uses to avert an accident.

Marron   *No Trouble For Grandpa*

A child with a disability helps his grandfather take care of his baby sister.

Shyer   *Welcome Home, Jellybean*

Neil and his family have a hard time when his retarded sister Gerri comes home to stay.

Smith *Kelly's Creek*

Nine-year-old Kelly thinks he is stupid because he can't read. His visits to a marsh and learning about marine life help him gain some confidence in himself.

Talbert *Toby*

Toby must convince the authorities that he wants to stay with his "slow" father and brain damaged mother, who love him very much.

Whitney *Nobody Likes Trina*

Sandy learns from her retarded friend, Trina, what love of nature really means.

Wrightson *A Racecourse For Andy*

Andy thinks he owns a racetrack and his friends have a hard time convincing him he does not.

Nonfiction

Friedberg *Accept Me As I Am: Best Books Of Juvenile Non-Fiction On Impairment and Disabilities*

This guide to juvenile nonfiction books about individuals with disabilities will be useful to people who deal with the disabled.

Baskin and Harris *Notes From A Different Drummer: A Guide To Juvenile Fiction Portraying The Handicapped*

The authors have written lengthy annotations and critiques of fiction works about handicapped people, not all learning disabled. Reading levels are included.

Baskin and Harris *More Notes From A Different Drummer*

This is a continuation of *Notes From A Different Drummer*, with books written after 1975.

Mather *Learning Can Be Child's Play*

For parents of developmentally-delayed children, this book tells how parents can help these children learn and develop through play experiences.

Bergman *On Our Own Terms*

Bergman describes the activities at the Caroline Hospital in Stockholm where handicapped children receive physiotherapy.

Brown *Someone Special, Just Like You*

Parents will want to share this with children, to help them accept and be more comfortable with children with disabilities. The author emphasizes the ways we are alike.

Cattoche *Computers For The Disabled*

The purpose of this book is to tell us how computers and computer devices are helping disabled people learn new skills and become more independent.

Emmert *I'm The Big Sister Now*

Nine-year-old Michelle describes the loving times and the special situations she and her family have with her sister who has cerebral palsy.

English *My Mommy's Special*

A little girl describes the things she does with her mother who is confined to a wheelchair.

Frevert *It's Okay To Look At Jamie*

Jamie was born with spina bifida and must learn to walk with braces on her legs.

Greenberg *What Is The Sign For Friend?*

Photographs and text depict the life of Shane, a deaf child who attends regular school.

Kaufman *Rajesh*

Handicapped Rajesh learns about the other children in his kindergarten class and they learn about him.

Meyer *Living With A Brother Or Sister With Special Needs: A Book For Sibs*

This is a helpful book for siblings of special children.

Bergman   *Finding A Common Language; Children Living With Deafness*

Bergman follows Linn, a deaf girl, in activities both in school and out. The final pages present questions and answers about deafness.

An Exceptional View Of Life: The Easter Seal Story

The words and pictures in this book are the works of exceptional children.

Larsen   *Don't Forget Tom*

The reader meets Tom, a mentally handicapped child.

Levine   *Lisa And Her Soundless World*

Born deaf, Lisa is able to hear with a hearing aid and learns to talk.

Peter   *Claire And Emma*

This is a true account of two little girls who were born deaf, Claire, four, and her sister Emma, two.

Sobol   *My Brother Steven Is Retarded*

Eleven-year-old Beth tells about the mixed feelings she has about her older mentally retarded brother.

Wolf   *Don't Feel Sorry For Paul*

Two weeks in the life of a handicapped boy are captured with photographs and text.

Binkard   *Disabled? . . . Yes, Able? . . . Also, Yes: A Count Me In Project*

Eight disabled teenagers would like people to be able to look beyond their disabilities.

Griswold   *Play Together; A Program Outline For Parents And Their Children Ages 3 Months To 3 Years Having Cerebral Palsy*

Thirty activities are described, together with objectives, motivating activity, and equipment.

Reprinted courtesy of the Tippecanoe County Public Library, Lafayette, Indiana.

Glossary

Affective The emotional aspects of an individual's inner life, including attitudes, feelings, dispositions, and outlooks, which tend to color interactions with others and with external activities.

Age Scores Scores that report an individual's performance in terms of typical performance of pupils at various age levels. An age score of 10–6 would mean that the individual's performance on the test is like that of a typical student ten years and six months of age.

Alternative One of the choices or options following the stem of a multiple-choice item.

Aptitude A hypothetical construct postulating the presence of special abilities or propensities that make it natural or easy for an individual to develop in a particular area.

Attitude A tendency to respond positively or negatively to specific activities, events, or aspects of the physical, social, and cultural environment.

Average Deviation A measure of variability obtained by summing all the deviations (ignoring the plus or minus sign) in a distribution and dividing by the number of cases.

CEEB Score A standard score that takes its name from the College Entrance Examination Board. CEEB scores have a mean of 500 and a standard deviation of 100. They are calculated by multiplying a z-score by 100 and adding 500.

Central Tendency The middle of a frequency distribution where a high concentration of scores can be observed. This point is indicated by the mean, median, or mode.

Coefficient Alpha A generalized form of the Kuder-Richardson Formula 20 that can be applied whether items are marked right-wrong or on a continuous scale, i.e., strongly agree, agree, etc. Coefficient alpha provides an estimate of test reliability based on the internal consistency of the items.

Cognitive Complexity A hypothetical continuum describing the way an individual perceives, organizes, and interprets events. At the low end, the events are discriminated into a few obvious elements and are combined in limited, stereotyped ways. At the high end, events are discriminated into many relevant features and a number of combinations and possibilities are constructed.

Computerized Adaptive Testing Testing administered by computers in which the flow of questions presented to the student is determined by the student's pass-fail record on preceding questions.

Concurrent Validity A procedure for establishing the validity of a test in which both the test data and the criterion data are collected concurrently, i.e., within the same time period.

Construct Validity The demonstration of a logical pattern of positive and negative correlations that would be expected on the basis of the theoretical nature of the trait the test purports to measure. Thus, a test of anxiety among adults might be expected to be positively related to a test of "fearfulness" and negatively related to "risk taking." See also convergent validity and discriminant validity.

Content Validity The extent to which the sample of items comprising a test adequately represents the underlying domain of all possible items that might have entered into the test. In achievement testing, it is particularly important that the test reflect a representative sample of the content that was actually taught, a condition that is not always met when tests constructed for national use are matched against a local curriculum.

Convergent Validity An aspect of construct validity marked by a set of positive correlations among a test and other indices of behavior, which would theoretically be associated with the construct that the test presumably measures.

Correction for Attenuation A formula for estimating the true relationship between two variables if they were measured with error-free tests. The formula increases the obtained correlation by correcting for the unreliability of the tests used to measure the variables.

Correlation Coefficient An index of the relationship between two variables; designated by the small letter r. Positive correlations (an increase in one variable accompanied by an increase in another) can reach a maximum of 1.0. Negative correlations (an increase in one variable accompanied by a decrease in another) can reach a maximum of −1.0.

Criterion A measure or index recognized as representing a reliable and valid index of the trait or ability of interest. For example, first semester grade point average might be considered a criterion measure for the construct "academic ability."

Criterion-Referenced Test A test designed to provide detailed coverage of a specific subject matter domain or skill, and for which a preset level of performance has been established to indicate mastery of the material.

Criterion Related Validity A procedure for validating a test in which the test is correlated with an accepted, established index of the behavior of interest. Thus, a test of manual dexterity might be correlated with the number of units assembled per hour (criterion) in a factory setting.

Critique A critical review or commentary. A test critique provides a critical discussion of its strengths and weaknesses.

Crystallized Intelligence A proposed aspect of intelligence characterized by past learning and measured by performance on such tests as vocabulary or general information.

Cumulative Frequency In a distribution of test scores, the number of students earning a given score and below. Cumulative frequency gives the number of students earning all scores up to and including the score for which the cumulative frequency is reported.

Cumulative Relative Frequency In a distribution of test scores, the percent of students earning a given score and below. Cumulative relative frequency gives the percent of students earning all scores up to and including the score for which the cumulative frequency is reported.

Derived Score A score obtained by converting a raw score to a more interpretable score, such as a percentile or stanine.

Describer-Explainer Continuum A proposed continuum for classifying responses of students asked to interpret a complex situation. Describers tend to repeat and paraphrase the original materials. Explainers tend to seek cause and effect relationships within the situation and bring in outside knowledge to help explain the events.

Descriptive Statistics Statistics, such as the mean and standard deviation, used to describe distributions of scores. Generally, descriptive statistics describe the central tendency, the variability of scores, and the shape of the distribution.

Deviation The amount that a given score deviates from the mean of the distribution; obtained by subtracting the mean from the score.

Deviation IQ A standard score having a mean of 100 and a standard deviation of 15 or 16. These standard scores are derived for each age level so that a deviation IQ of 100 can be interpreted as indicating that the individual has scored at the mean of other individuals in the norm group who are the same age.

Difficulty Level The proportion of students taking a test who passed a given item. The higher the difficulty level, the easier the item.

Discriminant Validity An aspect of construct validity marked by a set of low or insignificant correlations among a test and other indices of behavior, which theoretically bear no relationship to the construct that the test presumably measures.

Discrimination Index An index of the extent to which a test item differentiates students in approximately the top quarter and the bottom quarter in the distribution of total scores on the test. The discrimination index varies between 0 and 1 and can be interpreted as showing the difference in proportion of the two groups answering the item correctly; i.e., a discrimination index of .3 means that 30 percent more of the top group answered the item correctly than did the bottom group.

Distractors The incorrect alternative responses on a multiple-choice item. Distractors should be sufficiently plausible so that students who have not learned the relevant knowledge cannot eliminate them because of their remoteness to the topic or their absurdity.

Distribution A group of scores arranged from low to high showing the number of students earning each score. This term refers to a collection of scores arranged as a frequency distribution.

Dynamic Assessment A procedure for ascertaining the abilities, performance levels, and potentialities of an individual by alternating cycles of testing-teaching-testing with particular attention paid to the cognitive and affective processes that facilitate or impede acquisition of new learning.

Essay Test Tests requiring students to generate their own answers to questions rather than simply recognizing a correct answer. Essays tests can vary widely both in length of response required and in the amount of thinking versus recall demanded.

Expectancy Tables A table showing the percentage of people at any given test score who attained a given level of performance on a criterion measure. Expectancy tables are among the most useful ways of interpreting test scores.

Extrapolation The process of extending trends above and below the points actually observed. Extrapolation is often used in obtaining grade equivalent scores by projecting trends beyond the grades actually tested.

Face Validity A term referring to the appearance of a test; i.e., a test with face validity looks as if it measures what it claims to measure. Since appearance may not correspond with reality, face validity is not considered as evidence of the actual validity of a test.

Factor Analysis A family of mathematical procedures for determining which items of a test cluster together, thus suggesting that they are measuring the same underlying trait or ability. This procedure can also be applied to a collection of test scores.

Fluid Intelligence A proposed aspect of intelligence characterized by the ability to acquire new learning or solve new problems; measured by the ability to solve problems in number series, letter series, geometrical progressions, or matrices.

Formative Evaluation Evaluations obtained during the course of instruction to acquire feedback about the effectiveness of instructional approaches or individual progress so that appropriate changes can be made.

Frequency In a distribution of test scores, the number of students earning any given score; i.e., a count of how frequently a given score occurs.

Frequency Distribution A tabulation of a group of test scores arranged from low to high showing the number of students receiving each score.

Frequency Polygon A frequency distribution represented as a line graph, with the height of the line representing the number of students achieving each score.

Grade Equivalent Scores Scores that report an individual's performance in terms of typical performance of pupils at various grade levels in the norm group. A grade equivalent score of 6.3 would mean that the individual is performing on the test like a typical sixth grade pupil in the third month of school.

Higher Cognitive Processes   Within the framework of the Bloom Taxonomy, all the cognitive processes above the memory level. More generally, thinking involving such processes as comparisons, analysis, inferences, hypotheses, and generalizations.

Histogram   A frequency distribution represented as a bar graph, with the height of each bar indicating the number of students achieving each score.

Idiot Savant   An individual showing remarkable gifts in a single, limited field while showing marked deficiencies in most other areas of life.

Inferential Statistics   Statistics that apply to inferences made about the underlying population of scores from which a sample has been drawn. In educational research, it is frequently desirable to know whether the means of two groups are sufficiently different that it is unlikely they could have been drawn from a single underlying population. If the samples represent an experimental and a control group, the inference that the means are significantly different would suggest that the treatment of the experimental group produced the expected effects.

Information Processing Structures   Cognitive structures or mental habits that come into play when perceiving, organizing, and interpreting external events. Some individuals may have developed structures or habits that simplify perceptions and limit interpretations. Other individuals may have developed structures or habits that maintain the original complexity in the events and open the way for multiple interpretations.

Intellectual Development   As formulated by William Perry, based on observation of students during the college years, a transition from viewing the world in simple black-white categories supported by "authorities" to a perception of the world as holding multiple truths accompanied with a degree of uncertainty but providing a framework for making commitments.

Intelligence   A much-debated theoretical construct generally accepted to mean those clusters of mental abilities associated with school achievement. Historically, the most persistent argument is that intelligence represents a general ability marked by proficiency in grasping abstract concepts, seeing relationships, reasoning, judging, mentally manipulating the elements of a problem, and otherwise transforming information to arrive at solutions.

Intelligence Quotient   The original IQ, computed by dividing the mental age (determined by the intelligence test) by the chronological age and multiplying by 100. The more modern procedure is to convert the score earned on an intelligence test into a deviation IQ.

Intercorrelations   Correlation among the parts of a test or the scores of various tests in a battery. A pattern of high intercorrelations suggests that the separate subtests or scores may not be measuring independent abilities or achievements.

Interest   A preference for one activity over another. Interest inventories summarize a number of responses to questions about specific preferences.

Internal Consistency   A measure of test reliability obtained by determining the extent to which all items of a test are positively intercorrelated, suggesting that all items are measuring the same thing.

Interpolation   The process of estimating scores between two observed scores. In establishing grade equivalent scores for achievement tests, the test is given only once at a grade level and the intervening months are interpolated rather than observed points.

Interpretive Exercise   A form of test exercise in which a narrative description is followed by a number of inferences or generalizations that might be drawn from the narrative. Students show their ability to analyze or interpret the material by choosing the appropriate statements.

Interquartile Range   A measure of variability indicating the range of scores within which the middle 50 percent of the distribution lie. The interquartile range is less influenced by extreme scores than the range.

Interval Scale   A scale on which numbers represent equal intervals, but no true zero point. Test scores are assumed to be interval scales since each correct item adds one equal unit to the total score. A score of zero, however, may not mean that the student has absolutely no knowledge or ability in the area measured.

Item Analysis   A procedure for determining the difficulty level and discrimination index for each item of a test.

Item Response Theory   A sophisticated approach to item analysis using mathematical models to predict the probability of a correct response to an item based on the learner's ability (as indicated by performance on the test) and certain characteristics of the item.

Kuder-Richardson Reliability A procedure for calculating the reliability of a test based on the internal consistency of the items. The most widely applicable formula is the Kuder-Richardson Formula 20.

Learning Strategies Characteristic modes of approaching learning tasks or of processing, organizing, interpreting, and storing information during school learning.

Learning Styles Individual preferences or characteristics associated with learning behavior. Definitions vary widely, sometimes depending on psychological constructs (field dependence-field independence), sometimes on hemispheric specialization (right brain-left brain), and sometimes on conditions considered optimal for individual learners (quiet environment-noisy environment).

Likert Scale An item format widely used in the measurement of attitudes. A clear, strong statement of a particular attitude is followed by five response options: strongly agree, agree, undecided, disagree, and strongly disagree. Values of five to one are assigned the respective responses to score the item. These values are reversed when the stem reflects a negative attitude.

Matching Item Test item involving the matching of two lists such as inventors and inventions, historical events and dates, or labels and diagrams. Advantages include the ability to sample a large body of content and less guessing than a true-false format.

Mean An indication of the central tendency in a distribution of scores; obtained by summing the scores and dividing by the number of cases.

Measurement Errors Variations in test scores caused by unreliability, variations in sample of test items, changes in the individual, and other features associated with the act of measurement.

Median An indication of central tendency in a distribution of scores; obtained by counting to the middle score or interpolating to find the hypothetical middle score. The median is useful with data from an ordinal scale, skewed distributions, or distributions where a few high scores may distort the mean.

Mental Measurements Yearbooks A series of yearbooks issued every four to five years containing reviews of new or significantly revised tests appearing since the publication of the prior yearbook.

Mode An indication of central tendency in a distribution of scores; obtained by finding the most frequently occurring score. Score distributions exhibiting more than one mode are called bimodal. The mode is useful in reporting central tendency for data collected on nominal scales.

Motivation Orientation Orientations to school learning that reflect students' underlying reasons for exerting effort. Such motives may range from intrinsic interest in the school tasks to trying to avoid looking dumb among one's peers.

Multiple-Choice Item Test item consisting of the main part, or stem (question or incomplete statement), followed by three to five alternatives, one of which provides the best answer or most accurately completes the statement. Multiple-choice items are the most common item type and can be constructed to measure a wide variety of cognitive processes.

Nominal Scale A scale in which numbers represent categories. An example would be to code ethnic groups as White = 1, Black = 2, Hispanic = 3, and Other = 4. Nominal scales are not useful in arithmetic computations, but can be useful in identifying groups for further analysis.

Nominating Technique Any form of questionnaire in which students are asked to identify a classmate who fits a set of characteristics.

Norm Test norms are a set of tables for converting raw scores to scores that identify an individual's position in a large, presumably representative group.

Norm Group The large sample of individuals who have been chosen to represent the population of interest when the test is standardized. It is the group to whom the test is administered to obtain the scores used in constructing the norms of the test.

Norm-Referenced Test A test designed to differentiate students with various degrees of knowledge or skill in a specific domain, and for which scores are interpreted by comparing individual performance to that of other individuals in a group.

Normal Curve A mathematically defined, bell-shaped, symmetrical curve with known probabilities that a given number of cases will be included within any given area marked off in standard deviation units along the baseline.

Normal Curve Equivalents A form of standard score developed from percentile scores to convert them to a scale with equal intervals. The percentile score distributions are normalized and the mean of the distribution is set equal to 50 and the standard deviation to 21.06. This unique transformation makes Normal Curve Equivalents equal to percentile scores at three points, the 1st, 50th, and 99th percentiles. The Normal Curve Equivalents do not correspond to percentile scores at any other point and can best be understood by reference to discussions of standard scores.

Normal Distribution A hypothetical distribution of scores represented by a symmetrical, bell-shaped curve having known characterisitics.

Normalize A procedure generally used by test publishers to smooth irregularities in the results of testing a norm group so that the results take on the form of a normal curve.

Novel Situation A problem situation or set of conditions that has not previously been used as an example in teaching a concept or principle. Presenting novel situations to students in test items is an essential condition for measuring the ability to apply concepts and principles.

Objective Test Tests with clear, unambiguous scoring procedures; usually represented by multiple-choice and true-false tests.

Ordinal Scale A scale in which numbers represent rank order, but not absolute differences. Assigning an elephant, a giraffe, a dog, and a mouse each a rank from four to one indicates which animal is biggest and smallest, but does not tell how much difference there is between any two animals. Ordinal scales are poor candidates for statistical analysis.

Parallel Form Reliability A test reliability obtained by administering a similar form of the test and correlating the scores from the two administrations. Also called alternate form reliability.

Percentile Score An easily interpreted derived score, which indicates the percent of a norm group that an individual equals or exceeds.

Performance Assessment An approach to measuring school achievement based on demonstrations of what students can do when the testing situation is broadened to approximate real world conditions. Performance assessment tends to focus on cognitive processes and approaches used in arriving at solutions or products.

Portfolio A collection of work that documents a student's progress and accomplishments.

Predictive Validity A procedure for establishing the validity of a test in which the test data are collected at one point in time and then correlated with criterion data collected at a later point in time. Correlating test scores obtained when workers applied for a job with later performance records on the job would be an example of predictive validity.

Projective Techniques Procedures for eliciting various personality themes, concerns, and defense mechanisms of which the individual may have little or no conscious awareness. The procedures range from interpreting ambiguous ink blots to completing brief sentence stems such as "My mother . . .".

Range A measure of variability obtained by subtracting the lowest score from the highest score. The range has the disadvantage of conveying an inaccurate picture of distributions having outliers, which are single scores very much above or below the group as a whole.

Ratio Scale A scale with a true zero point on which numbers represent equal intervals. Although ratio scales are highly desirable, there are few true ratio scales in educational measurement.

Raw Scores The "number right" obtained by counting the correct answers on a test. Raw scores are frequently converted to more readily interpretable scores.

Relative Frequency In a distribution of test scores, the percent of students earning any given test score.

Reliability Refers to the precision of a measurement or to the ability of a test to provide consistent scores if the same individual were tested again.

Reliability Coefficient An index of test reliability obtained by correlating scores from two test administrations or from analysis of the internal consistency of the test items.

Representative Sample A sample of individuals selected in such a way that it contains about the same proportions of special groups (ethnic, rural-urban, socioeconomic, etc.) as is found in the total population.

Rubric A scoring rubric is a set of ordered categories to which a given piece of work can be compared. Scoring rubrics specify the qualities or processes that must be exhibited in order for a performance to be assigned a particular evaluative rating.

Scatterplot A graph representing the degree of relationship between two variables. For example, grades on an academic aptitude test may be plotted on the vertical axis and average grades earned during a semester plotted on the horizontal axis. A student's test score and grade average are represented by a single dot placed on the graph.

Scoring Rationale An explicit set of specifications indicating responses that will receive predetermined point values.

Self-Concept The evaluative perception of self representing a composite of feelings about one's appearance, behavior, achievements, social acceptance, abilities, and skills. At any given age, the role of one component may be more important in the self-concept than that of another.

Self-Report Inventories Inventories that ask respondents to report about their own feelings, attitudes, states of adjustment, etc.

Short Answer Item Test item requiring students to respond with a word, phrase, or sentence.

Skewed Distribution A nonsymmetrical distribution of scores in which most scores pile up near one end of the distribution rather than in the middle. Positively skewed distributions have long tails (few students) to the right. Negatively skewed distributions have long tails (few students) to the left.

Social Desirability Bias A tendency to respond to self-report items in a way that reflects social norms and ideas of acceptable attitudes and behavior.

Sociogram A graphic display of choices made when students are asked to identify classmates to share an activity. Such displays help identify isolated students and cliques that have formed within the class.

Sociometric Matrix A chart for organizing responses after students are asked to name classmates with whom they want to share a specific activity.

Spearman-Brown Prophecy Formula A formula for estimating the effects on test reliability of increasing or decreasing the number of items by any amount. This text presents the formula for the special case in which a test length is doubled. This simplified formula is used to estimate the reliability of a full-length test when a reliability coefficient has been calculated on two half-length tests obtained by splitting the original test.

Split-Half Reliability A test reliability obtained by splitting the test into two halves at the time the test is scored. The scores obtained on each half are correlated and the correlation is corrected using the Spearman-Brown formula.

Standard Deviation The most useful and commonly reported measure of variability. The standard deviation is calculated by obtaining the deviation of each score in the distribution, squaring the deviations, summing the squared deviations, dividing by the number of cases, and taking the square root of the results.

Standard Error of Measurement A very useful index of test reliability that indicates the amount of variation one might expect in a given score if the test were readministered. For 68 percent of the students, the score would vary within plus or minus one standard error; for 95 percent of the students, the score would vary within plus or minus two standard errors; and for virtually 100 percent of the students, the scores would vary within plus or minus three standard errors.

Standard Error of the Difference An index of the amount of difference between scores that might be expected because of measurement errors in each score. A difference within a range of plus or minus one standard error of the difference would be expected 68 percent of the time by chance alone and would not be interpreted as a significant difference. Some authors suggest that differences between two scores should be larger than two standard errors of difference to be considered significant.

Standard Score Any one of a family of scores that expresses a test score in terms of how many standard deviations above or below the mean the student has fallen. The z-score is the simplest standard score.

Standardized Test A test with explicit, fixed procedures for administering, scoring, and interpreting the test. Part and parcel to the definition is the concept that the test has been standardized or normed on a large, representative sample of individuals at specified grade levels. The test is standardized both in the sense of a common procedure for administering the test and common norms for interpreting the results.

Stanine A contraction of "standard nine" indicating a form of standard score in which the baseline of a frequency distribution is divided into nine sections. Raw scores are assigned to each section depending on where they fall in a frequency distribution. A stanine of five represents the performance of the middle 20 percent.

Summative Evaluation Evaluations obtained near the end of instruction or at the end of special projects to determine whether the objectives have been reached.

T Score A standard score that has the advantage over z-scores of having no decimals and no negative numbers. It is obtained by multiplying z-scores by 10 and adding 50.

Table of Specifications The organizing framework that guides the writing and selection of items for a test. The table specifies the major subdivisions of the content to be tested, the levels of cognitive processes that will be brought to bear on the content, and the number of items written to measure each content-process area.

Taxonomy A classification plan in which the elements are arranged hierarchically.

Test-Retest A procedure for obtaining the reliability of a test that involves readministering the original test after a period of time and correlating the scores from the two administrations.

True-False Item Test item consisting of a brief statement, which is judged to be true or false. True-false tests can efficiently sample a wide range of content but are highly susceptible to guessing.

True Score A perfectly accurate score obtained if an individual could be measured without measurement errors.

Validity The extent to which a test measures what it claims to measure. Validity is one of the essential characteristics of a good measurement instrument.

Variability The variation of scores within a distribution. Measures of variability include the range, the average deviation, and the standard deviation, all indicating the amount of scatter or variability around the mean.

Variance A measure of variability obtained by summing the squared deviations and dividing by the number of cases. Variance may also be defined as the standard deviation squared.

z-Score The most basic standard score. For all z-scores, the mean is set equal to zero and the standard deviation is set equal to one. Thus, a student who falls at the mean of a distribution of scores will have a z-score of zero. A student falling one standard deviation above the mean will have a z-score of one.

Bibliography

Aiken, L. R. (1987). Testing with multiple-choice items. *Journal of Research and Development in Education, 20*(4), 44–58.

Aiken, L. R. (1991). *Psychological testing and assessment.* Boston: Allyn & Bacon.

Anastasi, A. (1988). *Psychological testing* (6th ed.). New York: Macmillan.

Archbald, D. A., & Newmann, F. M. (1988). *Beyond standardized testing: Assessing authentic academic achievement in the secondary school.* Reston, VA: National Association of Secondary School Principals.

Arter, J. A. (1990). *Curriculum-referenced test development workshop series, addendum to workshops two and three: Using portfolios in instruction and assessment.* Portland, OR: Northwest Regional Educational Lab. (ERIC No. ED335364).

Ashburn, R. R. (1938). An experiment in the essay-type question. *Journal of Experimental Education, 7,* 1–3.

Asher, S. R., & Coie, J. D. (eds.) (1990). *Peer rejection in childhood.* Cambridge, England; New York: Cambridge University Press.

Asher, S. R., & Dodge, K. A. (1986). Identifying children who are rejected by their peers. *Developmental Psychology, 22*(4), 444–449.

Asher, S. R., Parkhurst, J. T., Hymel, S., & Williams, G. A. (1990). Peer rejection and loneliness in childhood. In S. R. Asher & J. D. Coie (eds.), *Peer rejection in childhood.* Cambridge, England; New York: Cambridge University Press.

Asher, S. R., & Wheeler, V. A. (1985). Children's loneliness: A comparison of rejected and neglected peer status. *Journal of Consulting and Clinical Psychology, 53,* 500–505.

Axline, V. M. (1947). Play therapy. New York: Houghton Mifflin.

Baldauf, G. S. (1990). *Career index: A selective bibliography for elementary schools.* New York: Greenwood Press.

Ball, W. W. R. (1956). Calculating prodigies. In J. Newman (ed.), *The world of mathematics,* Vol. 1. New York: Simon & Schuster.

Beden, I., Rohr, L., & Ellsworth, R. (1987). A public school validation study of the achievement sections of the Woodcock-Johnson Psycho-Educational Battery with learning disabled students. *Educational and Psychological Measurement, 47,* 711–717.

Bell, A., Burkhardt, H., & Swan, M. (1992). Moving the system: the contributions of assessment. In R. Lesh, & S. J. Lamon (eds.), *Assessment of authentic performance in school mathematics.* Washington, DC: American Association for the Advancement of Science.

Binet, A., & Simon, T. (1916a). Upon the necessity of establishing a scientific diagnosis of inferior states of intelligence. In A. Binet & T. Simon, *The development of intelligence in children* (E. S. Kite, Trans.). Publications of the Training School at Vineland, New Jersey, Department of Research, No. 11. Baltimore: Williams & Wilkins (Reprinted from *L'Annee Psychologique,* 1905, 163–191). Reprint edition 1973 by Arno Press, New York.

Binet, A., & Simon, T. (1916b). The development of intelligence in the child. In A. Binet & T. Simon, *The development of intelligence in children* (E. S. Kite, Trans.). Publications of the Training School at Vineland, New Jersey, Department of Research,

No. 11. Baltimore: Williams & Wilkins (Reprinted from *L'Annee Psychologique,* 1908, 1–90). Reprint edition 1973 by Arno Press, New York.

Binet, A., & Simon, T. (1916c). New investigations upon the measure of the intellectual level among school children. In A. Binet & T. Simon, *The development of intelligence in children* (E. S. Kite, Trans.). Publications of the Training School at Vineland, New Jersey, Department of Research, No. 11. Baltimore: Williams & Wilkins (Reprinted from *L'Annee Psychologique,* 1911, 145–201). Reprint edition 1973 by Arno Press, New York.

Bloom, B. S. (ed.) (1956). *Taxonomy of educational objectives, the classification of educational goals. Handbook I: Cognitive domain.* White Plains, NY: Longman Publishing Group.

Bloom, B. S. (1985). *Developing talent in young people.* New York: Ballantine Books.

The Bomb Factories. (1988). An ABC News Close-up Special Report. ABC Distribution Company. Capital Cities/ABC Video Enterprises, 825 7th Avenue, New York, NY 10019–6001.

Brown, F. G. (1983). *Principles of educational and psychological testing.* New York: Holt, Rinehart & Winston.

Browne, C. S. & Rife, J. C. (1991). Social, personality, and gender differences in at-risk and not-at-risk sixth grade students. *Journal of Early Adolescence, 11,* 482–485.

Brownell, W. A. (1946). *The measurement of understanding. Forty-fifth yearbook of the National Society for the Study of Education, Part I.* Chicago: University of Chicago Press.

California Assessment Program. (1989). *A question of thinking: A first look at students' performance on open-ended questions in mathematics.* Sacramento: California State Department of Education.

Campbell, D. T., & Fisk, D. W. (1959). Convergent and discriminate validation by the multitrait-multimethod matrix. *Psychological Bulletin, 56,* 81–105.

Campione, J. C., & Brown, A. L. (1990). Guided learning and transfer: Implications for approaches to assessment. In N. Frederiksen, R. Glaser, A. Lesgold, & M. G. Shafto (eds.), *Diagnostic monitoring of skill and knowledge acquisition* (pp.141–172). Hillsdale, NJ: Erlbaum.

Carroll, J. B. (1993). *Human cognitive abilities.* Cambridge, England; New York: Cambridge University Press.

Cattell, R. B. (1943). The measurement of adult intelligence. *Psychological Bulletin, 40,* 153–193.

Center for Children and Technology. (1990). *Applications in educational assessment: Future technologies.* Technical Report submitted to the Office of Technology Assessment. New York: Bank Street College of Education. (ED 340 773).

Chang, C. K., & McDaniel, E. (1993). *Information search strategies in a hypercard file.* Paper delivered at the Annual Meeting of the American Educational Research Association, Atlanta, GA.

Chase, C. I. (1978). *Measurement for educational evaluation.* Reading, MA: Addison-Wesley.

Chase, C. I. (1986). Essay test scoring: Interaction of relevant variables. *Journal of Educational Measurement, 23*(1), 33–41.

Coder, K. (1990). *Relationships between self-concept and anxiety among elementary school children.* Unpublished Ed.S. dissertation. Purdue University.

The Cognition and Technology Group at Vanderbilt. (in press). The Jasper series: A generative approach to improving mathematical thinking. In *This year in school science.* Washington, DC: American Association for the Advancement of Science.

Coie, J. D., & Koeppl, G. K. (1990). Adapting intervention to the problems of aggressive and disruptive rejected children. In S. R. Asher & J. D. Coie (eds.), *Peer rejection in childhood.* Cambridge, England; New York: Cambridge University Press.

Collins, A. (1990). Reformulating testing to measure learning and thinking. In N. Frederiksen, R. Glaser, A. Lesgold, & M. G. Shafto (eds.), *Diagnostic monitoring of skill and knowledge acquisition* (pp. 75–88). Hillsdale, NJ: Erlbaum.

Cook, W. W. (1951). The function of measurement in the facilitation of learning. In E. F. Lindquist (ed.), *Educational measurement.* Washington, DC: American Council on Education.

Cooley, C. H. (1902). *Human nature and the social order.* New York: Scribner's.

Cunningham, G. K. (1986). *Educational and psychological measurements.* New York: Macmillan.

De Vito, A. (1989). *Creative wellsprings for science teaching* (2nd ed.). West Lafayette, IN: Creative Ventures.

Dewey, J. (1916). *Democracy and education*. New York: Macmillan.

Differential Aptitude Tests, Fifth Edition, Technical Manual (1992). San Antonio, TX: The Psychological Corporation.

Ebel, R. L. (1972). *Essentials of educational measurement*. Englewood Cliffs, NJ: Prentice-Hall.

Ebel, R. L. & Frisbie, D. A. (1986). *Essentials of educational measurement* (4th ed.). Englewood Cliffs, NJ: Prentice-Hall.

Ebel, R. L., & Frisbie, D. A. (1991). *Essentials of educational measurement* (5th ed.). Englewood Cliffs, NJ: Prentice-Hall.

Educational Testing Service. (1973). *Multiple-choice questions: A close look*. Princeton, NJ: Educational Testing Service.

Ehrlich, V. (1968). *The dimensions of attitude toward school of elementary school children and grades three to six*. Unpublished doctoral dissertation, Columbia University, New York.

Eisner, E. (1985). *The art of educational evaluation*. Philadelphia, PA: Falmer Press.

Ennis, R. H. (1985). A logical basis for measuring critical thinking skills. *Educational Leadership, 43,* 44–48.

Ennis, R. H. (1991, April). *Critical thinking: A streamlined conception*. Paper presented at the meeting of the American Educational Research Association, Chicago.

Ennis, R. H., Millman, J., & Tomko, T. N. (1985). *Cornell Critical Thinking Tests, Level X & Level Z Manual*. Pacific Grove, CA: Midwest Publications.

Fennema, E., & Sherman, J. A. (1976). Fennema-Sherman mathematics attitude scale: Instruments designed to measure attitudes toward the learning of mathematics by females and males. *JSAS Catalog of Selected Documents in Psychology, 6* (31), Ms. No. 1225.

Feuerstein, R., Haywood, H. C., Rand, Y., Hoffman, M. B., & Jensen, M. R. (1986). *Learning Potential Assessment Device Manual*. Jerusalem: Hadassah-WIZO-Canada Research Institute.

Feuerstein, R., Rand, Y., Hoffman, M., & Miller, R. (1980). *Instructional enrichment*. Baltimore: University Park Press.

Fleming, G. M., & Chambers, B. A. (1983). Teacher-made tests: Windows on the classroom. *New directions for testing and measurement,* No. 19, 29–38.

Freeman, D. J., Kuhs, T. M., Porter, A. C., Floden, R. E., Schmidt, W. H., & Schwille, J. R. (1983). Do textbooks and tests define a national curriculum in elementary school mathematics? *The Elementary School Journal, 83*(5), 501–513.

Gabel, P. (1989). *Vietnam War: A hypercard history book* [Computer program]. Scotts Valley, CA: Paul Gabel Regeneration Software.

Galotti, K. M. (1989). Approaches to studying formal and everyday reasoning. *Psychological Bulletin, 105*(3), 331–351.

Gardner, H. (1983). *Frames of mind: The theory of multiple intelligences*. New York: Basic Books.

Gazzaniga, M. S., & LeDoux, J. E. (1978). *The integrated mind*. New York: Plenum Press.

Gerberich, J. R., Greene, H. A., & Jorgensen, A. N. (1962). *Measurement and evaluation in the modern school*. New York: David McKay.

Goddard, H. H. (1916). Editor's introduction. In A. Binet & T. Simon, *The development of intelligence in children* (E. S. Kite, Trans.). Publications of the Training School at Vineland, New Jersey, Department of Research, No. 11. Baltimore: Williams & Wilkins. Reprint edition 1973 by Arno Press, New York.

Gronlund, N. E. (1991). *How to write and use instructional objectives* (4th ed.). New York: Macmillan.

Gronlund, N. E., & Linn, R. L. (1990). *Measurement and evaluation in teaching* (6th ed.). New York: Macmillan.

Guthke, J., & Wingenfeld, S. (1992). In H. C. Haywood & D. Tzuriel (eds.), *Interactive assessment* (pp. 64–93). New York: Springer-Verlag.

Haertel, E. (1991). Form and function in assessing science education. In G. Kulm & S. M. Malcom (eds.), *Science assessment in the service of reform*. Washington, DC: American Association for the Advancement of Science.

Hagen, E., Delaney, E., & Hopkins, T. (1987). *Stanford-Binet Intelligence Scale examiner's handbook: An expanded guide for fourth edition users.* Chicago: Riverside.

Hakstian, A. R. (1971). The effects of type of examination anticipated on test preparation and performance. *Journal of Educational Research, 64* (7), 319–324.

Hampton, S. (1989, March). *A further word: The teaching of writing. Grades K–5.* Paper presented at the meeting of the Association for Supervision and Curriculum Development, Orlando, FL. (ERIC No. ED312648).

Hansen, J. C. (1987). Edward Kellog Strong, Jr.: First author of the Strong Interest Inventory. *Journal of Counseling and Development, 66,* 119–125.

Hansen, J. C., & Campbell, D. (1985). *Manual for the SVIB-SCII* (4th ed.). Stanford, CA: Stanford University Press.

Hattie, J. (1992). *Self-concept.* Hillsdale, NJ: Erlbaum.

Haywood, H. C., & Tzuriel, D. (eds.). (1992). *Interactive assessment.* New York: Springer-Verlag.

Henerson, M. E., Morris, L. L., & Fitz-Gibbon, C. T. (1978). *How to measure attitudes.* Beverly Hills, CA: Sage Publications.

Hinkle, D. G., Wiersma, W., & Jurs, S. G. (1988). *Basic behavioral statistics* (2nd ed.). Boston: Houghton Mifflin.

Holland, J. L. (1990). *The self-directed search* (1990 Revision). Odessa, FL: Psychological Assessment Resources.

The Holmes Group. (1990). *Tomorrow's schools.* East Lansing, MI: The Holmes Group.

Hopkins, K. D., Stanley, J. E., & Hopkins, B. R. (1990). *Educational and psychological measurement and evaluation.* Englewood Cliffs, NJ: Prentice-Hall.

Horn, J. L., & Cattell, R. B. (1966). Refinement of the theory of fluid and crystallized general intelligences. *Journal of Educational Psychology, 57,* 253–270.

Huey, E. B. (1910). The Binet scale for measuring intelligence and retardation. *Journal of Educational Psychology, 1,* 435–444.

Hughes, D. C., & Keeling, B. (1984). The use of model essays to reduce context effects in essay scoring. *Journal of Educational Measurement, 21*(3), 277–281.

Hughes, J. N. (1992). Review of Learning Style Inventory [Price Systems, Inc.]. In J. J. Kramer & J. C. Conoley (eds.), *The eleventh mental measurements year-*

book. Lincoln, NE: Buros Institute of Mental Measurements.

Hymes, J. L., Jr. (1949). *Teacher listen, the children speak . . .* New York: New York Committee on Mental Health of the State Charities Aid Association, 105 E. 22nd Street, New York, New York.

Jaeger, R. M., & Kehr, C. (1980). *Minimum competency achievement testing: Motives, models, measures, and consequences.* Berkeley, CA: McCutchan.

Jensen, A. R. (1981). *Straight talk about mental tests.* New York: Free Press.

Jensen, A. R. (1988). Review of the Armed Services Vocational Aptitude Battery. In J. Kapes & M. Mastie (eds.), *A counselor's guide to career assessment instruments.* Alexandria, VA: The National Career Development Association.

Jersild, A. T. (1952). *In search of self.* New York: Columbia University Press.

Jeske, R. J. (1985). Review of Piers-Harris Children's Self-Concept Scale (The Way I Feel About Myself). In James V. Mitchell, Jr. (ed.), *The ninth mental measurements yearbook.* Lincoln, NE: Buros Institute of Mental Measurements.

Just, M. A., & Carpenter, P. A. (1992). A capacity theory of comprehension: Individual differences in working memory. *Psychological Review, 99,* 1, 122–149.

Kachigan, S. K. (1982). *Multivariate statistical analysis: A conceptual introduction.* New York: Radius Press.

Kelley, T. L. (1939). The selection of upper and lower groups for the validation of test items. *Journal of Educational Psychology, 30,* 17–24.

Kelley, T. L., & Prey, A. C. (1934). *Tests and measurements in the social sciences.* Ann Arbor: University of Michigan Press.

Kerlinger, F. N. (1986). *Foundations of educational research* (3rd ed.). New York: Holt, Rinehart & Winston.

Kramer, J. J., & Conoley, J. C. (1992). *The eleventh mental measurements yearbook.* Lincoln, NE: Buros Institute of Mental Measurements.

Kuder, G. F., & Diamond, E. E. (1979). *Kuder Occupational Interest Survey. General Manual.* Chicago: Science Research Associates.

Lamon, S. J., & Lesh, R. (1992). Interpreting responses to problems with several levels and types of correct answers. In R. Lesh & S. J. Lamon (eds.), *Assessment of authentic performance in school mathematics.* Washington, DC: American Association for the Advancement of Science.

Lesh, R., & Lamon, S. J. (1992). Assessing authentic mathematical performance. In R. Lesh & S. J. Lamon (eds.), *Assessment of authentic performance in school mathematics.* Washington, DC: American Association for the Advancement of Science.

Linden, K. W., & Linden, J. D. (1968). *Modern mental measurement: A historical perspective.* Boston: Houghton Mifflin.

Linn, R. (1988). State-by comparisons of achievement: Suggestions for enhancing validity. *Educational Researcher, 17*(3), 6–9.

Linn, R. L., Baker, E. L., & Dunbar, S. B. (1991). Complex, performance-based assessment: Expectations and validation criteria. *Educational Researcher, 20*(5), pp. 15–21.

Lochman, J. E. (1985). Effects of different treatment lengths in cognitive behavioral interventions with aggressive boys. *Child Psychiatry and Human Development, 16,* 45–56.

Locurto, C. (1991). *Sense and non-sense about IQ.* New York: Praeger.

Macy, M. S. (1910). The subnormal child in New York city schools. *Journal of Educational Psychology, 1,* 132–144.

McDaniel, E. (1988). [Development of a multiple-choice test to measure cognitive complexity.] Unpublished raw data.

McDaniel, E., Ames, C., Anderson, J., Cicirelli, V., Feldhusen, J., Felsenthal, H., Kane, R., Lohmann, J., Moe, A., & Wheatley, G. (1973). *Longitudinal study of elementary school effects: Design, instruments and specifications for a field test.* Final report submitted to the U.S. Office of Education. West Lafayette, IN: Purdue Research Foundation. (ERIC No. ED100945).

McDaniel, E., & Lawrence, C. (1990). *Levels of cognitive complexity: An approach to the measurement of thinking.* New York: Springer-Verlag.

McDaniel, E., & Leddick, G. (1978, August). *Elementary children's self-concepts, factor structures, and teacher ratings.*

Paper presented at the meeting of the American Psychological Association, Toronto.

McDaniel, M. A., & Masson, M. E. J. (1985). Altering memory representation through retrieval. *Journal of Experimental Psychology: Learning, Memory and Cognition, 11,* 371–385.

Messick, S. (1989). Validity. In R. L. Linn (ed.), *Educational measurement.* New York: American Council on Education/Macmillan.

Midden, K. S. (n.d). *Environmental gaming simulation.* Carbondale, IL: Lands View Consulting.

Mitchell, R. (1992). *Testing for learning.* New York: The Free Press.

Mooney, R. L., & Gordon, L. V. (1950) Manual, *The Mooney Problem Checklists.* San Antonio, TX: The Psychological Corporation.

Mullis, I. V. S., & Jenkins, L. B. (1988). *The science report card.* Princeton, NJ: Educational Testing Service.

Nash, R., & Ducharme, E. (1983). Where there is no vision, the people perish: A nation at risk. *Journal of Teacher Education, 34*(4), 38–46.

Newman, J. R. (1956). Commentary on Sir Francis Galton. In J. Newman (Ed.), *The world of mathematics* (Vol. 2). New York: Simon & Schuster.

Nicholls, J. G. (1972). Creativity in the person who will never produce anything original or useful: The concept of creativity as a normally distributed trait. *American Psychologist, 27,* 717–727.

Nicholls, J. G. (1989). *The competitive ethos and democratic education.* Cambridge, MA: Harvard University Press.

Nolen, S. B., Haladyna, T., & Hass, N. (1992). Uses and abuses of achievement test scores. *Educational Measurement, 11*(2), 9–15.

Notes and News. (1910). *Journal of Educational Psychology, 1,* 55–57.

Oliverio, M. E. (1959). Review of Purdue Clerical Adaptability Test. In O. K. Buros (ed.), *The fifth mental measurements yearbook.* Highland Park, NJ: The Gryphon Press.

Owen, S. V., & Froman, R. D. (1987). What's wrong with three-option multiple-choice items? *Educational and Psychological Measurement, 47*(2), 513–522.

Paré, A. P. (1983–84). Developing students' higher-level reasoning skills through better social studies test questions. *Viewpoints—The Indiana Council for the Social Studies Newsletter, 11*(1), 9–11.

Patterson, G. R. (1971). *Living with children.* Champaign, IL: Research Press.

Paulson, F. L., & Paulson, P. R. (1991). *The making of a portfolio.* Unpublished manuscript available from the authors, 6800 Gable Parkway, Portland, OR 97225. (ERIC No. ED334251).

Paulson, F. L., & Paulson, P. R. (1992, August). *The making of a portfolio.* Revised and expanded draft. Available from the authors, 6800 Gable Parkway, Portland, OR 97225.

Pearson, K. (1924). *The life, letters, and labors of Francis Galton* (Vol. 2). Cambridge, England: Cambridge University Press.

Peel, E. A. (1971). *The nature of adolescent judgment.* New York: Wiley-Interscience.

Perry, W. G. (1970). *Forms of intellectual and ethical development in the college years: a scheme.* New York: Holt, Rinehart & Winston.

Peterson, N. S., Kolen, M. J., & Hoover, H. D. (1989). Scaling, norming, and equating. In R. L. Linn (ed.), *Educational measurement.* New York: American Council on Education/Macmillan.

Phillips, J. L., Jr. (1982). *Statistical thinking.* San Francisco: W. H. Freeman.

Piers, E. V., & Harris, D. B. (1969–84). *Manual of the Piers-Harris Children's Self-Concept Scale.* Los Angeles: Western Psychological Services.

Polson, P., & Jeffries, R. (1985). Instruction in general problem solving skills: An analysis of four programs. In J. W. Segal, S. F. Chipman, & R. Glaser (eds.), *Thinking and learning skills (Vol. 1) Relating instruction to research.* Hillsdale, NJ: Erlbaum.

Popham, W. J. (1978). *Criterion-referenced measurement.* Englewood Cliffs, NJ: Prentice-Hall.

Reynolds, C. R., & Richmond, B. O. (1987). *Revised Children's Manifest Anxiety Scale.* Los Angeles: Western Psychological Services.

Romano, T. (1991). *A time for immersion, a time for reflection: The multigenre research project and portfolio assessment.* Paper presented at the 1991 National Council of Teachers of English Spring Conference, Indianapolis. (ERIC No. ED333428).

Rothlisberg, B. A. (1990). The relationship of the Stanford-Binet: Fourth Edition to measurements of achievement: A concurrent validity study. *Psychology in the Schools, 27,* 2, 120–125.

Rowntree, D. (1977). *Assessing students: How shall we know them?* London: Harper & Row.

Rowntree, D. (1981). *Statistics without tears.* New York: Charles Scribner's Sons.

Samuels, M., Tzuriel, C., & Malloy-Miller, T. (1989). Dynamic assessment of children with learning difficulties. In R. T. Brown & M. Chazan (eds.), *Learning difficulties and emotional problems* (pp. 145–165). Calgary: Detselig Enterprises.

Schmeck, R. (1988). *Learning strategies and learning styles.* New York: Plenum.

Schmeck, R. R., Ribich, F. D., & Ramanaiah, N. (1977). Development of a self-report inventory for assessing individual differences in learning processes. *Applied Psychological Measurement, 1,* 413–431.

Schroder, H. M., Driver, M. J., & Streufert, S. (1967). *Human information processing: Individuals and groups functioning in complex social situations.* New York: Holt, Rinehart & Winston.

Schwab, J. J. (1974). The concept of the structure of a discipline. In E. W. Eisner & E. Vallance (eds.), *Conflicting conceptions of curriculum.* Berkeley, CA: McCutchan.

Seagoe, M. V. (1975). *Terman and the gifted.* Los Altos, CA: William Kaufmann.

Semonche, J. E. (1988). *Simulations in American history 1865: Should the Southern states be readmitted to the Union?* [Computer program]. San Diego: Harcourt Brace Jovanovich.

Shapiro, I. (1979). *The gift of magic sleep: Early experiments in anesthesia.* New York: Coward, McCann & Geoghegan.

Shavelson, R. J., Baxter, G. P., & Pine, J. (1992). Performance assessments, political rhetoric and measurement reality. *Educational Researcher, 21*(4), 22–27.

Shavelson, R. J., Bolus, R., & Keesling, J. W. (1980). Self-concept: Recent developments in theory and method. In D. A. Payne (ed.), *New directions for testing and measurements: Recent developments in affective measurements.* San Francisco: Jossey-Bass.

Shekerjian, D. (1990). *Uncommon genius.* New York: Viking.

Shepard, L. A. (1989). Identification of mild handicaps. In R. L. Linn (ed.), *Educational measurement*. New York: American Council on Education/Macmillan.

Shertzer, B., & Linden, J. D. (1979). *Fundamentals of individual appraisal*. Boston: Houghton Mifflin.

Spearman, C. (1930). Autobiography. In C. Murchison (ed.), *A history of psychology in autobiography,* Vol. 1 (pp. 299–334). Worcester, MA: Clark University Press.

Spearman, C. (1937). *Psychology down the ages,* Vol. II. London: Macmillan.

Spearman, C., & Jones, L. W. (1950). *Human ability.* London: Macmillan.

Spearritt, D. (1959). Review of Purdue Clerical Adaptability Test. In O. K. Buros (ed.), *The fifth mental measurements yearbook*. Highland Park, NJ: The Gryphon Press.

Speth, C., & Brown, R. (1990). Effects of college students' learning styles and gender on their test preparation strategies. *Applied Cognitive Psychology, 4,* 189–202.

Stalnaker, J. L. (1951). The essay type of examination. In E. Lindquist (ed.), *Educational measurement*. Washington, DC: American Council on Education.

Stanford Early School Achievement Test, Third Edition, SESAT, 1991 National Norms Booklet (1992). San Antonio, TX: The Psychological Corporation.

Sternberg, R. J. (1991). Theory-based testing of intellectual abilities: Rationale for the Triarchic Abilities Test. In H. A. H. Roe (ed.), *Intelligence: Reconceptualization and measurement*. Hillsdale, NJ: Erlbaum.

Strong, E. K., Jr. (1955). *Vocational interests 18 years after college*. Minneapolis: University of Minnesota Press.

Terman, L. M., & Oden, M. H. (1959). *Genetic studies of genius, Vol V. The gifted group at mid-life: Thirty-five years follow-up of the superior child*. Stanford, CA: Stanford University Press.

Test Collection, Educational Testing Service. (1991). *The ETS test collection catalog, Volume 5: Attitude tests*. Phoenix, AZ: Oryx Press.

Test Collection, Educational Testing Service. (1992). *The ETS test collection catalog, Volume 6: Affective measures and personality tests*. Phoenix, AZ: Oryx Press.

Tests in Print IV. (in press). Lincoln, NE: Buros Institute of Mental Measurements.

Thissen, D., & Mislevy, R. J. (1990). Testing algorithms. In H. Wainer, *Computerized adaptive testing: A primer* (pp. 103–136). Hillsdale, NJ: Erlbaum.

Thorndike, R. L., Hagen, E. P., & Sattler, J. M. (1986a). *The Stanford-Binet Intelligence Scale: Fourth Edition, Guide for administering and scoring*. Chicago: Riverside.

Thorndike, R. L., Hagen, E. P., & Sattler, J. M. (1986b). *The Stanford-Binet Intelligence Scale: Fourth Edition, Technical manual*. Chicago: Riverside.

Thorndike, R. M., Cunningham, G. K., Thorndike, R. L., & Hagen, E. P. (1991). *Measurement and evaluation in psychology and education* (5th ed.). New York: Macmillan.

Treffert, D. A. (1989). *Extraordinary people*. New York: Harper & Row.

Trevisan, M. S., Sax, G., & Michael, W. B. (1991). The effects of the number of options per item and student ability on test validity and reliability. *Educational and Psychological Measurement, 51,* 829–837.

Tzuriel, D., & Haywood, H. C. (1992). The development of interactive-dynamic approaches to assessment of learning potential. In H. C. Haywood & D. Tzuriel (eds.), *Interactive assessment* (pp. 3–37). New York: Springer-Verlag.

Vacca, R. T., & Rasinski, T. V. (1992). *Case studies in whole language*. Fort Worth: Harcourt Brace Jovanovich.

Vaught, S. (1989). *Interjudge agreement in dynamic assessment: Two instruments from the Learning Potential Assessment Device*. Unpublished master's thesis, Vanderbilt University, Nashville, TN.

Wainer, H. (1990). *Computerized adaptive testing: A primer*. Hillsdale, NJ: Erlbaum.

Wainer, H., & Mislevy, R. J. (1990). Item response theory, item calibration and proficiency estimation. In H. Wainer, *Computerized adaptive testing: A primer*. Hillsdale, NJ: Erlbaum.

Watson, G., & Glaser, E. M. (1980). *The Watson-Glaser Critical Thinking Appraisal*. San Antonio, TX: The Psychological Corporation.

Wechsler, D. (1991). *Wechsler Intelligence Scale for Children—Third edition. Manual*. San Antonio, TX: The Psychological Corporation.

Wesman, A. G. (1971). Writing the test item. In R. L. Thorndike (ed.), *Educational measurement*. Washington, DC: American Council on Education.

Whitehead, A. N. (1929). *The aims of education*. New York: Macmillan. Paperback edition published as a Mentor Book by The New American Library of World Literature, Inc., New York.

Wielkiewicz, R. M. (1990). Interpreting low scores on the WISC-R third factor: It's more than distractibility. *Psychological Assessment, 2,* 1, 91–97.

Wiggins, G. (1989). Teaching to the (authentic) test. *Educational Leadership, 46,* 7, 41–47.

Wolf, T. H. (1973). *Alfred Binet.* Chicago: The University of Chicago Press.

Woodcock, R. W., & Johnson, M. B. (1978). *Woodcock-Johnson Psycho-Educational Battery.* Boston: Teaching Resources.

Name Index

Subject Index

Correlation
negative or positive,
37–38
versus agreement, 38
versus causation, 39
Correlation coefficient, 3,
37–40
interpretation of, 39–40
predictive power of, 75
symbol and formula
for, 48
Correlation matrix, 71–72
Creativity, testing for, 277–78
Criterion, defined, 72
Criterion related validity,
72–74
Criterion-referenced test,
85–86
compared to norm-
referenced,
153–54
item analysis of, 161–62
Critical thinking/standardized
tests of, 207–8
Critiques, of tests, 113
Crystallized intelligence, 240
Cumulative frequency, 22, 23
Cumulative relative
frequency, 22, 23

Deep approach, to learning,
303–5
Derived score(s), 94–104
relationships among,
102–4
Describer-explainer
continuum,
209–10
Descriptive statistics, 3, 19
Developmental scales, and age
score, 97
Deviation, 29–30
average, 30
Deviation IQ, 101–2, 103
Differential Aptitude Tests, 266,
269–74
computerized adaptive
version, 334
validity of, 272–74
Difficulty level, of test item,
155–56, 157
Discriminant validity, 71

Discrimination level, of test
item, 155–56,
157–58, 161–62
Dispersion, 28
Distractibility, freedom from,
249
Distractors, and test answers,
148
Distribution, 21
normal (see Normal
curve)
types of, 25
Divergent thinking, and test
type, 171–72
Dynamic assessment, 9,
330–33
comments on, 332–33

Educational reform
movement, 11–12
and performance
assessment, 194
Ego-orientation, 301–30
English, mechanics of, and
essay scoring, 178
Environmental Gaming
Simulation,
199–201
Essay test, 5, 166
advantages of, 175–76
scoring of, 177–79
six-point scale for, 187
unreliability of, 173–75
versus multiple-choice
test, 169–72
writing questions, 176–77
ETS Test Collection Catalog,
The, 298
Evaluation
as educational objective,
133
formative, 85
summative, 87
test items for, 143–44
Expectancy tables, 104–7
Expressive objectives, 166–67
Extrapolation
of communication, 141
of score, 95

Face validity, 69, 74
Factor analysis, 237

Fluid intelligence, 240
Formative evaluation, 85
Frequency, 21, 22
Frequency distribution, 21,
22
Frequency polygon, 23–24,
25, 32

g factor, 234, 235–39
and tests of special ability,
272
Gaussian curve, 33
General Aptitude Test Battery
(GATB), 266,
274–76
Generalizability, in
performance
assessment,
192–93
"Genius" study, 227–28
Goals, and objectives, 138–39
Grade equivalent score,
94–97, 108
interpreting, 96
Grade placement, and grade-
equivalent score,
96
"Guess Who," 310

Histogram, 23, 24, 32
Holistic Scoring Rubric, 328,
329
Holmes Group, 11
Human abilities, nature of,
266–68

Idiot savant, 267
Individual adjustment
measure, 307–9
direct observation,
314–18
loneliness questionnaire,
313–14
nominating technique,
309–10
sociogram, 311–12
sociometric, 311–12
Individual differences, and
competency tests,
10–11
Inert ideas, 131

Inferential statistics, 19, 40–42
Information-processing, and
measuring
intelligence,
256–61
Information-processing
structures, 210–11
Instrumental Enrichment
program, 331
Integrated analysis, 213
Intellectual development, 210
Intelligence
concept of, 234
crystallized versus fluid,
240
general (g factor), 234,
235–39
specific (s factor), 235–39
Intelligence quotient (IQ),
101–10
creation of, 225
intelligence test, 6–7
and special class
placement,
255–56
Intelligence test(s), 101–2
for adults, 247
age-grading of, 224
Binet-Simon (1905), 223
early versions of, 220–25
group versus individual,
239
with high g loadings,
237–39
information-processing
approach, 256–61
Stanford-Binet, 225–28
thoughts about, 239–40
value of, 228–30
Wechsler, 246–47
Interest test(s), 7, 282–93
elementary level, 290–91
Self-Directed Search
(Holland), 289–90
Strong Interest Inventory,
284–86
Strong Vocational Interest
Blank (1927),
282–84, 287
Internal consistency, 51–52
Interpersonal intelligence, 236
Interpolation, of score, 95

Quantitative reasoning, test of, 242

Range, 28–29
Ratio scale, 20–21
Raven Progressive Matrices, 237, 238, 331
Raw score, 84
　converting to percentiles, 89–91
Reasoning, formal versus everyday, 209
Relative frequency, 22, 23
Reliability, 3–4
　coefficient alpha, 51–52
　of computer adaptive testing, 334
　correcting for underestimation of, 50–51
　and correction for attenuation, 63–64
　defined, 44
　determining, 46–55
　of dynamic assessment, 332–33
　and essay tests, 173–75
　Kuder-Richardson, 52–54
　of performance assessment, 185–86, 193
　retest, 47–49
　of SESAT 2, 121
　and single-administration testing, 49–53
　split-half, 50–51
　of *Stanford-Binet—Fourth Edition,* 243
　variation in estimating procedures, 54
　of *Watson-Glaser Critical Thinking Appraisal,* 207
　of *Wechsler Intelligence Scale for Children—Third Edition,* 251
Reliability coefficient, 47–49
　and group characteristics, 55
　guidelines for evaluating, 55–56

split-half, appropriate use of, 115
　using, 56–58
Remedial education/and IQ, 255–56
Representative sample, 91–93
Revised Children's Manifest Anxiety Scale, 307
Rorschach inkblot test, 297
Rubric, scoring, 186
　for logic problem, 189
　for open-ended questions, 188
　for performance assessment, 196

s factor, in intelligence, 235–39
Sample
　information, on essay test, 175
　representative, 91–93
Scales, types of, 18–21
Scatter, 28
Scatterplot, 37, 38
Scholastic Aptitude Test
　scoring of, 100–101
　validity of, 75
Schoolwork, and grade-equivalent score, 96–97
Science Research Associates inventory, 308
Scoring guide
　for essays, 177
　for performance tasks, 186
Self-concept
　and learning style, 305
　Piers-Harris scale, 305–7
　of young child, 306–7
Self-Directed Search (Holland), 289–90
Self-report inventory, 297
Semi-interquartile range, 29–30
Short-answer test items, 145–47
Significance level, 41
Simulation, use in performance assessment, 199–202

Skewness, of distribution, 25, 27, 28
Social desirability bias, 297
Sociogram, 311–12
Sociometric matrix, 311
Spearman-Brown Prophecy Formula, 50–51
Special education, and IQ, 255–56
Split-half reliability, 50–51
Spread, 28
Standard Age Score, 242–43
Standard deviation, 3, 31–32, 40
　in computing standard scores, 35–37
　formula for, 31
　and normal curve, 33–34
Standard error of measurement, 58–63
　formula for, 61
Standard error of the difference, 41
Standard error of the mean, 41
Standard score(s), 35–37, 99–102
　CEEB scores, 100–101, 103
　IQ scores, 101–2
　Normal Curve Equivalent, 101, 102
　on SESAT 2, 118–19
　stanine, 99, 103
　T score, 100, 103
　z-score, 36–37
Standardization
　evaluating of, 91–93
　importance of, 84
　of SESAT 2, 120–21
　of Stanford-Binet—Fourth Edition, 242–43
　of *Wechsler Intelligence Scale for Children—Third Edition* (WISC-III), 249–51
　See also Norms
Standardized test, of critical thinking, 207–8

Stanford Early School Achievement Test—Third Edition (SESAT 2), 116–24
　evaluation of, 120–24
Stanford-Binet—Fourth Edition, 241–46, 247
　correlation with achievement measures, 257
　fifteen tests of, 241–42
　reliability of, 243
　standardization procedure, 242–43
　validity of, 244–46
Stanford-Binet test, 6, 225–28
Stanines, 99, 103
Statistics
　basic concepts, 2–3, 18–19
　descriptive, 3, 19
　inferential, 19, 40–42
　significance level, 41
Stopping rule, in adaptive testing, 334
Strong Interest Inventory, 284–86
　interpreting scores on, 292
Strong Vocational Interest Blank (1927), 282–84, 287
Student, self-evaluation by, 326–27
Summative evaluation, 87
Surface approach to learning, 303–5
Synthesis
　as objective, 133
　test items for, 143–44

T score, 100, 103
Table of specifications, 5
　for achievement tests, 133–38
Task-orientation, 301–2
Taxonomy, defined, 132
Teacher
　and design of attitude test, 298